Lecture Notes in Computer Science   14630

Founding Editors

Gerhard Goos
Juris Hartmanis

The series Lecture Notes in Computer Science (LNCS), including its subseries Lecture Notes in Artificial Intelligence (LNAI) and Lecture Notes in Bioinformatics (LNBI), has established itself as a medium for the publication of new developments in computer science and information technology research, teaching, and education.

LNCS enjoys close cooperation with the computer science R & D community, the series counts many renowned academics among its volume editors and paper authors, and collaborates with prestigious societies. Its mission is to serve this international community by providing an invaluable service, mainly focused on the publication of conference and workshop proceedings and postproceedings. LNCS commenced publication in 1973.

Eugene Wallingford · Uwe Zdun ·
Christian Kohls
Editors

Transactions on
Pattern Languages
of Programming V

 Springer

Editors-in-Chief
Eugene Wallingford
University of Northern Iowa
Cedar Falls, IA, USA

Uwe Zdun (ID)
Universität Wien
Vienna, Austria

Guest Editor
Christian Kohls
Technische Hochschule Köln
Cologne, Germany

ISSN 0302-9743   ISSN 1611-3349 (electronic)
Lecture Notes in Computer Science
ISSN 1869-6015   ISSN 2511-6444 (electronic)
Transactions on Pattern Languages of Programming
ISBN 978-3-662-70809-5   ISBN 978-3-662-70810-1 (eBook)
https://doi.org/10.1007/978-3-662-70810-1

Preface

Welcome to the fifth issue of LNCS Transactions on Pattern Languages of Programming. Software patterns are an effective means for improving the quality of software design and engineering and for improving communication among the people building them. Patterns capture the best practices of software design, making them available to all software engineers.

LNCS Transactions on Pattern Languages of Programming publishes papers on patterns and pattern languages as applied to software design, development, and use. The primary focus of the LNCS Transactions on Pattern Languages of Programming is on patterns, pattern collections, and pattern languages themselves. The journal also includes reviews, survey articles, criticisms of patterns and pattern languages, as well as other research on patterns and pattern languages.

This issue includes papers on patterns and pattern languages for engineering specific kinds of application and for improving processes, as well as papers on the discovery, validation, and systemic use of patterns more broadly.

The seven articles in this issue went through two phases of review and improvement. First, the articles were workshopped at one of the PLoP conferences where, after an initial peer review, they received suggestions for improvement in a shepherding process prior to the conference and then in a writer's workshop at the conference itself. The articles were then substantially extended by the authors, and these extended versions were peer-reviewed again by at least three reviewers per article.

This edition of LNCS Transactions on Pattern Languages of Programming is the first under the new editors-in-chief. We thank the founding editors-in-chief of the series, James Noble and Ralph Johnson, for their efforts during the early years of LNCS Transactions on Pattern Languages of Programming and for James's continued guidance during the transition.

We thank the anonymous reviewers who helped in the peer review process of this issue.

November 2024

Eugene Wallingford
Uwe Zdun
Christian Kohls

Organization

Editors-in-Chief

Eugene Wallingford   University of Northern Iowa, USA
Uwe Zdun   Universität Wien, Austria

Managing Editor

Christian Kohls   Technische Hochschule Köln, Germany

Contents

A Pattern Language for Engineering Software for the Cloud

Tiago Boldt Sousa[✉], Hugo Sereno Ferreira, and Filipe Figueiredo Correia

Faculty of Engineering, INESC TEC, University of Porto, Porto, Portugal
{tbs,hugosf,filipe.correia}@fe.up.pt

Abstract. Software businesses are continuously increasing their presence in the cloud. While cloud computing is not a new research topic, designing software for the cloud is still challenging, requiring engineers to invest in research to become proficient at working with it.

Design patterns can be used to facilitate cloud adoption, as they provide valuable design knowledge and implementation guidelines for recurrent engineering problems.

This work introduces a pattern language for designing software for the cloud. We believe developers can significantly reduce their R&D time by adopting these patterns to bootstrap their cloud architecture. The language comprises 10 patterns, organized into four categories: Automated Infrastructure Management, Orchestration and Supervision, Monitoring, and Discovery and Communication.

1 Introduction

As of 2019, over 49% of the world population has access to one or more Internet-enabled devices [60]. Empowered by cloud computing, applications can reach users globally, with the public cloud services market surpassing US$204 billion in 2016 [43].

Software engineering is one of the fastest expanding branches of engineering, further motivated by the widespread of the Internet and the explosive growth of software businesses built on top of it. The demand for new engineers is growing faster than the pace at which they are graduating [96].

Using the cloud as a foundation for application development introduces new challenges but is essential for many modern businesses. Still, there is a clear lack of scientific research supporting development for the cloud, namely, identifying what forces drive successful cloud software, and the guidelines to balance them to craft better software.

The authors propose a language of patterns for building cloud software with this article. It is not part of the scope of this work to capture all the required knowledge for designing cloud software. Instead, it tries to be a foundation for an otherwise challenging task, which will continue to be pursued by the author and, hopefully, by the remaining members of the patterns community.

© The Author(s), under exclusive license to Springer-Verlag GmbH, DE, part of Springer Nature 2025
E. Wallingford et al. (Eds.): TPLOP V, LNCS 14630, pp. 1–66, 2025.
https://doi.org/10.1007/978-3-662-70810-1_1

This work consolidates design patterns for cloud development, which have been previously peer-reviewed in various *Pattern Languages of Programs* conferences since 2015 [13–17,94]. They complement endeavors by other researchers who have also been dedicated to documenting established solutions for the development of cloud software [1,3,4,19,34,69,87,88].

A study empirically evaluating some aspects of our patterns was published in a separate article [93] and the complete research is published as part of the first author's Ph.D. thesis [12].

2 A Pattern Language for Cloud Computing

The pattern language presented in this research is composed of twelve patterns, organized into four categories: *automated infrastructure management, orchestration and supervision, monitoring*, and *discovery and communication*.

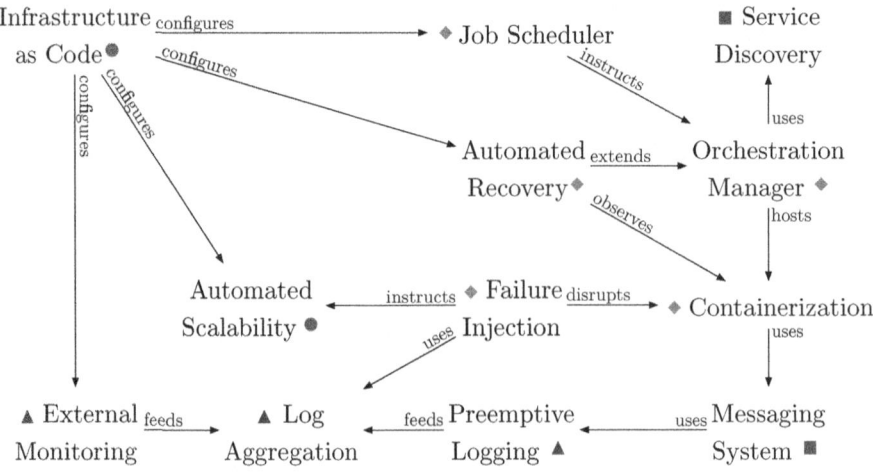

Fig. 1. The pattern language for engineering software for the cloud, depicting the relations between the patterns (arrows) and the categories that they fall into, *viz*: (■) Discovery and Communication, (♦) Orchestration and Supervision, (▲) Monitoring, and (●) Automated Infrastructure Management.

The patterns in the language and their relations are depicted by Fig. 1 and the next few sections briefly describe each category and associated patterns.

2.1 Automated Infrastructure Management

This category comprises two patterns that have already been extensively described in the literature but are essential for supporting the other patterns in the language: AUTOMATED SCALABILITY and INFRASTRUCTURE AS CODE.

Operations can be decisive for a product's success. Managing operations manually is slow, error-prone, and costly, rendering it hard to trace changes and evolve the infrastructure. In order for teams to be efficient, all their operations should also be automated. We have discussed how quality can be automated through the adoption of automated tests and CI. Operations should be equally automated, being implemented as part of the development process. This is the concept supported by the INFRASTRUCTURE AS CODE pattern [31,50,76].

Using a Microservice Architecture enables the separation of responsibility into multiple smaller services that can independently be designed, scaled or orchestrated. Multiple Microservices can be leveraged to create complex Cloud Applications [67,78,86].

Cloud applications can quickly move from being almost idle to serving millions of requests per second. When developing software for the cloud, keeping up with high traffic peaks is essential to ensure a smooth user experience. AUTOMATED SCALABILITY is essential to achieve continuous service performance. Resource usage should be monitored and used to decide when to automatically scale the system [37,97].

2.2   Orchestration and Supervision

With cloud infrastructure allocated, software developers are faced with the issue of allocating and operating their software on top of it. This category presents five patterns that help developers with this task.

Traditionally, deploying software in a host coupled it with the operative system, requiring dependencies to be installed and configurations to be set that could introduce side effects with other services in the same host. CONTAINERIZATION suggests the usage of containers to package and deploy services in isolation, avoiding their impact on each other or the host.

Deploying and updating software at scale is an error-prone, slow, and costly process. Such can be facilitated by adopting an ORCHESTRATION MANAGER to coordinate, manage, and properly distribute services while abstracting the underlying infrastructure. The orchestration can optionally monitor the running services and attempt an AUTOMATED RECOVERY to return the service to a functioning state. Finally, it can also be set to periodically run jobs in the infrastructure, using the JOB SCHEDULER pattern.

Has software uptime becomes more critical, developers tend to implement automated recovery strategies, some of which are described in the patterns above. Still, being software, the recovery strategies themselves are prone to failure and must be frequently exercised to ensure their accuracy, as described by FAILURE INJECTION.

2.3   Monitoring Patterns

Software running in the cloud is subject to an immense amount of traffic, which will eventually generate unexpected scenarios. While it is impossible to prevent issues from happening, developers should implement the required strategies to identify when and why issues happen, and to address them quickly and right from their first occurrence, preventing it from impacting the software again in the future.

PREEMPTIVE LOGGING describes a series of practices that ensure that run-time information is captured and made available for developers to address issues when they happen. LOG AGGREGATION then describes how these logs should be centralized, for facilitated access, mostly relevant for distributed systems.

The logged information will only become relevant once issues are detected. Automated monitoring strategies are recurrent and essential and can be internal or external to the infrastructure running the cloud software. EXTERNAL MONITOR describes how internal monitoring is subject to biased observation, incapable of detecting, for example, internet connectivity issues, given that it is testing the software from the same local network.

These patterns are further detailed in Sect. 4.

2.4 Discovery and Communication Patterns

When applications scale, they eventually need to do so vertically, resulting in the need to deploy additional replicates of the application or, often, to decompose it in multiple services. These services often need to cooperate in providing the entire application. Two common strategies are to use direct communication or an intermediary message passing system.

The SERVICE DISCOVERY describes how services can discover each other while using an ORCHESTRATION MANAGER, enabling direct service interaction.

In some scenarios, point-to-point communication might not be enough. Some architectures require a strategy to disseminate messages by a multitude of services. This can be implemented for addressing several requirements, such as a fine-grained control of what information each service can receive or implementing an underlying work queue, with a publisher-subscriber strategy. The MESSAGING SYSTEM addresses these requirements.

The two patterns introduced in this category facilitate the discovery and communication of services in a cloud environment, both using one-to-one or one-to-many strategies. They are further described in Sect. 5.

2.5 Adopting the Pattern Language

Resistance to change is by itself a pattern. Adopting a pattern language for developing software for the Cloud requires the need for teams to adapt their mindset regarding their organization, processes and software architectures. While it is imperative that the team is motivated to change, this pattern language eases its adoption as implementation can be partial and incremental. The team can identify its most critical problem and implement the pattern or set of patterns that solve it without addressing the whole pattern language.

This section was inspired by *The Unfolding of a Japanese Tea Garden* by Christopher Alexander [5]. It uses a sequence as a way to help the reader understand how the patterns relate and complement each other. Sequences describe a set of actions that should follow each other in order to achieve a specific goal.

Consider the scenario where a cloud *practitioner* needs to create and deploy a redundant Web Application, composed of a client-facing HTTP server and a database.

The *practitioner* should design his HTTP server and database as two cooperating microservices. By using CONTAINERIZATION and one service per container, he would create two container images, one of each service. These containers would be highly portable between multiple environments such as local, staging or production environments, configured using the available environment variables.

Using INFRASTRUCTURE AS CODE the *practitioner* would describe the infrastructure required to set up the system. By executing this programmatic description, the required infrastructure would become available. AUTOMATED SCALABILITY could be set up to ensure that the hardware where the web server executes would scale horizontally if needed according to the provided scalability rules.

To deploy his services in an isolated and scalable way, the infrastructure would be abstracted through ORCHESTRATION MANAGER, which would be responsible for allocating the container machines in the infrastructure optimally, taking into consideration the total and available resources in each machine.

JOB SCHEDULER would be responsible for executing the daily database backup process to an external site.

The web server would use the local network port 12345 to connect to the database. Such would be possible given SERVICE DISCOVERY was configured in all machines using a local reverse proxy that would expose a static service port for each service instantiated. This scenario would not require MESSAGING SYSTEM.

To ensure the service is working correctly, the *practitioner* would implement the following monitoring techniques.

EXTERNAL MONITOR service can monitor all public application endpoints, ensuring that they are both online and responding appropriately.

To further increase awareness of the system's state, PREEMPTIVE LOGGING could be adopted to configure the developed and adopted services to use an appropriate level of logging to make the required historical information available to the team to develop issues after they have happened. LOG AGGREGATION can bring all this information to a centralized, indexed, and queryable location for simple usage.

Finally, and in order to validate the resilience in the system, FAILURE INJECTION can exercise the resilience mechanisms by randomly introducing errors in the infrastructure, such as randomly shutting down machines, and verifying that the system recovers automatically.

3   Orchestration and Supervision Patterns

Cloud software requires a host environment where it is executed. In the past, configuring this environment required acquiring hardware, setting it all up, including the operative system, installing all dependencies, and installing the software itself. Today, most Cloud Providers use VIRTUALIZATION, enabling the creation and deletion of virtual machines on demand using APIs. Virtual machines are provided as an almost limitless resource, facilitating the allocation of computer power on demand. Platforms for setting up private cloud solutions also exist, enabling the same dynamic allocation of resources on top of private bare metal clusters using a similar API.

Creating development or production environments manually is a time-consuming process. The probability of error is high, given the commonly large number of dependencies and configurations required. Furthermore, these pollute the host, possibly preventing it from hosting multiple applications. While Virtualization can be used to create a portable environment of the entire hardware and software stack, it always virtualizes the whole hardware and software stack, which is very resource-demanding. CONTAINERIZATION is a better alternative, enabling the creation of immutable, reproducible, portable, and secure software execution environments. Containers are considerably lighter than full-stack virtualization, as there is no need to virtualize the Operative System layer. Containers prevent polluting the host with dependencies and configurations, making them easier to manage and deploy at scale [14,90]. This approach is also essential for individually scaling each service.

Infrastructure empowering Software in the Cloud is typically volatile and dynamically allocated. As such, orchestration plays a key role in dynamically identifying the execution setup and adapting the software to cope with it.

Servers in a cluster will differ in hardware details. While some might provide more CPU, others might have higher amounts of RAM available. Not all services are the same. As such, they need to be co-located with the hardware that better meets their requirements. Using TAGGED LOCAL RESOURCES, servers can make their resource details available for an orchestration manager, enabling it to make informed decisions and optimize service allocation in the cluster.

Services can also differ in requirements. While some might require a specific amount of memory to be available, others might need to be co-located in the same host for latency purposes. Again, allocating services must be carefully evaluated to ensure proper behavior. An ORCHESTRATION MANAGER should be responsible for allocating services to the proper hosts, considering their overall and available resources, and leveraging the allocation of other services.

Asynchronous tasks, such as database maintenance, sending emails, or performing backups, are often required to ensure that tasks are executed at the best possible time. These might run at a given frequency or at a single point in time. JOB SCHEDULER can be used to orchestrate the execution of these programs in a cluster and evaluate their result, generating error reports when needed.

Software fails. That assumption is even more relevant while orchestrating Software in the Cloud, given its large scale. Accepting that it is impossible to prevent software from failing, supervision ensures that services are running as expected, executing the proper action to recover them in case of failure.

Services running inside containers should be resilient in case of failure, providing AUTOMATED RECOVERY. Exploiting the immutability of containers, the container shall restart itself automatically to try to recover the service whenever it detects a malfunction. Advanced strategies might be applied to recover a service or set of services, such as restarting a list of services in a specific order. The Orchestration Manager should decide on the best strategy for each scenario.

Mechanisms for improving software resiliency can be built by accepting that software fails. By doing so, developers can hope that the system recovers in unexpected scenarios but cannot evaluate their confidence in them without testing unexpected scenarios. To ensure the system's reliability and resiliency, a FAILURE INJECTION mechanism can periodically or continuously inject unexpected events in the system, evaluating if it continues to behave appropriately. Fault injection can evaluate reliability by injecting unexpected values into the service and observing if any unexpected behavior occurs. Resiliency can be tested by randomly shutting servers down, ensuring they scale back up without impacting service quality.

3.1   Containerization

 Deploying a service to a host couples it with the operative system, possibly introducing side effects with other services in the same host, or the host itself. CONTAINERIZATION proposes the usage of containers to package the service and its dependencies and enable its isolated and programmatic deployment.

Context. Today's hardware, with multi-core and multi-CPU architectures, is built to execute multiple programs concurrently. Cloud computing often exploits resource sharing for executing multiple services in a single host. Sharing the host's operating system with the hosted services might introduce software incompatibilities between them or quickly clutter the host, as it must mutate its file system to accommodate each service's dependencies. Such introduced the need for isolated environments. Full stack virtualization quickly became the de facto standard approach to enabling resource sharing, allowing services to be executed in a dedicated installation of the operating system. Paravirtualization further improved that approach by exposing hardware resources directly to the virtualized environment. Still, isolation is achieved with an increased cost of hardware usage required to virtualize the operating system stack on each hosted environment.

Example. Consider a web application that has three services: an HTTP server, a database and an object caching service. These services share some core libraries, but each depend on different versions. The development team uses a few different Linux distributions for development but production environments are to use a specific distribution. All three services should be deployed on a temporary host for testing purposes and afterwards deployed in the production environment. It becomes a complex task to develop and deploy each service such that it is easily executed by each team member, as well as quickly installed in the development and production, despite existing configurations or the adopted distribution.

Problem. *Deploying a service to a host couples it with the operative system, possibly introducing side effects with other services in the same host, or the host itself.*

Software deployments tend to couple services with their host environment, modifying it according to their needs [61]. When hosting multiple services that share resources, namely file-system, CPU, memory and network availability, unexpected behavior might be observed as they compete for those resources. Furthermore, situations exist where two services cannot coexist in the same environment due to incompatible dependencies, either virtual or physical.

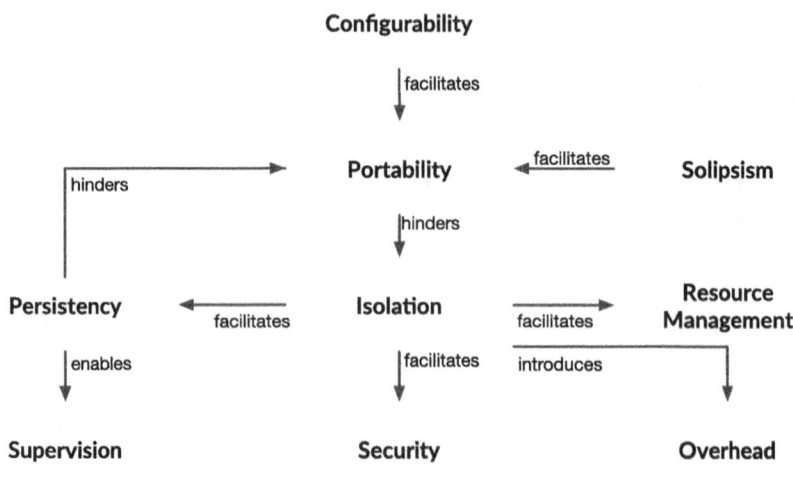

Fig. 2. Relationship between CONTAINERIZATION forces.

Forces. The following forces, represented in Fig. 2, need to be balanced while considering the adoption of this pattern:

Resource Management Not using all the resources is a server is not cost-efficient, while over-allocating services will degrade their performance.

Overhead Decoupling services from the operating system might lead to computation overheads.

Supervision The service status must be monitored, triggering a recovery on failures.

Isolation Installation of dependencies changes the host, possibly resulting in side effects with other services in the same host.

Portability Programmatic system deployment requires the packaged software to be easily deployed in different environments.

Configurability Programmatic system deployment requires a strategy for configuration in execution time.

Security Different approaches to isolation introduce different levels of security by default.

Solipsism Each running environment should only manage itself, communicating with external services resiliently.

Persistency Persist data in the host beyond the service's execution lifetime, possibly being reused in future executions.

Solution. *Use a container to package the service and its dependencies and enable its isolated programmatic deployment.*

Full stack virtualization provides isolated environment for running software. Despite that, the cost of virtualizing the operating system for each environment introduces considerable overheads in CPU, memory. Portability is also limited, given the increased disk usage. As such, this approach is not optimal solution for cloud software.

A better solution exists in operating system level virtualization, also known as containers. A container is a self-contained isolated environment with a virtual file-system, network and resources allocation which is executed within an host operating system [92].

The container can be created and started programmatically, with configurations provided to the inner software as environment variables, making it portable between hosts. Strict resource allocation ensures that the container will not overuse the available hardware resources. Figure 3 demonstrates how to configure and print environment variables for a container.

Persistent storage can be setup in the container by exposing files or folders from the hosting server inside the container. File system access is limited to those. When the container is deleted from the host, all its data is deleted as well, leaving behind only the files and folders created in the in the exposed storage to the container, if any.

On failure, it can restart itself with the same configurations and a clean environment.

There are multiple container implementations available today, with Docker[1] being the most adopted.

---

[1] Learn more about docker at https://www.docker.com/.

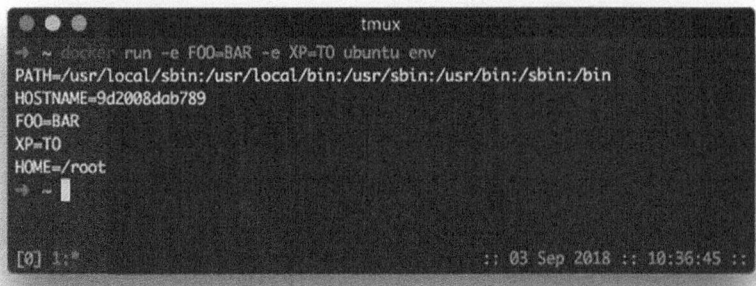

Fig. 3. Running a containerized Ubuntu image with injected environment variables. Environment variables are provided using the *-e* argument. This example executes the ENV command and exits, which simply prints the environment variables. Environment variables can be read by software running inside the container as a way of providing runtime configurations.

Example Resolved. Each service would be packaged into a separate container. In a development environment, the three containers could be started in the same host. A separate production environment could have each container being executed in an independent host. No changes would have to be made to the containers, other than starting them with the proper configuration as environment variables, which can easily be automated.

If needed, each service can be scaled independently from the others by increasing the number of instances for that specific container.

Resulting Context. This pattern introduces the following benefits:

- Resource use is optimized, with overheads being decreased when compared to full stack virtualization, as only a thin layer needs to be virtualized, improving the performance achievable by a host.
- Resources can be allocated to the container, leveraging the available host's resources between multiple containers, as well as what is exposed from the container to the host and vice-versa.
- Arguments can be provided to the container on execution to configure the service running inside it. Due to its immutability, in case of failure the container can restart with the original configuration.
- Isolated environment can be easily ported between development and production as the image size only packages the service and its dependencies, leaving out all operating system's components.

The pattern also introduces the following liabilities:

– Paravirtualization is a virtualization technique that exposes part of the host's hardware directly to the virtual machine. In some low-level hardware access scenarios, paravirtualization might provide increased performance.
– Packaging services as containers will still introduce overheads when compared to installing services directly in the host.

Related Patterns. Configuration might be required for a container to be adaptable to multiple hosts and scenarios. Using the ENVIRONMENT-BASED CONFIGURATION pattern it is possible to use environment variables to configure running services at execution time.

Some containers might have the need to persist information between executions in the host. That is the case of isolated databases that cannot lose their data if the machine reboots. With this goal in mind, the LOCAL VOLUMES pattern may be used to expose a folder from the host inside the container.

Known Uses. Containerization was first introduced in 1982 in the Seventh Edition Unix by Bell Labs, as a tool for testing the installation and build system of the operating system, providing an isolated file-system environment where services could be executed. By 2008 Linux Containers (LXC) were introduced in Linux Kernel version 2.6.24, reducing the virtualization overhead and increasing efficiency [38]. By 2013 Docker was built, based on LXC, in order to make containerization easier for a broader audience.

Docker is now the cloud standard for container-based deployment, with native support with multiple cloud providers, such as Amazon Web Services and Google Cloud Platform, both with native support for running docker containers [6,47]. A draft is being worked on to create a standard format for containers, with RunC being the reference implementation for it, which can also run Docker-created containers [59].

A study by DataDog in April 2018 showed that almost 25% of their clients were already using containers, with about 50% using some sort of ORCHESTRATION MANAGER [32].

Discussion. While container adoption is rising, virtual machines will always be part of cloud computing as the unit of provision of computation. For the development team, the question at hand is if services should be deployed at the virtual machine or container level, what their differences are and how to decide. This section sheds some light over this decision. Given the specific context of cloud computing, deploying natively is not within the scope of this discussion.

Providing some context over virtualization, it is built by leveraging a hypervisor to create and execute virtual machines. Hypervisors are responsible for the virtualization of the hardware in a virtual machine and are available in two different flavors: those who run on bare metal, such as Xen, and those who require an underlying operating system such as KVM[2]. In both scenarios, a virtual machine is a fully virtualized computing environment, meaning that every hardware component the virtual machine would see, namely the CPU, RAM or graphical card, would in fact be a virtual representation of such element. It is part of the hypervisor responsibility to them map those virtual components to the actual ones available.

Containers work differently, by having the hosted services sharing resources with the host environment, with the actual service execution being managed by the host's kernel, although in an isolated environment.

Performance. Performance is key in any system. Virtualization efficiency is typically inverse to the overhead introduced by the virtualization system. As previously described, each virtual machine requires its hypervisor to virtualize the hardware and operating system layers, which introduces an immense overhead. As such, virtualization is less efficient than containers. In fact, containers provide almost no overhead when compared to running in bare metal given that they actually share their host's operating System kernel and, at time, binaries and libraries as well. Theoretically, containers are a much more efficient solution to deploy multiple isolated environments in a server.

This theory has been validated by Xavier, whom made an extensive evaluation of native systems performance when compared to three container implementations (LXC, OpenVZ and VServer[3]) and the aforementioned Xen virtual environments [101], visually represented in Fig. 4.

Regarding computing performance, Xavier concluded that there were no statistically significant differences between native and the container implementations, but observed a 4.3% overhead with Xen virtualization.

The same study evaluated the memory performance of these three systems and also concluded that containers have similar performance to native, but observed a 31% overhead with Xen based virtualization. We identified this overhead to be a product of the hypervisor layer responsible for virtual machine to native memory address translation.

Finally, regarding disk IO, again containers presented a similar performance to native, with OpenVZ actually outperforming native. Xen on the other hand presented poor results with read and write performance being about 50% when compared to native.

Resource Isolation. When running multiple virtualized or containerized services in a server, they shouldn't negatively impact the performance of their neighbors. Such is possible by setting hard-limits on resource usage.

---

[2] Xen and KVM are both open source virtualization servers. Learn more about the projects at https://www.xenproject.org/ and https://www.linux-kvm.org/.

[3] LXC, OpenVZ and Vserver are three alternative container implementation. LXC was used internally by Docker until version 0.9, being replaced by lib-container since. You can learn more about these projects respectively at https://linuxcontainers.org/, https://openvz.org/ and http://linux-vserver.org/.

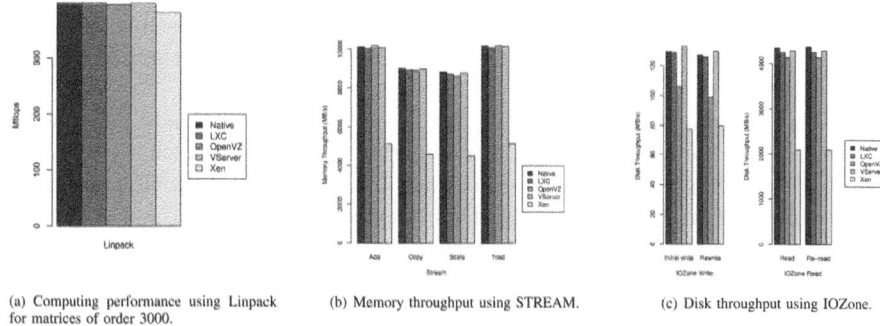

(a) Computing performance using Linpack for matrices of order 3000. (b) Memory throughput using STREAM. (c) Disk throughput using IOZone.

Fig. 4. Comparison of (a) computation performance, (b) memory management and (c) disk throughput, from Xavier's work.

With Xen, resource allocation is a requirement for the creation of the virtual machine. These resources are reserved by the hypervisor, which will only expose to the virtual machine the allocated resources.

Containers typically rely on the Linux Kernel Control Groups (cgroups) to enforce resource allocation. Control Groups allow the creation of a resource pool to be allocated to a given subsystem, enabling resource attribution to those. In practice, it limits the resources available to a service and it's descending processes [71].

Enforcing resource limitation introduces an overhead per se, which might have impact remaining existing systems. In his research, Xavier ran more than one virtualized or container systems, with one trying to use more resources than the ones allocated. He observed that for both Xen and LXC, CPU limitation is effective, not imposing any performance impact on the other hosted system. The same is not true for memory management, with the Xen hosted service having a minimal 0.9% performance impact, but with LXC presenting an impact of 88.2% [101]. Several other studies showed similar results, demonstrating that containers introduce negligible performance impact [38,84,92].

Security. Security is essential when executing services inside isolated environments. The service should not be able to access its host unless explicitly configured to do so.

Virtual machines, by design, provide optimal security to the host. A service running inside a virtual machine will not be able to understand if it is executing in a native or virtualized environment.

Opposed to virtual machines, containers do present an increased security thread. Given that the containerization engine is executed by the host's operating system kernel and that it requires *root* permissions, the kernel itself becomes an attack vector. In the Docker Security report [77], we listed a set of security measures recommended for container administrators, namely ensuring that the host's kernel is always using the latest version and that hosted containers are from trusted sources and do not present security flaws in them and that programs within them always executing using the least privilege possible, meaning that they should only have the required permissions to execute their functions.

Flexibility. Virtual machines provide the most flexibility for hosts and hosted environments. Given the existence of an hypervisor for a given machine, it will be able to create virtual machines and host any operating system with compatible architecture within it. As for containers, they currently only run natively in Linux systems, requiring some sort of virtualization in other operating systems to execute. Furthermore, and focusing on the Docker implementation, containers will only Linux as well [20].

Conclusion. We can conclude that container environments are still more prone to security flaws than virtual machines. New techniques for securing containers have been made available recently and more are expected to become available in the future, but it is imperative that the user acknowledges the problem and evaluate its risks while using containers.

3.2   Orchestration Manager

 Deploying and updating software at scale is an error-prone, slow and costly process. Such can be facilitated by adopting an ORCHESTRA-TION MANAGER to coordinate, manage and distribute multiple cloud services while abstracting the underlying infrastructure, fulfilling the service requirements.

Context. Along with cloud computing came very large applications, typically composed by several services, that needed to scale out to multiple servers.

Traditional teams would have an operations team that would deploy and operate the software built by the development team. This approach revealed itself impractical due to slow deployments and recurrent conflicts between the two teams [33] due to miscommunication and finger pointing. DevOps suggested merging both teams, having a single team responsible for the software life cycle. For that to happen, operations needed to be fully programmatic [33].

For achieving this level of automation, abstractions where required to facilitate building fully automated operation strategies. CONTAINERIZATION played an essential role in enabling programmatic deployment of software.

Example. An application is composed by two services that need to be orchestrated in an infrastructure with four servers. The service requirements might change with time and must be allocated into suitable hardware. Their current requirements are described in Table 1.

Table 1. List of services and their possible configurations for a production environment.

Service Name	CPUs	RAM	Disk Space	Instances	Constraints
HTTP	2	2 GB	5 GB	4	hostname=unique; location=Europe
Database	2	8 GB	50 GB	2	hostname=unique; SSD=true; location=Europe

The servers might also change with time, with more powerful or specialized hardware being allocated if need. The current servers available are described in Table 2.

Table 2. List of servers available in the infrastructure, along with their meta-data.

Server name	CPUs	RAM	Disk Space	Server Details
Alpha	4	4 GB	500 GB	location=Europe
Beta	4	4 GB	500 GB	location=Europe
Charlie	4	16 GB	1000 GB	SSD=true; location=Europe
Delta	4	16 GB	1000 GB	SSD=true; location=Europe

Problem. *Deploying and updating software at scale is an error-prone, slow and costly process.*

Multiple variants can constraint the allocation of services to servers in an infrastructure. Each service has its own requirements and each service provides a specific set of resources. Furthermore, given the wide adoption of continuous integration and deployment strategies, teams are increasing the frequency at which they deploy their services to several times per day [30], which demands automation in the deployment process.

A common requirement is to ensure that services are allocated to host machines which fulfills its hardware requirements and that this happens without human interaction. Such enables servers to run multiple services while ensuring their execution within the host's resource limits, guaranteeing the expected performance.

Cloud applications can also scale and the infrastructure empowering it must facilitate such scaling as well to adapt to a change in the volume of activity, while optimizing costs.

Forces. The following forces, represented in Fig. 5, need to be balanced while considering the adoption of this pattern:

Infrastructure Decoupling The development process should not be constraint by the running environment.

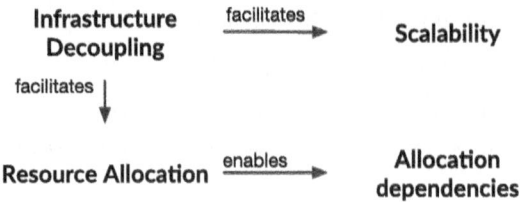

Fig. 5. Relationship between ORCHESTRATION MANAGER forces.

Resource Allocation Allocating services without ensuring their requirements will result in unexpected behavior.

Allocation dependencies Allocating services without ensuring their dependencies will result in unexpected behavior.

Scalability It must be possible to scale the system either up or down.

Solution. *Adopt an ORCHESTRATION MANAGER to coordinate, manage and distribute multiple cloud services while abstracting the underlying infrastructure, fulfilling the service requirements.*

Adopting an ORCHESTRATION MANAGER provides abstraction and automation over the orchestration of services. The abstraction is provided by having the ORCHESTRATION MANAGER evaluating each available server, service and its requirements and use that information to optimize service allocation. Automation is provided by exposing a programmatic interface that facilitates orchestrating software in the infrastructure.

Services can be deployed programmatically after being packaged using CONTAINERIZATION. Using a declarative strategy, the ORCHESTRATION MANAGER can be told what services need to be deployed and their requirements, leaving to it the responsibility of managing the allocation. Resource allocation is enforced, ensuring that all services are provided their required resources to execute properly. Most ORCHESTRATION MANAGER enable the specification of additional restrictions such as co-allocations or startup sequences. Listing 1 demonstrates how to tell the Kubernetes ORCHESTRATION MANAGER to instantiate two Nginx web servers [62].

ORCHESTRATION MANAGER work using a master-slave architecture, being the master elected automatically and responsible for handling service allocation. Deployment requests can often be issued to any slave, which proxies them to the master [73]. This approach facilitates electing a new master automatically if the current master fails.

Whenever a new slave joins the infrastructure, the master identifies its available resources. When a new service allocation request is received, the master decides where the service should be executed and instructs the slaves to start it. Figure 6 illustrates this interaction.

Listing 1. A Kubernetes specification for starting two instances of the Nginx web server.

```
1   apiVersion: apps/v1
2   kind: Deployment
3   metadata:
4     name: nginx-deployment
5   spec:
6     selector:
7       matchLabels:
8         app: nginx
9     replicas: 2 # tells deployment to run 2 pods matching the template
10    template:
11      metadata:
12        labels:
13          app: nginx
14      spec:
15        containers:
16        - name: nginx
17          image: nginx:1.7.9
18          ports:
19          - containerPort: 80
```

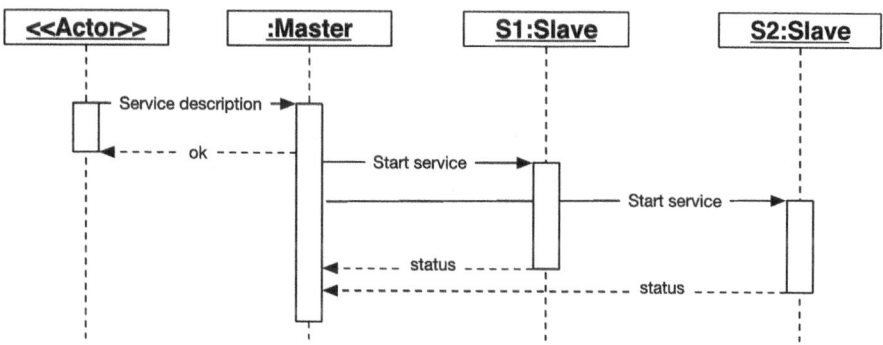

Fig. 6. Sequence diagram representing communication between master and slaves for service allocation.

If no slave is capable of hosting the service due to a mismatch on the service requirements and those available in the servers of requirements, the master periodically retries the service allocation until it succeeds.

Example Resolved. The team starts by deploying an ORCHESTRATION MANAGER that abstracts four existing servers. By doing so, one of the servers will be automatically elected as master, with the others proxying orchestration requests to it.

A descriptive file can be created for each service, describing how to obtain the respective container, as well as describing its requirements.

Finally, to deploy the services, a request similar to the one from Listing 1 is sent to the ORCHESTRATION MANAGER with each service description. The ORCHESTRATION MANAGER master evaluates the resources required by the services and the ones available in each server, instructing the selected servers to deploy the services.

In the example we can see that the hostname must be unique, meaning that it is not possible to deploy two HTTP or database servers in the same host. Also, the selected servers must be Europe, with the database service in a server with SSD storage.

Considering those restrictions, the ORCHESTRATION MANAGER would compute a viable solutions, which could be the one identified in Table 3.

Table 3. List of available servers in the infrastructure.

Service Name	Server Name	Applied constraints
http server	Alpha	`hostname=unique; location=Europe`
http server	Beta	`hostname=unique; location=Europe`
database	Charlie	`hostname=unique; SSD=true; location=Europe`
database	Delta	`hostname=unique; SSD=true; location=Europe`

In this example, when deploying the services, all servers are at full capacity and are able to fulfill the requested resources regarding CPU, RAM and disk space. When the service is deployed to Alpha and Beta, the ORCHESTRATION MANAGER subtract 2 CPUs, 2 GB RAM and 5 GB of storage from their available resources, influencing the allocation of services in the future. When deploying the database service, only European servers with SSD storage can be used, resulting in Charlie and Delta being the two only eligible hosts.

Resulting Context. This pattern introduces the following benefits:

Infrastructure decoupling Service development can be agnostic of the host where the service is going to be placed, describing only its requirements and packaging its dependencies using CONTAINERIZATION.

Resource allocation Services are allocated in servers that meet their requirements.

Allocation dependencies Dependencies are respected, managed as constraints for the allocation process.

Scalability Scalability is achieved by adding slaves to the infrastructure and individually change the number of instances for each service.

The pattern also introduces the following liabilities:

Suboptimal allocation Allocation using a greedy placement algorithm might result only in a locally-optimal solution.

Single point of failure In some implementation where the master is not automatically reelected in case of failure, using a single master node would result in a single point of failure.

Related Patterns. Some ORCHESTRATION MANAGER implementations might support additional strategies for running software, but CONTAINERIZATION is the most common strategy.

Known Uses. Kubernetes by Google is the fastest growing implementation of a ORCHESTRATION MANAGER. It abstracts a set of machines, receiving requests for allocating containers in the infrastructure. Kubernetes is under active development, widely adopted and supported across most cloud providers [46].

Mesos and Marathon together provide another robust solution for achieving the same goal. New services are submitted to the infrastructure using an HTTP API describing its requirements and constraints. With this information, the master communicates with the slaves, identifying a valid host and issuing the order for placing the service [54].

CoreOS offers similar technology, with a centralized registry made available using Etcd [28].

3.3   Automated Recovery

 Services may fail during execution and need to be recovered in a timely and orderly fashion. Including health checks and recovery configurations in the instructions used for the ORCHESTRATION MANAGER to orchestrate containers, enables it to monitor and recover failing containers.

Context. At the scale that cloud software is operated, it is reasonable to accept that it will eventually fail. Resilience is then an essential requirement while writing scalable cloud software. The development team must introduce the necessary strategies to ensure that the application is functioning properly or that, at least, it can recover back to a functioning state automatically.

This pattern extends the ORCHESTRATION MANAGER [14] pattern, responsible for executing services packaged using CONTAINERIZATION [14].

Example. Consider a web server exposing an API is running inside a container in an ORCHESTRATION MANAGER. Suppose that the service had a memory leak, which gradually consumed the memory allocated for the service, and thus making the service unresponsive. The ORCHESTRATION MANAGER sees the container running, but while it is still executing, it is unable to respond to requests.

Problem. *Services may fail during execution and need to be recovered in a timely and orderly fashion.*

Cloud software is exposed to variety of stress conditions, from public Internet exposure to dynamic cloud infrastructure. As such, software should be designed with resilience in mind to ensure it can to recover from failures.

With a traditional operations approach, a team member is responsible for identifying failures and deciding the best action to recover a failing system using the defined recovery protocol. This approach is troublesome as it requires manual intervention, which is slow and error prone.

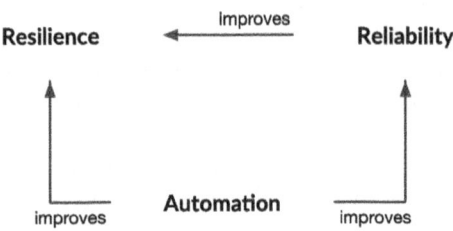

Fig. 7. Relationship between AUTOMATED RECOVERY forces.

Forces. The following forces, represented in Fig. 7, need to be balanced while considering the adoption of this pattern:

Resilience Failing containers should recover to an healthy state when failure is observed.
Reliability Monitoring strategies that are prone to false positives can trigger an unnecessary service recovery.
Automation Requiring manual intervention for recovering a failing service is error-prone, slow and costly.

Solution. *Including health checks and recovery configurations in the instructions used for the ORCHESTRATION MANAGER to orchestrate containers, enabling it monitor and recover failing containers.*

AUTOMATED RECOVERY is available in most ORCHESTRATION MANAGER implementations [65, 72]. The development team implements health checks for each container to verify if its service is behaving correctly. Most implementations provide at least plain TCP and HTTP checks. The health checks can be provided along with the service description directly to the ORCHESTRATION MANAGER.

To implement the recovery strategies the team needs to evaluate each service individually, deciding which check can be used to identify that the service is failing, how many times each check needs to be retried and how much time to wait between executing the checks and actually considering a service as failing.

A recovery protocol must be made available along with the health checks to be automatically executed by the ORCHESTRATION MANAGER to attempt the service recovery. Health checks and recovery protocols need to be considered part of the service's development process.

Health checks will be very specific to the service running in a container. These might range from checking if a port is receiving connections in the container, to more a advanced HTTP-based checks, to executing a command inside the container and monitoring its exit code.

TCP checks verify if a network port is open and accepting TCP connections. These are typically binary checks that just validate the service ability to receive connections.

HTTP checks are more advanced than their TCP counterparts since they can actually make HTTP requests and validate the HTTP return code and body, making way for more advanced tests.

Developers can implement dedicated health checking endpoints to be queried by AUTOMATED RECOVERY, providing responses that can be easily interpreted to verify the service's status.

While deciding on the supervision strategy, the team can leverage common features that prevent false positives from mistakenly restarting the service. A false positive might be a momentary request that fails to have a response, followed by normal service operation.

The recovery operation itself is prone to failure. Implementing this pattern is another step towards improving cloud software reliability, but cannot be relied upon as unbreakable.

When a failure is identified and that results in an AUTOMATED RECOVERY, the ORCHESTRATION MANAGER or the adopted AUTOMATED RECOVERY service will log that event and its details. The team can use this log as input for improving their software or to configure notifications to be aware as soon as they happen. This is relevant as restarting the container might only be a temporary solution or not able to fix the problem.

Listing 2 demonstrates how a service can be started using the Marathon ORCHESTRATION MANAGER, configuring an HTTP health check that verifies the response code from the /health endpoint. From this example, the parameters used are: *gracePeriodSeconds*, which ignores errors for a given number of seconds after the service starts; *intervalSeconds*, which configures the delay between checking the endpoint; *timeoutSeconds*, which configures the maximum time to wait for a response from the service; and *maxConsecutiveFailures*, which defines the number of times the health check can fail before being restarted.

While implementing this pattern, one needs to decide on how to balance:

Interface coverage We want to ensure the tests are as complete as possible, covering all application's interfaces, while balancing this investment with the available development effort.

Frequency We want to run the health checks as often as possible, while balancing this frequency with the increase in resource utilization.

Listing 2. A Marathon service description, describing the health check policies for AUTOMATED RECOVERY.

```
1   {
2     "id": "toggle",
3     "container": {
4       "docker": {
5         "image": "busybox"
6       }
7     },
8     "cpus": 2,
9     "mem": 32.0,
10    "healthChecks": [
11      {
12        "protocol": "HTTP",
13        "path": "/health",
14        "portIndex": 0,
15        "gracePeriodSeconds": 5,
16        "intervalSeconds": 10,
17        "timeoutSeconds": 10,
18        "maxConsecutiveFailures": 3
19      }
20    ]
21  }
```

Accuracy We want to prevent false positives by confirming issues redundantly, such as those who might result from a temporary slowdown in the system, automatically recovered inside the container.

Example Resolved. While deploying a service with an ORCHESTRATION MANAGER with support for AUTOMATED RECOVERY, the service definition specifies the set of health checks used to verify the service's status.

During execution, if a health check identifies a problem with a container, the respective container is restarted automatically. While the intrinsic issue might persist, the service will once again become available without team intervention. Given the notification sent to the team, they will be immediately aware of the issue and can focus on implementing a proper solution.

Resulting Context. This pattern introduces the following benefits:

Resilience The ORCHESTRATION MANAGER will be able to recover failing containers automatically.

Reliability Failing containers will be automatically identified using the implemented health checks, which can have an advanced strategy to prevent false positives.

Autonomy Failing services are restarted using the implemented recovery protocol, so that the system recovers its correct execution state automatically and without requiring manual intervention.

On the other hand, the following liabilities are also introduced:

Relaxation It might happen that the development team disregards software failures given that they are being automatically recovered.

Unawareness Without the proper monitoring and logging in place, considering that failing services are automatically recovered, it might happen that the team isn't aware of the failure in the system.

Performance degradation Running health checks against the container will introduce additional load in the system, which might result in performance degradation.

False positives It might happen that the health checks aren't accurate and the containers restarted while behaving correctly.

Unintended Consequences It might happen that the service is improperly designed and unable to be restarted, leaving it inconsistent and requiring manual intervention after a restart. In extreme scenarios each recovery attempt might further increase the problem. An example of such is the case where a backup system that is consistently failing during its execution will keep increasing the disk space it occupies without ever actually having a complete backup, until no more space is available.

Related Patterns. The ORCHESTRATION MANAGER pattern describes how containers can be orchestrated in an infrastructure automatically, leveraging allocation rules, container scaling and resource availability. AUTOMATED RECOVERY is commonly related with ORCHESTRATION MANAGER, given that most of its implementations provide some sort of supervision strategy to ensure the containers are working as expected [65,72].

AUTOMATED RECOVERY enables the automatic recovery of services if their health is degraded. This pattern is essential to implementing FAILURE INJECTION, where the reliability and resilience of the system is tested though a set of random inputs and events in order to identify possible attack vectors or failures in the system.

Dynamic Failure Detection and Recovery describes a subset of AUTOMATED RECOVERY, by proposing the existence of a resilient watchdog component that monitors IT resources and in case of failure notifies the team and attempts automated recovery [9].

Known Uses. Most ORCHESTRATION MANAGER pattern implementations provide AUTOMATED RECOVERY natively, as orchestration and supervision complement each other while deploying services in an infrastructure.

Marathon supports multiple health check strategies. TCP and HTTP are implemented as described in this pattern's solution. Additionally, Marathon supports the *COMMAND* check, which consists on running a command within a container and evaluate its output [72]. Listing 3 demonstrates how an health check can be configured for Kubernetes.

Kubernetes provides a similar approach to AUTOMATED RECOVERY [65], but with additional features to it. With Kubernetes, developers can set two flavors of health checks: readiness and liveliness. Readiness checks are considered only right after the container is instantiated and enable Kubernetes to check if the container is ready to start accepting traffic. Only after the readiness checks pass is the container considered healthy and ready to be used. Liveliness then work as health checks do in Marathon, periodically testing the container for its status, automatically restarting it when unhealthy.

Listing 3. A Kubernetes service description, describing the health check policies for HEALTH CHECK using HTTP.

```
1   apiVersion: v1
2   kind: Pod
3   metadata:
4     labels:
5       test: liveness
6     name: liveness-http
7   spec:
8     containers:
9     - name: liveness
10      image: k8s.gcr.io/liveness
11      args:
12      - /server
13      livenessProbe:
14        httpGet:
15          path: /healthz
16          port: 8080
17          httpHeaders:
18          - name: X-Custom-Header
19            value: Awesome
20        initialDelaySeconds: 3
21        periodSeconds: 3
```

Listing 4. A Dockerfile for building a container based on the Nginx image, leveraging Docker's implementation of AUTOMATED RECOVERY by periodically checking the web server's health.

```
1   from nginx
2
3   HEALTHCHECK --interval=5m --timeout=3s CMD curl -f http://localhost/ || exit 1
4
5   CMD nginx -g "daemon off;"
```

Just like with Marathon, health checks are defined with the service definition, along with the specification of what container to use and how to configure it, as demonstrated in Listing 3.

Docker has its own supervision mechanism. Docker's supervision provides a simple restart strategy, which automatically restarts a container either if it fails or when an health check is failing. Health checks can be specified while creating the container [35]. Docker health checks consist on the periodic of a command within the container, verifying its exit code. Listing 4 demonstrates how to create a Dockerfile which builds a Docker image using the Nginx image has base and simply executes Nginx on start, verifying every five minutes if the web server is responding to requests. If a request takes longer than three seconds to respond, the health check fails and the container is automatically restarted.

3.4   Job Scheduler

 Cloud applications require frequent short-running jobs to be scheduled, which must be orchestrated across a dynamic infrastructure without permanently allocating resources. A scheduler service running along with the ORCHESTRATION MANAGER can instruct it to allocate one time or periodic jobs, recovering their resources to the infrastructure when they complete.

Context. It is often required that jobs are executed on a periodic basis inside an infrastructure managed by an ORCHESTRATION MANAGER. These jobs can range from internal system verifications, maintenance, infrastructure scaling and many others. These are not long running services, hence, do not need to be continuously executing on the infrastructure, as doing so preallocates valuable resources that would be idle part of the time.

In a non-cloud context, job scheduling was typically provided by Cron (see Sect. 3.4) or similar application. In the context of the cloud Cron is not a viable option, given that it is local to a specific server and not aware of the whole infrastructure and its resource availability.

This pattern considers the adoption of CONTAINERIZATION for packaging the jobs to execute and the presence of an ORCHESTRATION MANAGER.

Example. Consider a distributed database, replicated between multiple servers. Despite the replication, keeping frequent backups in a secure remote location is relevant to recover the database from an unexpected scenario in the infrastructure. This backup must happen frequently and automatically, without the team's intervention.

Problem. *Cloud applications require frequent short-running jobs to be scheduled, which must be orchestrated across a dynamic infrastructure without permanently allocating resources.*

It is common for short-running jobs to be executed in a infrastructure, alongside the hosted microservices. These can vary from database backups to internal system checks. Traditionally, these operations would be the responsibility of the operations team. Some degree of automation could be achieved by leveraging a job scheduler, such as Cron. In the cloud using Cron is not ideal given that the infrastructure is continuously evolving, that containers are dynamically allocated to their host servers and that co-location with specific containers or resource allocation rules might exist for running these jobs. Also, using Cron while using CONTAINERIZATION would require a container to be running for the sole purpose of executing scheduled jobs, permanently reserving resources for the container, or using the host's Cron scheduler polluting the host, both less than ideal approaches.

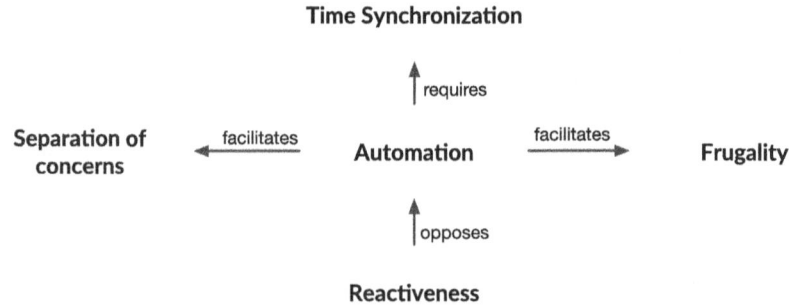

Fig. 8. Relationship between JOB SCHEDULER forces.

Forces. The following forces, represented in Fig. 8, need to be balanced while considering the adoption of this pattern:

Automation Manual intervention is error-prone, slow and costly.

Frugality Permanent resource allocation to idle containers that are only active periodically is not resource efficient for the infrastructure.

Reactiveness Some short-running jobs need to execute as a reaction to an external event (typically called triggers).

Separation of concerns Short-running jobs are bundled with the description of the resources they require to execute, without needing to know anything about the infrastructure where they will be executed.

Time synchronization Maintain machine clocks synchronized across the infrastructure to ensure that jobs are started at the correct time, despite what machine is starting the execution.

Execute one time or periodic jobs in the infrastructure.

Solution. *Deploy a scheduler service along with the* ORCHESTRATION MANAGER *that can instruct it to allocate one time or periodic jobs, recovering their resources to the infrastructure when they complete.*

A JOB SCHEDULER extends the ORCHESTRATION MANAGER pattern, responsible for executing services using CONTAINERIZATION, by enabling the scheduling and execution of one time or periodic jobs in the infrastructure. The pattern can be implemented by using a third-party JOB SCHEDULER that already integrates with the adopted ORCHESTRATION MANAGER.

The JOB SCHEDULER service can expose a programmatic, graphical or both, configuration interface to manage job scheduling. A job specification is composed by the instructions required to execute the job, along with its resource requirements and schedule details.

The exact information required for executing jobs will be specific to the adopted JOB SCHEDULER implementation, but will typically require the details of a container image to execute, along with list of environment variables to configure it, supervision criteria and required execution resources such as the required number of CPU cores or amount of RAM, just like any service would.

The JOB SCHEDULER should integrate with an ORCHESTRATION MANAGER, which is responsible for executing the scheduled job inside a container, honoring its requirement constraints. It does so by instructing the ORCHESTRATION MANAGER to execute a container for running the Job, while also providing the requirements for running it.

Allocated resources are freed upon the job completion, becoming available for executing other jobs. The integration with the ORCHESTRATION MANAGER ensures that jobs are only started if their required resources are available and restarted in case of unexpected failure, observed through the job's exit code.

An ORCHESTRATION MANAGER might also provide the possibility for restricting where jobs are executed in the infrastructure, by tagging the available servers and limiting allocation to servers who are tagged with a particular set of labels.

To ensure consistent behavior despite in which node the JOB SCHEDULER is deployed, the hosts should have their clocks synchronized using an external time server.

Example Resolved. Deploy the scheduler service within the infrastructure. The backup operation would be configured in the scheduler to execute every day. The ORCHESTRATION MANAGER would be responsible for ensuring that the container responsible for executing the job is placed in a server that provides the required resources to run the job, as well as, if needed, it is co-located with the server running the database, reducing network latency.

A retry mechanism can also be specified, ensuring that the backup job would automatically retry up to a certain number of times in case of failure. If the failure persists, the execution of the job is aborted and the team is notified of the issue.

To ensure that all machines share the same date and time, a time synchronization daemon should be present.

Resulting Context. This pattern introduces the following benefits:

Automation Jobs are automatically spawned on the infrastructure on their scheduled times, without requiring manual intervention.

Frugality Resources allocation is minimized for short-running jobs, being recovered by the infrastructure once the job finishes.

Separation of Concerns The scheduled job does not need to know details about the infrastructure, only describe its requirements. The ORCHESTRATION MANAGER will assume the responsibility of placing the container in the right host.

On the other hand, the following liabilities are introduced:

Dependency If a job depends on another service's status, if that service is degraded, the job may consistently fail.

Single point of failure When the scheduler fails, the ORCHESTRATION MANAGER will not be instructed about the jobs it needs to execute.

Synchronism Wrong clock synchronization or misconfigured timezones might result in jobs being executed outside their expected times, which might introduce unexpected results.

Reactiveness This solution does not address reactive job execution.

Related Patterns. Being an extension to ORCHESTRATION MANAGER, choosing a JOB SCHEDULER implementation typically is aligned with the ORCHESTRATION MANAGER choice.

Google also describes how to reliably schedule jobs using their cloud [48]. Using the Chronos JOB SCHEDULER on top of an Apache Mesos ORCHESTRATION MANAGER is explicitly described, as also seen in Sect. 3.4.

Microsoft describes the behavior for a scheduler pattern [75], but it only explains how to implement one. This pattern follows a different approach, detailing on how to use a JOB SCHEDULER with an ORCHESTRATION MANAGER rather then implementing one from scratch.

Known Uses. Most infrastructure management environments have a companion scheduler service, either bundled in or as a plug-in service.

Chronos is a distributed and fault-tolerant scheduler for the Apache Mesos framework [25]. It exposes an API and user interface with which jobs can be scheduled and monitored. Figure 9 shows the Chronos user interface, with four jobs configured. Their state and recurrence is easily perceived in the status and state column, respectively.

Kubernetes enables job scheduling by making available a built in scheduler service. Similar to Chronos, jobs can be managed using the user interface or API [63]. Kubernetes API uses the YAML[4] format to describe jobs, as demonstrated in Listing 5.

---

[4] YAML is a human friendly data serialization standard for all programming languages. Learn more at http://www.yaml.org/.

Fig. 9. The Chronos configuration user interface, showing four scheduled jobs. Chronos enables job scheduling on top of Mesos using a graphical user interface.

Listing 5. Kubernetes configuration for scheduling the execution of a container every minute.

```
1   apiVersion: batch/v1beta1
2   kind: CronJob
3   metadata:
4     name: hello
5   spec:
6     schedule: "*/1 * * * *"
7     jobTemplate:
8       spec:
9         template:
10          spec:
11            containers:
12            - name: hello
13              image: busybox
14              args:
15              - /bin/sh
16              - -c
17              - date; echo Hello from Kubernetes
18            restartPolicy: OnFailure
```

Without using a ORCHESTRATION MANAGER, but with a similar objective, cloud providers tend to provide their own implementation of a scheduler, which can be used to manipulate their environment or client applications directly [8, 75]. These typically enable calling the provider's API to start some action such as running an anonymous function or starting a virtual machine or container.

It was also observed that some companies use a scheduler to periodically evaluate the infrastructure's load and appropriately resize it to cope with the current incoming traffic.

Further Consideration. Most JOB SCHEDULER implementation respect the syntax specified by the POSIX utility Cron, as represented in Fig. 10 [57], for scheduling jobs. This syntax, despite not being a standard, has since been widely adopted as the de facto syntax for describing recurrent jobs, as seen in Sect. 3.4.

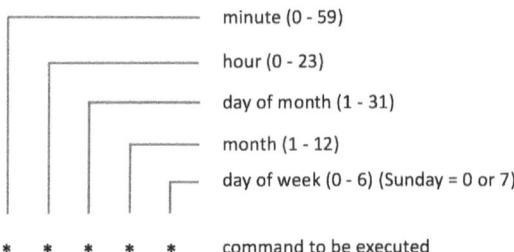

minute (0 - 59)
hour (0 - 23)
day of month (1 - 31)
month (1 - 12)
day of week (0 - 6) (Sunday = 0 or 7)

*   *   *   *   *   command to be executed

Fig. 10. Overview of the CRON format, a commonly adopted syntax used to specify the date and time at which a job should be executed and repeated.

While scheduling is an common approach to schedule one time and recurrent jobs, there is another approach to it. The event-driven community [41] defends that a reactive is the most efficient way to identify when jobs should be spawned [18]. With this approach, a JOB SCHEDULER would not be needed, but an additional component to register event subscription could be adopted, defining which jobs should be spawned after a specific event if observed. For the specific case of time-based execution, this component could react to the clock ticks.

3.5 Failure Injection

 Resilience mechanisms are triggered when software is failing. Since systems are designed to work correctly, the status quo prevents us to from continuously verifying the correctness of those mechanisms. We need additional strategies to minimize the probability of failure in production due to faulty resilience strategies. FAILURE INJECTION software can generate atypical events at both the application and infrastructure level, exercising the available recovery mechanisms, verifying the application's resilience.

Context. Software fails [24]. This assertion is widely accepted and the motivation for writing resilient software. Application failures can originate both from malfunctioning software or due to external conditions, which might be impossible to predict, such as network failures or defective hardware.

When running software at scale, issues are statistically guaranteed to happen [82]. As such, it is imperative that cloud software is designed with resilience in mind, meaning that the application should have a set of strategies to recover from problematic situations at both the application and infrastructure layers. Still, resilience strategies are themselves software, hence, prone to failure, limiting the confidence on their efficiency.

Example. Consider a online web application powered by a database. Such database is essential for the system to work. As such, the database is replicated in hot-standby mode, meaning that the second instance has a complete copy of the first, being used for failover. Furthermore, the database is frequently backed up to an off-site using AWS S3 and Azure disk snapshots.

Consider now that the second database has an issue and needs to be manually resynchronized. While doing so, by mistake, an operator manually deletes part of the production database, leaving both inconsistent and loosing production data. When trying to recover the database from the off-site backups, the operator identifies that the backups are not available and identifies that the backup procedure has not been running as expected. No recent backup is available and the operator will not be able to recover the database to a recent state, resulting in the actual loss of production data.

The example above is actually a simplified version of an event from early 2017, when a GitLab engineer accidentally deleted part of their production database, only to understand that the existing recovery mechanisms where not properly configured, leaving the system down for over 18 h and resulting in the actual loss of production data, namely in the changes to projects, comments, user accounts, issues and snippets, that took place between 17:20 and 00:00 UTC on January 31 [45].

Problem. *Resilience mechanisms are triggered when software is failing. Since systems are designed to work correctly, the status quo prevents us to from continuously verifying the correctness of those mechanisms. We need additional strategies to minimize the probability of failure in production due to faulty resilience strategies.*

It has been previously asserted that software fails. That was the main motivation behind the *let it crash* philosophy in the Erlang language and other actor models, where instead of defensively addressing all possible errors, the program was allowed to crash and restarted in an attempt to recover normal execution [29]. The Reactive Manifesto also addresses this type of recovery, with resilience through recovery as being one of the four characteristics of reactive systems [18].

By relying on software as a recovery mechanism for other software, it is possible that the recovery mechanisms might fail as well. For that matter, just like any other application, the recovery mechanisms themselves must be validated and frequently tested to ensure their correct behavior.

While designing resilience processes for cloud software, these processes them-selves should be monitored, ensuring that the system is able to properly recover from from failure.

Verifying resilience presents the same problem as verifying software: it is not possible to guarantee that the system is completely resilient, only that it endures the identified test scenarios. Furthermore, testing software for bugs is easier than testing resilience, as resilience might be influenced by the underlying infrastructure that hosts the application, which might not be under them team's control. As such, resilience testing is not an one time activity, but instead needs to be continuously improved during the lifetime of the application.

At its core, verifying resilience requires the implemented processes to be stressed, putting the application through unexpected scenarios and verifying how well it behaves. This might be problematic by itself if at some point the application is unable to recover without manual intervention, rendering it in a degraded state.

This problem becomes further complex as it is insufficient to verify resilience in a staging environment, given that resilience is highly influenced by a mul-titude variables in the infrastructure, such as number of resources allocated, for how long they have been allocated or how much load they are handling. While it is possible to create a similar staging environment, even the specific hardware allocated to production might present a different behavior from the staging environment. As such, the only way to increase trust over the resilience of a production environment is to actually test that environment.

Fig. 11. Relationships between FAILURE INJECTION force.

Forces. The following forces, represented in Fig. 11, need to be balanced while considering the adoption of this pattern:

Preemptive failure detection Identify failures in the application before they accidentally impact the application or are exploited by third parties.
Failure generation Known failures are less likely to cause impact in the system than artificially generated ones.
Resilience Failure injection might degrade the status of the system.

Solution. *Generate atypical events at both the application and infrastructure level, exercising the available recovery mechanisms to verify the application's resilience*

To ensure that the system will recover when a problem arises, its resilience strategies must be frequently exercised, even in production, ensuring that the system does in fact recover to the expected status when a failure happens.

An external piece of software can frequently generate unexpected events at both the application and infrastructure level and monitor how the system behaves, verifying it if it recovers as expected. These events can range from shutting down a container instance to a full virtual machine server. In both scenarios, the resilience strategies should be able to recover the application to the expected status, restarting the container in the first scenario or the machine and it's hosted services in the second.

The adopted strategy used for FAILURE INJECTION should be aware of the application and infrastructure's APIs and randomly inject invalid payloads or shutdown system components.

While implementing this pattern, one must consider:

Completeness failures can be injected at both the infrastructure and application level. Only by testing both can we maximize the level of confidence in the system's resiliency.

Frequency We need to decide how often we will exercise the resilience mechanisms, balancing how much resources we are willing to allocate, which directly impacts execution cost, with the level of trust we want to continuously have over the system.

Traceability We need to understand the impact of injecting failures in the system, by aggregating information from the failure injection system with the infrastructure and application logs, facilitating the evaluation of the impact of a failure injection on the system.

Programatic failure injection We want to enable the developer to programmatically describe his failures or failure generation logic, so that the failure injection can be automated and executed automatically, reducing the need for manual intervention while running failure injection tests.

There's a several attack vectors and liabilities introduced while testing resilience. The following scenarios should be considered:

Application misuse Generate random inputs to the application's interfaces, including its APIs.

Unexpected load Suddenly increase the system's load, by generating an abnormally high amount of traffic.

Network degradation Degrade or disable the network to a server, either by disabling the server's network card or use an application that consumes its bandwidth.

Resource depletion Deplete available disk, RAM or CPU from a server, by starting an application in the server that consumes such resources.

Unexpected component shutdown Shutting down random servers or other system components, up to disabling entire availability regions.

While exercising the recovery mechanisms with FAILURE INJECTION, the system is expected to be impacted, which should be carefully monitored by observing:

Latency Some tests will degrade or shutdown resources. While doing so, application latency should be monitored. An ideal resilience mechanism will recover from the injected time without increasing latency above the expected limit. Data from the EXTERNAL MONITOR pattern can be leveraged to observe the application's latency from the user's perspective.

Recovery time The application should recover within an expected duration. Infrastructural and application logs can be used to verify if a recovery is taking more time than expected, which will introduce the need to improve the resilience mechanisms.

Data A resilient application should be able to recover from a failure without losing or corrupting data.

Security During the recovery of the application, the system should remain secure, ensuring that no temporary attack vector is introduced.

Supervision and monitoring patterns such as EXTERNAL MONITOR are companions to FAILURE INJECTION. It is expected that some of the generated events will degrade the system, but its resilience should enable automatic recovery, preventing any impact on the application. If such doesn't happen, monitoring patterns should identify the degraded system state, providing the required information for the development team to recover the system and afterwards implement the required steps to improve its resilience.

It is arguable if FAILURE INJECTION should be applied to production environments given the risk to degrade them. To prevent impacting production systems, FAILURE INJECTION should first be thoroughly tested in a development or staging environment, being introduced into production when the level of confidence around the application's resilience if definitive. Furthermore, its execution in production environment should be constrained to work hours, under close supervision of the team.

While it is arguable if FAILURE INJECTION should be executed against production systems, exercising its recovery mechanisms is the only way to ensure that they are working properly.

Example Resolved. Adopt a FAILURE INJECTION tool and configure it to generate failures against the application's database and its infrastructure, insuring that the system is able to recover automatically.

By periodically exercising the database reliability, the team would have been able to identify earlier that the backup process was not working, just as well as it would be able to understand that the hot-standby replication was not optimally configured, improving it to be sure that the secondary server would be able to sustain the expected level of service required by the application.

Resulting Context. This pattern introduces the following benefits:

Automated Failure detection The adopted tool will generate and inject random events in the system, testing it thoroughly and continuously, identifying issues faster than any manual testing could.

Awareness Using the EXTERNAL MONITOR pattern, the team can be notified of a degradation whenever a FAILURE INJECTION impacts the system.

Preemptive failure detection By stressing the application with unexpected events, the team is able to preemptively identify failures that could happen in the wild otherwise.

On the other hand, the following limitations will be introduced:

Availability While testing reliability, it might be the case that an issue is identified and the system's performance degraded. The team should be immediately alerted and take the required actions to recover the system's stability, as well as implementing the required automations to recover from the newly identified scenario.

Resource usage Exercising resilience will only be possible when resilience mechanisms are available. Often resilience requires redundancy to be implemented, which will always increase the resources required to operate the application.

Unintended consequences While the system might be able to recover, it might do so while introducing unacceptable consequences. For example, a critical system might lose data during a recovery process.

Related Patterns. When implementing this pattern, SELF HEALING should have been implemented, enabling both the application and infrastructure to recover automatically. FAILURE INJECTION can also leverage LOG AGGREGATION for capturing its action.

The description of the responsibilities for a FAILURE INJECTION tool has been described the Software Failure Injection Pattern System [66].

Known Uses Netflix was one of the main motivators behind FAILURE INJECTION with the implementation of their open source tool ChaosMonkey. ChaosMonkey interacts with an AWS account and randomly shutting down infrastructure components. At Netflix, ChaosMonkey is executed against the production environment during business hours, randomly terminating virtual machines. Their rationale is that exposing engineers to failures motivates them to make their services more resilient [80]. ChaosMonkey is one of the many tools available in the Simian Army, a set of open source tools developed by Netflix to help engineers improve their software's reliability [79].

Motivated by the impact from the floods of Hurricane Sandy in 2012 in New Jersey, Project Storm is Facebook's approach to resilience testing. At its infancy, it was composed by a set of small drills lead by a reliability team that were designed to replicate the consequences of catastrophic natural events, just like Hurricane Sandy was, by degrading or disconnecting small parts of their infrastructure. By 2014, the team behind Project Storm upped their game, starting to disable entire data centers. The initial drills enabled the team to identify several unexpected points of failures [55].

FAILURE INJECTION is motivated by the Principles of Chaos Engineering. Quoting, "Chaos Engineering is the discipline of experimenting on a distributed system in order to build confidence in the system's capability to withstand turbulent conditions in production" [23]. In practice, it consists on experimenting with the moving parts of the application, looking for actions that might result in a system failure, such as crashing servers of malfunctioning hard drives.

Further Considerations. Chaos engineering practices are implemented against systems expected to be reliable, validating their reliability. It should be expected that failures are found and the system should recover without manual intervention. Still, for teams starting to implement FAILURE INJECTION, its execution should be carefully monitored, as some failures might result in non considered scenarios, leaving the system in an unrecoverable state and requiring manual intervention.

According to the Chaos Community, Chaos Engineer is based on the following principles [23].:

Build a Hypothesis around Steady State Behavior Focus on the measurable output of a system, rather than internal attributes of the system. Measurements of that output over a short period of time constitute a proxy for the system's steady state. The overall system's throughput, error rates, latency percentiles, etc.could all be metrics of interest representing steady state behavior. By focusing on systemic behavior patterns during experiments, Chaos verifies that the system does work, rather than trying to validate how it works.

Vary Real-world Events Chaos variables reflect real-world events. Prioritize events either by potential impact or estimated frequency. Consider events that correspond to hardware failures like servers dying, software failures like malformed responses, and non-failure events like a spike in traffic or a scaling event. Any event capable of disrupting steady state is a potential variable in a Chaos experiment.

Run Experiments in Production Systems behave differently depending on environment and traffic patterns. Since the behavior of utilization can change at any time, sampling real traffic is the only way to reliably capture the request path. To guarantee both authenticity of the way in which the system is exercised and relevance to the current deployed system, Chaos strongly prefers to experiment directly on production traffic.

Automate Experiments to Run Continuously Running   experiments manually is labor-intensive and ultimately unsustainable. Automate experiments and run them continuously. Chaos Engineering builds automation into the system to drive both orchestration and analysis.

Minimize Blast Radius Experimenting in production has the potential to cause unnecessary customer pain. While there must be an allowance for some short-term negative impact, it is the responsibility and obligation of the Chaos Engineer to ensure the fallout from experiments are minimized and contained.

3.6   Summary

This chapter introduced five patterns for orchestrating and supervising services in the cloud. CONTAINERIZATION provided a strategy for isolating and porting services. ORCHESTRATION MANAGER abstracted the underlying infrastructure, automating service placement using containers on top of it. AUTOMATED RECOVERY continuously monitored these services, evaluating if they were or were not responding as expected to specific inputs, restarting them on failure. JOB SCHEDULER enabled running transient jobs in the infrastructure at any given time and with a configured frequency, releasing the resources once the job completes. Finally, FAILURE INJECTION generates failures in the infrastructure and services, forcing them to recover as a strategy to validate their recovery mechanisms continuously. These patterns facilitate the orchestration of services in the cloud and ensure their continuous execution.

The next chapter introduces the monitoring patterns category, describing three patterns for observing service status and state.

4   Monitoring Patterns

Monitoring continuously evaluates the conditions under which the services are being executed. Monitoring can work reactively, detecting issues on data generated by the application, such as a log entry or an alarm, as well as active by interacting with the services directly, and evaluating their correct behavior.

Debugging an application in production requires as much information as possible in order to trace the actions that lead to an issue. Services should PREEMPTIVE LOGGING, producing verbose execution logs that should be kept for the longest period of time possible.

Having distributed services producing logs will require developers to leverage multiple log files to trace an issue. To prevent this, the team should adopt LOG AGGREGATION, by having a centralized view of all the logs generated by all services in a queryable format.

4.1   Preemptive Logging

 The information required to debug issues in software is often lost during their first occurrence due to insufficient log verbosity. By adjusting logging verbosity preemptively in services and servers within acceptable resource limits (CPU, storage, others), the team maximizes the probability of capturing relevant information for addressing future issues right from their first occurrence.

Context. It's often difficult to guarantee that software will behave as expected, but it can be designed for the worst. In those situations, information is key to debug applications, which makes having execution logs available after those unexpected scenarios the most relevant piece of information to understand what, how and why the software has failed.

Most third-party applications have adjustable verbosity logging capabilities, but first-party applications sometimes neglect that need, causing the developers to lack the required information to mitigate unexpected failures. Given that service cooperation is key in cloud software, and considering the uncertainty of the events that lead to unexpected errors, all services should equally generate logs that are the sole resource from developers to understand and mitigate the issue.

Example. Consider a database service in a microservices architecture. The service is responsible for persisting information important for other services in the infrastructure. At a given point in time, the database crashes. Automated operations practices should ensure that the service is automatically recovered, but, after a while, it crashes again. This behavior is recurrent and without explanation from the development team. The team is expected to identify and fix the issue, but is not being able to reproduce it outside the production environment. Without the proper information about the production system, the team is rendered incapable to properly addressing the issue.

Problem. *The information required to debug issues in software is often lost during their first occurrence due to insufficient log verbosity.*

Development teams tend to be conservative on their software instrumentation, undervaluing the importance of capturing runtime information. When software fails, it is common that the only debugging approach is to further instrumenting the software and await for the issue to repeat itself. This approach decreases the level of confidence on the software quality, as well as requires the team to knowingly leave a bug in their software given the lack of information to fix it.

Forces. The following forces, represented in Fig. 12, need to be balanced while considering the adoption of this pattern:

Traceability Development teams need as much data as possible to be available in order to identify the conditions that may have triggered issues in a service.

Execution Resources Increasing the logging level increases the amount of resources required to execute the service, such as CPU and memory.

Retention Policy Verbose logging can become expensive to collect and persist for large periods of time.

Verbosity Increasing the log verbosity provides additional information for posterior debug, but it also requires additional storage space and human effort to process.

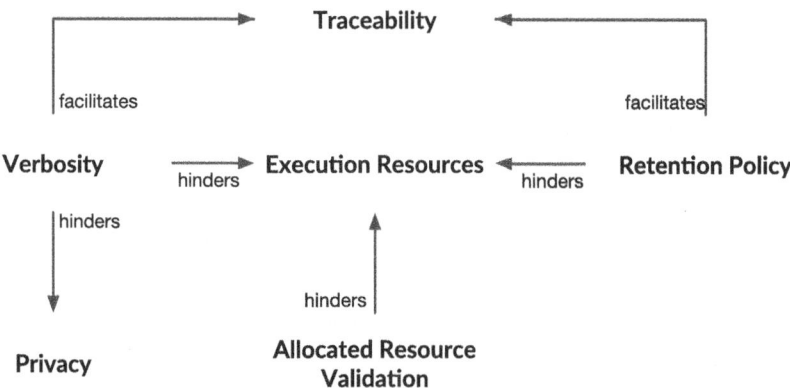

Fig. 12. Relationship between PREEMPTIVE LOGGING forces.

Allocated Resource Validation Resources might be over or under-allocated to a service, result in a poor usage of the available infrastructure resources.

Privacy Due to legislation, it might not be possible to persist some type of data.

Solution. *Adjust logging verbosity in services and servers within acceptable resource limits (CPU, storage, others), maximizing the probability of capturing relevant information for addressing future issues right from their first occurrence.*

Logging is often undervalued by less experienced developers, who are tempted to reduce log verbosity in production to keep the system leaner. By doing so, they unintentionally miss the opportunity of capturing information that would allow them to debug unexpected runtime problems. This may prevent the development team from effectively tackle such problems, unless they begin monitoring the service and server, hoping to observe the issue happening again and capture enough information to identify the reasons behind it.

PREEMPTIVE LOGGING insures that runtime information from both services and servers is captured, being an asset for debugging runtime issues.

To implement it, development teams should start by discussing and identifying all the information that can possible be extracted from the service and respective server. From there, the team should discard the items that will never be useful, setting the optimal log verbosity level for them.

While deciding on what data to keep, resource usage should be discussed, has the more information is persisted, the greater the resource impact in the system. A retention policy should also be set, as the information becomes less relevant with time.

A scenario where all system events can be captured is ideal, as these can be reproduced in a test environment to further debug issues. Also, once a bug is fixed, they can be replayed in the production environment some types of failures, e.g. one where a specific service is dropping the events sent to it.

Recent privacy trends such as the European GDPR regulation might prevent some event data to be physically persisted.

Example Resolved. The team responsible for the database service would discuss what metrics would be relevant to understand how the service is behaving. As an example, they could capture: number of incoming connections, number of incoming queries, query response times, programming exceptions and the incoming queries themselves. Server metrics would also be captured, namely disk IO, RAM, CPU or network usage.

If the service revealed an issue, they would access the generated log files and use them to understand what triggered it. They could start by understanding if the allocated resources where enough to accommodate the service. If that hypothesis is excluded, they could then dig into the service's own logs in order to understand when and why the service started to misbehave.

A retention policy can automatically archive or delete older log entries. When adjusting this policy the team should allow enough time to ensure the logs are available during the time period when they might be used, preventing them to get discarded too soon.

Resulting Context. By adopting PREEMPTIVE LOGGING, development teams will gain:

Reproducibility Service operations can be captured, facilitating the team to understand how it has behaved. The whole input stream can be captured and replicated in a controlled environment to understand how and why it reacted in a certain way to a given set of inputs.

Allocated Resource Validation Capturing logs from hardware usage from a server will enable the team to better understand how the service consumes resources and optimize resource allocation.

Security and Auditing The development team will be able to trace security problems and threads.

While configuring the service's logging levels, the following should be taken into consideration:

Resources Should be increased to cope with both the higher CPU and disk space demand of increasing the log verbosity.

Retention Policy An increased retention policy will keep the logs available for a long time period, but such will increase the required disk space required to persist the logs.

Verbosity Again, the verbosity level should be adjusted to a value that balances a relevant output, with the amount of disk space it will consume.

Security An attack on this component would expose information from all others.

Related Patterns. The team job's is simplified if it is able query log entries from multiple sources, understand what events where happening in each service. LOG AGGREGATION provides this functionality, by moving the logs from their origin to a centralized repository, where they are aggregated and indexed, facilitating their usage. COLLABORATIVE MONITORING AND LOGGING describes the importance of logging and its relevance while deployment software on the cloud [10]. Fernandez described how logs can be leveraged to audit security in the AUDIT LOG pattern [39].

Known Uses. Amazon Web Services' CloudTrail enables the capturing of all API interactions in an AWS account, providing complete traceability of all changes through it [7]. Azure provides a similar service [11]. Spinellis identified log verbosity as a parameter to manually tweak in production when looking for problems [42]. Fu elaborated on that problematic in his survey [42], theorizing automated log verbosity adjustment in production as a relevant research topic.

4.2   Log Aggregation

 Services orchestrated at scale produce disperse logs, resulting in a troublesome process to acquire and correlate those who come from multiple sources. This pattern suggests the Aggregation and indexing all service and server logs in a central repository, providing the team with a centralized system to query and visualize execution logs.

Context. At the scale at which cloud Computing is applied, and given the scalability of operations introduced by DevOps, a development team can easily be managing hundreds of services orchestrated on top of thousands servers. Both the hardware and their hosted services are continuously operating and producing relevant information, commonly via log files. Those files must be accessed often and it is not functional to keep them dispersed in the infrastructure, forcing developers to individual access each machine and file to gather the information they require.

Example. Consider the example from Sect. 5.1, where each service is running on its own dedicated server. The three services are producing log files, along with the operative system from their host. Imagine now that there was an issue with the AC service or server, rendering the service unresponsive. The developers need to remotely login to the server to access the required log file and debug the issue. Along this process, they understand that the issue was due to a communication error with the messaging service. They now need to access the machine hosting the messaging service in order to debug its log entries. This process must be repeated for each service and server involved in the issue, going back and forth until the problem is identified. This approach makes it difficult to correlate log entries from different sources and demands that the developer individually access each one of the machines.

Problem. *Services orchestrated at scale produce disperse logs, resulting in a troublesome process to acquire and correlate those who come from multiple sources.*

Teams deploying software at scale can easily see their infrastructure grow to tens of servers hosting hundreds of service instances. As suggested by PREEMPTIVE LOGGING, these services should be verbose at producing logs. At this scale, it is troublesome for developers to leverage this logs, given their sparsity across the infrastructure. The basic solution of individually accessing each server and service log file quickly becomes unmanageable.

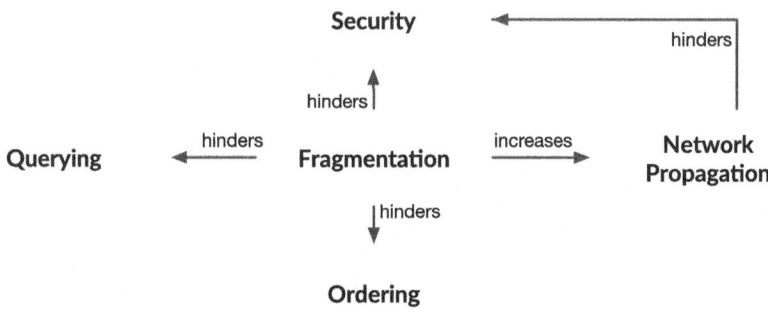

Fig. 13. Relationship between LOG AGGREGATION forces.

Forces. The following forces, represented in Fig. 13, need to be balanced while considering the adoption of this pattern:

Fragmentation Scattered log files across servers incur in extra effort for the developers to debug the application.

Network Propagation Transferring log data from its source to a central aggregation point requires additional bandwidth and might incur in additional data transfer costs.

Ordering Propagation of logs through the Internet and unaligned clocks might result in out of order log entries.

Querying Querying in a log stream is essential to quickly identify relevant information from large collections of logs.

Security Sending logs across the network should use a secure channel, insuring that sensitive information is never stolen. Also, the log storage should guarantee that they are not writable, preventing attackers or other software from changing them.

Solution. *Aggregate and index all service and server logs in a central repository, providing the team with a centralized system to query and visualize execution logs.*

Having logs available only at their source makes their usage troublesome, requiring the user to login into the system and either download them or use the set of tools remotely available to query them. At scale, when tracing how services cooperate with each other, this means that the user would have to replicate this process across all intervening servers and services.

LOG AGGREGATION solves this problem by providing a centralized system for aggregating and visualizing all logs in an infrastructure. This solution is applied as: (1) a log aggregation service is deployed in the infrastructure, enabling the querying and visualization of information from the logs and (2) each service daemon deployed along with it must forward its logs to the log aggregation service.

The centralized log service can persist the log entries in a database, exposing a query interface for them. This allows developers to mix and match events, better understanding what has happened in their infrastructure as a whole, or in a specific machine or server. Figure 14 represents the involved components in this process as a class diagram.

A secure channel should be used when sending logs from their origin to this centralized database. Also it should allow entries from being written, but prevent them from being changed, ensuring that logs are immutable.

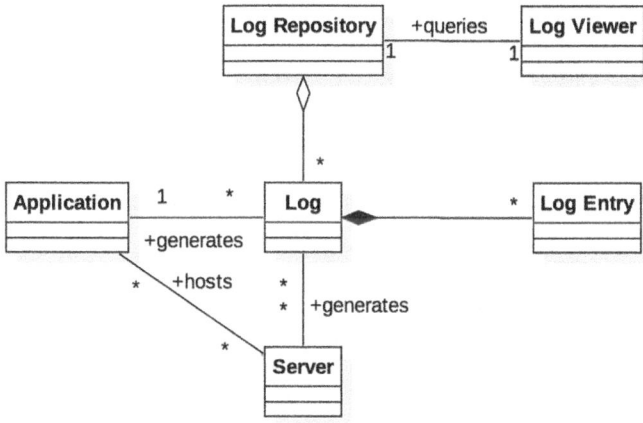

Fig. 14. Class diagram showing the entities involved in the log generation, persistence and querying process. Applications and Servers generate log files which are composed by multiple log entries. Each log entry has relevant information of the team to use in the future. Logs are persisted in a remote log repository. This repository aggregates all sources of information, allowing the log viewer to query a single location.

Example Resolved. Each service and server would send their logs to a centralized log repository service. This service would need to be instantiated in the infrastructure or adopted as an external service. Within it, the developer would have a global view of all logs from all services in the infrastructure. It would be possible to query those logs, filtering them specifically for any specific service at any given time.

Resulting Context. This pattern introduces the following benefits:

Fragmentation Developers can use a aggregation service to aggregate all the information they need from any service or server in the infrastructure.

Querying Once aggregated in a single location, data can be indexed, allowing developers to query the logs, finding the information they need for their specific task faster.

Security Communicating logs using a secure channel is essential for keeping sensitive data private. Also, the chosen log storage should also be secured to prevent data leakage.

While deciding the technologies to implement this pattern, the following should be taken into consideration:

Network Propagation In order to propagate logs to the aggregating server, additional bandwidth will be consumed.

Ordering Ordering will rely on the time stamp generated at the server. There might be some errors in cases where the server's clock isn't synchronized.

Single point of failure Without a redundant deployment, a failure in log aggregation system would revert this system's benefits.

Related Patterns. REPOSITORY describes a generic approach to a data repository [53]. Fernandez describes the application of log aggregation in the security context to trace user actions [39].

MESSAGING SYSTEM can be used as a communication channel to propagate logs to the log the aggregation service. This pattern is further useful if PREEMPTIVE LOGGING is applied in each service in the infrastructure.

LOG AGGREGATION can be used as a source of information for REACT, feeding it with the events used to trigger reactive actions.

Known Uses. Elastic, through their Elastic Stack, leverage Logstash as a tool for acquiring and propagating logs from applications. Logs are propagated to a remote Elasticsearch, an highly indexable JSON document storage. Information can then be queried and visualized using Kibana, a dash-boarding tool for captured data [36].

Loggly[5] is a subscription based log aggregation cloud service. It provides clients for acquiring logs from multiple platforms and services, making them available in a single time-based searchable history.

---

[5] Details at https://www.loggly.com/.

Roderick et all have described how their logging service acquired over 50 TB per year, making this data available for over 1000 users daily [89].

4.3   External Monitoring

 Monitoring an application from inside the infrastructure that hosts it will result in an incomplete and biased version of the reality, for example, given the inability to observe issues such as lack of Internet connectivity or abnormal latency to the application. EXTERNAL MONITOR suggest testing the application's public interfaces from an external source, providing an unbiased awareness of the application's status.

Context. While part of the development process is responsible to ensure resilience, just like it is impossible to ensure complete reliability using software testing [70], it is not possible to ensure that a system is 100% resilient. Accepting that it will eventually fail is important to accept the need to increase awareness about the system's status at all times. This is the motivation behind the adoption of monitoring systems. Frequently, monitoring systems live within the application's own infrastructure, which might bias the awareness about the actual state of the application, given all the external variables introduced by using the Internet as a distribution channel.

Example. Consider an authentication service, part of a larger application. Provided with a valid login, it should output an authentication token for interacting with the other services in the application. Consider the scenario where when used from within the infrastructure, the authentication service works as expected, but, when accessed from a remote application, the authentication service is inaccessible. Such discrepancy might have been caused by a misconfigured firewall.

This scenario demonstrates that a service can have different status when observed from within the application's infrastructure and a remote site.

Problem. *Monitoring an application from inside the infrastructure that hosts it will result in an incomplete and biased version of the reality, for example, given the inability to observe issues such as lack of Internet connectivity or abnormal latency to the application.*

Software failures can be catastrophic to business owners. Application downtime consequences can range from client complaints to loss of confidence in the application and, ultimately, user abandonment or contractual breach. Given the ever growing offer of online services, a failing application can easily be replaced by a competitor.

In case of failure, the development team should quickly be aware of the application's status, facilitating a quick reaction.

This awareness must not depend on the application or its infrastructure, as that would bias the observation. In the context of cloud computing, simply monitoring the application alongside its execution is not only biased, but prevents the detection of several unpredictable Internet-related issues, such as misconfigured or failing routers, CDN, DNS or firewalls, which would directly impact the client's access to the application.

In the example from Sect. 4.3, a misconfigured firewall is inadvertently blocking traffic from a valid source, leaving the service inaccessible from the outside. This issue would not be identified by monitoring the application from within the infrastructure, as the firewall would not be used between two internal services.

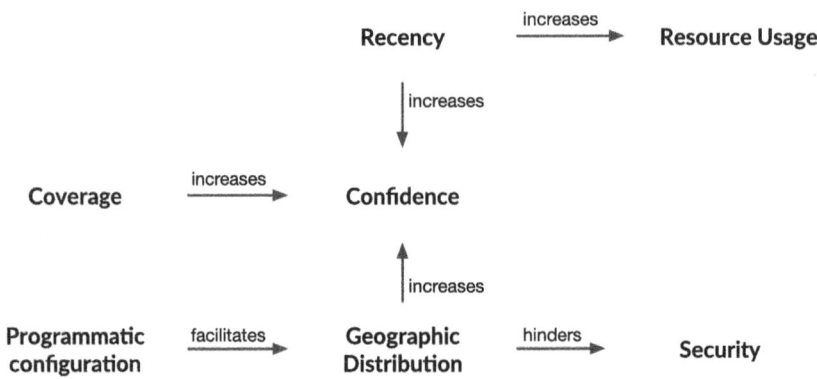

Fig. 15. EXTERNAL MONITOR forces relationships.

Forces. The following forces, represented in Fig. 15, need to be balanced while considering the adoption of this pattern:

Confidence Maintain awareness of the system's state without relying on its internal information or be biased by internal monitoring.

Recency Be notified as soon as a possible complication is identified in the application.

Coverage Confidence level is increased with the increase of test coverage.

Resource usage Minimize the impact from monitoring on the application's resource requirements, which will directly impact either performance or cost.

Security Minimize the attack vectors for the application. Exposing sensitive application details to additional external tools will create a new attack vectors.

Geographic description Running tests from different globe locations increases the level of confidence that the system is working worldwide.

Solution. *Test the application's public interfaces from an external source, providing an confidence over the application's status.*

Resilience is an essential requirement of any cloud software. Still, just like with software testing, it is impossible to guarantee that a system is fully resilient and that it will not fail. Besides improving the system's resilience, the development team should also invest in their awareness of the system's status in production, reducing the time required to detect a failure.

EXTERNAL MONITOR consists on the frequent execution of tests against the public interfaces of a live production system, evaluating if they are responding as expected. Tests are configured and executed from in a service running in a separate network environment from the application itself and run without any knowledge of the application's state (as a black-box test), providing an accurate observation of the system's status as seen from across the Internet.

Test coverage can range from a basic status check to see if the service is up to having a batch of tests covering all the application's public interfaces and their different uses. Such level of coverage could be seen as black-box integration tests executed against a live environment. It is up to the team to balance the level of coverage with the intended level con confidence in the system's status.

The team can either develop their own EXTERNAL MONITOR tool or adopt one of the many third party tools available. Developing a tool for external monitoring would require a considerable investment in development and operations. On the other hand, adopting a third party tool introduces a financial cost for using the service, as well as it widens the attack surface to the application, as sensible information such as user credentials need to be shared with the system. An hybrid approach could consider adopting an open-source tool for doing external monitoring, which will prevent sharing sensitive credentials with a third party while still requiring little investment in developing the software.

Some tests might require sensitive data to execute, such as user credentials. In case of an attack to the monitoring platform, this might hinder security, leaving those credentials exposed. Frequently rotating these credentials can help mitigate this issue.

While implementing this pattern, one must consider:

Recency We need to decide how often we will run the external monitoring tests, balancing how fast do we want to know when an issue appears with the system as the load introduced by the tests will increase resource usage.

Development effort We need to balance the completion of test coverage with the time required developing new tests.

Security We need to decide which, if any, credentials should be made available in the external system to test protected interfaces, at the cost of possibly exposing sensitive data.

Accuracy We want to prevent false positives by confirming issues redundantly, such as those who might result from latency or network partitioning.

Geographical distribution We might want to distribute tests globally, ensuring the the application is working within the specified parameters, despite where the traffic is originated. This enable verifying the correct behavior of components such as CDNs.

Traceability We want to understand why a test has failed, by evaluating the inputs and outputs used to identify the failure. LOG AGGREGATION pattern can be leveraged to combine logs from this patterns, as well as logs from FAILURE INJECTION and the remaining components of the system, providing an unified view over the system's behavior.

Programmatic configuration We want to manage monitoring tests automatically as part of the deployment process, eliminating the need for manual configuration, hence, increasing confidence in the tests.

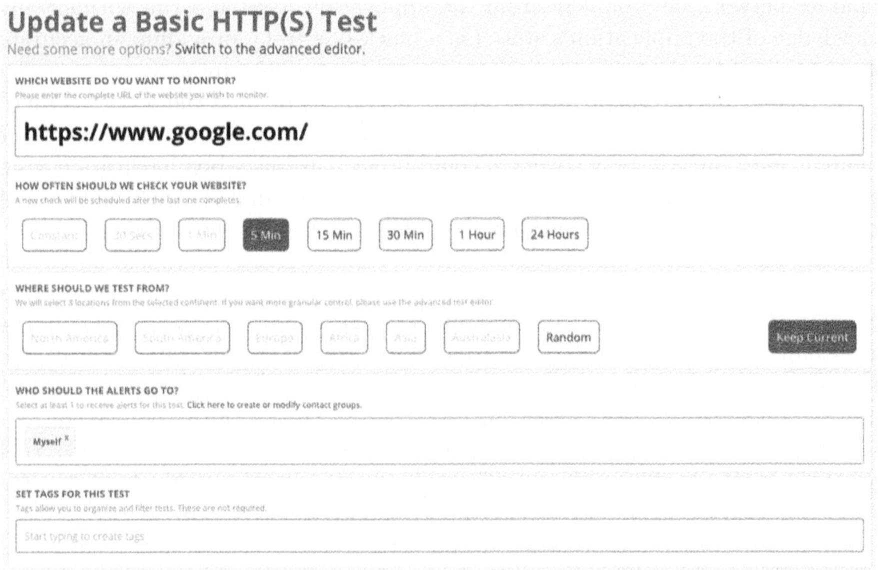

Fig. 16. Statuscake's HTTP(S) test creation interface, showing a basic HTTP test for Google's homepage, which will execute every 5 min from a random server.

Third party tools for implementing the pattern often allow tests to be created from both a graphic interface, as seen in Fig. 16 and a programmatic interface. The latter enables tests to be configured as part of the application's deployment process.

EXTERNAL MONITOR is not a recent subject to cloud computing. *Cloud monitoring: A survey* [2] thoroughly details why cloud computing is an important aspect of cloud applications and describes over twenty tools to implement it, ranging from commercial to open-source offers, being a good support for selecting the tool used to implement this pattern.

Example Resolved. Considering the example, this pattern would be implemented by adopting an EXTERNAL MONITOR system which would make an authentication request to the authentication system and confirm that the answer contained a proper authentication token. This test would be configured in the monitoring platform at the end of the deployment process, ensuring that the application is tested and working as expected right from the moment the deployment is complete.

Tests would be executed at a configured frequency and from different geographic locations to ensure that the application behaves correctly, despite from where a request has originated.

Possibly at a later stage, and for increasing test coverage, any other interface in the service could be tested as well.

To prevent configuring the external platform with actual user credentials, a mock user could be set up in the live system. This way, in the case of data leakage in the monitoring system, no significant impact would be observed on the monitored application. It is arguable that testing against a single user account that was created with the sole purpose of interacting with tests might bias the test results.

Resulting Context. By adopting EXTERNAL MONITOR, development teams will gain:

Confidence Given continuous independent monitoring, there is an added confidence that the system is behaving as expected if no alarm is raised.

Traceability The team will be able to understand what behavior was observed as response to any failing request using the EXTERNAL MONITOR logs.

Programmatic configuration The team will be able to evolve test scenarios along with their development, using the EXTERNAL MONITOR API to setup or update tests.

On the other hand, the following liabilities can be introduced:

Security When the communication channel is properly secure, no data leakage can occur by executing the tests from an EXTERNAL MONITOR provider. The team must trust the provider though. Given an attack against it, sensible information might be exposed. It is the team's responsibility to minimize or eliminate the need for sensible information such as credentials for executing the tests.

Resource usage If careless, the team might create a large volume of tests at a high frequency, which might generate enough load to degrade the application. It is up to the team to properly balance the volume of tests and their frequency.

Related Patterns. EXTERNAL MONITOR providers expose APIs which can be used to programmatically manage the tests. A team that adopts INFRASTRUCTURE AS CODE will be more efficient at managing their tests.

EXTERNAL MONITOR can be used to feed information for LOG AGGREGATION, facilitating a centralized view of the issues observed in the application from this monitoring strategy as well.

HEALTH ENDPOINT MONITORING from Microsoft is similar to this pattern proposes the creation of HTTP health checks exposed by the application, so that an external tool can verify the application status [74]. That implementation differs from EXTERNAL MONITOR, as it requires specific endpoints to be implemented and tested from the external health checking tool. Instead, EXTERNAL MONITOR proposes that the external tool interacts with the application as a client would, using any public interface, not limited to HTTP, validating that it is providing the expected answers.

The COLLABORATIVE MONITORING AND LOGGING pattern [37] describes how monitoring and logging activities can be coordinated between a cloud consumer and provider, describing that monitoring and auditing requirements can described by the consumer but observed by the provider. This approach is similar to EXTERNAL MONITOR, given that the monitoring behavior is extracted from the application the consumer is developing and executed with an external tool, managed by the cloud provider.

Known Uses. Multiple services are available providing the EXTERNAL MONITOR tool required to implement this pattern. StatusCake, Pingdom or NewRelic [81,85,95] are only three of those applications. Pricing and features set them apart, with most being able to test at the HTTP and TCP layers.

Further Considerations. Juvenal, a first century poet, in his *Satires* series of books wrote the famous Latin quote "Quis custodiet ipsos custodes?", roughly translated to *who watches the watchmen?* [99]. This quote can still today motivate discussion around cloud monitoring. By relying on an external tool to monitor the system, we are delegating the responsibility of capturing failures to an external system. What must be taken into consideration is that the external system is a piece of software as well, which might also. In such scenario, a failing system would not be detected, given that the monitoring system would also be unavailable.

4.4 Summary

This chapter introduced three patterns for observing cloud software status and state. PREEMPTIVE LOGGING recommends that developers preemptively adjust their logging level to ensure they capture relevant information to debug potential future issues with the system. LOG AGGREGATION facilitates working with logs from multiple sources, aggregating them in a centralized platform where developers can slice and dice it for quicker and more meaningful exploration. Finally, EXTERNAL MONITOR recommends the monitoring of the public service endpoints from an external location, ensuring that the system is monitored independently by interacting with the system as a user would, generating alarms for the team on failures. These patterns help developers increase their confidence in the correct operation of the application, providing the required data to dissect issues when they are observed.

The next chapter introduces two discovery patterns, which help developers design how their services can cooperate, both synchronously and asynchronously.

5   Discovery and Communication Patterns

In a microservice architecture, multiple services need to cooperate in order to achieve their goal as a whole. Being deployed in containers hosted in dynamically provisioned hardware, the services must first discover and create a communication channel before they can start to cooperate.

While using an Orchestration Manager that dynamically allocates containers, the exact network location at where a service will be running is unknown. Using a SERVICE DISCOVERY, a service can be abstracted through a local network port exposed on every machine that is always forwarded to one instance of the service, possibly balancing traffic between multiple instances [91]. This is easily achieved by preemptively creating a table that maps local ports to services. Whenever the port is mapped, the service is up and the communication can be established.

Some use cases require services to communicate amongst themselves synchronously for RPC and asynchronously for delegating information to collaborating services. A MESSAGING SYSTEM can be used to send both types of messages between micro-services, eliminating the complexity associated with service discovery [44].

5.1   Messaging System

 As service instances increase, communication between services needs to be abstracted, enabling proper balancing between instances. This communication strategy is required to be fault-tolerant and scalable to maintain the application's resiliency. As a solution, a MESSAGING SYSTEM, colloquially known as message queue, can abstract service placement and orchestrate messages with multiple routing strategies between them.

Context. The adoption of microservices as an architectural style introduced the need for services to cooperate in a decentralized and possibly unreliable environment. It is not guaranteed that every component is online at all time, nor that each service has a stable IP address (Internet Protocol) or number of instances running.

These intricacies of cloud computing introduce several requirements, namely, services need to *communicate* with each other in an ever-changing environment, the communication process must be fault-tolerant, ensuring that the system as a whole is *resilient* when confronted with irregular behavior from either side of the communication, and message passing should be *asynchronous, decoupled, evolvable*, using a *content-agnostic* communication channel.

Example. Consider an home automation solution that manages Air Conditioning (AC) systems. Three services compose the solution: *Sensor Reader*, *Data Receiver* and *AC Manager*. *Sensor Reader* is deployed inside the user's house. It is responsible for acquiring and forwarding temperature data. *Data Receiver* is a Web Server that receives temperature metrics and persists them in a database. *Data Receiver* is also able to provide aggregations over the data persisted in the database. *AC Manager* is responsible for managing AC units by evaluating the average temperature over the course of the past 10 min, configuring an AC to generate cold or warm air. The three services must cooperate to provide a complete solution for automated AC management. The expected interaction between them is depicted in Fig. 17.

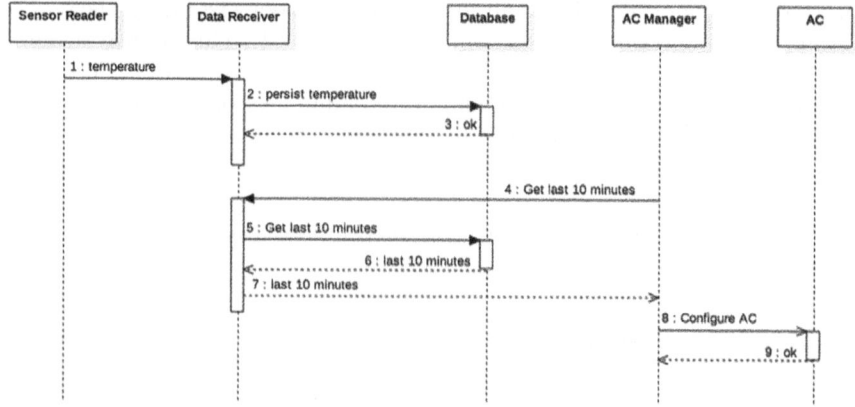

Fig. 17. A microservice architecture-based system to capture and persist temperature metrics from an home environment, later used to configure an AC system. The arrows in the sequence diagram represent the massages exchanged between the components.

Problem. *As service instances increase, communication between services needs to be abstracted, enabling proper balancing between instances. This communication strategy is required to be fault-tolerant and scalable to maintain the application's resiliency.*

Services in a cloud application need to communicate with each other to cooperate. A common communication strategy uses a client-server approach, limiting the communication to the two intervening service instances and requiring that the client knows how to connect to the server, namely its hostname and server port. Cloud application are deployed into dynamic hardware, which means that internal server's addresses are not available during development time, rendering troublesome to use direct communication between services. Furthermore, when multiple instances of a service exist, the traffic needs to be balanced between all instances.

Considering the above, the need for an abstraction over the communication between services is identified. Such channel must enable passing any type of messages and correctly identify the sender and receiver of such messages. Such communication channel must be scalable, ensuring that latency requirements are met even when handling large volumes of messages.

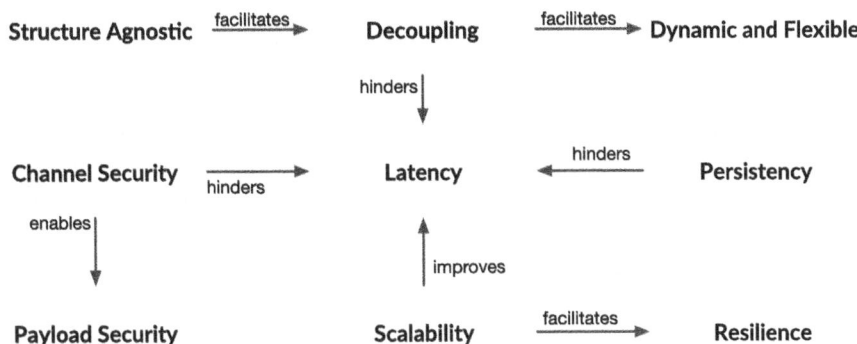

Fig. 18. Relationship between the MESSAGING SYSTEM forces.

Forces. The following forces, represented in Fig. 2, need to be balanced while considering the adoption of this pattern:

This pattern is influenced by the following forces:

Decoupling A sender doesn't need to know the network address of a receiving service to communicate with it.

Scalability The communication channel needs to be itself scalable.

Resilience Communication should be resilient, despite failures in the communication channel.

Persistency Messages between services should be persisted until there is a confirmation that they have been processed.

Structure Agnostic The communication channel should be agnostic to the messages it orchestrates.

Dynamic and Flexible The topology of the system will evolve with time, with new services joining existing ones, and others leaving in real time.

Payload security The communication channel should support encrypted messages.

Channel security The communication channel should itself encrypted.

Latency Introducing an indirection in communication increases the latency required for passing a message between two services.

Solution. *Use a* MESSAGING SYSTEM, *colloquially known as message queue, to abstract service placement and orchestrate messages with the optimal routing strategy between them.*

A MESSAGING SYSTEM is responsible for routing messages between services which can be both producers and consumers of messages. Messages can vary in size and contents, given that the channel is agnostic of their internal structure, as long as they respect the adopted protocol.

MESSAGING SYSTEM works by creating one or more queues that work as a first in, first out (FIFO) data structure. Some implementations provide the possibility of prioritizing messages in the queue. Quality of Service (QoS) policies can also be applied, forcing consumers to confirm that they have successful processed the message before it gets discarded from the queue. QoS ensures that a failing service won't remove a message from the queue without it actually being processed. If a service fails to acknowledge that the message has been processed in an acceptable time period, the message becomes available for another consumer to process.

Most implementations support multiple message delivery strategies. RabbitMQ, which is one of the most adopted implementation, supports simple queues, exchanges with multiples queues, routing, topic-based consumption and RPC [83].

When implementing Remote Procedure Call (RPC), services can issue requests to the message queue and block waiting for an answer. A consumer would pick up the request, process it, and send it back to the queue, destined to the request sender. That first server would then receive his request and resume his computation.

Moving the responsibility of handling all communications to the Message Queue service makes it a single point of failure. For this reason, messaging services are typically deployed with redundancy, ensuring that communications between services will continue to work if some instances fail.

The concept of message passing systems has been available for several years, as middleware that provide highly-observable communication strategies, namely one-to-many communication, providing dynamic connections among services. Initial reference to messaging applications as a mean of communication between servers was first introduced on the 2001 patent *Message Queue Server System* [102]. More recently, several standards have been introduced, namely the *Advanced Message Queuing Protocol* (AMQP) and the *Message Queue Telemetry Transport* (MQTT) [68].

Most implementations will enable the communication channel to use an encryption algorithm to protect the communication channel. Being agnostic to the message's contents, the payload itself can also be encrypted when needed, preventing data leaks even if the MESSAGING SYSTEM is compromised.

Example Resolved. Considering the example described in section Sect. 5.1, the three services can communicate using a message queue based distribution in a message system, as shown in Fig. 19. Message queues can be identified by a name and require consumers to subscribe the queues from which they want to receive messages.

Initially, the *Data Receiver* service would subscribe to queues *metrics* and *requests*. *AC Manager* would subscribe to a queue named after it, *manager*.

Inside the house *Sensor Reader* would capture temperature metrics and send them to the message queue using the *metrics* queue. Asynchronously, *Data Receiver* would consume these messages and persist them in the database.

Periodically, *AC Manager* would require the last 10 min of temperature metrics to the message queue in the *requests* queue. *Data Receiver* would consume that message, gather that information from the database and sent back to the message queue using the *manager* queue. Finally, *AC Manager* would consume those messages and configure the AC system with the appropriate behavior.

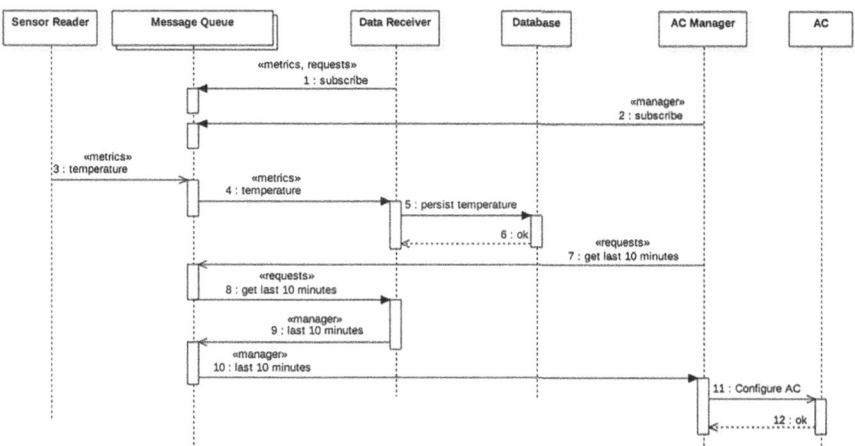

Fig. 19. Communication between the three described services, routed via a messaging system. No two services communicate directly. Arrows represent the messages exchanged in the systems.

Resulting Context. In the context of engineering software for the cloud, message queues can abstract where services are located, eliminating the need for discovery mechanisms between them. Each service can communicate directly with one or more queues, requiring only the address of the Message Queue service.

Using message queues also facilitates service scaling. Services receiving traffic from outside channels should be scaled in order to handle the traffic. These would then inject messages in queues which are being consumed by other services. In such architecture, the size of the queue can be used to understand if and how a service should be scaled, aiming at always keeping the message queue as small as possible.

This pattern can positively improve a cloud application as follows:

Decoupling services allow a faster integration of new services in the ecosystem.

Scalability is achieved by creating an infrastructure of Message Queue services, proportional to the number of services using it.

Resilience is improved as messages can be kept in the queue until a consumer service is available to process them. The message queue software might also be deployed in an infrastructure and keep the messages persisted in disk to improve its own resilience.

Availability for messages is ensured, with the message queue being able to persist the messages as long as needed until these are consumed.

Security is improved by obscurity, as the services receiving messages do not need to be reachable from the message sending services. Also, the communication channel use encryption to enforce a secure communication of all messages sent through it.

On the other hand, the following pitfalls are observable:

Complexity , by increasing the level of indirection, understanding how messages are being passed between service might become incredibly complex and hard to debug. For this reason, Facebook's Flux architecture which is partially event driven, explicitly disallows sending nested events.

Latency is increased, since an additional hop is required to get a message from its producer to the consumer. Modern message queues, when co-located with both services and given the appropriate network conditions, can still ensure latency under 50 milliseconds.

Single point of failure Without a redundant deployment, a failure in the messaging system will halt all interaction between the services.

Related Patterns. Message Queues are a more elaborate approach to Hohpe's Message Buses, which provided a basic communication channel between applications. In his book *Enterprise Integration Patterns*, additional communication patterns that most message queue implementations have adopted are described, such as PUBLISH-SUBSCRIBE CHANNEL or GUARANTEED DELIVERY [56].

Another version of the Publisher-Subscriber pattern was also documented by [21].

This pattern introduces an approach to allow services to communicate without knowing their peers location. This might not be acceptable at all times, mostly due to latency constraints. For those cases, SERVICE DISCOVERY [14] can be applied.

A similar strategy described by the IO GATEKEEPER and related patterns in the telecommunication domain for managing the interaction between humans and systems [51].

SERVICE DISCOVERY can also be used to discover where the message queue is available in the infrastructure.

Messaging systems can be used to implement LOG AGGREGATION, by having services communicating their logs as messages, which are then aggregated by the log centralization service.

Known Uses. MESSAGING SYSTEM has a wide range of adoptions. At CERN, it was used to make information available for multiple monitoring tools in multiple projects, namely in the LHC [22]. A similar environment to the one presented in Sect. 5.1 is described by Grgićm, along with details on how to instantiate it [49].

In another example, [52] demonstrates how message queues can be adopted to acquire real-time data from trains and be used with Reactive Blocks[6] to facilitate collaboration in development and maintenance of software systems.

5.2   Service Discovery

 Services might lack the network information required to communicate with other dynamically allocated services. Communication can be achieved by abstracting service network details by relying on an external mechanism that facilitates communication and balances traffic between two services.

Context. Cloud applications are commonly composed by a multitude of services, which may be spread over multiple physical servers in different networks. In order for services to cooperate they need to know how to communicate with each other, which implies the need for configuration or discovery of the hostname or IP and port where the required service can be reached. Furthermore, when a service has multiple instances, required in high availability setups, there might be the need to evenly distribute traffic between existing instances.

Example. An application server receives HTTP requests and queries a database server for information required to process the HTTP response. For scalability purposes, the database is distributed with multiple read replicas that vary in number of instances considering the average system load. Due to the dynamic allocation of database instances, the service has no information about how to the database servers can be reached. Figure 20 represent a possible distribution of services among the existing servers of such system.

Problem. *Services might lack the network information required to communicate with other dynamically allocated services.*

Service decoupling is required as software gets deployed and scaled automatically in the cloud, enabling the scaling of individual software components when using dynamically provisioned hardware. Deploying in these conditions leave the client services unaware of where other services are allocated, requiring a discovery strategy to enable synchronous communication between them.

---

[6] Project details available at www.bitreactive.com.

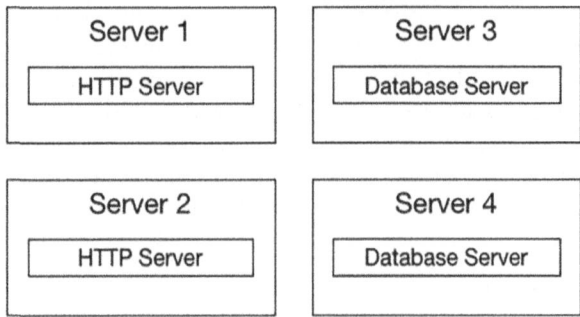

Fig. 20. The four members of an infrastructure, each hosting a service.

Forces. The following forces, represented in Fig. 21, need to be balanced while considering the adoption of this pattern:

Real-time discovery State must be updated when there is a change in the number of instances in a service.
Location decoupling Services do not need to know where others are deployed to communicate with them.
Protocol Agnostic Work at the network level, supporting any protocol adopted by the services.

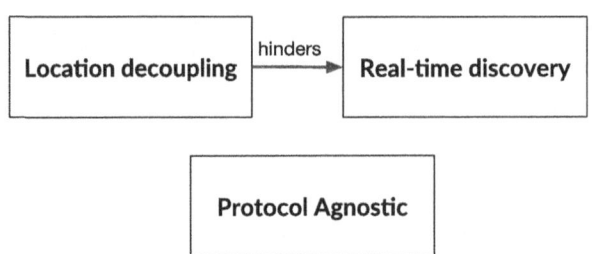

Fig. 21. Relationship between SERVICE DISCOVERY forces.

Solution. *Abstract service network details by relying on an external mechanism that facilitates communication and balances traffic between two services.*

Use an new component to instruct a client service on how to reach the destination service. Implementations can vary from using a DNS server of a reverse proxy within each server.

The first approach consists on using a DNS service that is aware of the service deployment, creating one DNS entry per service and keeping it up to date so that it will always resolve to the list of servers where the service is deployed. This approach requires forcing the deployed client services to use this DNS server.

The reverse proxy approach relies on deploying a proxy in each server. The proxy exposes a service port for each known service and is aware of the deployment state so that it forwards each local port to where the service is actually deployed within the infrastructure.

Proxies work at the network level, which makes them protocol agnostic, seamlessly handling TPC, UDP or HTTP.

Both strategies require that the proxy or DNS server be continuously aware of the deployment state. There are multiple strategies for doing so. One is to have a service registry where each service announces itself, along with a dedicated software that periodically reads this information and updates the proxies. Another alternative is to query this information from an ORCHESTRATION MANAGER.

Both proxy and DNS servers can be configured on how to route traffic When multiple instances of a service are available, acting as a load balancer. The balancing algorithm might work, for example, by distributing the requests using a round-robin technique or in a smarter way, according to the target's resource availability.

Example Resolved. This technique requires an external orchestration mechanism to keep meta-information on the services running in the infrastructure, regarding hosts and ports. Each host machine has a proxy that periodically queries the orchestration manager and forwards a known local port to the host(s) and port of where a service available in the infrastructure. The applications expect a specific port to be available locally that will abstract the exact port and host where the service is actually running. Consider the example previously described: a web application is deployed with two HTTP Servers receiving external requests, which must communicate with one of the two other Database Servers to create a reply. For the HTTP servers to communicate with the database, instead of establishing a direct connection, they connect to the local known port, leaving for the proxy to forward the request to an available Database server. Scalability is achieved by varying the number of Database or HTTP Servers independently, relying on the proxies on the HTTP side to properly identify available Database Servers and distribute load between them. This example is represented in Fig. 22.

Resulting Context. This pattern introduces the following benefits:

Real-time discovery Changes to the infrastructure are immediately identified by the orchestration manager, which will reconfigure the proxies.

Location decoupling Service development can ignore the actual physical location of other services it is integrating with, relying on the reverse proxy to forward traffic to where the service is executing.

Protocol agnostic Proxies work at the transport OSI layer or lower, hence, are protocol agnostic.

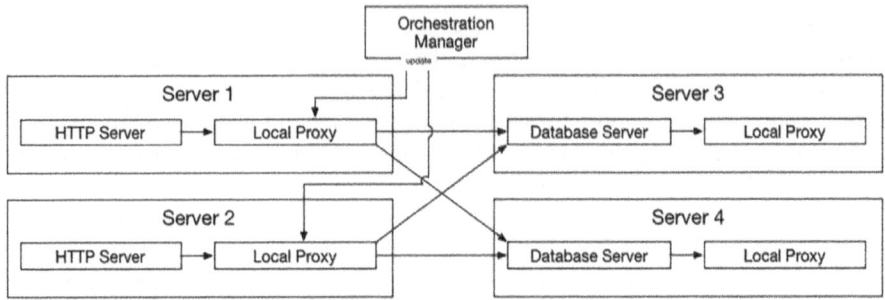

Fig. 22. Proxy configuration example.

The pattern also introduces the following liabilities:

Monitoring A mapping between a service and its running instances must be maintained at all time so that the reverse proxies are properly configured and only redirect traffic to active services.

Related Patterns. This pattern may be applied when CONTAINERIZATION is being used to isolate applications, facilitating communication between containers hosted in different servers, without requiring applications to individually integrate with discovery mechanisms. Information about service ports in each container can be injected using environment variables.

This pattern depends on an external mechanism that keeps track of each service in the infrastructure. An ORCHESTRATION MANAGER holds this information and could be queried for it.

Known Uses. A basic approach is presented by Wilder, keeping an Nginx reverse proxy updated according to meta-information extracted from running docker containers in the local machine [98].

The reverse proxy Vulcanproxy [27], together with the distributed key-value storage Etcd [26] provides a reverse proxy service agnostic to the software using it. By depending on Etcd, it is not an optimal solution as it requires services to register themselves with Etcd.

A better solution is based on Apache Mesos [40] which allow jobs to be spawned across multiple nodes, managing their allocation and Marathon, an infrastructure-wide init and control system for Mesos [Mesosphere 2015a]. Using meta-information available with Marathon, a script can periodically update a proxy server on each machine in the infrastructure, forwarding a TCP or UDP port, named the service port, to the actual address where the application is running, despite it being local or in a remote machine [100]. There are many implementations available to work with Marathon, including Bambo, an HAProxy auto-discovery and configuration tool for Marathon [100]. There is also a script that can configure a local HA proxy, made available by Marathon's team [58].

Kubernetes has implemented this pattern by providing an embedded DNS server that automatically exposes all services deployed with it [64].

5.3 Summary

This section introduced two patterns for supporting service cooperation. MESSAGING SYSTEM introduces a message passing as a strategy to asynchronously exchange messages between services, while SERVICE DISCOVERY facilitates service discovery in a cluster, supporting synchronous interaction. Service discovery and communication are essential to enable service cooperation and vertical service scaling.

Acknowledgements. The authors would like to express their gratitude to the PLoP, EuroPLoP, and SugarLoafPLoP conferences, where the contents of this article have been previously workshoped, and to the various individuals who contributed significantly to its development and refinement. Special thanks are extended to Robert Hanmer, Bogdana Botez, Eduardo Fernandez, and José Ruiz, for their insightful feedback during the shepherding of the original papers. Appreciation is also extended to the members of the writers workshops, including Tim Wellhausen, Andreas Seitz, Fei Li, Julio Moreno, Ralph Johnson, Joe Yoder, Antonio Tercero, Pedro Martos, Alessandro Leite, Renato Ferreira, Hironori Washizaki, Madiha Syed and Bharatkumar Sharma.

References

1. Cloud design patterns - Azure Architecture Center (2021). https://docs.microsoft.com/en-us/azure/architecture/patterns/index-patterns
2. Aceto, G., Botta, A., De Donato, W., Pescapè, A.: Cloud monitoring: a survey. Comput. Netw. **57**(9), 2093–2115 (2013). https://doi.org/10.1016/j.comnet.2013.04.001
3. Albuquerque, C., Correia, F.F.: Deployment tracking and exception tracking: monitoring design patterns for cloud-native applications. In: Proceedings of the 28th European Conference on Pattern Languages of Programs, pp. 1–10 (2023)
4. Albuquerque, C., Relvas, K., Correia, F.F., Brown, K.: Proactive monitoring design patterns for cloud-native applications. In: Proceedings of the 27th European Conference on Pattern Languages of Programs, pp. 1–13 (2022)
5. Alexander, C.: The Nature of Order, Book 2: The Process of Creating Life. Center for Environmental Structure (2002)
6. Amazon: Amazon EC2 Container Service (2015). https://aws.amazon.com/docker/
7. Amazon: Amazon Cloudtrail (2017). https://aws.amazon.com/cloudtrail/
8. Amazon: Scheduled Tasks (cron) (2017). http://docs.aws.amazon.com/AmazonECS/latest/developerguide/scheduled_tasks.html
9. Arcitura Education Inc: Dynamic Failure Detection and Recovery. http://cloudpatterns.org/design_patterns/dynamic_failure_detection_and_recovery
10. Arcitura Education Inc: Cloud Patterns (2019). https://patterns.arcitura.com/cloud-computing-patterns

11. Azure: Azure Logging and Auditing (2017). https://docs.microsoft.com/en-us/azure/security/azure-log-audit

12. Boldt Sousa, T.: Engineering Software for the Cloud: A Pattern Language. Ph.D. thesis (2020). https://repositorio-aberto.up.pt/handle/10216/127347

13. Boldt Sousa, T., Aguiar, A., Correia, F.F., Sereno Ferreira, H.: Engineering software for the cloud - patterns and sequences. In: 11th Latin American Conference on Pattern Languages of Programs Programs, Buenos Aires, Argentina, no. 11, p. 8 (2016)

14. Boldt Sousa, T., Correia, F.F., Sereno Ferreira, H.: Patterns for software orchestration on the cloud. In: 22nd Conference on Pattern Languages of Programs, Pittsburgh, Pennsylvania, USA. (2015)

15. Boldt Sousa, T., Ferreira, H.S., Correia, F.F., Aguiar, A.: Engineering software for the cloud: messaging systems and logging. In: 22nd European Conference on Pattern Languages of Programs, Irsee, Bavaria, Germany (2017). https://doi.org/10.1145/3147704.3147720

16. Boldt Sousa, T., Sereno Ferreira, H., Correia, F.F., Aguiar, A.: Engineering software for the cloud: automated recovery and scheduler. In: 23rd European Conference on Pattern Languages of Programs, Irsee, Bavaria, Germany (2018)

17. Boldt Sousa, T., Sereno Ferreira, H., Correia, F.F., Aguiar, A.: Engineering software for the cloud: external monitoring and fault injection. In: 23rd European Conference on Pattern Languages of Programs, Irsee, Bavaria, Germany (2018)

18. Bonér, J., Farley, D., Kuhn, R., Thompson, M.: The reactive manifesto (Version 2.0). Reactivemanifesto.Org 2(16 September 2014), 1–2 (2014). http://www.reactivemanifesto.org

19. Brown, K., Woolf, B., Yoder, J., Mitchell, I.J.: Patterns for Developers and Architects building for the cloud (2021). https://kgb1001001.github.io/cloudadoptionpatterns/

20. Bui, T.: Analysis of Docker Security. Computing Research Repository (2015). http://arxiv.org/abs/1501.02967

21. Bushmann, F., Meunier, R., Rohnert, H.: Pattern-oriented software architecture: A System of Patterns, vol. 1. Wiley Publishing, Hoboken (1996)

22. Casey, J., Cons, L., Lapka, W., Paladin, M., Skaburskas, K.: A messaging infrastructure for WLCG. J. Phys. Conf. Ser. 331(PART 6) (2011). https://doi.org/10.1088/1742-6596/331/6/062015

23. Chaos Community: Principles of Chaos Engineering (2017). http://principlesofchaos.org/

24. Charette, R.N.: Why Software Fails (2005). https://doi.org/10.1109/MSPEC.2005.1502528

25. Chronos: Chronos (2017). https://mesos.github.io/chronos/

26. Community, C.: Etcd Project Page (2015). https://github.com/coreos/etcd

27. Community, V.: Vulcanproxy Project Page (2015). http://www.vulcanproxy.com/

28. CoreOS Community: CoreOS Project Page (2015). https://coreos.com/

29. Cunningham, W.: Let It Crash (2014). http://wiki.c2.com/?LetItCrash

30. Cycligent: Continuous Delivery Patterns for Design and Deployment (2015). https://medium.com/@Cycligent/continuous-delivery-patterns-for-design-deployment-8f8744558401

31. Dadgar, A.: What is infrastructure as code and why is it important? (2018). https://www.hashicorp.com/resources/what-is-infrastructure-as-code

32. DataDog: Docker Adoption (2018). https://www.datadoghq.com/docker-adoption/

33. De Bayser, M., Azevedo, L.G., Cerqueira, R.: ResearchOps: the case for DevOps in scientific applications. In: Proceedings of the 2015 IFIP/IEEE International Symposium on Integrated Network Management, IM 2015, pp. 1398–1404 (2015). https://doi.org/10.1109/INM.2015.7140503

34. Dobaj, J., Schuss, M., Krisper, M., Boano, C.A., Macher, G.: Dependable mesh networking patterns, pp. 1–14 (2019). https://doi.org/10.1145/3361149.3361174

35. Docker: Dockerfile reference (2018). https://docs.docker.com/engine/reference/builder

36. Elastic: The Open Source Elastic Stack (2017). https://www.elastic.co/products

37. Erl, T., Cope, R., Naserpour, A.: Cloud Computing Design Patterns. Prentice Hall, Upper Saddle River (2015)

38. Felter, W., Ferreira, A., Rajamony, R., Rubio, J.: IBM Research Report An Updated Performance Comparison of VirtualMachines and Linux Containers. Technical report (2012). http://domino.watson.ibm.com/library/CyberDig.nsf/home

39. Fernandez, E.B.: Security Patterns in Practice: Designing Secure Architectures Using Software Patterns (2013)

40. Foundation, A.: Mesos Project Page (2015). http://mesos.apache.org/

41. Fowler, M.: What do you mean by "Event-Driven"? (2017). https://martinfowler.com/articles/201701-event-driven.html

42. Fu, Q., et al.: Where do developers log? an empirical study on logging practices in industry. 36th International Conference on Software Engineering, ICSE Companion 2014 - Proceedings, pp. 24–33 (2014). https://doi.org/10.1145/2591062.2591175

43. Gartner: Gartner Forecasts Worldwide Public Cloud Revenue to Grow 17.5 Percent in 2019. Technical report (2019). https://www.gartner.com/en/newsroom/press-releases/2019-04-02-gartner-forecasts-worldwide-public-cloud-revenue-to-g

44. Gawlick, D.: Message queuing for business integration. eAI J., 30–33 (2002)

45. Gitlab: Postmortem of database outage of January 31 (2017). https://about.gitlab.com/2017/02/10/postmortem-of-database-outage-of-january-31/

46. Goasguen, S.: Docker in the Cloud, 2nd edn. O'Reilly Media, Newton (2016)

47. Google: Google Cloud Container Service (2015). https://cloud.google.com/container-engine/

48. Google: Reliable Task Scheduling on Google Compute Engine (2018). https://cloud.google.com/solutions/reliable-task-scheduling-compute-engine

49. Grgić, K., Špeh, I., Hedi, I.: A web-based IoT solution for monitoring data using MQTT protocol. In: Proceedings of 2016 International Conference on Smart Systems and Technologies, SST 2016, pp. 249–253. IEEE Computer Society (2016). https://doi.org/10.1109/SST.2016.7765668

50. Guckenheimer, S.: What is Infrastructure as Code? (2017). https://docs.microsoft.com/en-us/azure/devops/learn/what-is-infrastructure-as-code

51. Hanmer, R.: An input and output pattern language. In: Design Patterns in Communications Software, no. c, pp. 95–129. Cambridge University Press, Cambridge (1998)

52. Herrmann, P., Svae, A., Svendsen, H.H., Blech, J.O.: Collaborative model-based development of a remote train monitoring system. In: ENASE 2016 - Proceedings of the 11th International Conference on Evaluation of Novel Software Approaches to Software Engineering, pp. 383–390 (2016). https://doi.org/10.5220/0005929403830390

53. Hieatt, E., Mee, R.: Repository Pattern. https://martinfowler.com/eaaCatalog/repository.html
54. Hindman, B., Konwinski, A., Zaharia, M.: Mesos: a platform for fine-grained resource sharing in the data center. In: Proceedings of the NSDI, p. 32 (2011). http://dl.acm.org/citation.cfm?id=1972457.1972488
55. Hof, R.: Meet Project Storm, Facebook's SWAT team for disaster-proofing data centers (2016). https://siliconangle.com/2016/08/31/meet-project-storm-facebooks-swat-team-for-disaster-proofing-data-centers/
56. Hohpe, G., Woolf, B.: Enterprise integration patterns: designing, building, and deploying messaging solutions. In: Enterprise Integration Patterns Designing Building and Deploying Messaging Solution, p. 736 (2003). https://doi.org/10.1525/vs.2009.4.3.toc
57. IEEE, Open, T.G.: crontab (2016). http://pubs.opengroup.org/onlinepubs/9699919799/utilities/crontab.html
58. Inc, M.: Mesosphere Service Discovery & Load Balancing (2015). https://mesosphere.github.io/marathon/docs/service-discovery-load-balancing.html
59. Initiative, O.C.: Open Containers Project Page (2015). http://www.opencontainers.org/
60. Internetlivestats.com: Number of Internet users in the world (2019). http://www.internetlivestats.com/internet-users/
61. Koutoupis, P.: Everything You Need to Know about Linux Containers, Part II: Working with Linux Containers (2018). https://www.linuxjournal.com/content/everything-you-need-know-about-linux-containers-part-ii-working-linux-containers-lxc
62. Kubernetes: Run a Stateless Application Using a Deployment. https://kubernetes.io/docs/tasks/run-application/run-stateless-application-deployment/
63. Kubernetes: Kubernetes Cron Jobs (2017). https://kubernetes.io/docs/concepts/workloads/controllers/cron-jobs/
64. Kubernetes: DNS for Services and Pods (2018). https://kubernetes.io/docs/concepts/services-networking/dns-pod-service/
65. Kubernetes: Pod Lifecycle (2018). https://kubernetes.io/docs/concepts/workloads/pods/pod-lifecycle/
66. Leme, N.G.M., Martins, E., Rubira, C.: A Software Fault Injection Pattern System. In: Pattern Languages of Programs (2001). https://hillside.net/plop/plop2001/accepted_submissions/PLoP2001/ngmleme3/PLoP2001_ngmleme3_3.pdf
67. Lewis, J., Fowler, M.: Microservices (2014). http://martinfowler.com/articles/microservices.html
68. Magnoni, L.: Modern messaging for distributed sytems. J. Phys: Conf. Ser. **608**(1), 012038 (2015). https://doi.org/10.1088/1742-6596/608/1/012038
69. Maia, T., Correia, F.: Service mesh patterns. In: Proceedings of the 27th European Conference on Pattern Languages of Programs. EuroPLoP 2022, Association for Computing Machinery, New York (2022)
70. Malaiya, Y.K., Li, M.N., Bieman, J.M., Karcich, R.: Software reliability growth with test coverage. IEEE Trans. Reliab. **51**(4), 420–426 (2002). https://doi.org/10.1109/TR.2002.804489
71. Menage, P.: CGROUPS. Technical report (2004). https://www.kernel.org/doc/Documentation/cgroup-v1/cgroups.txt
72. Mesosphere: Marathon Health Checks (2017). https://mesosphere.github.io/marathon/docs/health-checks.html

73. Mesosphere: Marathon API (2018). https://docs.mesosphere.com/1.11/deploying-services/marathon-api/

74. Microsoft: Health Endpoint Monitoring pattern (2017). https://docs.microsoft.com/en-us/azure/architecture/patterns/health-endpoint-monitoring

75. Microsoft: Microsoft Azure Scheduler (2017). https://azure.microsoft.com/en-us/services/scheduler/

76. Morris, K.: Infrastructure as Code. O'Reilly Media, Inc., Newton (2015)

77. Mouat, A.: Docker Security. Technical report (2015). http://www.oreilly.com/webops-perf/free/docker-security.csp

78. Namiot, D., Sneps-Sneppe, M.: On micro-services architecture. Int. J. Open Inf. Technol. **2**(9), 24–27 (2014)

79. Netflix: The Netflix Simian Army (2011). https://medium.com/netflix-techblog/the-netflix-simian-army-16e57fbab116

80. Netflix: Chaos Monkey (2017). https://github.com/Netflix/chaosmonkey

81. Pingdom: Pingdom (2017). https://www.pingdom.com/

82. Pinheiro, E., Weber, W., Barroso, L.: Failure trends in a large disk drive population. In: Proceedings of the 5th USENIX Conference on File and Storage Technologies (FAST 2007), vol. 7, pp. 17–29 (2007)

83. Pivotal: RabbitMQ Tutorials (2007). https://rabbitmq.docs.pivotal.io/35/rabbit-web-docs/tutorials/tutorial-one-java.html

84. Regola, N., Ducom, J.C.: Recommendations for virtualization technologies in high performance computing. In: Proceedings - 2nd IEEE International Conference on Cloud Computing Technology and Science, CloudCom 2010, pp. 409–416 (2010). https://doi.org/10.1109/CloudCom.2010.71

85. Relic, N.: New Relic (2017). https://newrelic.com/

86. Richards, M.: Software Architecture Patterns (DRAFT), vol. 32 (2014). https://doi.org/10.1097/NHH.0000000000000071

87. Richardson, C.: Microservices patterns: with examples in Java. Manning Publications Co., Shelter Island (2018)

88. Richardson, C.: A pattern language for microservices (2021). http://microservices.io/patterns/

89. Roderick, C., Burdzanowski, L., Kruk, G.: The CERN Accelerator Logging Service- 10 Years in Operation: A Look at the Past, Present and Future. Technical report, CERN (2013). http://cds.cern.ch/record/1611082

90. Scheepers, M.J.: Virtualization and containerization of application infrastructure : a comparison. In: 21st Twente Student Conference on IT, pp. 1–7 (2014)

91. Schumacher, M., Fernandez-Buglioni, E., Hybertson, D., Buschmann, F., Sommerlad, P.: Security Patterns: Integrating Security and Systems Engineering (2006)

92. Soltesz, S., Pötzl, H., Fiuczynski, M.E., Bavier, A., Peterson, L.: Container-based operating system virtualization. ACM SIGOPS Oper. Syst. Rev. **41**(3), 275 (2007). https://doi.org/10.1145/1272998.1273025

93. Sousa, T.B., Ferreira, H.S., Correia, F.: A Survey on the Adoption of Patterns for Engineering Software for the Cloud - dataset (2021). https://doi.org/10.5281/zenodo.4415778

94. Sousa, T.B., Ferreira, H.S., Correia, F.F.: Overview of a pattern language for engineering software for the cloud. In: 25th Conference on Pattern Languages of Programs, Portland, Oregon, USA (2018)

95. Statuscake: StatusCake (2017). https://www.statuscake.com/

96. Taft, D.: How the Skills Gap Is Threatening the Growth of App Economy (2015). http://www.eweek.com/developer/slideshows/how-the-skills-gap-is-threatening-the-growth-of-app-economy.html
97. Wilder, B.: Cloud Architecture Patterns: Using Microsoft Azure. Springer, Heidelberg (2012). https://books.google.com/books?id=X-d6JVHQwo8C&pgis=1
98. Wilder, J.: Automated Nginx Reverse Proxy for Docker (2015). http://jasonwilder.com/blog/2014/03/25/automated-nginx-reverse-proxy-for-docker/
99. Winstedt, E.O.: A bodleian MS. of juvenal. Class. Rev. **13**(4), 201–205 (1899). https://doi.org/10.1017/S0009840X00078409
100. Wuggazer, P.: Evaluation of an Architecture for a Scaling and Self-Healing Virtualization System. Ph.D. thesis, University of Magdeburg (2015)
101. Xavier, M.G., Neves, M.V., Rossi, F.D., Ferreto, T.C., Lange, T., De Rose, C.A.: Performance evaluation of container-based virtualization for high performance computing environments. In: Proceedings of the 2013 21st Euromicro International Conference on Parallel, Distributed, and Network-Based Processing, PDP 2013 (LXC), pp. 233–240 (2013). https://doi.org/10.1109/PDP.2013.41
102. Yarbrough, G., Hook, S.: Message Queue Server System (2002). https://www.google.com/patents/US20020004835

An Extended Pattern Collection
for Blockchain-Based Applications

Xiwei Xu[1,2(✉)], Cesare Pautasso[3], Sin Kuang Lo[1,2], Liming Zhu[1,2],
Qinghua Lu[1,2], and Ingo Weber[4,5]

[1] Data61, CSIRO, Sydney, Australia
{xiwei.xu,sin.lo,liming.zhu,qinghua.lu}@data61.csiro.au
[2] School of Computer Science and Engineering, University of New South Wales,
Kensington, Australia
[3] University of Lugano, Lugano, Switzerland
c.pautasso@ieee.org
[4] School of CIT, Technical University of Munich, Munich, Germany
ingo.weber@tum.de
[5] Fraunhofer-Gesellschaft, Munich, Germany

Abstract. Blockchain is an emerging technology that enables new forms
of decentralized software architectures, where distributed components
can reach agreements on shared system states without trusting a central
integration point. Blockchain provides a shared infrastructure to execute
programs, called smart contracts, and to store data. Since blockchain
technologies are at an early stage, there is a lack of a systematically organized knowledge providing a holistic view on designing software systems
that use blockchain. We view blockchain as a component of a bigger software system, which requires patterns for using blockchain in the design
of the software architecture. In this paper, we collect a list of patterns for
blockchain-based applications. The pattern collection is categorized into
five categories, including interaction with external world patterns, data
management patterns, security patterns, structural patterns of contracts,
and user interaction patterns. Some patterns are designed considering the
nature of blockchain and how blockchains can be specifically introduced
within real-world applications. Others are variants of existing design patterns applied in the context of blockchain-based applications and smart
contracts.

Keywords: Blockchain · Smart contract · Pattern

1 Introduction

Blockchain is the technology behind Bitcoin [17], which is a digital currency
based on a peer-to-peer network and cryptographic techniques. The blockchain
provides immutable, append-only, shared data storage, which only allows inserting transactions without updating or deleting any existing ones, thus preventing
any tampering or revision of previously stored data on blockchain as long as the

E. Wallingford et al. (Eds.): TPLOP V, LNCS 14630, pp. 67–117, 2025.
https://doi.org/10.1007/978-3-662-70810-1_2

majority of the network peers do not agree to allow such revision. The blockchain enables decentralization as new forms of distributed software architectures, where components can reach agreements on the historical log of shared states for decentralized and transactional data sharing, across a large network of untrusted participants without relying on a central integration point.

Financial transactions are the first, but far from the only use case being investigated for blockchain. Many start-ups, enterprises, and governments [20] are exploring blockchain-based applications in areas as diverse as supply chain, electronic health records, voting, energy supply, ownership management, and protecting critical civil infrastructure. Despite of the wide array of interest in blockchain technology, there is a lack of a systematic and holistic view when applying blockchain in the design of software applications.

Previous work has characterized blockchain from a software architecture perspective as a software connector [26] that provides a shared infrastructure for storing data and running programs (known as *smart contracts*). Blockchain guarantees unique properties including immutability, non-repudiation, data integrity, transparency, and equal rights. It also has two main limitations, namely, lack of privacy and poor performance [26]. The taxonomy presented in [27] discusses such properties for different types and configurations of blockchain technology. To better leverage the positive properties of blockchain and avoid or reduce the impact of its limitations, more architectural guidance on blockchain-based applications is needed.

In this paper, we present a set of patterns for the design of blockchain-based applications. In software engineering, a design pattern is a reusable design solution to a problem that commonly occurs within a given context during software design [4]. A design pattern defines constraints that restrict the roles of architectural elements (processing, connectors and data) and the interaction among those elements. Adopting a design pattern causes trade-offs among quality attributes. Our pattern collection includes four patterns about interaction between blockchain and the external world, four data management patterns, four security patterns, five structural patterns of smart contract and two user interaction patterns. The pattern collection provides an architectural guidance for developers to build applications on blockchain.

The remainder of the paper is organized as follows. Section 2 presents a background of blockchain and smart contracts. Section 3 gives an overview of the pattern collection, followed by detailed patterns discussed from Sect. 4 to Sect. 8. Related work on blockchain-based applications and design patterns is discussed in Sect. 9. Section 10 concludes the paper and outlines the future work.

2   Background

2.1   Blockchain

Blockchain is a data structure of an ordered list of blocks, where every block "chained" back to the previous block through containing a hash of a presentation of the previous block. Every block on blockchain contains a list of transactions (possibly empty). A transaction is a data package that stores information for money transfer, like sender, receiver, and monetary value, or the (compiled) code of smart contracts, or parameters of function calls of smart contracts. Due to the security properties of hash function, the historical transactions on blockchain can not be deleted or altered without invalidating the chain of hashes. In addition to the design of the data structure, there are computational constraints and consensus protocols applied to the creation of blocks. All together, blockchain can in practice prevent revision and tampering of the information on blockchain.

When using a blockchain, one design decision is the deployment, *i.e.*, whether to use a public blockchain, consortium/community blockchain or private blockchain [27]. Most cryptocurrencies use public blockchains, which can be accessed by anyone on the Internet. Using a public blockchain results in better information transparency and auditability, but sacrifices performance and has a different cost model compared with a conventional data storage. It costs monetary value to store data or execute code on a public blockchain. In a public blockchain, data privacy relies on encryption or cryptographic hashes. A consortium blockchain is used across multiple organizations. The consensus process in a consortium blockchain is controlled by a set of pre-authorised nodes. The right to read the blockchain may be public or may be restricted to specific participants. In a private blockchain network, write permission is kept within one organization, although this may include multiple divisions of a single organization.

Properties. The data contained in a transaction on blockckchain is seen as *immutable* in practice. The chain of immutable cryptographically-signed historical transactions provides *non-repudiation* of the stored data. Cryptographic techniques used by blockchain support data *integrity*, the public access provides data *transparency*, and *equal rights* allows every participant to have the same ability to manipulate the data on blockchain. Such rights can be weighted by the computational power (*Proof-of-work*) or stake (*Proof-of-stake*) owned by a node. *Trust* of the blockchain is built based on the interactions between nodes within the blockchain network. The participants of a blockchain network rely on the design of blockchain, the cryptographic techniques used by blockchain and the blockchain network itself rather than relying on trusted third-party to facilitate transactions.

Limitations. *Data privacy* and *scalability* are the main two limitations of public blockchains. Data privacy on public blockchain is limited because there is no privileged user, and every participant can join the network to access all the information on blockchain and validate new transactions. There are scalability limits on (i) the size of the data included into a transaction, (ii) the transaction processing rate, and (iii) the latency of data transmission and commits. Latency between submitting a transaction and it being committed on a blockchain is affected by the consensus protocol. This is around 1 h (10-min block interval with time for inclusion and 5-block confirmation) on Bitcoin, and around 3 min (14-second block interval with 11 confirmation blocks) on Ethereum[1]. Times in

---

[1] https://www.ethereum.org/.

practice can be even longer [21]. The number of transactions included in each block is also limited by the bandwidth of nodes participating in the network (for Bitcoin the current bandwidth per block is 1MB) [1]. Ethereum applies a so-called *gas* limit to blocks (*gas* is the internal pricing unit for executing a transaction or storing data), which limits the number and complexity of transactions that can fit into a block.

Blockchain as a Software Component. When used in a large software system, blockchain can be viewed as a software component [26]. In such software system, blockchain is responsible for storing and sharing data, and executing smart contracts. Due to the limitations of privacy and performance, there might be off-chain auxiliary databases used in the system. For example, private or large sized data can be stored in an internal database. There is normally a API layer between the data storage layer and the applications using the blockchain, which is same as with conventional technology. When blockchain interacts with other off-chain components, an "oracle" [13] is needed to bridge blockchain with the external world.

2.2   Smart Contract

The first generation of blockchains, like Bitcoin, provides a public ledger to store cryptographically-signed financial transactions [19]. There is very limited capability to support programmable transactions, and only very small pieces of auxiliary data could be embedded in the transactions to serve other purposes, such as representing other digital assets or physical assets.

The second generation of blockchains provides a general-purpose programmable infrastructure with a public ledger that records the computational results. Programs, known as *smart contracts* [18], can be deployed and run on a blockchain. Smart contracts can express triggers, conditions and business logic [22] to enable more complex programmable transactions. The signature of the transaction initiator authorizes the data payload of a transaction or the creation or execution of a smart contract. A common simple example of a smart contract-enabled service is escrow, which can hold funds until the obligations defined in the smart contract have been fulfilled. Smart contracts are pure functions by design, which cannot access the state of external systems directly.

Smart Contract Languages. *Script* used by Bitcoin is a simple stack-based scripting language[2], which is intentionally designed not to be Turing-complete. Script provides the flexibility to define conditions required to spend the Bitcoin associated with the transactions, for example, requiring multiple private keys to authorize the payment. Ethereum is currently the most widely-used blockchain that supports general-purpose (Turing-complete) smart contracts. The primary

---

[2] https://en.bitcoin.it/wiki/Script.

smart contract language used on Ethereum blockchain is *Solidity*[3]. DigitalAsset[4] proposed DAML[5]as a domain specific smart contract language for financial institutes. Smart contracts running on Hyperledger Fabric[6] are called Chaincode, which can be written in any programming language and executed in containers inside the fabric context layer.

3   Overview of Blockchain-Based Application Patterns

In this section, we discuss the overview of the blockchain-based application pattern collection, which currently includes nineteen design patterns that shape the architectural elements and their interactions in blockchain-based applications. Figure 1 gives an overview of these patterns as well as their mutual relationships. The arrows in Fig. 1 illustrate how to navigate through the pattern collection during a design process. Applying the patterns to an blockchain-based application can better align it with the unique properties provided by blockchain, avoid its limitations, and achieve other quality attributes.

The patterns about interaction between blockchain and the external world describe different ways for blockchain to communicate data with the external world, including *Centralized oracle* (Sect. 4.1), *Decentralized oracle* (Sect. 4.2), *Reverse oracle* (Sect. 4.4) and *Voting* (Sect. 4.3). The four data management patterns are about managing data on and off blockchain, including *Tokenisation* (Sect. 5.1), *Off-chain data storage* (Sect. 5.2), *State channel* (Sect. 5.3) and *Legal and smart contract pair* (Sect. 5.4). The four security patterns concern the security aspect of the blockchain-based applications. *Multiple authorization* (Sect. 6.2) and *Dynamic authorization* (Sect. 6.3) are aimed at adding dynamism to authorization of transactions and smart contracts. *Embedded permission* (Sect. 6.4) aims to improve security of smart contracts, and *On-chain Encryption* (Sect. 6.1) can be used to improve security of on-chain data.

The five contract structural patterns define the dependencies among smart contracts and behaviour of smart contract. Smart contracts on blockchain are immutable. Upgrading a smart contract to a new version is a challenge which hinders the evolution of blockchain-based applications. *Contract registry* (Sect. 7.1), *Factory contract* (Sect. 7.3) and *Data contract* (Sect. 7.2) can used together to improve upgradability of smart contracts. *Incentive execution* (Sect. 7.4) and *Security deposit* (Sect. 7.5) provide incentive mechanism for execution and maintenance of smart contracts. The two user interaction patterns summarise different ways for users to interact with DApps, including *DApp* (Sect. 8.1) and *Semi-DApp* (Sect. 8.2).

---

[3] https://solidity.readthedocs.io/.
[4] http://www.digitalasset.com/.
[5] https://daml.com/.
[6] https://www.hyperledger.org/use/fabric.

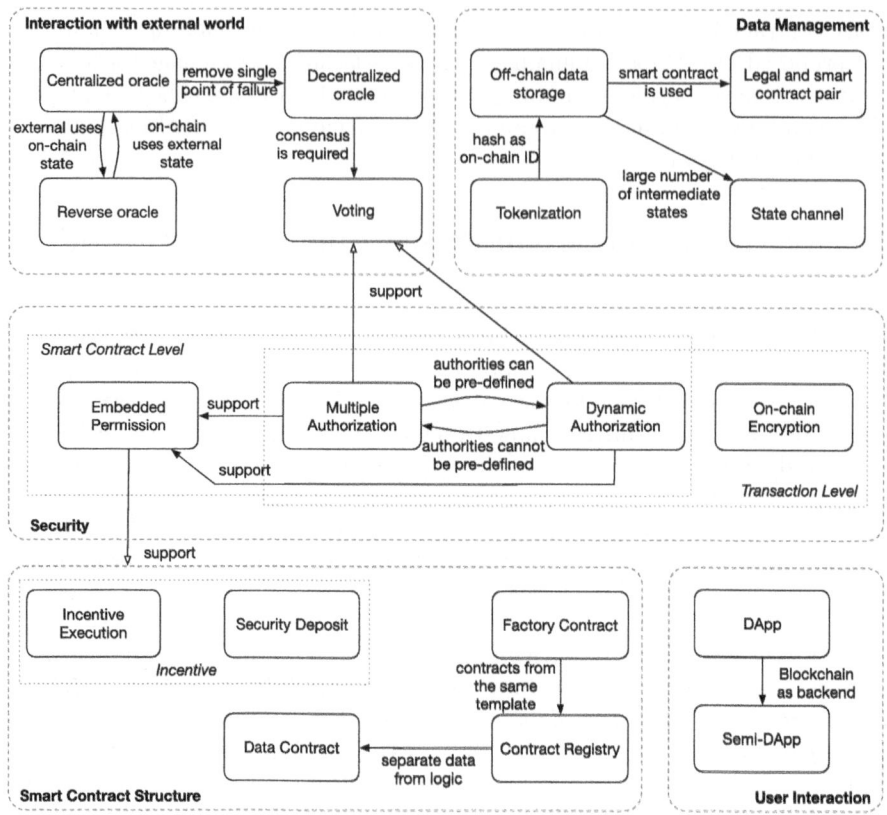

Fig. 1. Blockchain as a component within a software architecture

In this paper we follow the extended pattern form from [14], which includes the name of the pattern, a short summary, the context, the problem statement, an explicit discussion of the forces which make the problem difficult, the solution, its consequences, and some examples of real-world known uses of the pattern. Forces are identified with the corresponding quality attribute, as sometimes the solution will propose a trade-off between them. Regarding the consequences, we distinguish the benefits and drawbacks. Finally, we discuss features only applicable to a certain deployment of blockchain, such as monetary cost of data storage and code execution.

4   Interaction with External World Patterns

As a component of a big software system, blockchain needs to communicate data with other components within the software system. This section discuss four patterns applicable to the interaction between blockchain and external world.

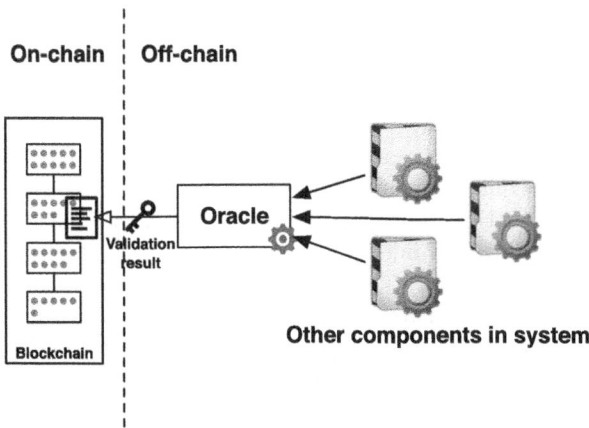

Fig. 2. Centralized Oracle Pattern

4.1   Pattern 1: Centralized Oracle

Summary: Introduce the state of external systems into the closed blockchain execution environment through a single centralized connector (called *oracle*). Figure 2 is a graphical representation of the pattern.

Context: From the software architecture perspective, blockchain can be viewed as a component or connector within a large software system [26]. In the case where blockchain is used as a distributed database for more general purposes other than financial services, the applications built on blockchain might need to interact with other external systems. Thus, the validation of transactions on blockchain might depend on states of external systems.

Problem: Smart contracts running on blockchain are pure functions by design. The execution environment of smart contract is self-contained. It can only access information present in the data and transactions on the blockchain. The state of external systems are not directly accessible to smart contracts. How can function calls in smart contracts be enabled to access the state of the external world from within smart contracts?

Forces: The problem requires to balance the following forces:

- *Closed environment.* Blockchain is a secure, self-contained environment, which is isolated from external systems. Smart contracts on blockchain cannot read the states of the external systems.
- *Connectivity.* In addition to the data found on the blockchain, general-purpose applications might require information from external systems. For example, a parcel tracking application needs context information like geo-location information, a gambling application might need weather data from a Web API[7].

---

[7] https://openweathermap.org/api.

Solution: To connect the closed execution environment of blockchain with the external world, *oracle* is introduced to assist in evaluating conditions that cannot be expressed in a smart contract running within the blockchain environment. If the information flows from blockchain to external world, Reverse Oracle (Sect. 4.4) should be used. An centralized oracle is a trusted third party that provides the smart contracts with information about the external world. When validation of a transaction depends on external state, the oracle is requested to check the external state and inject the result to the blockchain in a transaction signed using its own key pair. The validators (*miner*) take the result provided by the oracle into account when validating the transaction. From the perspective of validator, by introducing the oracle, the validation of transactions is based on the authentication of the oracle (through digital signature) rather than the external state because what provided by oracle is trusted by the validator. From the perspective of the validator, the data injected from oracle is no different from data provided (through embedding into a transaction or as a variable value) by other users. What validators can do is to ensure the data integrity by checking the digital signature of the sender and executing the smart contract based on the input data, but they cannot check the originality or correctness of the input data from external world. More technical details of implementing the pattern could be found in [16].

Consequences:

Benefits:

- *Connectivity.* The closed execution environment of blockchain is connected with external world through a centralized oracle. The applications based on blockchain can access external states through the oracle and use the external states to validate transactions.
- *Efficiency.* Centralized oracle is more efficient in terms of monetary and time cost. It is easier to manage compared with Decentralized Oracle (Sect. 4.2)

Drawbacks:

- *Trust.* Using a centralized oracle introduces a trusted third party into the system. The oracle selected to verify the external state needs to be trusted by all the participants involved in relevant transactions.
- *Validity.* The external states injected into the transactions can not be fully validated by miners. Thus, when miners validate the transaction including external state, they rely on the oracle to check the validity of the information from external world.
- *Long-term availability and validity.* It could happen that while transactions are immutable, the external state used to validate them may change after the transactions were originally appended to the blockchain.
- *Single point of failure.* A centralized oracle introduces a single trusted element, whose unavailability or failure may prevent the blockchain from successfully completing the transaction verification process.

Related Patterns:

- *Decentralized Oracle* (Sect. 4.1) can be used to avoid the single point of failure introduced by a centralized oracle.
- *Reverse Oracle* (Sect. 4.4) can be used when the information flows from blockchain to external components.

Known Uses:

- *Oracle* in Bitcoin is an instance of this pattern[8]. Oracle is a server outside the Bitcoin blockchain network, which can evaluate user-defined expressions based on the external state.
- *Provable*[9] is an oracle service provider, which utilises trusted hardware to directly fetch information from external trusted execution environment (TEE). Provable introduces three different proofs for fetching data from external data sources, namely, TLS-Notary, Ledger proof and Android proof.
- *Corda*[10] has a centralized oracle mechanism embedded in its platform. The oracle mechanism uses Intel Software Guard Extensions (SGX) for hardware attestation to prevent unauthorised access outside of the SGX environment.

4.2   Pattern 2: Decentralized Oracles

Summary: Introduce the state of external systems into the closed blockchain execution environment through a cluster of connectors (called *oracles*). Figure 3 is a graphical representation of the pattern.

Context: In the case where blockchain is used as a distributed database for more general purposes other than financial services, the applications built on blockchain might need to interact with other external systems. A centralized *oracle* (Sect. 4.1) can be applied to inject the states of external systems into blockchain.

Problem: A centralized oracle introduces a single trusted third party into the system, which might becomes a single point of failure of the whole software system.

Forces: The problem requires to balance the following forces:

- *Reliability and Availability.* A centralized oracle becomes a single point of failure from an architecture perspective. In the case that the status injected into the blockchain is a faulty status, the whole system might behave inaccurately. In the case that the oracle is unable to inject any state to the system, the whole system might be stuck and unavailable depending on how critical the state is.

---

[8] https://en.bitcoin.it/wiki/Contract#Example_4:_Using_external_state.
[9] https://provable.xyz/.
[10] https://www.corda.net/.

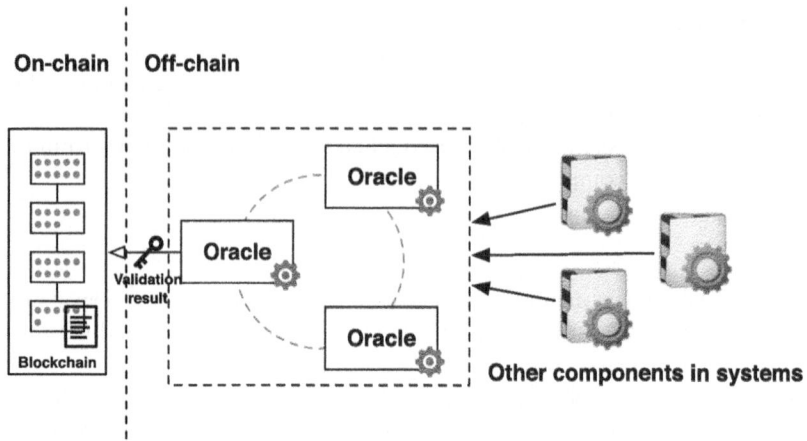

Fig. 3. Decentralized Oracle Pattern

- *Cost.* The cost of data retrieval from external world is proportional to the number of oracles.

Solution: To improve trustworthiness of the oracle, a decentralized oracle mechanism is introduced, which is based on multiple oracles. These oracles can get data from one data source or multiple independent data sources. *Voting* (Sect. 4.3) can be applied to decentralized oracle to reach a consensus on the status to be injected into the blockchain.

Consequences:
   Benefits:

- *Reliability and Availability.* By having multiple oracles retrieving data from external world, the risk of validating transactions based on faulty external data is reduced from a single centralized oracle. Acquiring data by multiple oracles also improves the reliability and the confidence of the final accepted value.

   Drawbacks:

- *Trust.* Although using decentralized oracle avoids the single-point-of-trust, it still introduces trusted third parties into the system. All the oracles that verify the external state needs to be trusted by all the participants involved in relevant transactions. So trust needs to be extended from a single entity to a cluster.
- *Cost.* Cost of using a piece of data from external world increases with the number of oracles being used.

- *Time.* It might take longer time for multiple oracles to get the required information and reach a consensus over the final result. If all oracles need to agree, the time is bound by the slowest oracle. If a subset of the oracles is sufficient, then the slowest oracles can be ignored, thus potentially speeding up the process.
- *Uncertainty.* Compared with centralized oracle, decentralized oracle introduces more uncertainties. When human is involved, the value what majority vote becomes the result, which might be different from the *truth* in the physical world.

Related Patterns:

- *Centralized Oracle* (Sect. 4.1) can be used if a single oracle is trusted by all the participants involved into a transaction.
- *Reverse Oracle* (Sect. 4.4) can be used when the information flows from blockchain to external componnets.
- *Voting* (Sect. 4.3) (Sect. 6.2) can be applied with decentralized oracles to achieve consensus among multiple oracles.

Known Uses:

- Orisi[11] on Bitcoin maintains a set of independent oracles. Orisi allows the participants involved in a transaction to select a set of oracles and define the value of M (number of oracles) before initiating a conditional transaction.
- Gnosis[12] is a decentralized prediction market that allows users to choose any oracle they trust, such as another user or a web service, *e.g.*, for weather forecasts. A human oracle is also called *arbitrator*, who is trusted by the interacting participants to resolve disputes or check external state.
- Augur[13] is another prediction market that leverages the capability of human oracles to do prediction and resolve disputes.

4.3   Pattern 3: Voting

Summary: To achieve an agreement on a state proposed on blockchain, anyone with blockchain account can propose tentative new state or vote for a proposed state by staking their tokens until a consensus is achieve. Figure 4 is a graphical representation of the pattern.

Context: The public access of blockchain provides *equal rights* that allow [27] every participant the same ability to access and manipulate the blockchain. This property of blockchain enables a way for blockchain users to make decisions together and achieve consensus on the result. During the consensus process, everyone has equal right to participate in decision making. In the context of

---

[11] http://orisi.org/.

[12] https://gnosis.io/.

[13] https://www.augur.net/.

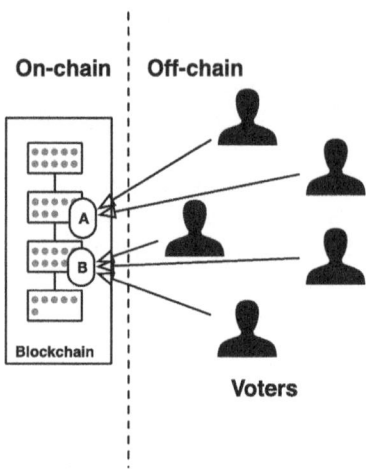

Fig. 4. Voting Pattern

decentralized oracle, especially the one using human oracles, blockchain users use different sources to report the result. They may have different preferences.

Problem: During a process to achieve an agreement on certain state on blockchain, what if the state proposed by an blockchain account (oracle or human) is disputed?

Forces: The problem requires to balance the following forces:

- *Fairness.* Every participant in blockchain network has a equal right to access and manipulate the blockchain. Each participant's vote should have the same weight as the others.
- *Consensus.* Multiple participants in different opinions need to reach an agreement to make decision. Participants also need to agree on which of the many paths leading to an outcome based on their preferences (e.g., simple or qualified majority) is taken.
- *Transparency/Auditability.* The voting process should be deterministic and auditable so that the outcome can be reproduced from the same input (which should not disappear after the vote).

Solution:
Voting is a mechanism commonly used by a group of participants to make a collective decision when the state originally proposed by participant is disputed. Anyone with a blockchain account that does not agree with the state can propose another state as tentative answer. To make a decision, every participant vote through sending transaction through her/his blockchain account. The voting

transaction is signed by the private key of the participant, which represents the right of the participant to make decision. Such right can be weighted by the resource owned by the participant, like the application-specific tokens. Normally, majority rule is used to select the alternative which has the most votes (or with heavier weight in terms of stake) among all alternatives.

One possible extension to the solution is to support secret voting by leveraging digital signatures. The voters can encrypt their choice when casting a vote, which can be decrypted using the corresponding public key when the votes are being counted. However, by linking the voting transaction with other transactions from and to the account, the anonymity of the user might be compromised. A more privacy-preserving way for the voter is to create a new account for voting only. It is debatable whether blockchain is a suitable technique to solve on-line voting security due to sociological issues that are outside of technical environment[14].

Consequences:
Benefits:

- *Equality.* Voting method allows the participants to use their right to participate decision making.
- *Consensus.* Multiple participants with different preferences can reach a consensus through voting.

Drawbacks:

- *Duplication* The vote is associated with the blockchain account. Smart contract can help to avoid duplicated votes from the same blockchain account, for example by counting only the most recent vote. But since blockchain is pseudonymous, every participant can own multiple blockchain addresses to gain additional voting power, which is similar to the Sybil attack at network layer.
- *Time.* Voting may take a long time due to long voting/dispute time windows

Related Patterns:

- *Decentralized Oracles* (Sect. 4.2) works with voting pattern to achieve consensus on the answer reported to blockchain.
- *Security Deposit* (Sect. 7.5) provides a mechanism for participants to weight their vote using their stake.
- *Multiple Authorization* (Sect. 6.2) is one on-chain mechanism to enable voting.
- *Dynamic Authorization* (Sect. 6.2) is one off-chain mechanism to enable voting.

---

[14] https://theconversation.com/blockchains-wont-fix-internet-voting-security-and-could-make-it-worse-104830.

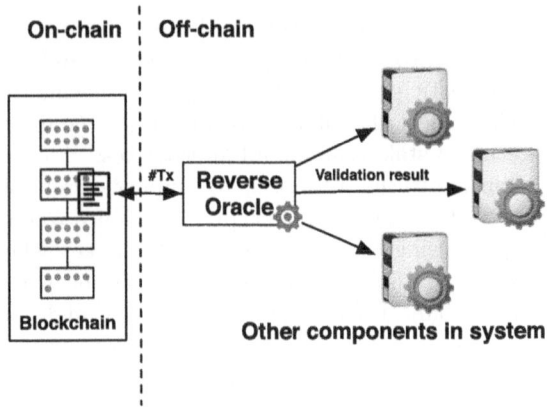

Fig. 5. Reverse Oracle Pattern

Known Uses:

- Voting mechanism is used in DAOs (Decentralised Autonomous Organisations)[15].
- In Gnosis (see footnote 12) prediction market, a voting mechanism is used if someone challenges the reported outcome. This voting mechanism allows users to vote on what the correct outcome was by betting Ether on that outcome.
- In Augur (see footnote 13) prediction market, a similar voting mechanism is used to resolve disputes on the outcome reported by oracles.

4.4   Pattern 4: Reverse Oracle

Summary: The reverse oracle of an existing system relies on smart contracts running on blockchain to validate requested data and check required status. Figure 5 is a graphical representation of the pattern.

Context: In a software system, where blockchain is one of the components, the off-chain components might need to use the data stored on the blockchain and the smart contracts running on the blockchain to check certain conditions.

Problem: Some domains use very large and mature (or even legacy) systems, which comply with existing standards. For such domain, how to integrate the existing complex systems with blockchain in an non-intrusive approach without changing the core of the existing systems?

Forces: The problem requires to balance the following forces:

- *Connectivity.* Integrating blockchain into an existing system to leverage the unique properties of blockchain, as discussed in Sect. 2.1.

---

[15] https://www.ethereum.org/dao.

– *Simplicity.* Introduce minimal changes to the existing system.

Solution: The unique ID of the transactions or blocks on blockchain is a piece of data that can be easily integrated into the existing systems so that they can refer to specific transactions as having taken place or address data permanently stored in specific blocks. Reverse Oracle is a component sitting between the blockchain and the other components in the system. Reverse Oracle is mainly reading data from the blockchain, and inserting the reference (ID of transaction) of this data into other components in the system. Oracle, however, is mainly writing data into the blockchain from other components. Validation of such data is implemented by smart contracts running on blockchain. Any off-chain component is required to query the blockchain through using the ID of the referenced data. More technical details of implementing the pattern could be found in [16].

Consequences:
Benefits:

– *Connectivity.* The blockchain is integrated into an existing system with minimal effort.

Drawbacks:

– *Non-intrusive.* It's not always possible to use blockchain in a non-intrusive way depending on the extensibility of the existing systems. Writing to and reading from the blockchain might need changing the existing system so that they can securely access the blockchain network.

Related Patterns:

– *Centralized Oracle* (Sect. 4.1) and *Decentralized Oracles* (Sect. 4.2) can be used when the information flows from external to blockchain.

Known Uses:

– *Identitii*[16] provides a solution to enrich the payments in banking systems with documents and tamper-proof attributes stored on a private blockchain. Identitii invents the concept of identity token stored on a blockchain. Every payment is associated with an identity token, which is used to exchange enriched information about a payment. The identity token is exchanged between the banks through being embedded into existing SWIFT protocol messages and can be verified against the copy in the blockchain.
– *Chaintrace*[17] records all the information about a wine, such as source, location, volume of the ingredients on blockchain. Chaintrace can be connected to external supply chain system and injects relevant information about a bottle of wine for cross verification.

---

[16] https://identitii.com/.
[17] https://chainflux.com/wine-traceability-using-blockchain/.

5   Data Management Patterns

Due to the unique properties and limitations of blockchain, the main architectural consideration for a blockchain-based software application is to decide what data and executable code (smart contract) should be kept on-chain, and what should be kept off-chain. Two factors need particular attention, namely performance and privacy. Performance highly depends on the type of deployment of the blockchain. For example, a consortium blockchain [27] can be configured to achieve much better performance than a public blockchain. This section discusses four data management patterns that manage data on and off blockchain.

5.1   Pattern 5: Tokenisation

Summary: Using tokens on blockchain to represent fungible goods for easier distribution.

Context: The concept of tokenisation has emerged centuries ago with the first currency systems. Tokenisation is a means to reduce risk in handling high value financial instruments by replacing them with equivalents, for example, the tokens used in casino. Tokens can represent a wide range of goods which are transferable and fungible, like shares, or tickets. Blockchain is a suitable technique for asset management because of its immutability and transparency.

Problem:
How to have a representative of assets to avoid repetition and decrease risk?

Forces: The problem requires to balance the following forces:

- *Risk.* Handling fungible financial assets with high value is risky, e.g., lost assets cannot be replaced.
- *Repetition.* An asset should be represented by only one token as the authoritative source.

Solution: Tokenisation is a process starting from an asset (*e.g.*, money) is locked under a custody (*e.g.*, a bank), and gets represented in the cryptographic world through a token. The ownership of the digital token matches the ownership of the corresponding asset. The reverse process can take place by which the user redeems the token to recover the value which is sitting within the bank.

Blockchain provides a trustworthy platform to realise tokenisation. There are different ways to implement tokenisation using blockchain. A token on blockchain is the authoritative source of the physical asset. Naive tokens on a blockchain (*e.g.*, BTC on Bitcoin, ETC on Ethereum) can be used to formulate a system where the tokens represent monetary value or other physical assets. The token is generally used to track title over the physical assets. Transactions on blockchain record the verifiable title transfer from one user to another. However, using the native token on blockchain for tokenisation is limited because it can only implement the title transfer of the physical assets, with limited conditions checking.

A more flexible way is to define a data structure in a smart contract to represent physical assets. By using smart contracts, some conditions can be implemented and associated with the ownership transfer.

Consequences:

Benefits:

- *Risk.* Tokenisation reduces risk in handling high value financial instruments by replacing them with equivalents.
- *Repetition.* Blockchain and smart contracts provide a trustworthy infrastructure to provide authorised tokens for the corresponding assets.

Drawbacks:

- *Integrity.* Integrity of the tokens is guaranteed by the blockchain infrastructure. But the authenticity of the corresponding physical/digital asset is not guaranteed automatically.
- *Standardisation.* 24% of the existing financial smart contracts on Ethereum uses this tokenisation pattern [3]. Given the popularity of this pattern, ERC20[18] (and ERC777[19] as an advanced version) has been proposed as a fungible token standard that describes the functions and events that a token smart contract has to implement. The new proposed fungible tokens should follow the standard.
- *Legal processes for ownership.* A token on a blockchain is not necessarily the authoritative source of information about the ownership of a physical asset. The owner of an asset may be entitled to sell the asset without being required to create a transaction on the blockchain. Also, legal processes such as court orders and bankruptcy proceedings can change the ownership of physical assets without any associated transaction being recorded on the blockchain.

Related Patterns:

- *Off-Chain Data Storage* (Sect. 5.2) can be used to add a hash of a digital asset as an ID on blockchain.

Known Uses:

- *Digix*[20] uses tokens to track the ownership of gold as a physical property.
- *Elevated Returns*[21] is an asset management firm that uses tokenisation to manage ownership on real estates.
- *CargoX*[22] creates a smart token to replace their bill of lading. The ownership of goods are claimed by using the smart token.

---

[18] https://eips.ethereum.org/EIPS/eip-20.
[19] https://eips.ethereum.org/EIPS/eip-777.
[20] https://digix.global/.
[21] https://www.elevatedreturns.com/.
[22] https://cargox.io/.

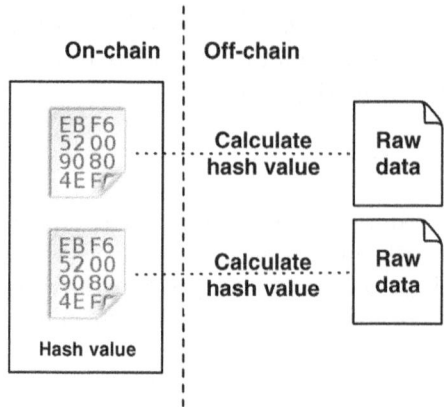

Fig. 6. Off-chain Data Storage Pattern

5.2   Pattern 6: Off-Chain Data Storage

Summary: Use hashing to ensure the integrity of arbitrarily large datasets which may not fit directly on the blockchain. Figure 6 is a graphical representation of the pattern solution.

Context: Some applications consider using the blockchain to guarantee the integrity of large amounts of data.

Problem: The blockchain, due to its full replication across all participants of the blockchain network, has limited storage capacity. Storing large amounts of data within a transaction may be impossible due to the limited size of the blocks of the blockchain (for example, the gas limit on Ethereum). Data cannot take advantage of the immutability or integrity guarantees without being stored on the blockchain. How to store data of arbitrary size and take advantage of the immutability and integrity guarantees provided by the blockchain?

Forces: The problem requires to balance the following forces:

- *Integrity.* Applications leverage blockchain to achieve data integrity.
- *Scalability.* Blockchain provides limited scalability because every bit of data is replicated across all nodes, where it is kept permanently.
- *Cost.* If a public blockchain is used, storing data on blockchain costs real money, although the cost is a one-time cost to write the data. This is in contrast to traditional distributed data storage, like cloud, which charge based on the amount of allocated storage space over time. A piece of data can be stored on blockchain through being embedded into a transaction, or as a variable of smart contract or as a log event. Embedding data into a transaction is the cheapest way, while storing data in a contract is more efficient to enable manipulation, but can be less flexible due to the potential constraints of the smart contract languages on the value types and length [27]. Different blockchain has different cost model for storing data.

– *Size.* There are limits of transaction size or block size. For example, on Bitcoin blockchain, The default Bitcoin client only relayed *OP_RETURN* transactions up to 80 bytes, which was reduced to 40 bytes in 2014[23]. Ethereum has a block gas limit that restricts the amount of gas which all transactions in a block are allowed to use.

Solution: The blockchain can be used as a general-purpose replicated database, as transactions logged in the blockchain can include arbitrary data on some blockchain platforms. For data of big size (essentially data that is bigger than its hash value), rather than storing the raw data directly on blockchain, a representation of the data with smaller size can be stored on blockchain with other small sized metadata about the data (*e.g.*, a URI pointing to it). The solution is to store a hash value (also called digest) of the raw data on chain. The value is generated by a hash function, *e.g.* one from the SHA2 [7] family, which maps data of arbitrary size to data of fixed size. Hash function is a one-way function which is easy to compute, but hard to invert given the output of a random input. If even one bit of the data changes, its corresponding hash value would change as well. The hash value is used for ensuring the integrity of the raw data stored off-chain, and the transaction on blockchain that includes the hash value guarantees the integrity of the hash value as well as the original raw data from which the hash was derived.

Consequences:
  Benefits:

– *Integrity.* Blockchain guarantees the integrity of the hash value that represents the raw data. The integrity of the raw data can be checked using the on-chain hash value.
– *Cost.* If a public blockchain is used, blockchain is utilized at a lower cost (fixed cost as the size of the hash value is fixed) for integrity of data with arbitrary size.

  Drawbacks:

– *Integrity.* The raw data is stored off-chain, where the off-chain data store might not be as secure as blockchain. The raw data may be changed without authorization. This change will be detected thanks to the hash of the original data stored on the blockchain. However, without additional measures, it will neither be possible to recover the original data nor to prevent the change from happening in the first place.
– *Availability.* Since the raw data is stored off-chain, it may be deleted or lost. Only its hash value remains permanently on the blockchain.
– *Data sharing.* The on-chain data can be shared through using blockchain platforms. Extra communication mechanisms and storage platforms are required for data sharing off-chain.

---

[23] https://github.com/bitcoin/bitcoin/pull/3737.

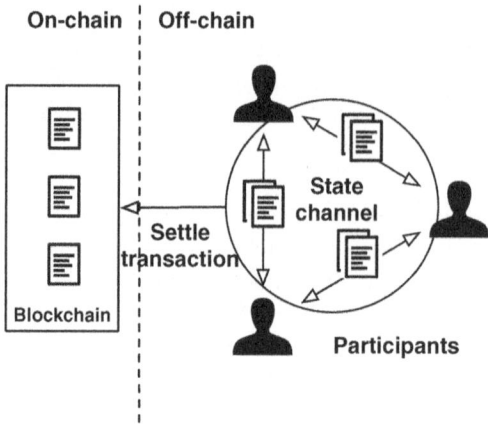

Fig. 7. State Channel Pattern

Related Patterns:

- *Tokenisation* (Sect. 5.1) can be used to add a authoritative representative of an asset on blockchain.
- *Legal and Smart Contract Pair* (Sect. 5.4) is enabled by *Off-Chain Data Storage*.

Known Uses:

- *Proof-of-Existence (POEX.IO[24])* allows entering an SHA-256 cryptographic hash of a document into the Bitcoin blockchain as a "proof-of-existence" of the document at a certain time. The hash value guarantees the data integrity of the document.
- *Chainy*[25] is a smart contract running on Ethereum blockchain. Chainy stores a short link to an off-chain file and its corresponding hash value in one place.

5.3   Pattern 7: State Channel

Summary: Micro-payments transactions are too expensive to be performed on-chain because the required transaction fee might be higher than the monetary value associated with the transaction assuming a public blockchain is used. Thus, micro-payments should be exchanged off-chain while periodically recording settlements for larger amounts on chain. Such a payment channel can be generalized for arbitrary state updates for more general purposes other than monetary value. Figure 7 is a graphical representation of the pattern.

---

[24] https://poex.io/.
[25] https://chainy.info/.

Context: Micro-payments are payments that can be as small as a few cents, *e.g.*, payment of a very small amount of money to a WiFi hot-spot for every 10 kilobytes of data usage. Blockchain has potential to be used for such financial transactions with tiny monetary value. The question is if it is necessary and cost effective to store all the micro-payment transactions on blockchain.

Problem: The decentralized design of blockchain has limited performance. Transactions can take several minutes or even one hour (for Bitcoin blockchain) to be *committed* on the blockchain [21]. Due to the long commit time and high transaction fees on a public blockchain (where fees are largely independent of the transacted amount), it is often infeasible to store every micro-payment transaction on the blockchain network. During a peak in demand, the average fee per transaction raised to the equivalent of US$55[26] on Bitcoin. On-chain transactions are suitable for transactions with medium to large monetary value, relative to the transaction fee.

Forces: The problem requires to balance the following forces:

- *Trustworthiness.* Payment transactions on the blockchain are trusted.
- *Latency.* Blockchain transactions may take a long time to be committed while users expect micro-payments to happen instantaneously.
- *Scalability.* Blockchain has limited scalability because every bit of data is replicated across all nodes, and kept permanently.
- *Cost.* Storing data on a public blockchain costs real money. The transaction fee of individual micro-payment transaction might be higher than the monetary value associated with the micro-payment transaction.

Solution: Storing every micro-payment transaction on blockchain is infeasible in certain contexts due to the small monetary value associated with it. Thus, a solution is to establish a payment channel between two participants, with a deposit from one or both sides of the participants locked up as security in a smart contract for the lifetime of the payment channel. The payment channel keeps the intermediate states of the micro-payment off-chain, and only stores the finalized payment on chain. The frequency of transaction settlement depends on the use case, and agreement between the two sides. For example, in scenarios around utilities, internet service providers or electricity companies can establish payment channel with their consumers for an agreed billing period, for example, a month. As the consumer uses data or energy daily, the intermediate state is stored in the channel until the end of the month, when the channel is closed to finalize the payment of that month. A network of micro-payment channels can be built where the transactions transferring small values occur off-chain. The individual transactions take place entirely off the blockchain and exclusively between the participants, across multiple hops where needed. Only the final transaction that settles the payment for a given channel or set of channels is

---

[26] https://bitinfocharts.com/comparison/bitcoin-transactionfees.html for 22 Dec 2017; accessed on 11/03/2021.

submitted to the blockchain. The technologies used to implement state channel are normally specific to blockchain platform. For example, Lightning network[27] on the Bitcoin blockchain is a proposed implementation of Hashed Timelock Contracts (HTLCs)[28] with bi-directional payment channels which allows secure payments across multiple peer-to-peer channels. A HTLC is a type of payments that use the features of Script, like *hashlocks* and *timelocks*, to require that the receiver of a payment acknowledges receiving the payment prior to a deadline by generating cryptographic proof.

Consequences:
  Benefits:

- *Speed.* Without involving blockchain for every transfer, the off-chain transactions can be settled without waiting for the blockchain network to process the transaction, generate a new block with the transaction and reach consensus, and the desired number of confirmation blocks.
- *Throughput.* The number of off-chain transactions that can be processed is not limited by the configuration of blockchain, such as the block size, block interval, gas limit, etc., and thus a much higher throughput can be achieved than for on-chain transactions.
- *Privacy.* Other than the final settlement transaction, the individual off-chain transactions do not show up in the public ledger, thus, the detail of these intermediate off-chain transactions is not publicly visible.
- *Cost.* If a public blockchain is used, only the final settlement transaction costs transaction fee to be included in the blockchain. Direct individual off-chain transactions do not cost any money. Multi-hop transactions may cost small transaction fees, which are typically charged as a percentage of the transacted amount.

  Drawbacks:

- *Trustworthiness.* The individual off-chain micro-payment transactions might not be as trustworthy as the on-chain transactions because the micro-payment transactions are not stored in an immutable data store. The intermediate state of payment channels might be lost after the payment channels are closed.
- *Liquidity.* To establish a payment channel, money from one or both sides of the channel needs to be locked up in a smart contract for the lifetime of the payment channel. The liquidity of the channel participants is thereby reduced.
- *Wallet.* A new wallet or extension to the existing wallet is needed to support the micro-payment protocol.

Related Patterns:

- *Off-Chain Data Storage* (Sect. 5.2) is another mechanism that reduces data on blockchain.

---

[27] https://lightning.network/.
[28] https://en.bitcoin.it/wiki/Hashed_Timelock_Contracts.

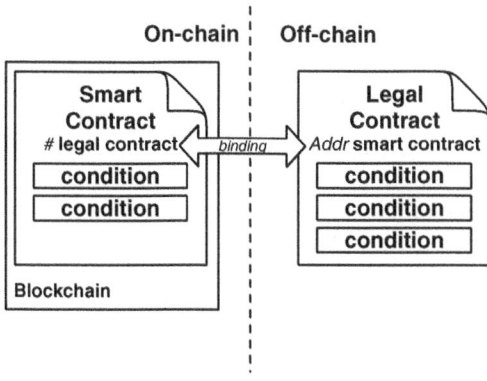

Fig. 8. Legal and Smart Contract Pair Pattern

Known Uses:

– The *Lightning network* uses an off-chain protocol to enable micro-payments of Bitcoin and several other crypto-currencies.
– The *Raiden network*[29] on the Ethereum blockchain is a similar solution as lightning network. The basic idea is to avoid the consensus bottleneck by leveraging a network of off-chain payment channels that allow to securely transfer monetary value. Smart contracts are used to deposit value into the payment channels.
– *State channel* on Ethereum[30] and *Gnosis Go*[31] offer a more generalized form of state channels that support exchanging state for general-purpose applications.

5.4   Pattern 8: Legal and Smart Contract Pair

Summary: A bidirectional binding is established between a legal agreement and the corresponding smart contract. Figure 8 is a graphical representation of the pattern.

Context: The legal industry is becoming digitized, for example, using digital signatures has become a valid way to sign legal agreements. The Ricardian contract [10] was developed in the mid 1990s to interpret legal contracts digitally without losing the value of the legal prose. Digital legal agreements need to be executed and enforced.

Problem: An independent trustworthy execution platform trusted by all the involved participants is needed to execute the digital legal agreement. How to

---

[29] https://raiden.network/.
[30] http://www.jeffcoleman.ca/state-channels/.
[31] https://forum.gnosis.pm/t/how-offchain-trading-will-work/63.

bind a legal agreement to the corresponding smart contract on a trusted execution environment to ensure a 1-to-1 mapping?

Forces: The problem requires to balance the following forces:

- *Authoritative source.* A 1-to-1 mapping is required between a legal contract and its corresponding smart contract to make the smart contract as the authoritative source of the legal contract.
- *Secure storage.* A secure and trustworthy data storage is required to keep the legal agreement.
- *Secure execution.* A trustworthy computational platform is required to execute digital agreements to enforce certain conditions as defined in a legal contract.

Solution:
Blockchain can be an ideal trusted platform to run digital legal agreements, which are bound with the corresponding on-chain smart contracts. The smart contract implements conditions defined in the legal agreement. When deployed, there is a variable to store the hash value of the legal agreement, but is initially a blank value. The address of the smart contract is included in the legal agreement, and then the hash of the legal agreement is calculated and added to the contract variable. By binding a physical agreement with a smart contract, the bridge between the off-chain physical agreement and the on-chain smart contract is established. The two directional binding makes sure that the legal agreement and smart contract have a 1-to-1 mapping.

The smart contract digitizes the conditions defined within the legal agreement. Thus, these conditions can be checked and enforced automatically by the smart contract. However, not all the legal terms can be easily digitalized. The smart contract can also enable automated regulatory compliance checking in terms of the required information and process. However, the capability of compliance checking might be limited due to the constraints of smart contract programming language.

Consequences:
Benefits:

- *Automation.* Some of the conditions defined in the legal contract, for example, a conditional payment, can be automatically enforced by blockchain.
- *Audit trail.* Blockchain permanently records all historical transactions related to the legal contract and the contract itself. This immutable data enables auditing at anytime in future.
- *Clarification.* Encoding legal terms expressed in natural language into smart contracts will require to give them a clear interpretation.

Drawbacks:

- *Expressiveness.* Smart contracts are written in programming languages. The smart contract languages might have limited expressiveness to express contractual terms of arbitrary complexity. The capability of regulatory compliance checking also depends on the expressiveness of the smart contracts. A regulation may regulate the process, for example, what should or should not be done by whom at what stage.

- *Enforceability.* If a public blockchain is used, there is no central administering authority to decide a dispute, or perform the enforcement of a court judgment.
- *Interpretability.* There might be different ways to interpret a certain legal term and to encode them in the smart contract. Ambiguity of natural language makes it a challenge to accurately implement a certain legal term in a way that is agreed upon by all the involved participants.

Related Patterns:

- *Legal and Smart Contract Pair* is enabled by *Off-Chain Data Storage* (Sect. 5.2).

Known Uses:

- *OpenLaw*[32] is a platform that allows lawyers to make legally binding and self-executable agreements on the Ethereum blockchain. The legal agreement templates are stored on a decentralized data storage, IPFS[33]. Users can create customized contracts for specific uses.
- *Smart Contract Template* proposed by Barclays[34] uses legal document templates to facilitate smart contracts running on Corda (see footnote 10) blockchain platform [5,6].
- Specific proposals for the representation of machine-interpretable legal terms have been explored in KWM's project on digital and analog (*DnA*) contracts[35] and in the *Accord Project*[36].

6 Security Patterns

This section discusses four security patterns that mainly concern the security aspect [9] of the blockchain-based applications.

6.1 Pattern 9: On-Chain Encryption

Summary: Ensure confidentiality of the data stored on blockchain by encrypting it. Figure 9 is a graphical representation of the pattern.

Context: For some applications on blockchain, there might be commercially critical data that should be only accessible to the involved participants. An example would be a special discount price offered by a service provider to a

---

[32] http://openlaw.io/.
[33] https://ipfs.io/.
[34] https://www.barclays.co.uk/.
[35] https://github.com/KingandWoodMallesonsAU/Project-DnA.
[36] https://www.accordproject.org/.

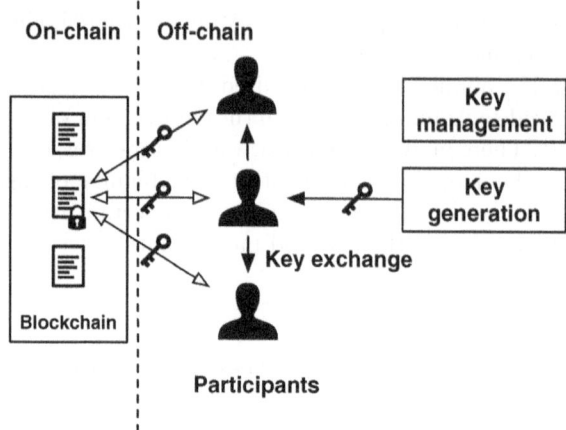

Fig. 9. Encrypting On-chain Data Pattern

subset of its users. Such information should not be accessible to the other users who do not get the discount.

Problem: The lack of data privacy is one of the main limitations of blockchain. All the information on blockchain is publicly available to the participants of the blockchain network. There is no privileged user within the blockchain network, no matter the blockchain is public, consortium or private. On a public blockchain, new participants can join the blockchain network freely and access all the information recorded on blockchain. Any confidential data on public blockchain is exposed to the public.

Forces: The problem requires to balance the following forces:

- *Transparency.* Every participant within a blockchain network is able to access all the historical transactions on blockchain, which is required to enable them to validate previous transactions. The transactions on a public blockchain are also accessible to everyone with access to the internet, simply using tools like a blockchain explorer such as Etherscan[37].
- *Lack of confidentiality.* Since all the information on blockchain is publicly available to everyone in the network, commercially sensitive data meant to be kept confidential should not be stored on blockchain, at least not in plain form.

Solution: To preserve the privacy of the involved participants, symmetric or asymmetric encryption can be used to encrypt data before inserting the data into blockchain. One possible design for sharing encrypted data among multiple participants is as follows. First, one of the involved participants creates a secret key for encrypting data and distributes it during an initial key exchange. When

---

[37] http://etherscan.io.

one of the participants needs to add a new data item to the blockchain, they first symmetrically encrypt it using the secret key. Only the participants allowed to access the transaction have the secret key and can decrypt the information.

Consequences:

Benefits:

- *Confidentiality.* Using encryption, the publicly accessible information on blockchain is encrypted, so that is useless to anyone who does not hold the secret key.

Drawbacks:

- *Compromised key.* Both symmetric and asymmetric encryption require off-chain key management. If key management is not done properly, it can lead to compromise and disclosure of private or secret keys. If the required private key or secret key is compromised, the encryption mechanism does not guarantee the confidentiality nor the integrity of the data.
- *Access revocation.* Revoking read access is a challenge after the encrypted data has been published to the blockchain. The encrypted data on blockchain is immutable. Thus, as long as the participant keeps the secret key used to encrypt the data, it has access to the encrypted data forever.
- *Immutable data.* Even if stored in encrypted form, the critical data will remain in the blockchain forever. In addition to the risk of key compromise, the encrypted data may be subject to brute force decryption attacks at any time in the future, or breakthroughs in technology like quantum computing might render current encryption technologies ineffective. So even if the data is considered to be secure with a given key size when it is stored in the blockchain, this may no longer be the case in the future.
- *Key sharing.* The encryption key needs to be shared off-chain before submitting any relevant transaction to the blockchain secretly. Although blockchain can be used as a software connector [26] to communicate data, secret keys can not be shared through blockchain because the shared key would be publicly accessible if being communicated through blockchain.

Related Patterns:

- *Off-Chain Data Storage* (Sect. 5.2) also provides data confidentiality because the raw data is not stored on blockchain.

Known Uses:

- Encrypted queries from *Provable* (see footnote 14). Provable is a smart contract running on Ethereum public blockchain, which provides a service to access state from external world. Provable allows smart contract developers to encrypt the parameters of their queries locally by using a public key before passing them to a smart contract. The only one who can decrypt the call parameters is Provable with the paired private key.

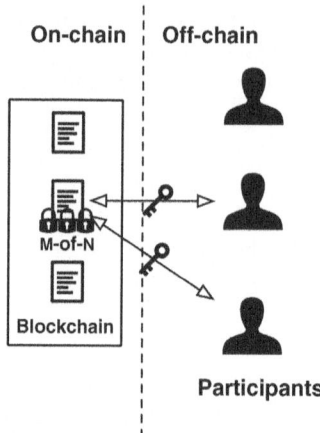

Fig. 10. Multiple Authorization Pattern

- *Crypto digital signature* is suggested by *MLGBlockchain*[38] to encrypt data and share the data between the parties who interact and transmit data through blockchain.
- Hawk [11] is a smart contract system that stores transactions as encrypted data on blockchain to retain the privacy of the transactions. The compiler of Hawk can automatically generate a cryptographic protocol for a smart contract. The involved participants interact with the blockchain following the cryptographic protocol.

6.2   Pattern 10: Multiple Authorization

Summary: A set of blockchain addresses which can authorise a transaction is pre-defined. Only a subset of the addresses is required to authorize transactions. Figure 10 is a graphical representation of the pattern.

Context: In blockchain-based applications, activities might need to be authorized by multiple blockchain addresses. For example, a monetary transaction may require authorization from multiple blockchain addresses.

Problem: The actual addresses that authorize an activity might not be able to be decided due to the availability of the authorities. How to allow multiple authorities to dynamically authorize a transaction based on their availability?

Forces: The problem requires to balance the following forces:

- *Flexibility.* The actual authorities who authorize the transaction can be from a set of pre-defined authorities.

---

[38] https://mlgblockchain.com/crypto-signature.html.

– *Tolerance of compromised or lost private key* Authentication on blockchain uses digital signature. However, blockchain does not offer any mechanism to recover a lost or a compromised private key. Losing a key results in permanent loss of control over an account, and potentially smart contracts that refer to it.

Solution: It would enable more dynamism if the set of blockchain addresses for authorization are not decided before the corresponding transaction being submited into the blockchain network, or the corresponding smart contract being deployed on blockchain. On the Bitcoin blockchain, a multi-signature mechanism can be used to require more than one private key to authorize a Bitcoin transaction. In Ethereum, smart contract can mimic multi-signature mechanism.

Consequences:
  Benefits:

– *Flexibility.* This pattern enables flexible binding of authorities, but depends on the availability of authorities when the activity is proceeded.
– *Lost key tolerant.* One participant can own more than one blockchain address to reduce the risk of losing control over their smart contracts due to a lost private key. There could be a function that can update the list of allowed authorities, and the threshold of the authorization. In the case that the update function also requires threshold-based authorization, the list of the update addresses can be also updated through authorization from at least the minimum number of addresses.

  Drawbacks:

– *Pre-defined authorities.* Although the pattern enables flexible binding, all the possible authorities still need to be known in advance of any decision or update.
– *Lost key.* At least a minimum number of private keys should be safely kept to avoid losing control.
– *Cost of dynamism.* If a public blockchain is used, updating the list of authorities costs money, as does deploying the logic for multiple authorities. Besides, it costs more to store multiple addresses as the possible authorities than storing only one.

Related Patterns:

– *Dynamic Authorization* (Sect. 6.3). An off-chain secret enabled dynamic authorization pattern is used when the possible authorities are unknown beforehand.
– *Voting* (Sect. 4.3) can be enabled by Multiple Authorization.

Known Uses:

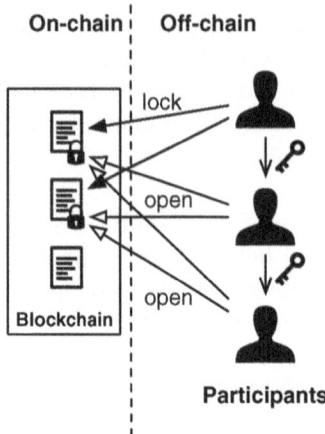

Fig. 11. Off-chain Secret Enabled Dynamic Authorization Pattern

- Multi-Signature mechanism provided by Bitcoin[39].
- Multi-signature wallet, written in Solidity, running on Ethereum blochchain and is available in the Ethereum DApp browser Mist[40].

6.3 Pattern 11: Dynamic Authorization

Summary: Using a hash created off-chain to dynamically bind authority for a transaction. Figure 11 is a graphical representation of the pattern. This solution is sometimes referred to as *Hashlock*.

Context: In blockchain-based applications, some activities need to be authorized by one or more participants that are unknown when a first transaction is submitted to blockchain.

Problem: Sometimes, the authority who can authorize a given activity is unknown when the corresponding smart contract is deployed, or the corresponding transaction is submitted to the blockchain. Blockchain uses digital signature for authentication and transaction authorization. Blockchain does not support dynamic binding with an address of a participant which is not defined in the respective transaction or smart contract. All accounts that can authorize a second transaction have to be defined in the first transaction before that transaction is added to the blockchain. How to allow one or more unknown authorities to dynamically authorize a transaction?

Forces: The problem requires to balance the following forces:

---

[39] https://en.bitcoin.it/wiki/Multisignature.
[40] https://github.com/ethereum/mist.

- *Dynamism.* Dynamic binding one or more unknown authorities with a second transaction representing an activity after the first transaction submitted to blockchain.
- *Pre-defined authorities.* Using only on-chain mechanisms, all the possible authorities are required to be defined beforehand.

Solution: An off-chain secret can be used to enable a dynamic authorization when the participant authorizing a transaction is unknown beforehand. In the context of payment, for example, a smart contract can be used as an escrow. When the sender deposits the money to an escrow smart contract, a hash of a secret (for example, a random string, called pre-image) is submitted with the money as well. Whoever receives the secret off-chain can claim the money from the escrow smart contract by revealing the secret. With this solution, the receiver of the money does not need to be defined beforehand in the escrow contract. This can be generalized to any transaction that needs authorization from a dynamically bound participant. Note that since the secret is revealed, it cannot be reused. One variant is to lock multiple transactions with the same secret – by unlocking one, all of them are unlocked.

Consequences:
  Benefits:

- *Dynamism.* This pattern enables dynamic binding of unknown authorities after the transaction is added into the blockchain.
- *Lost key tolerant.* No specific private key is required to authorize transactions.
- *Routability.* This pattern has the useful property that once the secret is revealed, any other transactions secured using the same secret can also be opened. This makes it possible to create multiple transactions that are all locked by the same secret. This property is used by micro-payment channels (Sect. 5.3) to enable multi-hop transfers where the money hosted by every hop and secured by a same secret can be released after the end receiver claims the money with the secret (*i.e.* the secret is revealed). The secret can be exchanged through an off-chain channel to every hop.
- *Interoperability.* There is no need for a special protocol to exchange the secret. The secret can be exchanged in any ways off-chain. It provides a mechanism for other systems to trigger events on blockchain.

  Drawbacks:

- *One-off secret.* The secret used in this pattern is a one-off secret. Verification of the secret is on-chain. Thus, once a secret is embedded in a transaction submitted to the blockchain, the secret is revealed.
- *Combination of signature and secret.* Because this pattern has the property that once the secret is revealed, any other transactions secured using the same secret can also be opened, sometimes the transaction protected by the secret should also be associated with a public key so that both a correct secret and an appropriate signature with the respective private key are required to authorize the transaction. This is applicable to the situation where a large set of authorities are known beforehand, but not all of them are allowed

to authorize a certain activity/transaction. Thus, a hash secret is used to dynamically bind one or multiple authorities from the larger pre-defined set of authorities.

- *Lost secret.* The sender/initiator of a transaction takes the risk of losing the off-chainsecret. If the secret is lost, the transaction cannot be authorized and being proceeded anymore. In the case of money transfer, the money associated with the transaction would be locked forever if the transaction cannot be authorized properly.

Related Patterns:

- *Multiple Authorization* (Sect. 6.2). The multiple authorization pattern is used when all the possible authorities are known beforehand. Multiple authorization pattern is an on-chain mechanism.
- *Voting* (Sect. 4.3) can be enabled by Dynamic Authorization.
- Dynamic Authorization enables routability for *State channel* (Sect. 5.3) in the financial transaction scenarios.

Known Uses:

- *Raiden network* (see footnote 29) is a network of off-chain payment channels on top of Ethereum blockchain network, which enables secure value transfer. The multi-hop transfer mechanism in Raiden Network uses *hashlocked* transactions to securely router payment through a middleman.
- In the Bitcoin ecosystem, *atomic cross-chain trading*[41] allows one crytocurrency (for example, Bitcoin) to be traded for another cryptocurrency (for example, tokens on a Bitcoin sidechain) using a off-chain hash secret.

6.4   Pattern 12: Embedded Permission

Summary: Smart contracts use an embedded permission control to restrict access to the invocation of the functions defined in the smart contracts. Figure 12 is a graphical representation of the pattern.

Context: All the smart contracts running on blockchain can be accessed and called by all the blockchain participants and other smart contracts by default, because there are no privileged users in blockchain network. In the case of public blockchain, every one with internet access can join the network to access all the information and code stored and running on blockchain.

Problem: A smart contract by default has no owner, meaning that once deployed the author of the smart contract has no special privilege on the smart contract. A permission-less function can be triggered by unauthorized users accidentally. Such a permission-less function becomes vulnerability of blockchain-based application. For example, a permission-less function which is discovered

---

[41] https://en.bitcoin.it/wiki/Atomic_cross-chain_trading.

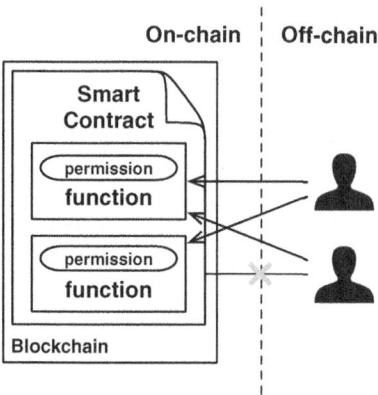

Fig. 12. Embedded Permission Pattern

in a smart contract library used by the Parity multi-signature wallet, caused the freezing of about 500K Ethers[42]. 7% smart contract on public Ethereum can be terminated without authority [21].

Forces: The problem requires to balance the following forces:

– *Security.* The functions defined in the smart contracts should be called only by the authorized participants. Due to the transparency of public blockchains, all the smart contracts are also publicly available to everyone connecting to the Internet. In contrast, in a conventional software system, the internal logic is normally not visible to the end uses. Interaction with the software system is either through a user interface or API, where it is possible to enforce access control policies.

Solution: Adding permission control to every smart contract function to check permissions for every caller that triggers the functions defined in the smart contract based on the blockchain addresses of the caller. This can be done by checking the authorization of the caller before executing the logic of the function: unauthorized calls are rejected and the execution of the function terminated before reaching the core logic of the function.

Consequences:
  Benefits:

– *Security.* Only the participants and smart contracts that are authorized by the smart contract can call the corresponding functions successfully.
– *Secure authorization.* Authorization is implemented in smart contracts running on blockchain, which leverages the properties provided by blockchain.

---

[42] https://paritytech.io/a-postmortem-on-the-parity-multi-sig-library-self-destruct/.

Drawbacks:

- *Cost.* On a public blockchain, extra code that implements the permission control mechanism also has additional monetary cost for deployment and execution.
- *Lack of flexibility.* Such permissions are defined in the smart contract before its deployment, therefore they are difficult to change. However, permissions may be required to be dynamic. A mechanism is needed to support dynamic granting and removal of permissions.

Related Patterns:

- *Multiple authorization* (Sect. 6.2) is one way of implementing embedded permission pattern.
- *Dynamic authorization* (Sect. 6.3) is another way of implementing embedded permission pattern.

Known Uses:

- The Mortal contract discussed in the Solidity tutorial[43] restricts the permission of invoking the *selfdestruct* function to the "owner" of the contract – where "owner" is a variable defined in the contract code itself.
- The *Restrict access* pattern suggested in the Solidity tutorial[44] uses *modifier* to restrict who can make modifications to the state of the contract or call the functions of the contract. *Modifier* is a mechanism that adds a piece of code before the function to check certain conditions.

7   Contract Structural Patterns

This section discusses five smart contracts patterns. Essentially, smart contracts are programs running on blockchain, thus some of the existing design patterns and programming principles for conventional software environments are also applicable to smart contracts. If a public blockchain is used, the structural design of the smart contract has large impact on its deployment and execution cost. The cost of deploying a smart contract depends on the size of the smart contract(s) because the code is stored on blockchain, resulting in a data storage fee that is proportional to the size of the smart contract. Thus, a structural design with more lines of compiled code costs more money. A consortium blockchain does not necessarily have tokens/currency; therefore monetary cost is typically not an issue for a consortium blockchain. However, blockchain size is still a design concern because the total size of the blockchain keeps growing as more blocks are appended to it and no block can ever be detached from it, and every participant stores a full replica of blockchain. Besides, different structural designs of smart contracts may affect performance because more or less transactions may be required.

---

[43] http://solidity.readthedocs.io/en/develop/contracts.html.
[44] http://solidity.readthedocs.io/en/develop/common-patterns.html.

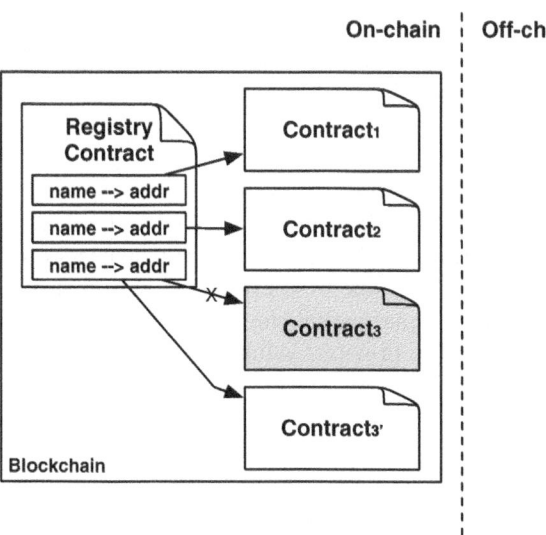

Fig. 13. Contract Registry Pattern

7.1 Pattern 13: Contract Registry

Summary: Before invoking it, the address of the latest version of a smart contract is located by looking up its name on a contract registry. Figure 13 is a graphical representation of the pattern.

Context: As any software application, blockchain-based applications need to be upgraded to new versions. To do so, the on-chain functions defined in smart contracts need to be updated to fix bugs as well as to fulfill new requirements.

Problem: Smart contracts deployed on blockchain cannot be upgraded because the code of the smart contracts as a type of data, stored on blockchain is immutable. How to perform upgrades of smart contracts?

Forces: The problem requires to balance the following forces:

- *Immutability.* Every bit of data, including deployed smart contracts, stored on blockchain is immutable.
- *Upgradability.* There is a fundamental need to upgrade all but short-lived applications and their smart contracts over time.
- *Human-readable contract identifier.* The identifier of a smart contract on blockchain platforms, like Ethereum, is hexadecimal address, which is not human-readable.

Solution: An on-chain registry contract is used to maintain a mapping between user-defined symbolic names and the blockchain addresses of the registered contracts. The address of the registry contract needs to be advertised off-chain. The creator of a contract can register the name and the address of the new contract to the registry contract after the new contract being deployed. The invoker of a registered contract retrieves the latest version of the new smart contract from the registry contract. The corresponding functions provided by the registered contract can be upgraded by replacing the address of the old version contract in the registry contract with the address of a new version without breaking the dependency between the upgraded smart contract and other smart contracts that depend on its functions. The address of a contract is stored as a variable in the registry contract. The value of contract variables can be updated. The registry contract can have a permission control module to maintain the writing permission. Note that all the previous values of the variable are still stored on the blockchain.

Consequences:

Benefits:

- *Human-readable contract name.* The registry contract maintains a mapping between human-readable names and the hexadecimal addresses of the smart contracts. A human readable form of smart contract names is desired, for example, to be exposed to the user interface. A human readable name is also useful for developers.
- *Constant contract name.* The smart contract associated with a registered name can be updated without changing its name. This way dependencies relying on the name of the smart contract do not get broken.
- *Upgradability.* The smart contract associated with a registered name could be replaced by a new version without breaking the dependencies based on the human-readable name.
- *Version control.* Version control can be integrated in the registry contract as well to allow a look-up based on the name and version of a smart contract. Old versions of a smart contract that are no longer needed should be terminated.

Drawbacks:

- *Upgradability.* Upgradability is still limited if the functions defined in the smart contract are called by other contracts. Although the implementation of the function can be upgraded, the interface (that is function signature) cannot be modified without breaking the link to dependent smart contracts. Similar methods as for API/service interface management need to be implemented, *e.g.* through versioning and depreciation flags.
- *Cost.* There is an additional cost to maintain a registry that contains the mapping between the contract names and their addresses. Furthermore, all the inter-contract function calls require a registry look-up to find the latest version of the smart contract to be invoked.

Related Patterns:

- *Embedded permission* (Sect. 6.4) can be used to define writing permission.

– *Data contract* (Sect. 7.2) and this pattern can work together to further improve upgradability of smart contracts.

Known Uses:

– ENS[45] is a name service on Ethereum blockchain, which is implemented as smart contracts. ENS maintains a mapping between both smart contracts on-chain and resources off-chain and simple, human-readable names. ENS can be viewed as a contract registry built on Ethereum blockchain, which is accessible to everyone. A blockchain-based application can also maintain a separate registry contract for the application.
– *KairosFuture*[46] experimented using blockchain smart contract as a replacement for land registry. All the signed contracts are recorded by a registry contract on the blockchain.
– *Kaleido*[47] proposed a enterprise-level smart contract management solution. The core function of their management solution is the contract registry that is accessible to every participants in Kaleido network.

7.2   Pattern 14: Data Contract

Summary: Store data in a separate smart contract. Figure 14 is a graphical representation of the pattern.

Context: The need to upgrade a blockchain-based application over time is ultimately necessary, so as the smart contracts used by the application. In general, logic and data change at different times and with different frequencies. There are different ways to store a data on blockchain, as discussed in *Off-chain Data Storage* pattern (Sect. 5.2).

Problem: Storing data on blockchain is expensive and there is a limitation on the amount of data and amount of computation a transaction can contain. In the context of upgrading smart contracts, the upgrading transactions might contain a large data storage for copying the data from the old version of the smart contract to the new version of the smart contract. Porting data to a new version might even require multiple transactions, *e.g.* when the block gas limit on Ethereum prevents an overly complex data migration transaction.

Forces: The problem requires to balance the following forces:

– *Coupling.* Smart contracts can live forever on blockchain if not being explicitly terminated. If a smart contract is deactivated in this way, the data stored in the smart contract cannot be accessed through the smart contract functions any more – although it can still be accessed with some effort, *e.g.* for provenance or audit purposes.

---

[45] https://ens.domains.
[46] https://www.kairosfuture.com/publications/reports/the-land-registry-in-the-block-chain-testbed/.
[47] https://www.kaleido.io/blockchain-blog/smart-contract-management-solution-how-it-works-why-you-need-it.

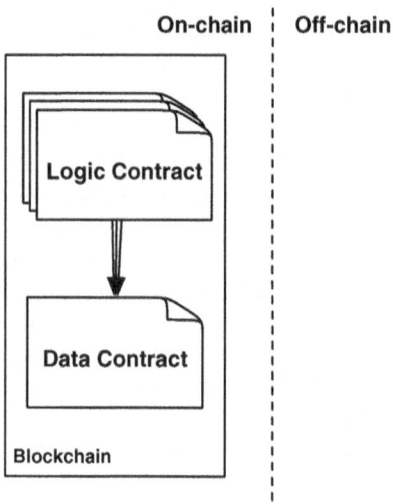

Fig. 14. Data Contract Pattern

- *Upgradability.* The need to upgrade the application and the smart contracts supporting the application over time is ultimately necessary for many applications.
- *Cost.* If a public blockchain is used, storing data on blockchain costs money. Thus copying data from an old version of a smart contract to a new version should be avoid or minimized.

Solution: To avoid moving data during upgrades of smart contracts, the data store is isolated from the rest of the code. In the context of blockchain, data could be separately stored in different smart contracts to enable isolation. Depending on the circumstances of the application, how large of a data store it needs and whether the data structure is expected to change often, the data store could use a strict definition or a loosely typed flat store. The more generic and flexible data structure can be used by all the other logic smart contracts and is unlikely to require changes. One example of a generic data structure is a mapping to store SHA-256 key and value pairs.

Consequences:
  Benefits:

- *Upgradability.* By separating data from the rest of the code, the logic of the application is able to be upgraded without affecting the data contract.
- *Cost.* Since the data is separated from the rest of the code, there is no cost for migrating data when the application is upgraded.
- *Generality.* If the data can be cleanly separated and generalized, there would be an additional benefit: the generic data contract can be used by all related logic smart contracts.

Drawbacks:

- *Cost.* If a public blockchain is used, storing a piece of data in a generic data structure costs more money than a strictly defined data structure. For example, as mentioned earlier, a generic data structure maintains a mapping between SHA-256 key and value pairs, but a more strictly defined data structure can be of smaller size, *e.g.* not requiring the key to be stored. Querying the data is also less straightforward. This is the cost of a generalized solution.

Related Patterns:

- *Contract registry* (Sect. 7.1) and Data Contract can work together to further improve upgradability of smart contracts.

Known Uses:

- *Chronobank*[48] is a blockchain project that tokenizes labour and provides a market for professionals to trade their labour time with businesses. It uses a smart contract with a generic data structure as the data store used by all the other logic smart contracts.
- *Colony*[49], a platform for open organizations running on Ethereum. Similar to Chronobank, Colony has a data contract with a generic data structure.

7.3 Pattern 15: Factory Contract

Summary: An on-chain template contract is used as a factory that generates contract instances from the template. Figure 15 is a graphical representation of the pattern.

Context: Applications based on blockchain might need to use multiple instances of a standard contract with customization. Each contract instance is created by instantiating a contract template. For example, in a business process management system, each of the business process instances might be represented by a smart contract being generated from a contract template representing the business process model [22]. The template can be stored off-chain in a code repository, or on-chain, within its own smart contract.

Problem: Keeping the contract template off-chain cannot guarantee consistency between different smart contract instances created from the same template because the source code of the template can be independently modified.

Forces: The problem requires to balance the following forces:

- *Dependency management.* Storing the source code of smart contract off-chain in a code repository introduces the issue of integrating more systems into the blockchain-based application.

---

[48] https://chronobank.io/.
[49] https://colony.io/.

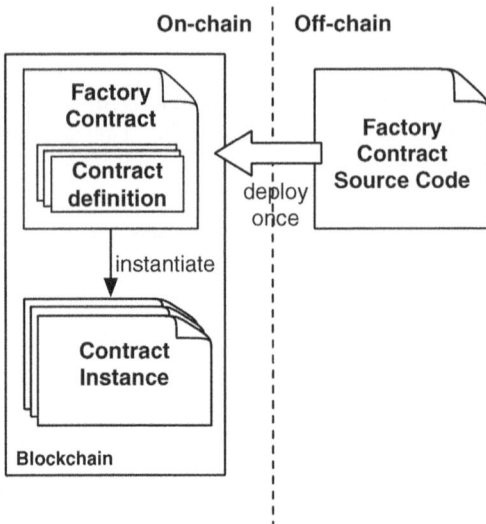

Fig. 15. Factory Contract Pattern

- *Secure code sharing.* The source code smart contract should be stored in a secure storage.
- *Deployment.* If a public code repository, like Github, is used to store the source code of a smart contract, a component is needed to implement the function of deploying smart contract on blockchain, otherwise, the end users need to understand how to deploy smart contracts.

Solution: Smart contracts are created from a contract factory deployed on blockchain. The factory contract is deployed once from the off-chain source code. The factory may contain the definition of multiple smart contracts. Smart contract instances are generated by passing parameters to the contract factory to instantiate customized smart contract instances. Factory contract is analogous to a *Class* in an object-oriented programming language. Every transaction that generates a smart contract instance essentially instantiates an object of the factory contract class. This contract instance (the object) will maintain its own properties independently of the other instances but with a structure consistent with its original template.

Consequences:
    Benefits:

- *Security.* Keeping the factory contract on-chain guarantees the consistency of the contract definition. Blockchain provides a secure platform to share code of smart contracts. As opposed to a traditional code repository, changes of code deployed on a smart contract can be strictly limited or prohibited.

– *Efficiency.* If the contract definition is kept on-chain in a factory contract, smart contract instances are generated by calling a function defined in the factory contract.

   Drawbacks:

– *Deployment cost.* If a public blockchain is used, using factory contract requires extra cost to deploy the factory contract.
– *Function call cost.* If a public blockchain is used, creating a new smart contract instance requires extra cost to call a function defined in the factory contract.

Related Patterns:

– *Contract registry* (Sect. 7.1) can be used to store the addresses of all the smart contract instances generated from a factory contract. The factory and instance registry can be implemented in the same contract, although that limits upgradability.

Known Uses:

– A tutorial from Ethereum developers[50] about how to create a contract factory from which smart contract instances can be created.
– Factory pattern has been applied in a real-world blockchain-based health care application [28].
– The business process management system in an academic work [22] uses a contract factory to generate process instances.

7.4   Pattern 16: Incentive Execution

Summary: Reward is provided to the caller of the contract function for invoking the execution. Figure 16 is a graphical representation of the pattern.

Context: Smart contracts are event-driven programs, which cannot execute autonomously. All the functions defined in a smart contract need to be triggered either by a transaction from external account or another smart contract to execute. Other than the functions that provide regular services to users, some functions need to run asynchronously from regular user interaction, for example, to clean up the expired records, or make dividend payouts etc. Such accessorial functions usually involve a time, after which the function should start.

Problem: Users of a smart contract have no direct benefit from calling the accessorial functions. If a public blockchain is used, executing these functions causes extra monetary cost. Some accessorial functions are expensive to execute. How to make sure the accessorial functions are invoked?

Forces: The problem requires to balance the following forces:

---

[50] https://ethereumdev.io/manage-several-contracts-with-factories/.

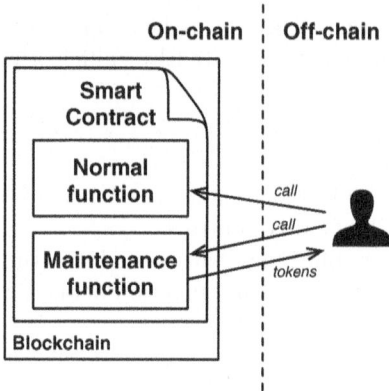

Fig. 16. Incentive Execution Pattern

– *Completeness.* The regular services provided by a smart contract are supported by some accessorial functions.
– *Cost.* Execution of accessorial functions causes extra costs from the users.

Solution: Reward the caller of a function defined in a smart contract for invoking the execution, for example, sending back a percentage of payout to the caller to reimburse the (gas) execution cost.

Consequences:
   Benefits:

– *Completeness.* The execution of the accessorial functions helps to complete the regular services provided by the smart contract.
– *Cost.* The users, who spends extra to execute the accessorial functions, are compensated by the reward associated with the execution.

   Drawbacks:

– *Execution.* Execution cannot be guaranteed even with incentive. Thus, another option is to embed the logic of accessorial functions into other regular functions that users have to call to use the services.

Related Patterns:

– Both *Security Deposit* (Sect. 7.5) and Incentive Execution provide incentive mechanisms.

Known Uses:

– *Ethereum alarm clock*[51] is a service provided by a smart contract running on Ethereum. It facilitates scheduling function calls for a specified block in the future and provides incentive for users to execute the scheduled function.

---

[51] http://www.ethereum-alarm-clock.com/.

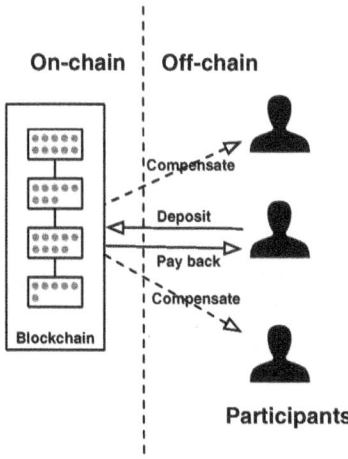

Fig. 17. Security Deposit Pattern

7.5   Pattern 17: Security Deposit

Summary: A user put aside a certain amount of money, which will be paid back to the user for her honesty or given to the other parties to compensate them for the dishonesty of the user. Figure 17 is a graphical representation of the pattern.

Context: In a decentralized environment like blockchain, trust in the blockchain-based application is achieved from the interactions between participants within the network. A blockchain-based application rely on all the users rather than relying on trusted third-party organisations to facilitate transactions.

Problem: The *equal rights* property of blockchain allows every participant the same ability to access and manipulate the blockchain and the decentralized applications running on blockchain. How can a certain participant proves to others that he/she behaves honestly?

Forces: The problem requires to balance the following forces:

- *Security.* The security of a decentralized application relies on the behaviour of all the participants of the application.
- *Incentive.* In a decentralized application, participants can be incentivised to behave honestly.

Solution: Initially, participant is required to put aside amount of tokens, which will be paid back to the participant if she behave honestly, otherwise the deposit is given to the other parties to compensate them for their loss. Such security deposit is recorded on blockchain, which is publicly available to other parties. Security deposit is a way to reduce the risk of participants in the network misbehave by temporarily sacrificing some of her stake.

Consequences:

Benefits:

– *Security.* The security of the application is obtained through security deposit because the deposit will be paid back to the participant only if the participant behaves honestly.

Drawbacks:

– *Access.* The security deposit is normally larger than the potential profit the participant gain from her/his dishonesty. If the required deposit is large, it restricts some participants to access the application.
– *Liquidity.* Similarly as above, the liquidity of the application participants is reduced due to the deposit.

Related Patterns:

– Both *Incentive Execution* (Sect. 7.4) and Security Deposit provide incentive mechanisms.

Known Uses:

– The notion of "deposits" has already been used in *Bitcoin*'s contract[52], where deposit is bought by a party with no reputation as a proof of her trust.
– *Ethereum alarm clock* (see footnote 51) enables scheduling of transactions for delayed execution in the future. Before the execution window, there is a claim window when the request may be claimed by a participant for execution. To claim a request, the participant is required to put down a deposit. If the claimer fulfils their commitment to execute the request, the deposit is returned to them, otherwise, the deposit is given to someone else that executes the request as an additional reward.

8 User Interaction Patterns

This section illustrates two patterns regarding user interacting with smart contracts.

8.1 Pattern 18: DApp

Summary: Decentralized applications (DApps) are applications running on P2P network rather than a single computer. DApps are blockchain-based web applications that allow users to interact with smart contracts deployed on blockchain. Figure 18 is a graphical representation of the pattern.

---

[52] https://en.bitcoin.it/wiki/Contract#Example_1:_Providing_a_deposit.

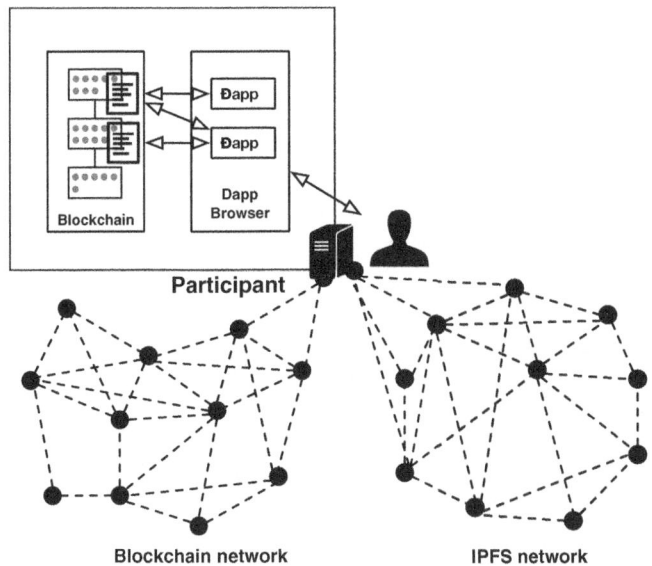

Fig. 18. DApp Pattern

Context: Users interact with smart contracts through sending transactions to invoke the functions defined in smart contracts. In order for the users to understand how to interact with a smart contract, the source code of the smart contract is open source and visible to users. Second, the application binary interface (ABI) of the smart contract is also publicly accessible so that users can send transactions to it.

Problem: Users need a strong technical understanding of blockchain and smart contract to be able to generate transactions calling smart contracts. Such process is error-prone and with a bad user experience [23]. How to call a smart contract in a trustless environment?

Forces: The problem requires to balance the following forces:

- *Learning Curve.* Users need to understand the functionality of a smart contract before being able to interact with it. To understand the input required and the output produced by a smart contract, users need to read the documentation or the source code of the smart contract.
- *Convenience.* Manually generating transactions to interact with an smart contract is an error-prone process despite the understanding of the smart contract. Depending on whether many transactions need to be sent, it may be worth to invest into automating the transaction submission process.
- *Trust.* The user needs to trust the provider of such automated transaction submission process.

Solution: DApp provides a front-end user interface for users to easily interact with smart contracts. The frond end uses the same technology as conventional web applications to render web pages. The difference is that DApps can be hosted on a decentralized storage, like IPFS, and are rendered by DApp browsers, like Ethereum Mist (see footnote 40) or a plug-in to a web application browser, like MetaMask[53]. Both the smart contract on blockchain and the DApp is deployed on a local node. The transactions calling smart contracts are generated by DApps, and are presented to the users for further verification before being sent to the blockchain.

Consequences:

Benefits:

– *Convenience.* Users interact with smart contract through a front-end provided by the DApp provider instead of reverse engineering how to submit transactions from the source code of the smart contract. The user experience of using the front-end of a DApp are much better as it requires less technical understanding of the smart contract. Assuming the DApp is correct, it is also less error-prone than manually generating transactions to interact with smart contracts.

Drawbacks:

– *Trust.* Using DApps imposes trust to the DApp provider because the transactions are generated by the DApp on behalf of the user. However, the impact of the execution is not explicit without understanding the smart contracts underneath, especially if the source code of the contract or ABI is not published.
– *Learning Curve.* Basic technical knowledge regarding transactions and *gas* are still required by users to use DApps and verify the transactions generated by the DApps.

Related Patterns:

– *Semi-DApp* (Sect. 8.2) can be browsed using a conventional web browser without any DApp plugin.

Known Uses:

– *State of the DApps*[54] provides a directory of the DApps on Ethereum blockchain. There are 1800+ DApps with different levels of maturity registered to the directory. *DappRadar*[55] also provides a directory of DApps, not only on Ethereum blockchain but also included DApps deployed on EOS[56] and TRON[57].

---

[53] https://metamask.io/.
[54] https://www.stateofthedapps.com/.
[55] https://dappradar.com/.
[56] https://eos.io/.
[57] https://tron.network/index?lng=en.

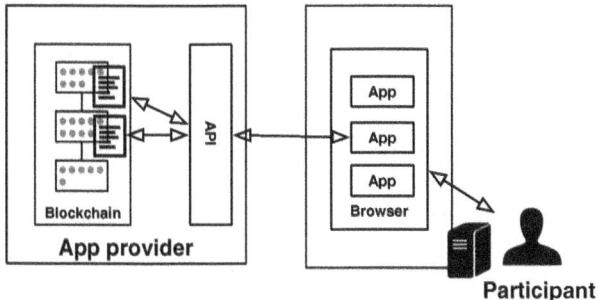

Fig. 19. Hybrid-DApp Pattern

– *Remix*[58] is an open source smart contract compiler that allow user to write and interact with Solidity contracts from the browser.

8.2   Pattern 19: Semi-DApp

Summary: Semi-DApp provider offers a web application, which can be browsed using a conventional web browser without any DApp plugin (like MetaMask). Figure 19 is a graphical representation of the pattern.

Context: Users interact with smart contracts through sending transactions to invoke the functions defined in smart contracts. In order for the users to interact with a smart contract, the source code of the smart contract is open source and visible to users. Second, the application binary interface (ABI) of the smart contract is also publicly accessible.

Problem: Users need a strong technical understanding of blockchain and smart contract to be able to generate transactions and interact with smart contracts. Such process is error-prone, with a bad user experience [23]. Even with a front-end that assists the user to interact with smart contracts, some basic technical knowledge regarding transactions and *gas* is still required by users to use DApps and verify the transactions generated by the DApps (Sect. 8.1). It is not feasible for non-technical user to learn and understand the source code of smart contract to use it.

Forces: The problem requires to balance the following forces:

– *Learning Curve.* Users need some basic technical knowledge of smart contracts in order to use DApps.
– *User Experience.* Due to the decentralization nature of DApps, the front-end of most DApps is quite simple, and exposes too many technical details of the underlying smart contract, which not all users are capable to grasp.

---

[58] https://remix.ethereum.org.

Solution: Semi-DApp provider offers a standard web application for users to easily interact with smart contracts. The web application keeps the technical details of the corresponding smart contracts opaque to the users. The website communicates with the backend through RESTful API calls Thus, the backend is responsible for interacting with the smart contracts on behalf of the user who is not able to inspect nor validate the transactions being sent to the blockchain. The transaction ID is normally returned to the user for the user to check the transaction on blockchain using blockchain explorer, like EtherScan (see footnote 42).

Consequences:

   Benefits:

– *Convenience.* Users interact with smart contracts through a web application provided by the Semi-DApp provider. The user experience of using the front-end of such a DApp is as same as using the front-end of a conventional web application. This solution offers the maximum convenience and the most gentle learning curve.

   Drawbacks:

– *Trust.* Users need to completely trust the Semi-DApp provider who is responsible for managing their private keys. One example is a Japan-based Bitcoin exchange, Mt. Gox[59]. Launched in 2010, Mt. Gox used to be the largest Bitcoin exchange in the world, which handles over 70% of all Bitcoin transactions worldwide. In June 2011, Mt. Gox announced that approximately 850,000 Bitcoins (an amount valued at more than $450 million at the time) belonging to customers and the company disappeared, most likely due to a compromised internal computer.

Related Patterns:

– *DApp* (Sect. 8.1) allows users to interact with smart contracts.

Known Uses:

– Cryptocurrency exchanges are common examples of this patterns as they always interact with the blockchain on behalf of the users. *Kraken*[60] is a San Francisco-based Bitcoin exchange.
– *Binance*[61] is a cryptocurrency exchange founded in China.

---

[59] https://en.wikipedia.org/wiki/Mt._Gox.
[60] https://www.kraken.com/.
[61] https://www.binance.com/.

9   Related Work

To document the reusable solutions for blockchain-based application design, blockchain patterns have been summarized [2,8,12,15,16,23]. Some of them are generic and can be applied for general purposes [8,16,23]. For example, five patterns are proposed for blockchain-based applications in [8], which focus on what data and computation should be on-chain and what should be kept off-chain. Other documented patterns apply to specific use cases [2,12]. There are also design patterns for writing smart contracts from both academia and industry[62]. The binary code of a smart contract deployed on a public blockchain is publicly accessible, and for many, the code is also open-source. Empirical analysis has been conducted using smart contracts from different public blockchain platforms to identify the common programming patterns [3,24,25]. Existing patterns from conventional programming languages have been also applied to smart contract programming, for example, four existing object-oriented software patterns were applied to smart contract programming in the context of a blockchain-based health case application [28].

Compared with the above existing work, our paper covers system-level design patterns about interaction between blockchain and other components within a big software system, data management patterns, security patterns, structural patterns for smart contracts and user interaction patterns. Some structural patterns are new and some are modifications of the existing design patterns. More importantly, we provide use cases from the real world with each of the patterns. There is some overlap between the existing works and our paper. For example the *Proxy* pattern from [28] is a more generic pattern compared with our *Off-chain data storage* pattern. The *Off-chain signatures* pattern from [8] is similar to our *State channel* pattern. The *Authorization* pattern from [3] is similar to our *Embedded permission* pattern. *Self-Confirmed transactions* pattern from [23] is similar to our *DApps* pattern and *Delegated transactions pattern* is similar to our *Semi-DApps* patter.

10   Conclusions

We view the blockchain as a fundamental building block of large-scale decentralized software systems. For effective use of blockchain to this end, patterns are needed that show how to make good use of the blockchain in the design of systems and applications. In this paper, we propose a pattern collection for blockchain-based applications. Our pattern collection includes four patterns about interaction between blockchain and the external world, four data management patterns, four security patterns, five contract structural patterns and two user interaction patterns. The pattern collection provides an architectural guidance for developers to build applications on blockchain. Some patterns are designed specifically for blockchain-based applications considering the unique properties of blockchain. Others are variants of existing software patterns applied to smart contracts.

---

[62] https://consensys.github.io/smart-contract-best-practices/.

Acknowledge. We want to thank Tim Wellhausen, the shepherd for our Euro-PLoP2018 patterns paper, and the anonymous reviewers of our paper for their helpful comments.

References

1. Ali, M., Nelson, J., Shea, R., Freedman, M.J.: Blockstack: a global naming and storage system secured by blockchains. In: USENIX ATC, Santa Clara, CA, pp. 181–194. USENIX Association (2016)
2. Bandara, H.M.N.D., Xu, X., Weber, I.: Patterns for blockchain data migration. In: Proceedings of 25th European Conference on Pattern Languages of Programs (EuroPLoP 2020) (2020)
3. Bartoletti, M., Pompianu, L.: An empirical analysis of smart contracts: platforms, applications, and design patterns. In: Financial Cryptography and Data Security, pp. 494–509. Springer, Cham (2017)
4. Beck, K., Cunningham, W.: Using pattern languages for object oriented programs. In: Conference on Object-Oriented Programming, Systems, Languages, and Applications (OOPSLA), Orlando, FL, USA. ACM (1987)
5. Clack, C.D., Bakshi, V.A., Braine, L.: Smart Contract Templates: essential requirements and design options (2016)
6. Clack, C.D., Bakshi, V.A., Braine, L.: Smart Contract Templates: foundations, design landscape and research directions (2016)
7. US Department of Commerce: National Institute of Standards and Technology
8. Eberhardt, J., Tai, S.: On or off the blockchain? Insights on off-chaining computation and data. In: 6th European Conference on Service-Oriented and Cloud Computing (ESOCC 2017), Oslo, Norway, pp. 3–15. Springer (2017)
9. Fernandez-Buglioni, E.: Security Patterns in Practice: Designing Secure Architectures Using Software Patterns. Wiley (2013)
10. Grigg, I.: The ricardian contract. In: The 1st IEEE International Workshop on Electronic Contracting (WEC 2004), San Diego, California, pp. 25–31. IEEE (2004)
11. Kosba, A., Miller, A., Shi, E., Wen, Z., Papamanthou, C.: Hawk: the blockchain model of cryptography and privacy-preserving smart contracts. In: 37th IEEE Symposium on Security and Privacy (S&P 2016), Fairmont, SAN JOSE, CA, pp. 839–858. IEEE (2016). https://doi.org/10.1109/SP.2016.55
12. Liu, Y., Lu, Q., Paik, H.Y., Xu, X.: Design patterns for blockchain-based self-sovereign identity. In: Proceedings of 25th European Conference on Pattern Languages of Programs (EuroPLoP 2020) (2020)
13. Lo, S.K., Xu, X., Staples, M., Yao, L.: Reliability analysis for blockchain oracles. Comput. Electr. Eng. **83**, 106582 (2020)
14. Meszaros, G., et al.: A pattern language for pattern writing. Pattern Lang. Program Des. **3**, 529–574 (1998)
15. Moreno, J., Fernandez, E.B., Fernandez-Medina, E., Serrano, M.A.: Blockbd: a security pattern to incorporate blockchain in big data ecosystems. In: Proceedings of the 24th European Conference on Pattern Languages of Programs. EuroPLop 2019. Association for Computing Machinery, New York (2019). https://doi.org/10.1145/3361149.3361166
16. Mühlberger, R., Bachhofner, S., Di Ciccio, C., Weber, I., Wöhrer, M., Zdun, U.: Foundational oracle patterns: connecting blockchain to the off-chain world. In: Blockchain Forum of the International Conference on Business Process Management (BPM) (2020)

17. Nakamoto, S.: Bitcoin: a peer-to-peer electronic cash system (2008). https:// bitcoin.org/bitcoin.pdf
18. Omohundro, S.: Cryptocurrencies, smart contracts, and artificial intelligence. AI Matters **1**(2), 2685334 (2014). https://doi.org/10.1145/2685328.2685334. http:// doi.acm.org/10.1145/2685328.2685334
19. Swan, M.: Blockchain: Blueprint for a New Economy. O'Reilly, US (2015)
20. UK Government Chief Scientific Adviser: Distributed ledger technology: beyond blockchain. Technical report, UK Government (2016)
21. Weber, I., et al.: On availability for blockchain-based systems. In: SRDS 2017: IEEE International Symposium on Reliable Distributed Systems, Hong Kong, China, pp. 64–73. IEEE (2017)
22. Weber, I., Xu, X., Riveret, R., Governatori, G., Ponomarev, A., Mendling, J.: Untrusted business process monitoring and execution using blockchain. In: BPM, Rio de Janeiro, Brazil, pp. 329–347. Springer (2016)
23. Wessling, F., Gruhn, V.: Engineering software architectures of blockchain-oriented applications. In: 2018 IEEE International Conference on Software Architecture Companion (ICSA-C), Seattle, USA, pp. 45–46 (2018)
24. Wöhrer, M., Zdun, U.: Design patterns for smart contracts in the Ethereum ecosystem. In: 2018 IEEE International Conference on Internet of Things (iThings) and IEEE Green Computing and Communications (GreenCom) and IEEE Cyber, Physical and Social Computing (CPSCom) and IEEE Smart Data (SmartData), pp. 1513–1520 (2018)
25. Wöhrer, M., Zdun, U.: Smart contracts: security patterns in the Ethereum ecosystem and Solidity. In: International Workshop on Blockchain Oriented Software Engineering (IWBOSE), pp. 2–8 (2018)
26. Xu, X., et al.: The blockchain as a software connector. In: 13th Working IEEE/IFIP Conference on Software Architecture (WICSA 2016), Gothenburg, Sweden, pp. 182–191. IEEE (2016)
27. Xu, X., et al.: A taxonomy of blockchain-based systems for architecture design. In: ICSA 2017, Gothenburg, Sweden, pp. 243–252. IEEE (2017)
28. Zhang, P., White, J., Schmidt, D.C., Lenz, G.: Design of blockchain-based apps using familiar software patterns with a healthcare focus. In: Proceedings of the 24th Conference on Pattern Languages of Programs. PLoP 2017, The Hillside Group, USA (2017)

Anti-patterns and Code Smells
for Multi-language Systems

Mouna Abidi[1]([✉]), Manel Grichi[1], Foutse Khomh[1], and Yann-Gaël Guéhéneuc[2]

[1] Polytechnique Montreal, Montreal, Canada
mouna.abidi@polymtl.ca
[2] Concordia University, Montreal, Canada

Abstract. Software quality becomes a necessity and no longer an advantage. In fact, with the advancement of technologies, companies must provide software with good quality. Many studies introduce the use of design patterns as improving software quality and discuss the presence of occurrences of design defects as decreasing software quality. Code smells include low-level problems in source code, and poor coding decisions that are symptoms of the presence of anti-patterns in the code. Most of the studies present in the literature discuss the occurrences of design defects for mono-language systems. However, nowadays most of the systems are developed using a combination of several programming languages, to use particular features of each of them. As the number of languages increases, so does the number of design defects. They generally do not prevent the program from functioning correctly, but they indicate a higher risk of future bugs and make the code less readable and harder to maintain. We analysed open-source systems, developers' documentation, bug reports, and programming language specifications to extract bad practices of multi-language systems usage. We encoded and cataloged these practices in the form of code smells and design anti-patterns. We report in this paper six anti-patterns and 12 code smells.

Keywords: Anti-patterns · code smells · multi-language systems · software quality

1 Introduction

Nowadays, most of the systems are written using a combination of several programming languages and technologies. The core of an application might be written in Java, while it has some routines written in C, with a user interface written in PHP, JavaScript, and HTML [1]. Most of the systems with which we interact daily are built using a combination of programming languages, such as Facebook, Youtube, etc. [2]. Developers can reuse existing modules without re-implementing the source code from scratch [3]. They often choose the programming language suitable for their needs, instead of having all the tasks written in a single language [4–6]. Consequently, software systems became more complex, and their maintenance became more challenging [7].

© The Author(s), under exclusive license to Springer-Verlag GmbH, DE, part of Springer Nature 2025
E. Wallingford et al. (Eds.): TPLOP V, LNCS 14630, pp. 118–161, 2025.
https://doi.org/10.1007/978-3-662-70810-1_3

Software quality presents one of the most important concerns during software development, providing software with high quality could reduce maintenance and testing costs [8,9]. Software quality has been widely studied in the literature and has been often directly related to the presence of design patterns, anti-patterns, and code smells. Design patterns are defined in the GOF as reusable good solutions to recurring design problems [10]. Design defects are known as the opposite of design patterns [11]. They include anti-patterns, which are higher-level design defects, and code smells, which are lower-level defects [12]. Code smells include low-level problems in source code, and poor coding decisions that are symptoms of the presence of anti-patterns in the code. As code smells are error-prone and change-prone, it is important to detect and correct them as soon as possible.

Several studies in the literature studied occurrences of anti-patterns and code smells and their impact on software quality with studies mostly focusing on a single programming language [13–16]. Few studies investigated such good or bad practices for multi-language systems [3,17]. Some studies also focused on the design patterns related to such systems [18–21]. To improve the software quality of multi-language systems, we extracted, encoded, and cataloged good and bad practices in the development, maintenance, and evolution of multi-language systems. We analysed the source code of open-source multi-language systems as well as developers' documentation, and programming-language specifications. These systems contain mainly Java/C(++) but also include other programming languages e.g. Python, JavaScript, Lua, etc. We observed good and bad practices in the code as well as issues reported in the developers' documentation and bug reports. We encoded and cataloged these observed practices and reported our findings in the form of anti-patterns and code smells. These anti-patterns and code smells could apply to microservices or, rather, to the implementation of microservices, as to any other pieces of code in which such poor design or implementation choice could appear. We have focused our efforts on designing anti-patterns and code smells to complement the previous work on identifying design patterns for multi-language systems [18–21].

The remainder of this paper is organised as follows: Sect. 2 discusses the background of multi-language systems and related works. Section 3 describes our methodology for gathering good and bad practices. Section 4 reports multi-language systems Anti-patterns, while Sect. 5 reports multi-language systems code smells. Section 6 summarises threats to the validity of our methodology. Section 7 concludes the paper and discusses future works.

2 Background and Related Work

We now present a brief background about multi-language systems, patterns, and anti-patterns, in general. We then discuss some related works.

Multi-language Systems: Developed using more than one programming language. Most of the systems with which we interact daily integrate components written in several, different programming languages. Developers of these systems attempt to choose the "right" programming language for each component. The adjective "right" covers every choice, from using the most appropriate programming language instead of trying to solve all problems with a single language [2], to using the programming language that some particular developers know best. The resulting heterogeneous components usually communicate through Foreign Function Interfaces (FFIs) [22]. Some of the multi-language systems also rely on language binding which are wrapper libraries offering a bridge between two programming languages, so that a library written for one language can be used in another language.

Patterns and Anti-patterns: Patterns were introduced in the domain of architecture by Alexander [23]. "Each pattern describes a problem which occurs over and over again in our environment and then describes the core of the solution to that problem, In such a way that you can use this solution a million times over, without ever doing it the same way twice" [23, p267]. From architecture, design patterns were introduced in software engineering by Gamma et al. [24]. In their landmark book, Coplien et al. [10] provided an overview of practical guidelines for design pattern usage. They presented design patterns as a means to meet the goal of capturing the design of complex object-oriented systems. These design patterns are based on the developers' experiences when facing recurrent problems and applying "good" solutions to solve these problems. The goal of encoding and cataloging design patterns is to preserve, share, reuse, and improve design knowledge and take the benefits from similar, past situations [10, 25].

Anti-patterns are "opposite" to design patterns. They document "poor" solutions to recurring problems [26,27]. In the literature, there are two main types of such bad practices: anti-patterns and code smells [26–28]. Several studies showed that the presence of anti-patterns makes the evolution of the software more difficult. They affect software comprehensibility and increase change- and fault-proneness and increase the effort needed to perform maintenance activities [29,30]. For example, classes including design defects are significantly more fault-prone and change-prone compared to classes without those occurrences [13,31].

Encoding and Cataloguing: There exist several templates in the literature to encode patterns and anti-patterns. The template that we used in this paper is inspired by the *WikiWikiWeb*[1]. We adapted the template to the specificity of our work as follows:

- Anti-pattern/Code Smells: We describe in the title the name to identify the anti-pattern or the code smell.
- Context: The context in which this particular anti-pattern or code smell applies, for example, real-time systems or communication systems.
- Problem: It introduces the initial problem that is being solved or the problem that may lead to the wrong solution. It can be illustrated by a simple concrete example.

---

[1] http://wiki.c2.com/.

- Supposed Solution: The supposed solution is the solution solving the problem on first thought but that has other negative impacts on software quality.
- Forces Toward: Used in the anti-pattern section, they describe common reasons and choices that may lead to the application of the bad solution. We relied on the forces discussed in the anti-pattern book to write the forces [26]. They are based on the Software Design-Level Model (SDM) that are the general forces ignored, misused, or overused in the Anti-pattern. They can also be contextual motivating factors that influence design choices.
- Consequences of the Anti-Pattern: These consequences describe the impact of applying the "poor" solution to solve the problem.
- Forces Away: Used in the anti-pattern section, the forces away provide the decisions and reasons to avoid the bad solution. Similar to the *Forces Toward*, these forces are inspired by Brown's book and can be related to the management of functionality, performance, complexity, changes, resources, and technology transfer [26].
- Refactoring: This solution (or solutions) presents the better solution that can be applied to remove the anti-patterns or code smells. It includes the steps that can be followed to apply the solution.
- Benefits of the Refactoring: These benefits are the consequences describing the positive impact of applying the refactoring to remove the occurrences of the code smells and–or anti-patterns.
- Related Anti-Patterns: If any, specify the names of related code smells and–or anti-patterns.
- Related Patterns: If any, specify the names of patterns that could be used in the refactoring. In this paper, we specify the names of the patterns that could be applied in the refactored solution. In future work, we will examine the effectiveness of those solutions.
- Examples: These examples provide code and–or diagrams showing the anti-pattern or code smell in context. When possible, the example is taken from real systems or is a Minimal, Complete, and Verifiable example. In some cases, we provided a small fictive example. In other cases, we did not add examples, especially where, the anti-pattern or code smell seems evident, or cannot be well illustrated with only one example. We used a detailed description to illustrate the situation.

Related Work: Several studies in the literature investigated the quality of multi-language systems.

Neitsch et al. [19] studied five multi-language software packages from Ubuntu 9.10. They provided common build patterns and anti-patterns that summarise the key problems related to the build of multi-language systems.

Goedicke et al. [18] proposed five architectural patterns based on well-known design patterns. These patterns are defined to wrap legacy components as black-box entities. Most of the defined patterns can be used with different programming languages. To assess the legacy migration and the wrapping techniques, the authors also presented a pilot project. They also provided a detailed definition of these patterns. The pattern *Object System Layer* provides a highly flexible object system as a layer built on top of a given language [32]. It makes components that are not object-oriented or that are implemented in another language, accessible through *Object System Layer*. These components can then be treated as black boxes. The pattern *Message Redirector* ensures a simple indirection architecture that maps the calls to a message implementation [33]. It also provides callback methods around the calls.

Malinova [20] attempted to connect some well-known design patterns e.g. Adapter, Proxy, and Wrapper Facade, to the process of Java wrapping of native legacy codes. In this paper, design patterns were studied in the context of invoking native applications from Java code.

Kondoh et al. [34] focused on four kinds of common JNI mistakes made by developers. They proposed BEAM, a static analysis tool to find mistakes about error checking, virtual machine resources, invalid local references, and JNI methods in critical code sections. They did not propose recommendations to avoid and–or fix these mistakes.

Osmani et al. [35] presented the Lazy Initialisation pattern which describes how to execute Ajax requests in JavaScript, where the Ajax request includes a URL and some data, possibly in JSON or XML, to communicate with a server, likely implemented in C/C++.

Li and Tan [36] highlighted the risks caused by the exception mechanisms in Java, which can lead to failures in JNI implementation functions and affect security. They defined a pattern of mishandling JNI exceptions. This paper focused mainly on JNI but can also be adapted to other FFIs, such as the Python/C and the OCaml/C interface.

Tan et al. [3] studied the JNI usages in the JDK source code. They examined a range of bug patterns in the native code and they identified six bugs related to the use of JNI methods in the JDK. Bugs identified can cause a JVM crash or can open the JVM to some security breaches. They found that bugs are possible due to language mismatches and the assumptions made by the Java code regarding the C(++) code. As an example, the native method *java.util.zip.Deflater.deflatesByte()* assumes that its Java callers check bounds, which could lead to buffer overflows.

Ayers et al. [37] proposed TraceBack a tool that collects and analyses bugs in multi-language systems by storing data through runtime instrumentation of control-flow blocks. They collected the data by statically rewriting the libraries and instrumenting the intermediate languages to generate a unified trace of the components' execution.

Mayer and Schroeder [38] studied the dependencies in multi-language systems. They proposed a technique to identify dependencies among multi-language components, warn of potential missing dependencies, and propagate renaming among multi-language code.

3   Study Design

In this section, we detail the setup of our study. We present the steps followed to collect the anti-patterns and code smells. Figure 1 presents an overview of our methodology. We believe that the following steps could be used for a replication purpose as well as for any future study investigating new design patterns and anti-patterns.

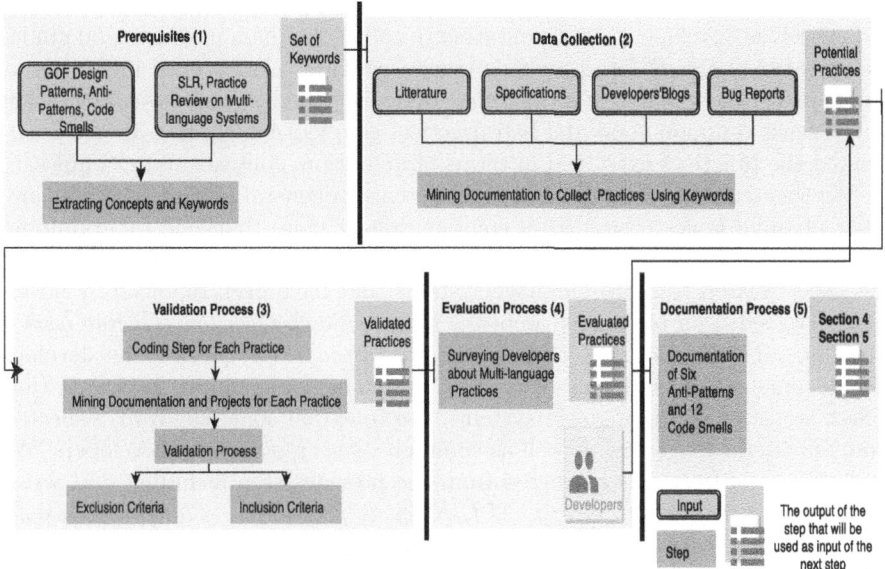

Fig. 1. Overview of the methodology used to collect and document the anti-patterns and code smells for multi-language systems.

Prerequisites: We believe that to investigate and collect good practices, design patterns, idioms—and bad practices—design anti-patterns and code smells for multi-language systems, it is important to have enough knowledge and experience with both multi-language systems and design patterns and anti-patterns. From previous studies and our literature review, we already had good background and knowledge of design patterns, design anti-patterns, and code smells for mono-language systems. Two of the authors of this paper have also experience in developing tools to detect occurrences of design patterns, design anti-patterns, and code smells. We performed in a prior study a systematic literature review and a practice review to investigate and compare the usage of multi-language systems in the literature and real systems hosted in GitHub. This step gave us good knowledge about multi-language systems and their challenges as well as design patterns and anti-patterns. It helped us to collect some keywords that can be used to retrieve challenges and issues related to multi-language systems.

It also allowed us to better distinguish between a simple habit and a possible pattern or code smells.

Data Collection: Once we decided to collect and document anti-patterns and code smells for multi-language systems. We started by mining all possible sources of documentation. We searched the literature, language specification, developers' blog as well as bug reports. From our systematic literature review on multi-language systems. We found that the most studied combination of languages is Java/C(++). For that, We decided to start with this combination and then include other languages. We deeply read the Java Native Interface specification [17] as well as developers' documentation to collect common practices and guidelines related to the JNI and multi-language systems. We searched in Google as well for JNI practices and found a couple of developers' blogs and documentation that discuss common good and bad practices (see footnotes 2 and 3). We documented the practices extracted in terms of definition, context, and examples.

We then considered multi-language systems in general and searched for any other possible issues related to a combination of more than one programming language. We analysed bug reports and developers' documentation to extract the issues related to multi-language systems that have been reported by developers. We relied on often used websites such us *Stack Overflow*, *GitHub issues*, *Bugzilla*, *IBM Developers*[2], and *developer.android*[3]. We queried the developers' documentation and bug reports by searching for common keywords that reflect issues in multi-language systems. We relied on some keywords collected from our literature review as well as common issues reported by developers. We used the set of keywords extracted from the previous step including *JNI issue*, *Python/C issue*, *foreign library*, *API*, *polyglot*, *programming languages issues*, *incompatibility*, *compilation errors*, *memory issues*, *performance issues*, *security issues*, *foreign function interface*. As an example, when searching for *JNI issue* in *Bugzilla*, our query returned 23 results, among them we considered only two as possible bad practices. One was related to the library loading, and the other was related to the management of exceptions[4,5]. From *Stack Overflow*, for the keywords *JNI issue* and *Python/C issue*, we had for each of these keywords 500 results, we searched manually only for issues that have been already discussed in the developers' documentation (see footnotes 2 and 3).

We documented all of the reported issues and possible practices in our list of potential practices. This list is then used as input to the next step, which is the validation process. We believe that our research method to collect practices was not exhaustive and that there are many other good practices, design patterns, idioms—and bad practices—design anti-patterns and code smells that can be extracted as well. In future work, we plan to extract more practices from these sources. We considered as practices a common situation that was reported

---

[2] https://www.ibm.com/developerworks/library/j-jni/index.html.
[3] https://developer.android.com/training/articles/perf-jni.
[4] https://bugzilla.redhat.com/show_bug.cgi?id=529919.
[5] https://bugzilla.redhat.com/show_bug.cgi?id=1045623.

more than three times in any kind of documentation, including literature, the developers' documentation, or bug report.

Data Validation: For each of the practices reported in our list of potential practices, we performed a coding process in which, we provided a definition and explanation of the practice. The explanation was in terms of what are the contexts, situations, and possible examples that we should look for to retrieve occurrences of the practices. We performed a discussion between the authors to validate the explanations provided for the potential practices. We performed the validation process through different sources of information following inclusion and exclusion criteria. Through this step, we aimed to verify if the potential reported practices have been used or discussed in at least three situations and or examples in open-source systems. We searched for occurrences of these practices in different sources of information (e.g. GitHub, Developers' Blog, Bug Report).

We defined a set of inclusion and exclusion criteria. As inclusion criteria, we considered a practice that was discussed in at least three situations. In the case of literature or any other type of documentation, we searched for similar situations that have been reported by developers and discussed in bug reports or developers' blogs. Another inclusion criteria were when analysing the source code of multi-language systems. We searched if the good or bad practices discussed in the literature were present in at least three classes, source code files, or systems. We also considered the case where that practice was discussed as a good one but was not followed in some open source systems (e.g. The code smell *Not Checking Exceptions* that was discussed in developers' documentation (see footnote 2) and in some articles but was not followed in most of the systems that we analysed). As exclusion criteria, we considered a practice for which, we were not able to find at least three of its occurrences in any of the sources of information, including open-source systems. We also considered exclusion criteria practices that seem more likely to be a simple habit than a potential code smell or anti-pattern.

We manually searched the source of information (e.g. bug reports, developers' blog, developers' documentation) to find at least three situations where the potential practices were discussed. We also used data already extracted from one of our prior studies focusing on JNI usage. The data consists of 100 multi-language open-source systems. We extracted these systems from OpenHub using Python Scripts. We then downloaded the projects and manually analysed their source code. These systems were mainly JNI systems but also contained other languages. OpenHub provided the list of all the languages used in the project. These systems contained not only Java/C(++) but also Python, JavaScript, Lua, etc. (e.g. *OpenCv* is mainly written in C(++) but contains 25.239 Python lines of code, 24.427 Java lines of code, and other languages). Here are some systems in which we mainly focused more during this study: *libgdx, Google toolkit, Openj9, Rocksdb, JMonkeyEng, OpenVRML, PortAudio Java Bindings, jpostal, JavaSMT, Jna, ZMQ, reactNative, Telegram, OpenCV, Tenserflow, JatoVM, SQLlite, Frostwire, Godot, python-telegram-bot*. We provide in Sects. 4 and 5 the sources and-or names of the projects from which we extracted the code smells and-or anti-patterns.

We manually and qualitatively analysed the source code of the multi-language systems collected from GitHub to extract occurrences of good and/or bad practices. We also checked if the common guidelines and practices reported in the literature are followed by the developers in practice. Most of them were not, in that case, we reported it as a possible bad practice. In our case, we considered multi-language systems practice as a piece of code that is involved in the multi-language systems and participating in the interaction between two or more languages and that has been documented in the literature as bad practice or that has been reported in bug reports or developers' documentation as causing issues or negatively impacting the system. We considered practices in a similar situation and-or that were observed more than three times and was discussed in the programming language specification, or developers documentation as being a wise practice.

Data Evaluation: To evaluate our set of anti-patterns and code smells, we asked in our survey on multi-language systems if developers have faced these practices. We also asked them in this survey about any good or bad practices that they are adopting or avoiding when using multi-language programming. We added the proposed good and bad practices to our list of possible practices so they can be used in future work as input to the validation process. We will use this survey for future work to investigate the challenges related to multi-language systems as well as the practices used by developers to cope with those challenges.

Anti-patterns and Code Smells Documentation: We reported all the observed practices and performed a discussion between the authors to validate if the practices are really valuable and should be documented in the form of anti-patterns or code smells, or if they are only a simple practice or developers' habit. We discussed each case until a consensus was reached. We used an available template to document our results in the form of six anti-patterns and 12 code smells as presented in Sect. 2. We believe that these practices could help researchers and developers cope with the challenges introduced by multi-language systems. In future work, we will investigate more practices and document them in the form of design patterns, anti-patterns, and code smells. Figure 2 presents a pattern overview of the collected anti-patterns and code smells and the relationships between them.

4 Anti-patterns for Multi-language Systems

In this section, we present a catalog of the extracted good and bad practices in the form of anti-patterns following the template detailed in Sect. 2.

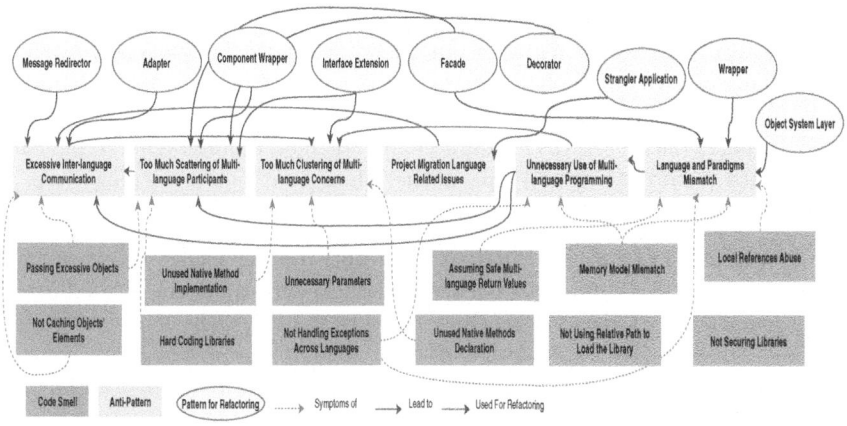

Fig. 2. Pattern Overview Diagram

4.1   Excessive Inter-language Communication

Context: Supposing we are in a context in which we must implement a task or add a new feature that is already available as a library implemented in another language. This can also be illustrated with a situation when a single language is not suitable to implement all the tasks. It may appear in the context of embedded systems, or systems in which we need an important number of communication between different layers or modules of the application.

Problem: Some projects may require important communication between components written in different programming languages. Other projects may be integrated with another module with high reuse of features which results in several calls. The problem is that developers or maintainers do not always know how to deal with such communication between heterogeneous languages and components. Usually, different teams may be involved separately to contribute to these components in a way that developers do not have enough knowledge about the whole architecture of the system.

Supposed Solution: Connect existing modules that are implemented using different languages and/or technologies. Reuse existing codes or modules implemented in different languages to benefit from the reuse of code or it can simply be related to the fact that some tasks are easier implemented in a specific language or are already available and ready to be used. The bad solution would be, to add the foreign code and access features from one language to another each time in the program we need to access foreign objects without considering the number of calls from one language to another.

Forces Toward: (1) Wrong partitioning of parts in the languages; (2) Trying to benefit from the performance of another lower-level language; (3) Using a scripting language to enable non-programmers to participate; (4) Providing several wrappers to access the features of the system; (5) Not separating all the multi-language concerns; (6) During a change or new requirement, design decision tends to introduce several calls rather than to refactor working code; (7) Classes designed with high coupling.

Consequences of the Anti-Pattern: This anti-pattern will result in an excessive passage of objects and calls between the host and the foreign language. In a study focusing on JNI systems, they found that calling the native code from Java code can take five times longer than a regular method call (see footnote 2). Similarly, calling Java code from the native code can take substantial time. If the partitioning of tasks between the foreign and the host languages is not used properly, this can cause a dispersion of the responsibility to perform a simple task between several languages. In some cases we can have excessive calls and passage of parameters from one language to another, These calls add more complexity to the program and negatively impact the first reported observation related to the performance of the system that we presented in Sect. 1.

Forces Away: (1) Design components with high cohesion; (2) Separate the concerns; (3) Ensure efficiency and management of the resources by limiting the number of methods calls and messages sent between components; (4) Information hiding and avoid indecent exposition.

Refactoring: To refactor this anti-pattern, start by locating the classes and objects involving excessive communication. Identify related attributes and operations. Then try to split the responsibility in a way that minimises the calls between the different languages but also with considering high cohesion. Decide which tasks are better implemented in which language. A good solution would be to separate the responsibility and identify the common concerns. If needed isolate the module involving the excessive calls or provide a wrapper to minimise the calls when we need to access from one language features available in another language.

Benefits of the Refactoring: Refactor this anti-pattern ensure high cohesion and low coupling. A better performance by reducing the number of calls from one language to another. It also reduces the complexity, by limiting and splitting the responsibility between the host and the foreign code. Another benefit is to avoid unnecessary broken code related to a nonseparation of concerns when applying changes.

Related Anti-Patterns: Circular dependency.

Related Patterns: Message Redirector [33] and Adapter [10].

Examples: Occurrences of this anti-pattern are generally observed in systems involving different layers or components. For example, the same object can be used and-or modified in more than one module written in different languages.

Each time we need the object, we pass it from one language to another or we call the foreign method to perform specific tasks in the object. The solution would be to separate the responsibilities and minimise the calls between the languages. It is better to focus each time on a single language to implement the tasks. Some examples of this anti-pattern have been observed in *Godot, PortAudio Java Bindings, OpenResty*. In *Godot*, The function *process()* is called at each time delta. The time delta is a small period of time that the game does not process anything i.e. the engine does other things than game logic out of this time range. The foreign function *process()* is called multiple times per second, in this case once per frame[6]. Another example in *PortAudio Java Bindings*, where they used raw buffers between Java and C++. In this example, they copy data between buffers which makes way for more communication than needed. Java supports memory-mapped input/output for this purpose, with this raw buffers can be used between language barriers[7]. We present in Fig. 3, an example of occurrences of this anti-pattern extracted from *OpenResty*. We found a situation, in which a developer introduced several calls from one Lua file to the Nginx. In this example, the developer was excessively calling the function ngx.exec() from the Lua file and getting values from the configuration file. A good solution is also present in the same system. They usually provide access as an entry point to ensure a better way of communication between Nginx and Lua[8].

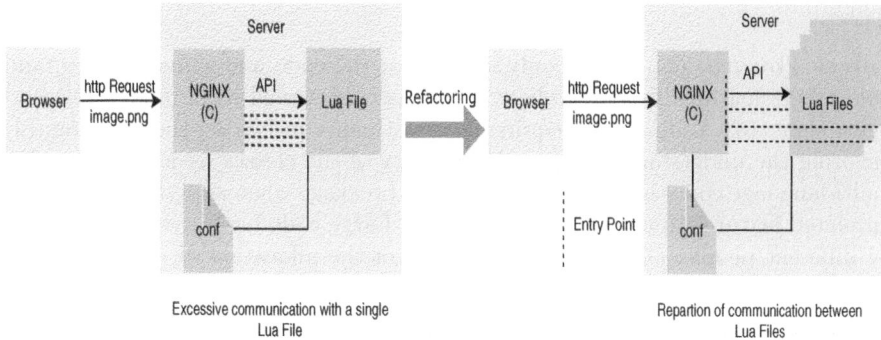

Fig. 3. Illustration Anti-Pattern - Excessive Inter-language Communication

---

[6] https://github.com/godotengine/godot-demo-projects/blob/master/2d/pong/paddle.gd.

[7] https://github.com/rjeschke/jpa/blob/master/src/main/native/jpa.c#L84.

[8] https://github.com/openresty/lua-nginx-module.

4.2   Too Much Scattering of Multi-language Participants

Context: We are maintaining a system, migrating a project from one language to another, or adding new functionality and features available in other languages. In multi-language systems usually, several teams are involved in the same project. This can also be faced in microservices architecture and feature-based decomposition where several teams are working on different features.

Problem: Under time pressure developers want to add multi-language systems code, the problem is that developers in these situations are not always sure where they should add the code. Especially since developers or maintainers do not always have a global idea about the overall architecture and design of the system. When several developers or teams are involved in the same project bugs related to changes may occur. Developers and managers would avoid these breakages in unrelated features, if the features are mixed, a change to the behavior of one may cause a bug in another feature.

Supposed Solution: Try to always separate multi-language classes to avoid breakage in unrelated features without considering the concerns. Add the foreign code without considering the concerns and architecture of the project. Each time we estimate that the use of multi-language programming can make it easier to perform a specific task, we add the foreign code without considering the classes already participating in the multi-language code and the responsibilities of each class.

Forces Toward: (1) Expose only subpart of the code and some features, and hide others features from the client; (2) Classes designed to be too simple and lightweight; (3) Adding new requirements without considering the coupling; (4) Favoring the understandability and simplicity of the classes by introducing few multi-language codes in each class; (5) Avoid breakage when applying a change in unrelated features that are mixed; (6) Build Large code bases over long periods by different people; (7) Wrong partitioning of the allocation of responsibilities of classes participating in the multi-language code.

Consequences of the Anti-pattern: The methods and classes participating in the foreign interaction are spread through the code in a way that determines which classes are participating and which require some effort. This code will be more difficult to maintain and refactor. It would be hard to know which classes are participating in the multi-language programming and which are not. It becomes difficult to locate and fix issues related to multi-language programming.

Forces Away: (1) Ensure a high cohesion and low coupling; (2) Merge the multi-language code in specific classes to improve the maintainability; (3) Ensure better encapsulation and Open/Closed principle; (4) Promote abstraction among classes and components.

Refactoring: To refactor this anti-pattern, start by investigating the architecture of the project, and which classes and packages are better involved in the multi-language programming concept. Then identify the multi-language code (e.g. methods, attributes, etc.) that is scattered through the code and that could be grouped in terms of concerns. Once the above is located, try to isolate the foreign code and limit the number of classes participating in the multi-language programming. Such Classes should be easily located in both languages, so they can easily be refactored or modified. It is better to concentrate on the code participating in the multi-language programming, so we have classes with and classes without.

Benefits of the Refactoring: When applying a change, developers or maintainers can easily locate the code related to the same feature. The refactored solution will ensure high cohesion and low coupling. Another benefit is to isolate the foreign code and limit the number of multi-language classes.

Related Anti-patterns: Functional Decomposition [26].

Related Patterns: Component Wrapper [18], Interface Extension [39], Facade, and Decorator [10].

Examples: This anti-pattern can be observed in a system where we have many classes participating in the multi-language programming and most of them contain only a small part involving foreign code as illustrated in Fig. 4. These classes are mainly mono-language but contain few foreign codes. A good solution would be to refactor the code and isolate the foreign code in a way that some classes mainly participate in multi-language programming and others involve only one language. We present a simple example in Fig. 4 to illustrate the excess of classes participating in multi-language programming. In this example, we have three classes each of which contains two native methods declarations. A good solution would be to move these methods or add a superclass if needed, that will contain all the native declaration methods, and keep these classes as inherited from this superclass. This will reduce the number of native method declarations by removing the duplicated ones. This will also reduce the scattering of multi-language participants and concerns by keeping the multi-language code concentrated only in specific classes. In the same vein, in the system *jpostal*, the classes *AddressParser* and *AddressExpander* contain a few native declaration methods that could be grouped into the same class[9]. Especially that the implementation of most of these native methods are duplicated between both of them. Other classes also from the same package contain one to two native method declarations. Another example of this anti-pattern is present in *Frostwire*. For example, the method *getWindowHandleNative()* is the only function written in C, and the window handle is used for displaying video using mplayer[10]. This method could have been grouped with other native methods to reduce the number of classes participating in the multi-language code. There are also other ways of doing this in Java by using a video player made for Java.

---

[9] https://github.com/openvenues/jpostal/tree/master/src/main/java/com/mapzen/jpostal.

[10] https://github.com/frostwire/frostwire/blob/7414e3be2ef5ced88a775df7831b7ae382fcf966/desktop/lib/native-src/linux/SystemUtilities.cpp.

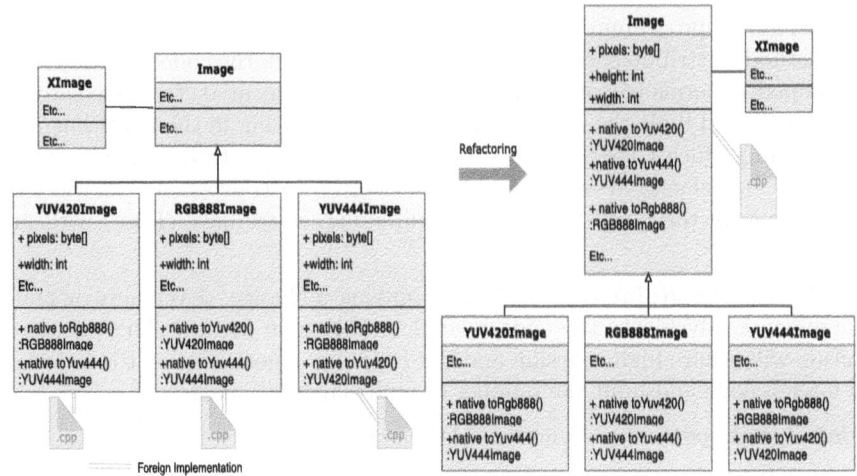

Fig. 4. Illustration Anti-Pattern - Too Much Scattering of Multi-language Concerns

4.3   Too Much Clustering of Multi-language Concerns

Context: In a situation where we are developing a new system or a system that has been released, we are asked to add new features. We are considering that the system is a multi-language system. The features to add may be in the same foreign language but are not related to each other. Each one of them is related to a specific task.

Problem: The problem is that under pressure, developers may excessively try to limit the classes participating in the multi-language programming which may violate the separating of concerns principle. This may be related to concerns in terms of tasks as well as concerns in terms of programming languages. Multi-language code is difficult to maintain and understand, having multi-language code scattered through the project may negatively impact the maintenance activities. For that, developers may choose to always limit the classes containing the multi-language code.

Supposed Solution: The bad solution would be to always try to concentrate as much as possible on the multi-language code in the same classes without considering the responsibilities related to each class. This situation can also be defined by merging the multi-language code in a single class in a way that results in high coupling and low cohesion. The occurrence of this anti-pattern would appear if we do not consider the concerns when adding new features or functionalities that involve the use of a multi-language code. The allocation of responsibilities between the multi-language classes is not well managed during system evolution so that one module becomes predominant regarding the other modules.

Forces Toward: (1) Inappropriate requirements allocation; (2) Class or module is given responsibilities that overlap most other parts of the project; (3) Class designed to touch multiple domains which must be decoupled from each other; (4) Iterative development where proof-of-concept code evolves over time into a prototype, and eventually, a production system evolution; (5) Classes in the project designed mainly for control or management; (6) Adding new requirements without considering the cohesion; (7) Wrong management of changes in the project by adding multi-language code to classes that are already multi-language instead of loading libraries or APIs in new classes.

Consequences of the Anti-pattern: As a consequence of this anti-pattern, there would be a negative impact on maintainability, as applying a change would require an important effort due to the complexity of understanding such code. There is also a loose of portability and reusability as the module has more than one responsibility. If we do not consider the cohesion and concerns when adding the code, this can result in a high coupling with low cohesion.

Forces Away: (1) Depending on the number of calls decide whether components that need to talk can have direct references to each other without having to go through the manager or controller class; (2) Promote simplicity and readability of the classes; (3) High cohesion and low coupling.

Refactoring: To refactor this anti-pattern, start by identifying and grouping related attributes and operations in terms of concerns. Then, search or create classes that could host these attributes and operations and ensure high cohesion. Then eliminate unnecessary coupling and indirect associations to have a high cohesion with low coupling. We encourage decoupling the code into distinct units with well-defined responsibilities. Always separate the concerns. When the concerns are properly separated, we can have different teams working in parallel on a given feature. A component with a solid separation of concerns can ensure greater collaboration between developers, maintainers, designers, etc. They can work at the same time on the same component. We also recommend ensuring cohesion between the programming languages and not only a cohesion of responsibilities. Depending on the programming languages, a possible solution would also be to expose services of a specific language and use extensions to invoke each programming language.

Benefits of the Refactoring: Refactor this anti-pattern will introduce several benefits, including the separation of the concerns and having simple and readable classes. This can also reduce maintainability efforts by keeping classes clean. Another benefit would be to allow high cohesion and low coupling.

Related Anti-patterns: Too Much Scattering of Multi-language Participants, Blob, and Swiss Army Knife [26].

Related Patterns: Interface Extension [39].

Examples: This anti-pattern can be identified in multi-language systems when the multi-language code is mixed in the same classes or files without any common concerns. We believe that it is a good practice to not spread the multi-language code through the system, but this should be balanced between the context. A good solution would be to find a compromise between separating the concerns and not dispersing the multi-language code. When a change needs to be applied we should be able to easily locate the code directly associated with the change. If the concerns are well separated between the languages, it is easier for developers to work separately on different tasks or modules. Separating the concerns also helps to avoid breakage in unrelated features, if the features are mixed a change to the behavior of one may cause a bug in another feature. One of the examples could be *React*, as it was reported to violate the separating of concerns by mixing *JavaScript* code with *HTML*, and *CSS*[11]. We present in Fig. 5 an example extracted from *ZMQ JNI*[12]. In this example, native methods related to cryptographic operations are mixed in the same class as the methods used for network communication. This merging of concerns resulted in a blob multi-language class that contains 29 native declaration methods and 78 attributes. Another example is the class GodotLib which contains 25 native declaration methods[13].

4.4   Unnecessary Use of Multi-language Programming

Context: This anti-pattern can be observed when the task can be completed in a single language in such a way that we are not taking benefit if we introduce the usage of multi-language programming but we are adding unnecessary complexity. Excessive usage of multi-language programming may result in a loose of their benefits and add more unnecessary complexity to the project.

Problem: This anti-pattern can result from a situation in which we are implementing a simple task or adding new features to an existing system. These features or tasks may be already available in other languages or as libraries. However, their development presents a simple task and does not require too much effort. This can also be related to the developer's experience with the programming languages. Developers have different experiences and levels of interest in different programming languages. The problem is that developers do not always have a great idea about the architecture of the system to decide whether in that specific case introducing multi-language programming worth it or not.

Supposed Solution: Always favor the reuse of code. If a feature or module is already available even if in another language, then integrate the module and make your program multi-language. If we are more comfortable in a specific language that differs from the language used to implement the application, use that specific language to implement the tasks.

---

[11] http://krasimirtsonev.com/blog/article/react-separation-of-concerns.

[12] https://github.com/zeromq/zmq-jni/blob/master/src/main/java/org/zeromq/jni/ZMQ.java.

[13] https://github.com/godotengine/godot/blob/60d910b1916305c4b0ac5f924150839 95b4f7c7a/platform/android/java/src/org/godotengine/godot/GodotLib.javanati vemethods.

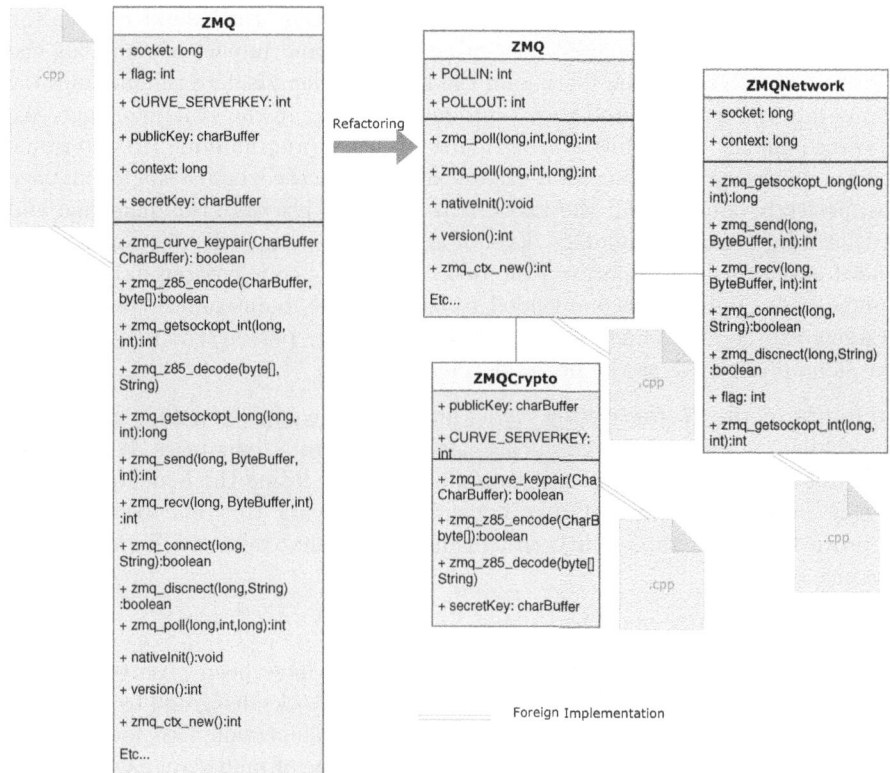

Fig. 5. Illustration Anti-Pattern - Too Much Clustering of Multi-language Concerns

Forces Toward: (1) Reuse of existing resources; (2) Pressure of time delivery; (3) Management of technologies and following the trends; (4) Reuse of existing code to save the development time; (5) Take the benefit of the different programming languages; (6) Avoid reinventing the wheel; (7) Start from a working example even if implemented in another language and adapt it to the specific needs.

Consequences of the Anti-pattern: Those kinds of systems will be difficult to maintain and understand. Especially, as reported in our fourth observation presented in Sect. 1, systems are usually developed and maintained by different people. A maintainer may not be as comfortable with multi-language systems and may not understand why they have been used in such situations.

Forces Away: (1) Reuse components and APIs implemented in the same language as the host project; (2) Improve the reusability and portability; (3) Avoid unnecessary complexity by introducing multi-language code.

Refactoring: To refactor this anti-pattern, identify the tasks or modules that could have been written in the same language. Search for existing implementations or modules implemented in the same language that could replace the foreign code. Then, we suggest measuring the cost and impact of removing the foreign code regarding the lifetime of the project. Then, isolate the modules try to migrate the features, and even reproduce the bugs in the same language. We also recommend before introducing multi-language programming, to determine if we are reducing or adding more complexity. In the case where a single language can perfectly complete all the tasks, it is better to use only this language and not introduce another language. Even if at that time, a specific developer would find it easier for him to perform the tasks by reusing code written in a different language. It is always recommended to consider the maintenance cost. All the systems will be maintained and probably by another person who may not have the same preferences as the initial developer.

Benefits of the Refactoring: Avoid unnecessary complexity. This will reduce the challenges related to introducing new programming languages. It is important to avoid multi-language programming if we are losing the benefits of introducing several languages. Other benefits of applying the refactoring are to improve the understandability and readability of the code and Reduce maintenance efforts.

Related Anti-patterns: Overengineering.

Examples: Some occurrences of this anti-pattern have been observed in JNI systems that we analysed, in which we found simple tasks delegated to JNI code. This was also discussed in some developers' documentation (see footnote 3). Figure 6 presents a possible case of unnecessary usage of multi-language systems extracted from *JniHelpers*. In some cases, the introduction of multi-language programming presents several benefits and can be justified. For example, in the case of mathematical operations like compression or encryption, or shared library that could be better written in a language available on all platforms. In these cases, we can reduce the maintenance cost and development cost by using the existing library written in C language for example instead of re-writing the same code in several languages. However, we should always keep in mind that native code might be faster under specific circumstances. But in the case of a bunch of arrays, loops, and arithmetic operations, there is no difference in performance between using Java and native or a different language[14]. The solution would be when a task can be perfectly implemented in a single language always go for that language. We also found in *Telegram* occurrences of this anti-pattern. It packages *SQLite* while there are other database types implemented in Java and recommended to be used within Java. Shipping *SQLite* opens the application to more vulnerabilities and bugs. The same goes for shipping *FFmpeg*. It is also recommended to not mix between Media playback and security concerns. Several bugs and vulnerabilities related to *FFmpeg* have been discussed in developers' blogs and bug reports[15]. Another example found in *JniCompressions*, where

---

[14] https://www.reddit.com/r/java/comments/vr250/the_jni_is_it_worth_it/.

[15] https://www.cvedetails.com/vulnerability-list/vendor_id-3611/Ffmpeg.html.

```
/* Java */
native void createJavaString();
native void nativeCreateJavaStringFromJavaString(String s);
void createJavaStringFromJavaString() throws Exception {
nativeCreateJavaStringFromJavaString(TestConstants.STRING); }
```

Fig. 6. Anti-Pattern - Unnecessary Use of Multi-language Programming

native implementation where used, while their functionality is already available as Apache common libraries for Java[16].

4.5   Language and Paradigms Mismatch

Context: In some cases, we can face tasks that may be better implemented in a specific language/paradigm. Also, the chosen programming language or paradigm might be inefficient for some specific tasks due to the limitations of that particular language. However, the developer may be more comfortable with that specific language or paradigm.

Problem: Each programming language has its own benefits and may be more efficient for specific tasks. The choice of the programming language to use depends on how the solution is modeled and the design decision applied. Some models work better with objects, some would best be done in an iterative solution, etc. However, design decisions may change during the software development phase and the same as the programming language used in the project. These languages have different paradigms that may introduce some incompatibilities once combined. In the same vein, developers do not have the same preferences and competencies in terms of programming languages. Many languages or environment decisions are made by "if you have a hammer, everything looks like a nail", developers tend to use the programming languages or tools they are familiar with.

Supposed Solution: The bad solution would be to implement the task in the language or paradigm that is easier to use but may not be the best language for that task or may introduce incompatibilities. This case may occur if we favor mono-language programming but also in the case of multi-language systems. If we do not choose the best language for the best task but always prefer to use language and paradigms with which we are more comfortable.

Forces Toward: (1) Coexistence with other software; (2) Introduce benefits from low-level programming languages; (3) Ensure efficiency implementation for specific tasks; (4) Reuse of similar or same features already implemented in another language; (5) Use of available resources; (6) A prototype or a part of the code was already written in the other language and developers prefer to reuse

---

[16] https://commons.apache.org/proper/commons-compress/javadocs/api-release/org/apache/commons/compress/compressors/lz4/package-summary.html.

what was already available; (7) An old project that is still used but developers avoid to refactor or migrate it to new technologies.

Consequences of the Anti-pattern: This anti-pattern can introduce problems during maintenance phases and also performance problems. As not all the languages are better used for the same tasks[17]. The same task could be written in four lines of code in Python language, however, require more than 10 lines of Java code. This may impact the understandability and maintainability of the system. Especially in the case of multi-language systems, this may cause additional overhead while debugging and maintenance of the system. Bad solutions like these contribute to the technical debt of the developers. This anti-pattern is related to our second observation presented in Sect. 1.

Forces Away: (1) Multi-threaded safety and robustness; (2) Ensure performance and calculation time; (3) Use each language for the best purpose; (4) Ensure performance by using low-level memory for specific tasks.

Refactoring: It might be possible that a certain task can be implemented more efficiently using another comparatively lower-level programming language than the primary programming language for the project. To refactor this anti-pattern we first recommend deeply verifying if the task can be isolated appropriately. If yes, then depending on the task, decide which language can be better suitable for this situation. Once the choice of the language is made, search for an existing module or library implemented in that language that provides the same features. The use of another programming language or paradigm for these tasks can boost the system's overall efficiency. We suggest isolating the task to a level that any problem caused by a task can be easily traced back to the code for this task. If there is no existing library or module that can be used, the task can be programmed using the chosen programming language with proper logs and documentation that can ease the usage of the library in the system. This methodology ensures the separation of concerns and the availability of reusable code in different modules or even projects.

Benefits of the Refactoring: Take the benefit from each programming language and use each language for the best purpose. This can also ensure security by using programming languages that present fewer vulnerabilities. Another benefit is related to improving performance by using another lower-level language for embedded programming or OS programming.

Related Anti-patterns: Blob [26].

Related Patterns: Object System Layer [32], Wrapper, and Facade [10].

Examples: One of the observed examples of occurrences of this anti-pattern was while sending files in Python. The system *python-telegram-bot* also contains occurrences of this anti-pattern. Several issues have been reported when sending

---

[17] https://stackoverflow.com/questions/1912408/appropriate%2Dprogramming %2Dlanguages%2Dfor%2Ddifferent%2Dproblems.

files in Python[18]. In the case where packets are checked for an acknowledgment then the transmission speed in Python is much lower than that of C programming language and may lead to timeout issues. File transmission is a task that can be easily isolated, and therefore programmed in C language, which can be converted into a dynamic library for use in Python. In this kind of situation, it would be better to isolate the task and provide an external library. We will benefit from the advantage that is introduced by the different programming languages and we use the right language for the right task. We present in Fig. 7 another example of occurrences of this code smell extracted from *jMonkeyEngine*[19]. In this example, JMonkeyEngine uses Java to process a lot of mathematical operations mostly related to terrain generation using the method *load()*. This could have been offloaded to C(++) and ensure better performance for each device as the system already involves the C(++) language.

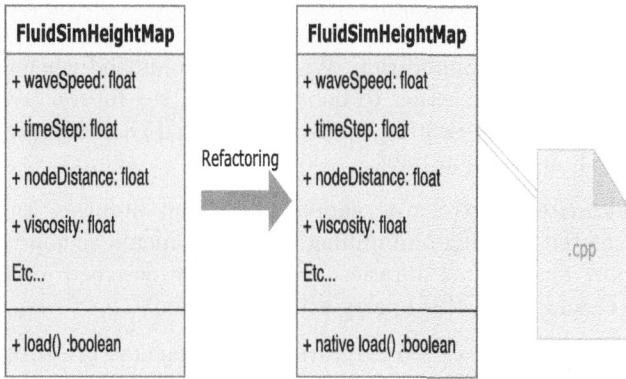

Fig. 7. Illustration Anti-Pattern - Language and Paradigms Mismatch

4.6 Project Migration Language Related Issues

Context: Developers and companies frequently face situations where projects fail or introduce several issues to be migrated. This can also be faced when modernising applications from old technologies to the new trends and advantages available in the market. Another case is, where applications or websites were designed as a prototype or for internal usage. But then started to be used by an important number of users. For this kind of reason, companies often migrate their applications. Another illustration of this anti-pattern is that some utility tools are not updated to support the latest and advanced features of new technologies. This can cause restrictions on advancements and updates to the project if these

---

[18] https://github.com/python-telegram-bot/python-telegram-bot/issues/533.
[19] https://github.com/jMonkeyEngine/jmonkeyengine/blob/master/jme3-terrain/src/main/java/com/jme3/terrain/heightmap/FluidSimHeightMap.java.

tools are not replaced. Some other tools may be migrated from one language to another from one technology to another. These systems, often become multi-language systems as a subset of the system remains in the old language and new features should be implemented in another language.

Problem: Usually systems are implemented under time delivery pressure or are designed as a prototype for internal usage. These systems are usually not implemented in a way that easily allows future migration and compatibility with new technologies. New programming languages and technologies also appear every day and with time, these technologies often become obsolete. When migrating a project it is also challenging to migrate business rules. In some cases, the programming language or technologies used in the past, may not be still used by an important number of developers. Martin Fowler discussed this common problem as it is more complex to migrate systems than it seems[20]. He explained that even when adding new features, old stuff has to remain, including old bugs that need to be added to the migrated version of the system. He introduced the concept of a strangler application pattern as a way of handling the release of the refactored code in a large application. We highly recommend when developing a new application to make it easier to be strangled in the future. Several studies also in the literature discussed the common issues and challenges related to the migration of such applications [40].

Supposed Solution: If the tool supports external libraries, then dynamic libraries are created focusing on fulfilling the requirements at hand. If the tools have no support for external libraries, new tools are designed for that specific requirement, or additional third-party software is used.

Forces Toward: (1) Legacy Configurations; (2) Business pressure; (3) Prioritising the delivery of a working version and not considering the maintenance activities and evolution after delivery; (4) The project designed as a prototype or one-time project not designated to add new features or be migrated with new technologies; (5) Not considering the extensibility, only the delivery process in that present time; (6) Design not oriented to support important changes and allowing evolvability and openness; (7) Project-based entirely upon marketing and industry need, and not consider future needs; (8) Lack of process management; (9) Companies looking for a quick and cheap transition to a client/server architecture.

Consequences of the Anti-pattern: In long-term projects, generally some utility/third-party tools are developed and used to interact with the primary system. These tools are developed with a specific aim in mind, and their design might not have been given enough attention to supporting extensions according to the latest technology trends and new programming languages. As new concepts are being implemented in the form of packages and libraries constantly, if the project dependency on these obsolete tools is high, then the entire project can become obsolete. The libraries might be developed to solve specific problems

---

[20] https://www.martinfowler.com/bliki/StranglerApplication.html.

at hand, but the lack of updates and bad design for a tool in most cases causes additional problems with time. Moreover, in most cases, whenever a third-party tool or library is used, only a small subset of its overall features is used in the project, which results in additional technical overhead for the people working with it. Migration issues are a common discussion between developers. Especially when migrating a project from one language to another (e.g. from COBOL to Java), developers are usually asking for any learned lessons or practices to avoid common migration issues[21].

Forces Away: (1) Adapt to a changing world and technologies; (2) Coexistence with other software and technologies; (3) Allow extensibility and reusability; (4) Incremental design process; (5) Choose language with active and important community; (5) Preserve several years of development, while greatly enhancing performance and flexibility.

Refactoring: To refactor this anti-pattern, we recommend first to understand the whole architecture of the system to be migrated. Then, choose the languages and technologies that will be used for the new version. Depending on the languages and technologies, there may be some existing tools that can help during the migration phase. It is also important, to consider making the system more flexible to future migrations. Martin Fowler introduced a possible solution to consider a strangler application over a cut-over rewrite. He also suggested good practice when designing a new application to make it easier to be strangled in the future. A good solution would be to always keep a future vision when implementing a system. New technologies and languages appear every day. Each of them introduces new advantages and may solve specific challenges. The systems should be designed in a way to allow extensions, especially for multi-language systems usage. This will allow for the smooth addition of future modifications and new features. Developers should ensure that tool support is always as good as expected.

Benefits of the Refactoring: Consider future extensions and reduce the costs and risks of project migration. This also allows the project to stay in the market and easily migrate to new technologies. Another benefit is related to the post-delivery as it ensures a better lifetime of the project once delivered.

Related Anti-patterns: Continuous Obsolescence and Autogenerated Stovepipe [26].

Related Patterns: Strangler Application [41].

Examples: An example of this anti-pattern would exist in each application that failed or introduced high cost, to be migrated from one technology or language to another. Martin Fowler also discussed examples of this anti-pattern. One example of this anti-pattern could be faced by a company with COBOL systems that cannot be migrated to new hardware for lack of appropriate compilers.

---

[21] https://stackoverflow.com/questions/1029974/experience-migrating-legacy-cobol-pl1-to-java.

Developers would have to deal with different tools and languages due to this migration issue[22]. Some of these issues were reported in one of our current studies in which we surveyed developers about the challenges of multi-language systems. The legacy tools should be replaced with the latest feature-rich technologies that will provide more areas for improvement and innovation. It would always be better to develop and maintain one utility tool with new technology than to maintain multiple legacy tools using a different set of technologies. Another example of this anti-pattern is the features that are available in one language but in the other language. As an example, we have the code assistance in Java but not in C language. In the literature, we also found occurrences of this anti-pattern presented as an industrial report when migrating an airport management system from a Bull mainframe using COBOL programming language and IDS as a database to a distributed UNIX platform using Java and Oracle [40]. They presented the challenges and issues related to such migration. Previously, two attempts have already been made to migrate this application from COBOL to Java but both of them failed. They also argued that it is much more difficult to migrate an existing application than to develop a new one starting from scratch. As in commercial applications, users are expecting to have all of the old features plus new ones. Another example of this situation was the case for *Microsoft*, when they rewrote their compiler[23]. The same for *Facebook*, with the increase of its popularity, PHP could not support the volumes they process. For that, they migrated the PHP into C++ thence machine code[24].

5   Code Smells for Multi-language Systems

In this section, we introduce the extracted good and bad practices in the form of code smells.

5.1   Passing Excessive Objects

Context: We have some attributes from classes and objects in the host language that we must access and use in the foreign code.

Problem: Developers do not have enough knowledge about the performance cost when integrating several programming languages. They usually make design and coding choices considering a single paradigm and do not consider that combining distinct paradigms may change those decisions.

Supposed Solution: We usually have to decide whether we pass an object that has multiple fields or pass the fields individually. The bad solution would be

---

[22] https://stackoverflow.com/questions/1029974/experience-migrating-legacy-cobol-pl1-to-java.

[23] https://medium.com/microsoft-open-source-stories/how-microsoft-rewrote-its-c-compiler-in-c-and-made-it-open-source-4ebed5646f98.

[24] https://softwareengineering.stackexchange.com/questions/176435/why-does-facebook-convert-php-code-to-c.

to always favor passing a whole object instead of passing parameters; i.e., each time we pass the whole object instead of passing the parameters of interest. If we consider passing the whole object in the context of the object-oriented principle, this provides better encapsulation. However, in the case of multi-language systems, it is better to consider the performance cost between the two solutions when combining different paradigms and languages.

Consequences of the Code Smell: Passing an object from one language to another may require an important effort of performance and implicate intermediate methods to access the native code as not all the languages have or treat similarly the types. In some cases, the native code uses several foreign calls to get the value of each field. Such additional calls add extra costs. Calls from native code to host language code are more expensive than a normal method call and may negatively impact the performance. Other consequences are that the methods implicated by this code smell will not have many parameters and will favor the encapsulation.

Refactoring: To remove this code smell, a good solution would be when a few parameters need to be accessed, favor passing them separately instead of passing the whole object. Depending on the languages, it may require additional effort to access the fields if they are not passed as parameters.

Benefits of the Refactoring: This will improve the performance in the case where passing a whole object is a consuming task. It also improves the readability by having the parameters of interest instead of whole objects. Another benefit is to avoid calling heavy methods to extract the parameters from the object, especially when the programming languages differ in terms of types and paradigms.

Examples: An example of occurrences of this code smell has been discussed in *IBM website* (see footnote 2). In the case of JNI, when we pass objects, it results in many calls to get the value for each of the individual fields. This kind of call adds an extra cost as the interactions between the native code and the Java code are generally more expensive than a method call. It may negatively impact performance. Figure 8 presents an example of occurrences of this code smell. Figure 9 presents a possible refactoring to remove this code smell. Depending on the programming language this code smell may also occur in Python/C and other sets and pairs of languages.

5.2   Unnecessary Parameters

Context: When adding new features or modifying an existing project, it may happen that we are not sure which parameters to keep and which ones to remove. This can also happen when passing parameters to and from one language to another which were never been used in the other language.

Problem: Several teams and developers are involved in the same projects. These projects are then maintained by other developers who do not have enough knowledge about the architecture of the project.

```
/* C++ */
int sumValues (JNIEnv* env,jobject obj,jobject allVal)
{ jint avalue= (*env)->GetIntField(env,allVal,a);
  jint bvalue= (*env)->GetIntField(env,allVal,b);
  jint cvalue= (*env)->GetIntField(env,allVal,c);
  return avalue + bvalue + cvalue;}
```

Fig. 8. Code Smell - Passing Excessive Objects

```
/* C++ */
 int sumValues (JNIEnv* env, jobject obj, jint a, jint b,jint c){ return
     a + b + c;}
```

Fig. 9. Refactoring - Passing Excessive Objects

Supposed Solution: A bad solution would be when applying a change to always keep the parameters already existing as they may be used in the other language while they are no longer used. This can also appear when we pass all the parameters that we believe can be used to complete the task while concretely not all of them are used.

Consequences of the Code Smell: Having unused parameters from one language to another may add complexity to the code, especially in maintenance activities. Developers may not be sure which parameters should be used and which not as they are related to another language. Multi-language systems are by nature more difficult to understand, adding unnecessary parameters or applying a change and not removing the corresponding parameters will introduce more complexity to the system. Some developers may go through this solution as once all the parameters are defined and passed from one language to the other, it is easier to use them or apply changes that involve these parameters.

Refactoring: To remove this code smell, Keep only the parameters that are used to avoid introducing unnecessary complexity and improve the readability.

Benefits of the Refactoring: Improve the understandability and maintainability as the method will contain only the parameters used. This also avoids dead code and Keeps only the parameters needed.

Examples: Figure 10 presents an example of occurrences of this code smell. The parameter *acceleration* is defined in the native method signature. However, it is not used by the native code. The solution would be to remove the unused parameters.

5.3   Unused Native Methods Declaration

Context: When we have some methods declaration in the host language that has never been implemented in the foreign language.

```
/* C++ */
JNIEXPORT jfloat JNICALL Java_jni_distance
  (JNIEnv *env, jobject thisObject,
  jfloat time, jfloat speed,
  jfloat acceleration) {
    return time * speed;}
```

Fig. 10. Code Smell - Unnecessary Parameters

Problem: Requirement or functionalities changes may lead to unused code. Usually, different teams may be involved separately to contribute to each programming language. These teams do not have a global view of the whole system, which methods are used and which are not.

Supposed Solution: A bad solution would be when applying a change to always keep the native methods declared without additional checking as they may be used in the other language while they are no longer used.

Consequences of the Code Smell: If a future modification involves implementing these methods, it will be easier as they are already declared. However, this code smell can result in unused and unnecessary code. It may add some complexity to the code and introduce more difficulty when reading and maintaining the code. Depending on the language, this kind of method may not crash the system or display an error, as these methods are never called or used. However, for a maintainer, it would require additional effort to investigate which methods are used in the multi-language systems and which are not.

Refactoring: To remove this code smell, keep only the methods that are used in the multi-language systems' interaction. An unused code may negatively impact the quality of a system, the impact may be important when we are dealing with multi-language systems. Depending on the size of the system, it may be difficult for a maintainer to identify the methods used. To retrace or fix a bug this may require more effort.

Benefits of the Refactoring: Improve the understandability and maintainability as the code will contain only the methods that are used. This also avoids dead code by providing clean code and Keeping only the methods used. Another benefit is that it would be easier for a maintainer or new developer to locate the code used.

Examples: An example of this code smell was perceived when we analyzed JNI systems and collected the number of method implementations and the number of method declarations. In most of the system, the number was the same between both of these metrics. However, we found examples where some native methods have been declared but have never been used.

5.4   Unused Native Method Implementation

Context: When we have the method declaration and its corresponding implementation. However, it is never called from the host language. In the case of multi-language programming, it is hard for a developer working on a specific part of the project implemented in a single language, to know which methods are used in the other language. Some implementations could also be provided by different Dynamic Link Library not written in the same language. These systems usually involve several developers or teams to work separately in the project and access only a subpart of it.

Problem: Several developers working on the same code and maintainers do not have enough knowledge about the project to confirm whether the code is used or not. It can also be in situations where a project was migrated or refactored. This can also be related to a planned extension that never happened or a renaming that failed. In the case of multi-language systems, it can be more difficult to locate these methods as they are implemented in one language or component and used in another one. Developers should have a complete vision of the architecture of the systems to know which methods are used or are planned to be used in near future releases. Depending on the programming language and paradigm, we may face situations where the foreign method is not called using the same name as the one used in the implementation or with the same signature.

Supposed Solution: Always keep the native methods implementations without additional checking as they may be used in the other language. Avoid breakages related to removing code that is still called or used somewhere on the project.

Consequences of the Code Smell: If a future modification involves using these methods, it will be easier as they are already implemented. However, this code smell adds more complexity and may result in huge classes in which we have an implementation of methods that are never called from the other language. When fixing bugs or adding new features, the developers may go through these methods and will not be aware that they are not used.

Refactoring: To remove this code smell, remove all unnecessary and unused code to reduce the complexity and keep in each class only the methods that are used. To prevent occurrences of this code smell, it is also important to always remove all the code related to the multi-language programming if it is no longer used. These systems usually involve different developers or teams working separately and it may be more difficult for them to know if the code is used somewhere in the project or not.

Benefits of the Refactoring: Improve the understandability and maintainability as the code will contain only the methods that are used. This also avoids dead code by having clean code and Keeping only the methods used. It may also be easier for a maintainer or new developer to locate the code used.

Examples: An example of this code smell was initially perceived when we manually analysed JNI systems and found some native methods that have been declared and implemented but are never called. It may be due to changes or refactoring in which they introduced another method. These methods introduced some doubt as we were confused about where they were used, but then we semi-automatically checked if they were called using *grep* command but we did not find any calls to these methods.

5.5   Not Handling Exceptions Across Languages

Context: In the case of multi-language systems, depending on the language we may not have the same way to manage the exception.

Problem: The management of exceptions is not automatically ensured in all the languages. Some programming languages, require developers to explicitly implement the exception-handling flow after an exception has occurred. If the exception is not explicitly implemented and handled by the developer this may introduce bugs. Developers may also not be aware of the consequences of not managing the exceptions, especially in the case of multi-language programming.

Supposed Solution: The bad solution would be to always rely on the exception provided by the other language and not necessarily implement the exception handling.

Consequences of the Code Smell: If the exception is not explicitly implemented and handled by the developer. This may result in bugs and unchecked exceptions will introduce faults in the system that will be hardly debugged or retraced to the origin of the bug. This code smell is related to the third observation presented in Sect. 1 related to the correctness.

Refactoring: To remove this code smell, always check whether an exception has been thrown after invoking any foreign methods that may throw an exception. Multi-language systems introduce more complexity than mono-language systems and need more effort to fix bugs and issues, it is important to consider checking and handling exceptions to prevent issues related to no checking exceptions. In the case of multi-language systems, it is much easier to prevent crashes by implementing the exception than to debug after the crash occurred. Upon handling the exception, we should also clear it depending on the language. For JNI, we should use the *ExceptionClear* function to inform the Java VM that the exception is handled and JNI can resume serving requests to Java space. If the host language provides the handling and management of exceptions, it is possible to simply check if an exception has occurred in the foreign code and if so return immediately to the host code so that the exception is thrown. It will then be either handled or displayed using the exception-handling process provided by the host language.

Benefits of the Refactoring: The refactored solution introduces several benefits, including preventing crashes, separating error-handling code from regular code, and differentiating error types.

Examples: Examples of occurrences of this code smell have been discussed in developers' documentation as a wise practice (see footnote 2)[25]. Most of the systems that we analysed were not always implementing a proper way to handle the exception as shown in Fig. 11, this code may cause a crash if the charField field no longer exists. For the JNI case, one good example was *Libgdx*, where they catch Java exceptions in native code using the JNI API call ExceptionOccurred. Figure 12 presents a refactoring example extracted from *IBM Developer Site* (see footnote 2). Occurrences of this code smell will not block the execution of the native code. However, any calls to JNI API will silently fail. As the actual exception does not leave any traces behind, it is hard to debug.

```
/* C++ */
jclass objectClass;
jfieldID fieldID;
jchar result = 0;
objectClass= (*env)->GetObjectClass(env, obj);
fieldID= (*env)->GetFieldID(env, objectClass, "charField", "C");
result= (*env)->GetCharField(env, obj, fieldID);
```

Fig. 11. Code Smell - Not Handling Exceptions Across Languages

```
/* C++ */
jclass objectClass;
jfieldID fieldID;
jchar result = 0;
objectClass = (*env)->GetObjectClass(env, obj);
fieldID = (*env)->GetFieldID(env, objectClass, "charField", "C");
if((*env)->ExceptionOccurred(env)) {return;}
result = (*env)->GetCharField(env, obj, fieldID);
```

Fig. 12. Refactoring - Not Handling Exceptions Across Languages

5.6 Assuming Safe Multi-language Return Values

Context: Typically when we are implementing a multi-language system, we need to access and transfer data and information between different languages. We usually pass and return values from one language to another.

Problem: Exceptions are extensions of the programming language for developers to report and handle exceptional events that require special processing

---

[25] https://nachtimwald.com/2017/07/09/jni-is-not-your-friend/.

outside the actual flow of the application. However, the management of exceptions is not supported by all the languages. The same for return values that are used to transfer data from one language to another. Some developers assume that return values are safe, while others are not aware of the consequences of not checking multi-language return values.

Supposed Solution: We may need to implement a specific task in a certain language and need to have the value returned to the other language. In most of the cases, we are just returning the value without performing specific checks. The bad solution in the case of multi-language systems is to implement the method in the foreign language and have its result returned to the main language assuming that return values are safe without considering additional checks.

Consequences of the Code Smell: It is important to consider the return values as exceptions to verify that the interaction between the languages was well performed. Otherwise, it may result in introducing faults and bugs in the program. As some values may be wrong or simply empty which can cause problems when returned to the other language. This code smell is related to the third observation presented in Sect. 1 related to the correctness.

Refactoring: To remove this code smell, a good solution would be to never assume that it is safe to use a value returned by a language API call, which must always be checked to make sure that the call was successfully executed and the proper usable value is returned to the native function. Multi-language methods usually have a return value that indicates whether the call succeeded or failed. A common bad practice, similar to not checking for exceptions, is to assume that the return values are safe. API functions rely on their return values instead to indicate any errors during the execution of the API call.

Benefits of the Refactoring: Ensure that the interaction between the languages was well performed. Other benefits are to ensure that the usable value is returned to the foreign code and avoid introducing bugs and faults.

Examples: Examples of occurrences of this code smell have been observed in most of the open-source systems that we analyzed. This was also reported in several developers' documentation and bug reports[26]. Depending on the languages involved in the multi-language systems, it is mostly recommended to always check the return values from one language to another. As in most cases, we use another language to perform a calculation or specific features that will be then used by the main language. It is recommended to always check the value before returning it to the host language. As illustrated in Fig. 13 extracted from *Libgdx*, if the class *NIOAccess* or one of its methods is not found, the native code will cause a crash. We are not applying any checks to handle the problems related to the return values. A good solution to remove this code smell is to add a check that handles the situations in which problems may occur with the return values. Figure 14 is a good example to illustrate a possible refactored solution.

---

[26] https://www.developer.com/java/data/exception-handling-in-jni.html.

```
/* C++ */
staticvoid nativeClassInitBuffer(JNIEnv *_env){
 jclass nioAccessClassLocal= _env->FindClass("java/nio/NIOAccess");
 nioAccessClass=(jclass) _env->NewGlobalRef(nioAccessClassLocal);
 bufferClass=(jclass) _env->NewGlobalRef(bufferClassLocal);
 positionID= _env->GetFieldID(bufferClass, "position", "I");
```

Fig. 13. Code Smell - Assuming Safe Multi-language Return Values

```
/* C++ */
//Checking the Return Value of JNI API Calls
jclass clazz;
...
clazz = env->FindClass("java/lang/String");
if (0 == clazz) {/* Class could not be found. */
} else { /* Class is found, we can use the return %value.*/ }
```

Fig. 14. Refactoring - Assuming Safe Multi-language Return Values

5.7   Not Caching Objects' Elements

Context: When implementing a multi-language system, we need to pass objects and variables from one language to the other. In this case, we want to access an object's field and methods from the foreign code.

Problem: Developers do not have enough knowledge of how the fields and methods are retrieved when passing from one language to another. They may consider using the most simple way to access foreign code and do not consider the performance cost.

Supposed Solution: Depending on the language, use the available methods to access the object fields and methods. Each time we need one of the object's fields, call the methods to retrieve the field as if it is the first time we access the field. For example, to access Java objects' fields and their methods, the native code performs calls to FindClass(), GetFieldID(), GetMethodId(), and GetStaticMethodID().

Consequences of the Code Smell: Depending on the language, it may require an important effort to use available methods to access the object fields and methods. Although these methods may be used frequently in multi-language applications, they may be heavy function calls by their nature. These functions traverse the entire inheritance chain for the class to identify the ID to return. The IDs returned for a class using GetFieldID(), GetMethodID(), and GetStaticMethodID(), do not change during the lifetime of the JVM process. However, this may be expensive in terms of performance. For that, we recommend to look them and reuse them once needed.

Refactoring: Neither the Class object, the Class inheritance, nor the fieldID can be changed during the execution of the system. These values are cached in the native layer for subsequent accesses. The return type of the FindClass function is a local reference, so to cache its values, developers must create a global reference first through the NewGlobalRef function when it is needed. The return value of GetFieldID is jfieldID, which is an integer that can be cached as it is. To remove this code smell, developers should focus on caching both the field and method IDs that are accessed multiple times during the execution of the application, this practice improves the execution time.

Benefits of the Refactoring: he IDs are often pointers to internal runtime data structures. Looking them up may require several string comparisons. Once we have them the call to get the field or the method does not take an important time. This also improves performance by avoiding several lockups and avoiding calling heavy functions.

Examples: Examples of occurrences of this code smell have been observed in JNI systems. Some developers' documentation also reported this common bad practice as negatively impacting the performance as shown in Fig. 15 (see footnote 2). In the case of JNI, the correct way to initialise the IDs is to Create a method in the C(++) code that performs the ID lookups. The code will be executed once when the class is initialised. If the class is ever unloaded and then reloaded, it will be executed again. If commonly used classes, fields IDs, and methods IDs are not properly cached, we lose the benefit of using the C(++). This code smell negatively impacts our first observation discussed in the introduction, related to the performance. As presented in the example (see footnote 2), using caching field IDs will take 3,572 ms to run 10,000,000 times Fig. 15. However, without using the cache as illustrated in Fig. 16, it takes 86,217 ms. Using this code smell the task takes 24 times longer than without the occurrences of this code smell.

```
/* C++ */
int sumVal (JNIEnv* env,jobject obj,jobject allVal){
   jclass cls=(*env)->GetObjectClass(env,allVal);
   jfieldID a=(*env)->GetFieldID(env,cls,"a","I");
   jfieldID b=(*env)->GetFieldID(env,cls,"b","I");
   jfieldID c=(*env)->GetFieldID(env,cls,"c","I");
   jint aval=(*env)->GetIntField(env,allVal,a);
   jint bval=(*env)->GetIntField(env,allVal,b);
   jint cval=(*env)->GetIntField(env,allVal,c);
   return aval + bval + cval;}
```

Fig. 15. Code Smell - Not Caching Objects' Elements

```
/* C++ */
  jint aval=(*env)->GetIntField(env,allVal,a);
  jint bval=(*env)->GetIntField(env,allVal,b);
  jint cval=(*env)->GetIntField(env,allVal,c);
  return aval + bval + cval;
```

Fig. 16. Refactoring - Not Caching Objects' Elements

5.8   Not Securing Libraries

Context: We want to access foreign libraries or an API available in another language. We aim to integrate an external library with the main application developed in a different language.

Problem: Developers are not always aware of the consequences of insecure code or do not provide enough intention.

Supposed Solution: When developing multi-language systems, we always need to access some API or libraries implemented in another language. We load the native library or API directly in the code without any security checking or restriction.

Consequences of the Code Smell: As a consequence of the occurrence of this code smell, several problems may occur due to the leak of security. An unauthorised code may access and load the libraries. Malicious code may use this vulnerable code to access the system. Depending on the domain of application in which the multi-language systems have been involved, this may have an important impact. As for mobile applications or embedded systems, a fault in the security may have an impact at the human level.

Refactoring: To remove this code smell, always ensure that the libraries cannot be loaded without permission. It is important to ensure that the loading of external libraries is written in a secured block of code to guarantee access only to those who are allowed to. Depending on the language some predefined classes may ensure security and prevent undesirable access to the system. As for the Java language, it is recommended to always load libraries in static blocks, wrapped in a call to *AccessController.doPrivileged* or use the *securityManager*.

Benefits of the Refactoring: One of the main benefits is to ensure that the libraries cannot be loaded without permission. This also avoids malicious attacks and secures the load of the library and the project.

Examples: The occurrences of this code smell have been observed on most of the analyzed systems. In the JNI case, we found the usage of the secure library only with the *JDK* and *Openj9*. In these systems, the loading library is always performed in a static block and using the *AccessController*. *AccessController* presents a safe way to load a library because it ensures that the library cannot be loaded without permissions, as shown in Fig. 17. Depending on the languages, we recommend always securing the loading library by using available methods for the specific language.

```
/* Java */
 static { AccessController.doPrivileged(
         new PrivilegedAction<Void>() {
         public Void run() {
         System.loadLibrary("osxsecurity");
         return null; } } ); }
```

Fig. 17. Securing Library Loading

5.9   Hard Coding Libraries

Context: We are loading different libraries for different OS, the same code can not run on all the platforms. we need to customize the loading according to the OS. For that, we hard-code the loading according to the OS.

Problem: The Project was designed as a prototype and does not consider future extensions and adaption to new platforms.

Supposed Solution: Depending on the used language, some of them are expected to run on all platforms, but in other languages, there must be different native code libraries for different platforms, which must be loaded according to the target OS. To ensure loading the libraries according to the OS the loading libraries are hard-coded in the code.

Consequences of the Code Smell: When the libraries are hard-coded, it is difficult for a maintainer to know which library is loaded at which time. Even to handle bugs and errors this would require more time to locate the errors. As a consequence of this code smell, developers may require additional effort to distinguish between the different libraries. This also may impact the understandability and readability of the system.

Refactoring: To remove this code smell, a clean way to load the library would be to handle all targeted OS on which the library is available. This ensures better code readability, letting the code Reader directly know what libraries are being loaded. Also, loading in a way to take care of the OS makes sure that all cases are properly covered and if a code is running on a new OS, errors are easy to locate.

Benefits of the Refactoring: One of the main benefits is to ensure readability by making the libraries easily defined for each operating system. It also ensures the handling of all targeted OS on which the library is available and improves understandability.

Examples: Examples of occurrences of this code smell as well as the good solution have been observed respectively in JavaSmt and Frostwire. In JavaSmt, most of the loading libraries were hard-coded in a way that it was difficult for us to know which library was related to which OS. As shown in Fig. 18. Some of the comments were explaining the OS related to the library. However, it is better if the way to load the library can be self-efficient and reflect which library is loaded. It is important when loading libraries to take care of the OS as shown in Fig. 19. This ensures that all platforms are covered and those missing libraries can be easily identified.

```Java
/* Java */
public static synchronized Z3SolverContext create(
try { System.loadLibrary("z3"); System.loadLibrary("z3java");
} catch (UnsatisfiedLinkError e1) {
try { System.loadLibrary("libz3");
      System.loadLibrary("libz3java");
} catch (UnsatisfiedLinkError e2) {...}
```

Fig. 18. Code Smells - Hard Coding Libraries

```Java
/* Java */
/*for Windows*/
if (OSUtils.isWindows() && OSUtils.isGoodWindows()) {
if (OSUtils.isMachineX64()) {
System.loadLibrary("SystemUtilitiesX64";}
else { System.loadLibrary("SystemUtilities");}
/*for Mac OS*/
public final class GURLHandler {
System.loadLibrary("GURLLeopard");
public class MacOSXUtils {
System.loadLibrary("MacOSXUtilsLeopard");
```

Fig. 19. Refactoring - Hard Coding Libraries

5.10   Not Using Relative Path to Load the Library

Context: When implementing a multi-language system, we need to load foreign code and then use external libraries or API. We have to specify the name of the library that we are going to load.

Problem: The project was designed as a prototype, not for future reuse. This can also be related to a situation where the project was initially used locally by a single or few developers.

Supposed Solution: In multi-language systems we usually need to access or integrate foreign libraries or APIs. For that, we need to specify the name or path to access the library. A bad solution would be to load the external library by only specifying the name of the library without providing the full path.

Consequences of the Code Smell: When using the relative path the loading and installation of the library can be done everywhere. But if we just put the name, this may impact the reuse of code or maintenance as the library cannot be accessed in the same way from everywhere if we do not specify the path. This code smell also impacts the reusability of the code, as the library cannot be reused from anywhere without providing the full path.

Refactoring: A good solution to remove this code smell would be to use relative or absolute Path to load a library. When using a native library, a relative path must be used to allow installation anywhere. A flag can specify if an absolute or relative path must be used. To avoid issues it is better to use an absolute path as it points to the same location in a file system, regardless of the current working directory. This will ensure the reusability and improve the maintainability as in case of issues related to this library, any future developer can directly locate the library.

Benefits of the Refactoring: One of the main benefits is to ensure reusability as the library can be used from anywhere. Maintainers or developers can also easily locate the library. This also improves maintainability.

Examples: We perceived examples of occurrences of this code smell when analysing JNI systems. Only a few of the systems that we analysed followed the practice of using a relative path. The systems `Conscrypt` and `JatoVm` are mainly relying on the relative path to load the library, while most of the systems that we analysed only specify the name of the library. Figure 20 presents an example of refactoring to remove this code smell extracted from `JatoVm`.

```
/* Java */
public class JNITest extends TestCase {
 static {System.load("./test/functional/jni/libjnitest.so"); }
```

Fig. 20. Refactoring - Not Using Relative Path to Load the Library

5.11 Memory Management Mismatch

Context: We are implementing a multi-language system in which we are passing reference types from one language to another. Depending on the languages, these types may be considered as pointers when used in other languages.

Problem: The management of the types and memory is not the same from one language to another. In some languages like C(++), the management of the memory is not done automatically. Depending on the language, it may be the developers' responsibility to care about the management of the memory. As in the case of JNI, if we are using a *String* we should be the one taking care of releasing it after its usage. However, developers do not have enough knowledge of the characteristics of the programming languages involved. They are usually dealing with programming languages that automatically handle the management of the memory.

Consequences of the Code Smell: The management of the memory may not be the same from one language to another. Memory leaks can occur if the developers forget to take care of releasing such reference types.

Refactoring: To remove this code smell, a good solution would be to always take care of the management of such reference types. It is better to assume that in foreign communication, the management of the memory is not always done automatically, and may be considered by the developers. Especially the allocation and release of memory that needs to be explicitly done by the developers. It becomes their responsibility when dealing with more than one programming language.

Benefits of the Refactoring: One of the main benefits is to avoid problems due to a leak of the memory. This also avoids performance issues and frees the memory allocated to objects that are no longer used.

Examples: Examples of occurrences of this code smell have been observed in a few JNI systems and developers' documentation, where problems related to the leak of memory occurred due to not releasing the memory. Developers should take care of such memory management in multi-language systems. For the JNI case, Java strings are handled by the JNI as reference types. Those reference types are not null-terminated C char arrays (C strings). When the Java string is converted to a C string, it simply becomes a pointer to a null-terminated character array. It is the developers' responsibility to explicitly release the arrays using the ReleaseString or ReleaseStringUTF functions. Figure 21 presents an example of the refactored solution to remove this code smell. An example of occurrences of this code smell is the non-release of the memory using `ReleaseString` or `ReleaseStringUTF`.

```
/* C++ */
str = env->GetStringUTFChars(javaString, &isCopy);
if (0 != str) {env->ReleaseStringUTFChars(javaString, str);
str = 0; }
```

Fig. 21. Refactoring - Memory Management Mismatch

5.12   Local References Abuse

Context: Depending on the programming language, the management of the memory is not the same. For this code smell, we are considering the references. For the Java code, JVM keeps an eye on the available references to the allocated memory regions. When JVM detects that an allocated memory region can no longer be reached by the application code. It releases the memory automatically through garbage collection leaving the developer free from memory management. However, JVM garbage collector boundaries are limited to the Java space only.

Problem: The lifespan of a local reference is limited to the native method itself. Depending on the language, garbage collector boundaries are limited to a specific space only, so the garbage collector cannot free the memory that the application allocates in the native space. The management of the memory may differ from one language to another. Thus, developers should always consider taking care of memory when using local and global references. For the JNI case, memory models and their management defer between Java and C. It is the developers' responsibility to manage the application's memory in the native space properly.

Supposed Solution: The bad solution would be to use local and global references without considering the management of the memory.

Consequences of the Code Smell: If we do not consider the management of memory and the criteria when using references from one language to another, this can cause memory leaks.

Refactoring: To remove this code smell, always take care of releasing the memory once using global or local references and never assume that their release will be done automatically. For the JNI case, it creates references for all object arguments passed into native methods, as well as all objects returned from JNI functions. These references will keep Java objects from being garbage collected. To make sure that Java objects can eventually be freed, the JNI by default creates local references. Local references become invalid when the execution returns from the native method in which the local reference is created.

Benefits of the Refactoring: One of the main benefits is to ensure releasing the memory once using global or local references. This avoids memory allocation bugs and makes sure to free the memory for reuse when no longer needed.

Examples: Occurrences of this code smell have been observed in JNI systems and the good practice of releasing the memory has been discussed in several developers' documentation as well as the JNI specification. Each time we return an object by a JNI function, local references are created. For example, as shown in Fig. 22 calling GetObjectArrayElement() will return a local reference to each object in the array. It is important to delete each reference when it is no longer required. A native method must not store away a local reference and expect to reuse it in subsequent invocations. so whenever a state is to be maintained during JNI calls, global references are a must. However, JNI global references are prone to memory leaks, as they are not automatically garbage collected, and the programmer must explicitly free them but they are necessary. Depending on the programming language, to reuse a reference, the developer must explicitly create a global reference based on the local reference using the New-GlobalRef JNI API call. The global reference can be released when it is no longer needed using the *DeleteGlobalRef* function. An example of refactoring is: env->DeleteLocalRef(globalObject).

```
/* C++ */
for (i=0; i < count; i++) {
jobject element = (*env)->GetObjectArrayElement(env, array, i);
if((*env)->ExceptionOccurred(env)) { break;}
```

Fig. 22. Code smell - Local References Abuse

6   Threats to Validity

We now discuss threats to the validity of our methodology and the reported anti-patterns and code smells.

Threats to Internal Validity: We used the well-know, open-source repositories *GitHub* and *OpenHub* to identify and obtain multi-language systems. We also used well-known developers' documentation, bug reports, and developers' blogs, such as *StackOverflow*, *IBM Developers*, *developer.android*, and *Bugzilla* to extract practices. Hence, we limited threats to the internal validity, although we did not identify exhaustively all existing anti-patterns/code smells. Moreover, we followed a systematic method to identify and report multi-language anti-patterns and code smells.

Threats to Conclusion Validity: The code smells and anti-patterns presented in this paper went through several rounds of a shepherding process. In this process, a pattern expert provided three rounds of meaningful comments to refine and improve the code smells and anti-patterns. The catalog of smells went then through the writers' workshop process, in which five researchers carefully read the paper and provided detailed comments for each code smell and anti-pattern. During the writers' workshop, each smell was examined in detail along with their definition and concrete examples [42,43].

Threats to External Validity: We observed each one of the anti-patterns more than three times in multiple systems. However, depending on the language, some of the anti-patterns or code smells may not exist or may have different consequences. Hence, we believe that our study is repeatable but could give different results for different programming languages.

Threats to Reliability Validity: We attempted to provide all the necessary information needed to reproduce our study here and online[27], including our developers' survey. Hence, we believe it to have minimised threats to its reliability.

7   Conclusions and Future Work

The development of multi-language systems has become very prevalent nowadays, it offers many opportunities, developers can reuse existing code and take advantage of existing libraries and modules written in several programming languages [2]. However, multi-language systems also present challenges to developers: they are difficult to develop, maintain, and evolve because they are more complex than mono-language systems.

Software quality is achieved partly by following good practices and avoiding bad ones. While several studies discussed the benefits and challenges of multi-language systems, only a few reported good and bad practices that developers should adopt when dealing with such systems [18–21].

Therefore, in this paper, we present the steps followed for studying these resources and report on 12 code smells and six anti-patterns that we borrowed, observed, and–or inferred from these resources. These practices should help developers and researchers handle the complexity of multi-language systems. We followed and adapted the template provided by *WikiWikiWeb*.

In future work, we will (1) survey developers about these anti-patterns and code smells, (2) combine multi-language design patterns and anti-patterns to relate them with one another, (3) create a pattern language that could relate multi-language design patterns, design anti-patterns, idioms, and code smells with one another, (4) investigate their impact on quality attributes, and (5) implement tools to identify and correct their occurrences.

References

1. Matthews, J., Findler, R.B.: Operational semantics for multi-language programs. ACM Trans. Program. Lang. Syst. (TOPLAS) **31**(3), 12 (2009)
2. Kochhar, P.S., Wijedasa, D., Lo, D.: A large scale study of multiple programming languages and code quality. In: 2016 IEEE 23rd International Conference on Software Analysis, Evolution, and Reengineering (SANER), vol. 1, pp. 563–573. IEEE (2016)
3. Tan, G., Croft, J.: An empirical security study of the native code in the JDK. In: Proceedings of the 17th Conference on Security Symposium, ser. SS 2008, pp. 365–377. USENIX Association, Berkeley (2008)
4. Tomassetti, F., Torchiano, M.: An empirical assessment of polyglot-ism in github. In: Proceedings of the 18th International Conference on Evaluation and Assessment in Software Engineering, ser. EASE 2014, pp. 17:1–17:4. ACM, New York (2014)
5. Pfeiffer, R.-H., Wkasowski, A.: Texmo: a multi-language development environment. In: Proceedings of the 8th European Conference on Modelling Foundations and Applications, ser. ECMFA 2012, pp. 178–193. Springer, Heidelberg (2012)

---

[27] http://www.ptidej.net/downloads/replications/europlop19/.

6. Mushtaq, Z., Rasool, G.: Multilingual source code analysis: state of the art and challenges. In: 2015 International Conference on Open Source Systems Technologies (ICOSST), pp. 170–175 (2015)
7. Boughanmi, F.: Multi-language and heterogeneously-licensed software analysis. In: 17th Working Conference on Reverse Engineering (2010)
8. Galin, D.: Software Quality Assurance: From Theory to Implementation. Pearson Education India (2004)
9. Shihab, E.: Practical software quality prediction. In: 2014 IEEE International Conference on Software Maintenance and Evolution (ICSME), pp. 639–644. IEEE (2014)
10. Vlissides, J., Helm, R., Johnson, R., Gamma, E.: Design patterns: elements of reusable object-oriented software, vol. 49, no. 120, p. 11. Addison-Wesley, Reading (1995)
11. Guéhéneuc, Y.-G., Albin-Amiot, H.: Using design patterns and constraints to automate the detection and correction of inter-class design defects. In: 39th International Conference and Exhibition on Technology of Object-Oriented Languages and Systems, 2001. TOOLS 39, pp. 296–305. IEEE (2001)
12. Czibula, G., Marian, Z., Czibula, I.G.: Detecting software design defects using relational association rule mining. Knowl. Inf. Syst. **42**(3), 545–577 (2015)
13. Khomh, F., Di Penta, M., Gueheneuc, Y.-G.: An exploratory study of the impact of code smells on software change-proneness. In: 16th Working Conference on Reverse Engineering, 2009. WCRE 2009, pp. 75–84. IEEE (2009)
14. van Emden, E., Moonen, L.: Java quality assurance by detecting code smells. In: Ninth Working Conference on Reverse Engineering, 2002. Proceedings, pp. 97–106 (2002)
15. Khomh, F., Di Penta, M., Gueheneuc, Y.: An exploratory study of the impact of code smells on software change-proneness. In: 2009 16th Working Conference on Reverse Engineering, pp. 75–84 (2009)
16. Abbes, M., Khomh, F., Gueheneuc, Y., Antoniol, G.: An empirical study of the impact of two antipatterns, blob and spaghetti code, on program comprehension. In: 2011 15th European Conference on Software Maintenance and Reengineering, pp. 181–190 (2011)
17. Liang, S.: Java Native Interface: Programmer's Guide and Reference. Addison-Wesley Longman Publishing Co., Inc. (1999)
18. Goedicke, M., Zdun, U.: Piecemeal legacy migrating with an architectural pattern language: a case study. J. Softw. Maint. Evol. Res. Pract. **14**(1), 1–30 (2002)
19. Neitsch, A., Wong, K., Godfrey, M.W.: Build system issues in multilanguage software. In: 2012 28th IEEE International Conference on Software Maintenance (ICSM), pp. 140–149. IEEE (2012)
20. Malinova, A.: Design approaches to wrapping native legacy codes. Sci. Works Plovdiv Univ. **36**, 89–100 (2008)
21. Neumann, G., Zdun, U.: Pattern-based design and implementation of an XML and RDF parser and interpreter: a case study. In: European Conference on Object-Oriented Programming, pp. 392–414. Springer (2002)
22. Furr, M., Foster, J.S.: Checking type safety of foreign function calls. In: Proceedings of the 2005 ACM SIGPLAN Conference on Programming Language Design and Implementation, ser. PLDI 2005, pp. 62–72. ACM (2005)
23. Alexander, C., Ishikawa, S., Silverstein, M., i Ramió, J.R., Jacobson, M., Fiksdahl-King, I.: A pattern language. Gustavo Gili (1977)

24. Gamma, E., Helm, R., Johnson, R., Vlissides, J.: Design Patterns: Elements of Reusable Object-Oriented Software. Addison-Wesley Longman Publishing Co., Inc., Boston (1995)
25. Martin, R.C.: Agile Software Development: Principles, Patterns, and Practices. Prentice Hall (2002)
26. Brown, W.H., Malveau, R.C., McCormick, H.W., Mowbray, T.J.: AntiPatterns: Refactoring Software, Architectures, and Projects in Crisis. Wiley (1998)
27. Fowler, M., Beck, K.: Refactoring: Improving the Design of Existing Code. Addison-Wesley Professional (1999)
28. Webster, B.F.: Pitfalls of object oriented development. Book (1995)
29. Soh, Z., Yamashita, A., Khomh, F., Guéhéneuc, Y.-G.: Do code smells impact the effort of different maintenance programming activities? In: 2016 IEEE 23rd International Conference on Software Analysis, Evolution, and Reengineering (SANER), vol. 1, pp. 393–402. IEEE (2016)
30. Yamashita, A., Moonen, L.: Do developers care about code smells? An exploratory survey. In: 2013 20th Working Conference on Reverse Engineering (WCRE), pp. 242–251. IEEE (2013)
31. Romano, D., Raila, P., Pinzger, M., Khomh, F.: Analyzing the impact of antipatterns on change-proneness using fine-grained source code changes. In: 2012 19th Working Conference on Reverse Engineering (WCRE), pp. 437–446. IEEE (2012)
32. Goedicke, M., Neumann, G., Zdun, U.: Object system layer. In: 5th European Conference on Pattern Languages of Programms (EuroPLoP 2000) (2000)
33. Goedicke, M., Neumann, G., Zdun, U.: Message redirector. In: 6th European Conference on Pattern Languages of Programms (EuroPLoP 2001) (2001)
34. Kondoh, G., Onodera, T.: Finding bugs in java native interface programs. In: Proceedings of the 2008 International Symposium on Software Testing and Analysis, ser. ISSTA 2008, pp. 109–118. ACM, New York (2008)
35. Osmani, A.: Learning JavaScript Design Patterns: A JavaScript and jQuery Developer's Guide. O'Reilly Media, Inc. (2012)
36. Li, S., Tan, G.: Finding bugs in exceptional situations of JNI programs. In: Proceedings of the 16th ACM Conference on Computer and Communications Security, ser. CCS 2009, pp. 442–452. ACM, New York (2009)
37. Ayers, A., Schooler, R., Metcalf, C., Agarwal, A., Rhee, J., Witchel, E.: Traceback: first fault diagnosis by reconstruction of distributed control flow. In: ACM SIGPLAN Notices, vol. 40, no. 6, pp. 201–212. ACM (2005)
38. Mayer, P., Schroeder, A.: Cross-language code analysis and refactoring. In: 2012 IEEE 12th International Working Conference on Source Code Analysis and Manipulation, pp. 94–103. IEEE (2012)
39. Schmidt, D.C., Stal, M., Rohnert, H., Buschmann, F.: Pattern-Oriented Software Architecture, Patterns for Concurrent and Networked Objects, vol. 2. Wiley (2013)
40. Sneed, H.M.: Migrating from cobol to java. In: 2010 IEEE International Conference on Software Maintenance, pp. 1–7. IEEE (2010)
41. Fowler, M.: Strangler application (2004). https://martinfowler.com/bliki/StranglerFigApplication.html
42. Abidi, M., Khomh, F., Guéhéneuc, Y.-G.: Anti-patterns for multi-language systems. In: Proceedings of the 24th European Conference on Pattern Languages of Programs, pp. 1–14 (2019)
43. Abidi, M., Grichi, M., Khomh, F., Guéhéneuc, Y.-G.: Code smells for multi-language systems. In: Proceedings of the 24th European Conference on Pattern Languages of Programs, pp. 1–13 (2019)

Pattern Language for Lightweight and Interactive Software Analytics Process

Joelma Choma[1]([✉]) [iD], Tiago Silva da Silva[2] [iD], and Eduardo M. Guerra[3] [iD]

[1] Federal University of São Carlos - UFSCAR, Sorocaba, SP, Brazil
jh.choma@hotmail.com
[2] Federal University of São Paulo - UNIFESP, São José dos Campos, SP, Brazil
[3] Free University of Bozen-Bolzano, Bozen-Bolzano, BZ, Italy

Abstract. Software analytics is a data-driven approach to decision-making, which allows software practitioners to leverage valuable insights from data about software to achieve higher development process productivity and improve many aspects of the software quality. Although widely adopted by large companies, software analytics has not yet reached its full potential for broad industrial adoption. Usually, software practitioners do not use analytics of data generated during the software development process to inform their decisions. Decisions based on practitioners' feelings and intuition can lead to wasted resources and increase the cost of building and maintaining the software. This paper presents a Pattern Language for supporting software analytics activities implementation in practice. The proposed patterns focus on recurring solutions about how to incorporate software analytics on an interactive and continuous basis to inform the decision-making process of software practitioners. The main contribution of patterns is to encourage and guide the software teams to develop software analytics activities lightly so as not to disrupt the production process.

Keywords: software quality · software analytics · software measurement · software metric · software data

1 Introduction

More and more companies around the world are looking for data information to make decisions about their business with the primary goal of becoming more competitive. For some years now, data analytics has been widely used in marketing to achieve and better understand customer behavior and consumption patterns. Analytics is related to the use of analysis, data, and systematic reasoning to make better decisions [14].

In recent years, the application of analytics in software development has also become increasingly popular due to the growing complexity of software projects. Software Analytics (SA) allows software practitioners (developers,

E. Wallingford et al. (Eds.): TPLOP V, LNCS 14630, pp. 162–189, 2025.
https://doi.org/10.1007/978-3-662-70810-1_4

testers, designers, and managers, to name a few) to leverage insightful information (accurate and in-depth) and actionable (with real practical value) for completing various tasks around software systems, software users, and software development processes [58].

Although widely adopted by large companies, software analytics has not yet reached its full potential for broad industrial adoption. For small companies, software analytics is an open question and rarely addressed [44]. Furthermore, to the best of our knowledge, there is no consolidated approach regarding how to introduce software analytics concepts and practices into an agile development context.

Focusing on delivering value, changes for agile teams are the opportunity to improve the product at any time in the development process [5]. In this sense, software analytics can support agile teams to make more appropriate changes based on actual data, rather than only on their personal experiences or intuitions. Process improvement is one of the main reasons for measurement in agile software development, as long as it is immediate and straightforward [25]. Metrics can be used to assess different aspects in agile projects [15,16]. While software metrics are parameters for measuring a certain aspect or attribute of software, software analytics is a broader approach, as it encompasses monitoring and understanding of software data through analytical reasoning on top of the results of a measurement that may have involved a set of metrics [46,57].

In the last years, many tools were developed to support data-driven software improvement process. However, the complexity and effort required to set up such tools often discourage the agile teams to establish a measurement program to track their development processes [29]. If on the one hand there is a lack of tools to facilitate the implementation of software analytics, on the other hand, many teams – under pressure due to the lack of time and the urgency of the product delivery – still need to be convinced of the gains of making decisions informed in software data. To successfully implement a software analytics process, our research was based on the following assumptions: (1) every measurement should be done for a reason; (2) all members of the development team need to be aware of the software analytics process; (3) the software project cannot be stopped just to implement the software analytics; and (4) the expected results of the analytics should be decisions and actions, rather than data only.

Considering software analytics an essential practice for leveraging value delivery in agile software development contexts, we conducted a systematic mapping study in the literature to identify typical issues addressed to that field, as well as practices on how to incorporate software analytics activities, on an interactive and continuous basis. Based on some third-party reports obtained from the literature, as well as our own experience working with software practitioners, we drew a set of candidate patterns for supporting software analytics implementation into agile contexts, which were previously presented and discussed at Conferences on Pattern Languages of Programs [10,11].

In this paper, we present the complete set of SA patterns documented in a pattern language. Although the software analytics tasks can be labor-intensive, we have drawn this pattern language to provide a lightweight and interactive software analytics process in adherence to the rapid iteration pace of agile environments. Our intended audience is software practitioners—including project managers, analysts, and software developers from small, large, or multiple teams.

2   Background

2.1   Software Analytics

The SA process comprehends monitoring, analysis, and understanding of software data to support the decision-making process throughout the different phases of the software lifecycle [57]. By software data, we mean the data generated from source code, bug reports, and test executions recorded in software repositories such as version control systems and issue-tracking systems, as well as the information about usage data typically stored in the log files [46].

In a software development context, many decisions related to a software system (e.g., allocation of development and test resources) can be based on software data analysis. However, software practitioners – owners, maintainers, and developers – tend to make many daily decisions based on their experience, feelings, and intuitions – e.g., determining which parts of software need to increase test coverage, or which parts of software should be refactored. Often, the lack of accurate information to support the decisions of professionals can lead to a waste of resources and an increase in the cost of building and maintaining the software [26].

Analytics has been used in software data to address a different type of concerns, such as issues related to the source code quality [9], bug proneness, number of defects, and amount of effort to fix bugs [41,50], productivity and ROI [44,53], software evolution [20], software runtime properties (e.g., performance, number of transactions and error log) [1,36], and users' behavior [38]. However, as far as we know, no previous study has presented patterns addressing the implementation of software analytics, nor related patterns for similar practices in agile teams.

2.2   Patterns in Software Analytics Area

In our literature review, we found few studies on patterns related to specific domains of software analytics. McGrath et al. [32] identified a pattern to trace code changes from user requests to change implementation by analyzing mailing lists and code repositories called CONCEPT TO COMMIT. First, they suggest how to reduce the volume of data, and then how to analyze both emails and commits descriptions using basic text mining by performing the steps: tokenization, stemming, and document matrix creation. For this activity, they indicated some tools such as RapidMiner[1] or any statistical software program like R software[2] Finally, frequency analysis can be performed using word cloud, heat map, or a dendrogram chart. This pattern suggests solutions to a very common problem within the context of *software analytics* that involves the analysis of unstructured data.

Giger and Gall [19] presented a pattern called EFFECT SIZE ANALYSIS related to significance testing used to determine whether the collected data support or not the researchers' hypothesis. They describe how significance testing can be extended by an analysis of the magnitude. This pattern is indicated for researchers want to draw more general conclusions and valid results using a restricted data subset. By addressing issues in the context of statistical decision making, researchers could rethink costly actions in response to such a comparatively small effect size.

Souza et al. [47] identified two patterns for recurring problems related to cleaning up invalid bug data – LOOK OUT FOR MASS UPDATES and OLD WINE TASTES BETTER [47]. Both patterns provide best practices to deal with missing or inaccurate data stored in bug tracking systems. The first pattern is indicated to determine which changes to bug reports were the result of a mass update, while the second one is to determine bug reports that are too recent to be classified.

Baysal et al. [4] introduced a pattern called ARTIFACT LIFECYCLE MODEL to facilitate the analysis of software artifacts and its evolution throughout development. Such models are used to capture the dynamic nature of how certain development artifacts changed over time. For example, the status of the tasks, modifications to lines of code, or bugs fixing status.

The patterns mentioned above were proposed primarily to support data analysis activities. That is, their scopes do not cover other activities concerning software analytics projects. As we mentioned earlier, data analysis is just part of the process that aims to generate insights and support decisions. In addition to analysis, software analytics activities also rely on gathering, measuring and monitoring, and visualizing information [8]. Moreover, we can notice that the mentioned patterns address data analysis from a more technological perspective. In contrast, the patterns documented in this study are focused on a human perspective with respect to the decision-making process.

3   Pattern Language Overview

Patterns are for capturing successful solutions to recurring problems by documenting experiences. In general, patterns describe the context for the problem, and the forces that weigh upon the problem-solver and suggest a proven solution to it [43]. However, patterns can be written in various forms. In this work, we adopted a most usual way based on Christopher Alexander style [2]. The pattern writing format adopted is composed of the following elements:

– Name: a short description or a single significant word.

---

[1] Source: https://rapidminer.com/.
[2] Source: https://www.r-project.org/.

- Context: where the pattern might apply.
- Problem: what problem could be solved with the pattern.
- Forces: considerations on constraints/limitations conflicting with the goals.
- Solution: what to do to solve the problem, how to achieve the goal.
- Examples: one or more applications using the pattern.
- Consequences: positive and negative effects of applying the pattern.
- Known uses: it describes known uses that confirm the pattern recurrence.
- Related patterns: patterns that are dealing with correlated issues.

Next, we provide a summary of the solutions of the eight patterns focused on solutions about how to embed software analytics activities into an agile context, further detailed in the next section.

(1) WHAT YOU NEED TO KNOW - Define the key issues that the team wants to focus on and introduce improvements regarding software throughout the process.
(2) CHOOSE THE MEANS - Define the most appropriate means, such as metrics, tools, techniques, and other approaches for extracting software data that will be useful for informing your decisions.
(3) PLAN ANALYTICS IMPLEMENTATION - Plan software analytics activities by adding the associated tasks in the backlog and then prioritizing them along with the regular project tasks over time.
(4) SMALL STEPS FOR ANALYTICS - Estimate the size and complexity of the software analytics tasks and adjust them within the team roadmap by breaking them down into smaller portions to be conducted in multi-steps.
(5) REACHABLE GOALS - Take insights and define reachable goals to plan further actionable steps from the software analytics findings.
(6) LEARNING FROM EXPERIMENTS - Conduct experiments to test hypotheses by comparing possible solutions to solve existing software issues.
(7) DEFINE QUALITY STANDARDS - Define quality standards by establishing minimal or maximum thresholds for any software aspect that the team intends to track for a while.
(8) SUSPEND MEASUREMENT - Put the measurements on standby that have already fulfilled their initial objective, or those that are costly to monitor continuously, or those that do not represent a value for the team at that moment.

These patterns could be applied in isolation. Nonetheless, patterns are commonly applied together from a language to solve a given problem. The group of interconnected patterns that fit together and fully address a topic or specific domain is named *pattern language* [7]. Figure 1 presents an overview of our pattern language for the software analytics domain. In this figure, the SA patterns are presented in a way that shows how they relate to each other. The blocks in black refer to the patterns representing steps recommended for the implementation of software analytics. The dashed blocks represent the expected outputs from the application of the patterns. And, the questions included among the patterns refer to factor that motivates the application of the pattern.

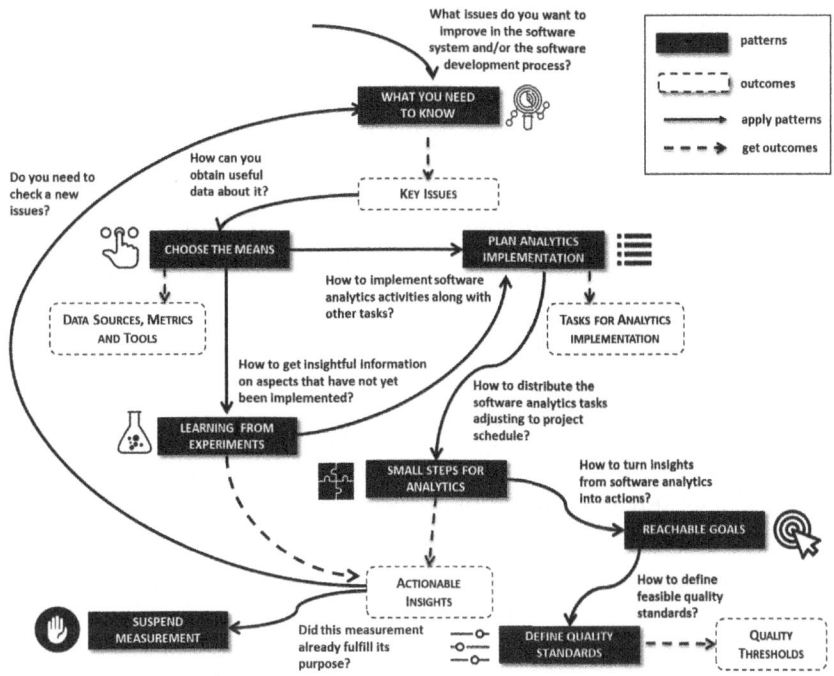

Fig. 1. Overview of the patterns and their relationships.

According to our pattern language, the first step towards implementing the software analytics process is to define WHAT YOU NEED TO KNOW. After that, to answer the raised issues, the team needs to CHOOSE THE MEANS that will be used for data gathering and analysis. LEARNING FROM EXPERIMENTS can be a way of testing a particular solution that the team is not sure is the best way from a practical standpoint. During the SOFTWARE ANALYTICS PLANNING, the team plans the analytics activities and prioritizes the tasks in their to-do list along with other development tasks.

Because analytics activities can be time-consuming, the team does not have to deploy them at once. Then, the team can set SMALL STEPS FOR ANALYTICS, according to the delivery schedule. Based on actionable insights, the team needs to define REACHABLE IMPROVEMENT GOALS to implement the improvements in software or its development process. Towards continuous improvement, the team DEFINE QUALITY STANDARDS to guide their improvement actions. The team can apply the pattern SUSPEND MEASUREMENT when measurements no longer make sense or when they have other priorities at the moment.

4 Software Analytics Patterns

4.1 What you Need to Know

Also known as Focus on Key Issues, Highlight Your Questions, What You Want to Improve
Development teams know that metrics and other kinds of information can be extracted from their systems to support decision-making. Development activities generate a large amount of data. Various software artifacts including source code, bug reports, commit history, test executions, etc. could provide valuable insights about software projects. Several tools can extract such data from the development environment at runtime. Although teams are aware of the existence of software data to be explored, they often do not know where to start to leverage it in their software improvement activities.

How can we employ software analytics to improve the software aspects and/or our development process?

– Software practitioners produce different data-rich software artifacts, but they usually do not use the data to support their decisions.
– Many tools were developed to support the software analytics deployment, but most of them can be time-consuming to install and configure.
– For many development teams, it may be difficult to start a software analytics project because of lack of time, but they need to consider their benefits for software improvement.
– Some tools can generate a huge amount of data by default from the development environment at runtime, but the team should just focus on the data that will be useful to solve a given issue.

Therefore:

Define the key issues that the development team wants to focus on, to improve the software throughout the project.

During the development of the product, issues around software aspects arise to be solved. The team frequently makes decisions to solve them based on experiences and intuitions. However, the team may not have enough information to solve a given issue. Such an issue can be related to the structure of the source code, the development process, or the business rules. By defining the key issues that need to be addressed, the team can focus on efforts to solve them through a data-driven investigation to obtain meaningful information to support any decisions.

Some decisions might lead to one-time action, for instance, when the team needs to prioritize the implementation of an architectural component to improve the system's performance. Or it might be a series of continuous decisions and actions that need to be performed through the iterations, such as for what part of the system we need to prioritize refactoring. A guiding question at this stage could be "What should we measure now?"

As an example, imagine that a development team wants to improve their tests and needs to decide where in the system they should put their effort. Using WHAT YOU NEED TO KNOW, *a possible question highlighted by the development team might be "What data is required to verify software test adequacy?". By answering this question, the team can avoid unnecessary data gathering, and plan better on how to collect useful data to investigate the issue.*

As a consequence, the team will understand the reason behind the data being collected, making better use of them. Additionally, unnecessary data will not be collected and will not take away the focus of the team on what is more important. Sometimes, tools can detect unexpected problems based on measurements that do not have a known reason. Focusing only on a subset of that information, the team can fail to notice a potential problem.

⋄ ⋄ ⋄

Jian-Guang Lou et al. formulated questions about incident-management as a software-analytics problem [30]. *For them, incident management of an online service requires the service provider to take action immediately to resolve the incident, since the cost of each hour's service downtime is high. As the use of debuggers to conduct diagnosis on services is usually impracticable, the teams need to highlight other questions to detect anomalies and quality issues at runtime of the service.*

Robert L. Nord et al. presented a series of questions related to measurement and analysis for software architecture and about how to meet the business goals of software [37]. *According to them, there is an increasing need to provide ongoing insight into the quality of the system being developed. Thus, the team's questions might be, for instance, about how to improve feedback between development and deployment through means to measure intrinsic quality, value, and cost. In the case presented by Gregorio Robles et al., the information about the development effort invested in a project was considered a business strategy* [45]. *And, the question highlighted by the development team was related to how to obtain software development estimations with a bounded margin of error.*

⋄ ⋄ ⋄

The pattern FIND ESSENTIAL QUALITIES [56] focused on quality assurance is linked to this pattern. Since software analytics is not just addressed to solve quality issues, our pattern also encompasses other software aspects, from the development process to business requirements. As an example of supporting strategic and tactical decisions, an issue to solve could be the need for a reduction in the overwork of developers. After defining WHAT YOU NEED TO KNOW, in the next step, the team needs to CHOOSE THE MEANS to solve the related issue.

4.2   Choose the Means

Also known as Approach to Answer, Choose the most Appropriate Means, Choose the Right Means
To solve the issues around WHAT YOU NEED TO KNOW, the team can conduct a data-driven investigation by collecting data related to such issues to support their decisions. If software practitioners trust only in their experiences and intuitions, they risk having a bad experience in the future because chose the wrong path. There is a plethora of data that can be collected from the development environment at runtime, which could provide concrete evidence and reasons to inform decision-making.

How can you extract useful data regarding the issues that you need to solve?

– The team can solve some problems based on their experience and intuition, but not always that decisions will be based on true premises.
– Some needs for change and improvement in software can be difficult to justify to stakeholders, but an analysis of these issues based on actual data can strengthen the team's arguments.
– Different data mining tools and methods can be used to discover patterns in large data sets, but the team needs to know which of them is most appropriate for each case.
– Several tools can extract data from different types of software artifacts, but such tools need to be properly configured to extract useful data.

Therefore:

Define the most appropriate means, such as metrics, tools, techniques, and other approaches for extracting data from software artifacts that will be useful in future decisions.

Focusing on the issue that should be solved, the developers can identify data that are useful in providing concrete evidence to support their decisions. This data can come from different sources – e.g., development tools, software repositories, issue-tracking systems, etc. As an example, developers could retrieve information about execution time from the software components to verify points that should be modified aimed at improving the performance of the system. As another example, commit history for bug correction, object-oriented metrics, and frequency of modification could be used to explore which parts of source code need to be prioritized for refactoring. Yet another example could be an analysis of usage data logs for estimating the impact of a new feature.

After identifying what data is needed to explore a given issue, the team needs to find tools and/or approaches that can be used to extract them from the system. There may be ready-to-use tools, but sometimes the team will have to develop their tool to retrieve data in a more specific scenario. Note that, at the first moment, the team will not yet have to implement any method or setting any tool, but only identify and define the more appropriate instruments for both data collection and analysis.

A few steps can be needed to extract accurate information from the raw data initially collected. Sometimes, raw data need to be filtered, interpreted, or yet combined with other information to meet WHAT YOU NEED TO KNOW. However, the approach for this does not need to be defined at this point, but it is important to discuss what kind of information do you expect to have at the end. At this stage, the team thinks about "How should we measure?"

Considering the running example, the development team wants to improve their tests and needs to decide where they should put their effort. By using CHOOSE THE MEANS, *developers defined that they needed to extract two kinds of information: the testing coverage values and the number of commits that modified each class. From this information, they intend to prioritize classes that are highly modified and that have low test coverage. To collect testing coverage data, they can use a test coverage tool that is available in their continuous integration environment. However, they do not know a ready-to-use tool to count the commits for each class. A viable solution could be to create a script to collect and record such data in a CSV file for further analysis. In the next step, the team will need to analyze classes with low test coverage and with a high modification frequency.*

As a consequence, the team can have an overview of how they can obtain concrete evidence for a decision. From this overview, they could consider whether it is worth following a software analytics approach by weighing the cost of the decision and the penalty for choosing the wrong alternative. Stakeholders would be able to understand better technical tasks and their impact on data analytics results. However, this process might consume precious time from the team, taking away the focus from the main software development tasks.

◇ ◇ ◇

According to Stella Pachidi et al., the collecting of usage data logs is an important means to monitor which applications are being most often used, which features were underutilized, and which features could be improved [38]. *Usage data can provide valuable information about how end-users are using the software, and whether the services are meeting their needs.*

Luigi Cerulo et al. proposed extracting data from developers' communication – as contained in emails, issue trackers, and forums – to improve the software development process [9].

Suonsyrjä et al. proposed a framework to support practitioners in finding a suitable technological approach for automated collecting of usage data within the process of data-driven software development [49].

◇ ◇ ◇

The pattern MEASURABLE SYSTEM QUALITIES [56] is related to this pattern especially when the issues are related to software quality. The most common quality attributes are performance, reliability, and usability. However, any internal or external attributes related to process, business, and/or resources (e.g., effort, number of coding faults found, cost-effectiveness, communication level, system structure, etc.) can be objects of measurement to solve an open issue addressed with software analytics. Moreover, the measurements can be used for both software evaluation and prediction. Note that, some attributes may be relatively easy to measure, while others may be difficult or costly to measure. After CHOOSE THE MEANS to investigate WHAT YOU NEED TO KNOW, in the next step, the team should PLAN ANALYTICS IMPLEMENTATION based on issues to solve.

4.3   Plan Analytics Implementation

Also known as Analytics in the Backlog, Software Analytics Planning
Towards understanding factors or causes contributing to the unwanted situation related to the software project, the team has already discussed which data is required for answering their questions and which means will be used in the process of collecting and analyzing. The team may encounter, however, some resistance from stakeholders because a task that is not related to the implementation of the software functionality may consume precious time and delay the project. On the other hand, it may be difficult to explain to the stakeholders that the number of unresolved software issues can also grow over time.

How to carry out the software analytics activities along with other development tasks?

- Software analytics tasks such as the implementation of methods and configuration of tools for data collection and analysis can be time-consuming, but the team does not have to do everything all at once.
- Tasks related to extracting and analyzing data can be planned along with development tasks, but it cannot take the team's attention off their delivery schedule.
- Data analytics can provide valuable information to help solve issues related to technical debts, but improvement actions will also need to be scheduled.
- Software analytics results surely lead to better decisions, but the cost of implementing it cannot be greater than the added value.

Therefore:

Plan analytics implementation by adding tasks related to the software analytics in the backlog to be prioritized with the regular project tasks.

The tasks identified when the team used the pattern CHOOSE THE MEANS should be planned. Tasks related to the extraction, filtering, and analysis of data should be estimated and prioritized. At this point, the team needs to consider whether the cost of implementing software analytics will not be greater than the value added to the product after the possible improvements.

Many analytics tasks can be selectively performed throughout the project, or when the decision-making is required. For instance, considering a decision that will be necessary to be made in two months, the implementation of analytics to support that decision is not a priority for the next iteration, then it can be postponed. At this stage, a guiding question could be "How should we plan the measurement?"

In the running example, developers want accurate information to improve the testing process. They chose means to investigate the testing coverage and the number of commits that modified each class. As part of the planning, they estimated the time for installing the tool for measuring test coverage and found that it would not consume much time. However, they would take considerable time to create the script for extracting the most modified classes, as well as to make a crossover analysis of the coverage data with the modified classes. Since the number of classes was not yet large at the moment, the team along with stakeholders decided to add only the task of setting the test coverage tool to the next iteration. Hence, the script creation task and data crossover analysis remained in the project backlog because were not considered a priority at that point.

As a consequence, the activities of software analytics will be planned and prioritized in the to-do list along with development tasks. Since tasks will be distributed throughout the project, it may be easier to manage the project without the risk of delays. However, some analytics tasks defined with low priority are at risk of remaining in the backlog indefinitely and never being done. To avoid this, the stakeholders need to be aware of how that effort can bring value to the project.

◇ ◇ ◇

Defect prediction is one common application of software analytics. Taneli Taipale et al. reported the challenges of deploying a defect prediction model into practice [51]. They proposed a defect prediction model based on different modes of information representative of the data, such as a commit hotness ranking, an error probability mapping, and an approach to the visualization of interactions among teams.

Antonio Gonzalez-Torres et al. focused on software maintenance issues that required the comprehension of project details [21]. Thus, they proposed a visual software analytics tool for the exploration and comparison of project structural, interface implementation, class hierarchy data, and the correlation of structural data with metrics, as well as socio-technical relationships.

Minelli and Lanza developed a visual web-based software analytics platform for mobile applications [35]. This tool supports the mining task and uses a set of visualization techniques to facilitate the data analysis task.

⋄ ⋄ ⋄

This pattern can be complemented with the SYSTEM QUALITY DASHBOARDS [56] pattern since it refers to a solution that facilitates the monitoring of the software measurements. By adopting dashboards, the team can visually identify potential risks at runtime and plan action to solve or mitigate them. After PLAN THE ANALYTICS IMPLEMENTATION, the team may resolve to perform SMALL STEPS FOR ANALYTICS, one at a time.

4.4   Small Steps for Analytics

Also known as Analytics Tasks in Multi-steps, Analytics in Small Steps
While recognizing the value of software analytics, the team's priority is always to develop the target software. Some tasks to implement a software analytics project can be extremely complex. Software measurement implementation, the configuration of the tools in the development environment, and data analysis can be time-consuming. The set of software data can provide valuable information, but it can be hard to analyze and interpret. Receiving much information at once, the team may not be able to turn it into information with real practical value (actionable) promptly.

How to implement software analytics at a pace that does not over-burden the team?

- Because of the tight schedule, the team may not have time to implement software analytics tasks, but they are aware that technical debts tend to accumulate and make the situation more complicated.
- Some tools in default configuration may generate a lot of information about the system, but the team is not able to handle so much information at once.
- It is important to keep an overview of the software analytics project and have a plan step-by-step outlined from beginning to end, but the team can go back and re-evaluate the tasks' priorities whenever necessary.
- There may be big and complex analytics tasks to be done in a short period, but breaking such tasks into smaller tasks helps everyone on the team stay on schedule.

Therefore:

Adjust software analytics tasks within the team schedule by breaking them down into smaller portions to be carried out in multi-steps.

By using the pattern to PLAN ANALYTICS IMPLEMENTATION, the team will have an overview of the analytics tasks and planning of how to perform them step by step. Certain tasks, however, can be complex and time-consuming. The team cannot take additional commitments on analytics that compromise their delivery schedule. However, the team would be postponing the solution of a relevant issue or failing to settle a technical debt when postponing any software analytics task. Instead, the team defines SMALL STEPS FOR ANALYTICS breaking down complex tasks into smaller portions to be carried out in multi-steps. This strategy can help to avoid delays and increase team satisfaction with the task done.

Some analytics tools have built-in features to support the monitoring of diverse software aspects collected from different sources. Such tools can generate a lot of information for developers at once. It will take much more time and effort to manipulate a great amount of information. In order not to overcharge the team with excessive and unnecessary information, the tool can be set to provide only specific information to complete a prioritized task. At this stage, the guide question is "How are we going to perform the measurement tasks?"

Considering the running example, the team decided to implement the Sonar-Qube[3] that can produce a test coverage report integrated into the continuous integration server. This tool can generate many other kinds of information, such as object-oriented metrics and bad practice detection. Based on this pattern, the team decided to disable the extraction of other kinds of information that would not be used by the team right now. Moving on to other tasks, other tool features might be enabled in the next iterations.

As a consequence, the team can move forward with the software analytics project without harming other development activities. Little by little, they will be able to solve key issues and decrease technical debts based on accurate information. However, critical problems can be detected late due to a slower project pace. Moreover, measurements that have been paused to avoid an overload of information might be needed to support other decisions.

◇ ◇ ◇

Olga Baysal et al. argued that modern issue tracking systems provide an immense amount of raw information that sometimes is irrelevant in a given situation [3]. They suggest personalized development tools that highlight only the most important information for developers by reducing information overload.

Pinto et al. proposed a tool that provides architectural compliance checking as part of the continuous integration process [39]. When violations are detected, this tool can lock the integration to the software repository.

Regarding useful information, Turhan and Kuutti state that a simpler analysis to answer a simpler question can provide more actionable insights to the team than a more complex alternative [52].

◇ ◇ ◇

The PLAN ANALYTICS IMPLEMENTATION pattern is related to this pattern because having an overview of the project is necessary to manage tasks and adjust them to fit the team schedule. Following this pattern, the team can review

---

[3] https://www.sonarqube.org.

and prioritize tasks as needed. Also, the amount of information can be controlled. As SMALL STEPS FOR ANALYTICS are executed, the team can set REACHABLE GOALS to put into practice the solutions that emerge from their findings.

4.5   Reachable Goals

Also known as Actionable Insights, Achievable Targets
Metrics indicate that always something could be better. Through an automated analytics tool, the team can detect several points of improvement. However, faced with many issues to solve, the team is a risk of losing focus on what they wish to achieve. Moreover, they can have the sensation that are not moving forward when they fail to reach the minimum quality boundaries set far above reality.

How to improve software aspects from software analytics measurements so that the team realizes that they are making progress with their actions?

- Software analytics can generate a lot of interesting insights, but the team needs to set clear and actionable goals they want to achieve.
- The team can identify many points of improvement from the analysis of software data, but they may lose focus on what are the project priorities when setting many goals.
- The result from analytics can identify a huge number of existing issues to fix, but not all issues can be solved right away, given the tight team's schedule.
- An ambitious goal can be achieved, but sometimes it takes it can take a long time, and the team may have the feeling that they are not evolving concerning the improvement issues.

Therefore:

Analyze the measurement findings, identify actionable insights to improve software aspects, and set goals that can be achieved in the short term.

Based on ideas emerging from software analytics with real practical value, the team should define the goals they want to achieve. For bolder goals, the team must adjust the action steps needed to achieve them. This prevents the team from becoming unmotivated every time they can't reach a goal. Both team and stakeholders should realize the benefits of software analytics taking into account implemented improvements actions. At this stage, the guiding question is "How can we plan our improvement actions for the short term?"

It is worthwhile noting that an improvement action sometimes does not have to be fully implemented in a single iteration. That is, the improvement actions can be planned to be carried out in multiple steps. For each step, the team sets achievable goals adjusted to their delivery schedule.

Considering the running example, imagine that through software analytics the team found three controllers modified frequently that had less than 20% code coverage. Now, the team can prioritize which classes need test coverage more urgently. However, the tests might be gradually implemented when, for example, this activity involves many features. As a reachable goal, the team defined to increase their code coverage to at least 50% in the next iteration. To evaluate the effects of their actions and manage the work in progress, the team decided to keep this issue in continuous monitoring.

As a consequence, the development team ends up establishing a culture of continuous improvement. By balancing the amount of work in progress, the team avoids accumulating uncompleted work. Sometimes, the team may not be able to deal with the extra amount of work needed to act on software analytics insights and take advantage of its benefits. And, if this work is not well planned, the technical debt may even increase rather than reduce.

◇ ◇ ◇

Haron and Syed-Mohamad proposed a plug-in for IDE that integrates test coverage, number of defects, number of unresolved defects, defects severity, and lines of codes, aiming to provide an analytical view for practitioners to assess and validate the testing results [24].

As to continuously monitoring and measuring activities, Rodrigo Souza et al. noted that improving automated testing tools and using integration repositories are two measures that can improve any project [48]. *However, they pointed out the importance of easier access to up-to-date information about the process, to evaluate the impact of yet-to-be-made decisions.*

As a practice of continuous inspection, Guerra and Aniche have recommended the use of static and dynamic analysis tools that retrieve information about important quality attributes from the source code, such as test coverage, complexity, and decoupling [23]. *Based on this information, the developers continuously can evaluate and refactoring small portions of code – one piece at a time.*

◇ ◇ ◇

A related pattern is CHUNKING [54] which shows how to analyze the set of changes made to a software system over time. This analysis aimed at identifying sets of code that have the property that a change that touches a chunk touches only that chunk. This pattern may be useful to help the team coordinate and optimize its improvement actions. In this pattern, authors provided an algorithm to identify uncoupled pieces of software (chunks) where each one represents a module on which an individual or a small team can work independently. In addition to defining REACHABLE GOALS, the team can also DEFINE QUALITY STANDARDS to track ongoing software improvements.

4.6 Learning from Experiments

Also known as Run Experiments, Measure with Experiments
The issues that emerge in software analytics can be related to different needs. At the development process level, the team may need to evaluate for instance new methods, tools, or practices. At the product level, the team may need to evaluate the requirements, features, or usage data. At the user experience level, they may need to evaluate product usability, user satisfaction, design aspects, etc. Some of these issues can be investigated through data collected from the development environment and software artifacts such as source code, bug reports, test cases, usage logs, documentation, etc. For other issues, however, the team may need to evaluate the usability of a feature that has not yet been implemented. Even further, the team may have implemented a feature that needs to be improved but does not know how to improve it. In both these situations, the team has nowhere yet to collect and analyze data to support their decisions.

How can we obtain information to make informed decisions about software issues on some aspect we have not yet implemented or we need to redesign?

- The team often has more than one way of implementing the same feature, using different methods and tools for development, and adopting different alternatives of architectural design, but they need to seek to make their choices as successful as possible.
- Sometimes the team makes a decision that will be simple to reverse if it does not work out, but some solutions are worth experimenting with before implementation to avoid wasting resources and rework.
- Experiments can fail, but the team can improve the experiment design by analyzing what went wrong.
- Sometimes, experiments can produce inconsistent results, but the team can investigate the cause of such inconsistencies and then conduct new experiments if they prove feasible.

Therefore:

Create an alternative solution and perform an experiment collecting data that allows the comparison with the current solution.

Experiments allow us to test our hypotheses for better decision-making. Results from experiments can provide us with relevant information to find the best alternatives for design, tools, approaches to development, and test methods, among others. Through experiments, we can compare two different approaches, where the control group can be an existing solution in use. That is, we can verify whether an idea is promising or it makes no sense to continue with it. At this stage, a guiding question could be "How should we test our ideas?"

Experiments can have a low cost of implementation. However, before opting for experimentation, the team always needs to weigh the cost of doing one or more experiments with the cost of re-engineering or redesigning after you implement something. The team needs to have a clear purpose for the experiment and have a reasonable hypothesis to test. The experimental design should be carefully planned, and the experimenters should know which aspects of the software or process will be observed.

During the experimental design planning, the team should be especially careful also to defining the experiment size, as large experiments can be costly and unfeasible. Both ROI and the time to implement an experiment are important factors to be considered by the team before adopting them. Sometimes experiments may not work out, and sometimes they can produce conflicting or unclear results. When an experiment does not provide useful information or has unclear results, the team decides if new experiments should be carried out from the lessons learned. Replicating an experiment may be impractical depending on its cost and size. Small experiments tend to be cheaper and easier to replicate. About experimenting and learning, worth taking into consideration Linda Rising's advice:

> *"You can't realistically plan anything from the beginning; the only way to reach your long-term goals or solve your big problems is to try a small thing and learn from the experience. That's how we have always learned. Babies do this from the start. It's the basis for the scientific approach. Experiment and learn."* [42]

As an example, imagine that a development team wants to increase the number of hits/clicks on related products in an e-commerce application. Currently, in this application, the products are merely recommended according to the category. The team has the following idea: an algorithm to recommend products that were recently bought with the product being searched. Additionally, the team wants to rearrange products on the user interface. They do not know how much it will be pleasing to the end-user. To save time and effort, the team develops some prototypes and runs an experiment with a limited number of users, representing the target audience. From the experiment results, they were able to know which was the best option for the user interface redesign.

As a consequence, the results of experimentation can produce insightful information about the product or the development process, that is, the reliable and valuable knowledge needed to make better decisions. Sometimes, team members can be biased in how they interpret the results of an experiment. If it doesn't produce the results they expect, they may discount the results or find ways to invalidate the experiment. Other times, the results of an experiment may be inconclusive. In that case, the team must decide whether to perform another experiment to pick among equally viable options. Also, an experiment can provide misleading information which did not test the hypothesis. In that case, the team may have to spend time figuring out why something you thought would improve the system did not.

◇ ◇ ◇

Kim et al. *investigated the competencies and working styles of data scientists in software-oriented data analytics context* [28]. *They reported an increase in the randomized two-variant experiments called A/B testing to assess the requirements and utility of new software features. Because of numerous possibilities for alternative software designs, data scientists along with engineering teams have built software systems to inject the changes, called flighting.*

Gousios et al. [22] *introduced the concept of streaming software analytics and proposed a data analytics infrastructure that unifies the representation of historical and current data as streams and enables high-level aggregation and summarization using a common query. This approach can facilitate the execution of experiments, as well as data collection and correlation of the results of applying specific design and development decisions and their outcomes.*

Liechti et al. *introduced the idea of test analytics to help an agile development team improve their test process* [29]. *Focusing on collaborative practices, they organized a series of workshops to train the team and started with small experiments on simple features which allowed them to evaluate and select a set of tools and to create a collection of examples.*

◇ ◇ ◇

BUILD PROTOTYPES [13] is a related pattern that highlights the usefulness of prototypes in experiments to understand requirements, validate requirements with customers, explore human/computer interactions for the system, or explore the cost and benefits of design decisions. EARLY VALIDATIONS is another pattern addressed for software startups [33]. In that pattern, experiments are performed to validate or reject an initial hypothesis and make decisions about the direction of the project based on acquired knowledge. LEARNING FROM EXPERIMENTS is a way to test ideas and possible solutions in response to WHAT YOU NEED TO KNOW.

4.7   Define Quality Standards

Also known as Define Quality Boundaries, Set Quality Thresholds
By using an analytics approach, the team collects data about a given issue. From the analysis of data, they discuss possible solutions and have insights to take action on. Based on these insights, the team defines which goals they want to achieve concerning critical issues. The improvement actions more audacious can be implemented in a stepwise fashion. However, the team needs to establish milestones to achieve the goals and evaluate the impact of the changes.

How you can achieve and maintain a good level of quality for important software aspects?

– By analyzing software data, developers can make better decisions about improving the development process and software quality, but the quality of some aspects will need to be continuously monitored.

- The culture of continuous improvement is stimulated by achieved goals and the satisfaction of stakeholders, but it may not be easy to convince stakeholders about the tradeoffs of continuous inspection.
- The process of continuous improvement helps sustain the software evolution and maintenance; the team must have reachable goals and define quality standards.

Therefore:

Define quality standards and then establish minimal or maximum thresholds for any software aspect that the team intends to monitor.

When investigating a given issue, the team might obtain information needed to take steps to solve it based on actual data. To maintain the quality achieved, some software aspects can be monitored longer. For this purpose, the quality metrics can assess software aspects such as code quality, testing coverage, performance, bug fixing, productivity, and user satisfaction.

Following a quality standard, the team should establish quality thresholds for aspects that they want to monitor. Quality thresholds can be defined whenever there is a need for continuous inspection. For example, for issues related to coverage testing, the response time cannot exceed 2 s (maximum acceptable value) or the test coverage must be at least 70% (minimum acceptable value). However, the minimum or maximum value established for an attribute should be periodically analyzed and can be redefined focusing on continuous improvement. Moreover, the team may need to make trade-offs between different software aspects – e.g., performance, security, and usability. Thus, the threshold value of an aspect can be redefined so that another aspect can work. At this stage, a guiding question could be "What are good or bad values to monitor?"

As an example, let's suppose that the team wants to automate more of their tests, but they do not know where to start, once there is an immense amount of classes. Their key issue is "Where should we focus our test efforts?". To answer this question, they identified the need to investigate two data sources: the code source to verify current test coverage, and the code repository to verify the percentage of commits related to fixing bugs and the classes with the highest number of changes to identify the classes with more problems. As data-gathering mechanisms they decided (a) to adopt SonarQube for code coverage; (b) to find a tool to collect the number of changes, and (c) to develop a script to relate commit messages with bug issues. When analyzing the collected data and looking for insights, the team found that "Web controllers have a high change rate and a low coverage" and "many changes in DAOs were related to bug fixes". Then, as part of an incremental goal, they established a minimum class coverage for Web Controllers of 60%; and minimum class coverage for DAOs of 80%. Moving forward, they set a threshold of at least 80% coverage for new classes.

As a consequence, as new requirements come in, the team is engaged in evolving the software, while maintaining a quality standard. By setting the boundary values, the team assumes a commitment to meet some pre-established quality standards. If these boundaries do not comply, the team must identify the causes because they have failed and if necessary redefine new achievable goals. Sometimes, the team attempting to reach a certain target can unknowingly fail to notice other issues.

◇ ◇ ◇

Feldt et al. [17] *reported how visualization and correlation between test and code measurements can support decisions on software quality improvements, based on a case study where heatmaps were employed to visualize and monitor changes and identify recurring patterns of an embedded control system.*

Foidl and Felderer [18] *discussed the challenges related to defect prevention and highlighted the importance of software analytics to improve the quality assurance of Internet of Things (IoT) applications. They recommend the usage of data mining algorithms and techniques (e.g., classification, association, and clustering) as well as predictive modeling to support the quality assurance of IoT solutions.*

Martínez-Fernández et al. [31] *proposed a quality model called Q-Rapids. The model encompasses four quality aspects. Maintainability, reliability, and functional suitability are quality aspects of ISO 25010 and refer to the quality of the software system, while productivity refers to the quality of the software development process. In this model, quality aspects are calculated based on product and process factors. Both product and process factors are calculated based on the assessed metrics. And, metrics are calculated from raw data, which may come from heterogeneous data sources.*

◇ ◇ ◇

The SYSTEM QUALITY DASHBOARDS pattern [56] recommends the use of dashboards to monitor important quality aspects from values established by the team. Tools for monitoring systems such as SonarCube allow you to configure alerts and notifications when measured values cross a threshold. The CONTINUOUS INSPECTION pattern [34] captures the overall practice of continuous inspection to preserve the quality of the source code and its alignment with the architecture in an agile environment. DEFINE QUALITY STANDARDS can help the team monitor their REACHABLE GOALS.

4.8 Suspend Measurement

Also known as Standby Measurement, Hold Measurement
When investigating a critical issue using software analytics, the team first performs data gathering to obtain accurate and in-depth information about it. And then, they analyze the data to find out the best way to solve that issue. In some instances, the information may be insufficient and the team will need to collect more data. Sometimes, a greater effort may be required to automate data collection and analysis when the team defines that a particular issue needs to be monitored continuously. However, there may be issues with a low likelihood of recurrence; or even issues that are no longer a priority for the team.

How the team should handle a measurement that requires additional effort to be continuously monitored but is not adding value anymore?

- It is crucial that the development team make decisions in its process based on evidence, but the software analytics activities need to be carefully planned and evaluated over time because they can consume a lot of team effort.
- Critical issues need an immediate investigation to avoid software operation failures and information inconsistency, but the team has other priorities in the project.
- A given issue that has been the subject of measurement may have achieved the primary goal and, for the next interactions new measurements will be unnecessary. Achieve a goal could be to prioritize the software maintenance tasks by identifying classes with the highest number of bugs, for example.
- Once a metric has been obtained through scripts, such as a static log analysis or a SQL query, it can be costly to add it into a continuous monitoring mechanism or to execute it frequently. The integration of this measurement in the deployment or build environment collecting live data might demand considerable effort.
- It may be difficult for the team to maintain continuous monitoring of a particular aspect of the software. However, the amount of value added may outweigh the team effort. Moreover, some tools can facilitate the process of automating reducing the effort significantly in the continuous monitoring implementation.

Therefore:

Put on standby the measurements that already fulfilled their initial goal, are costly to be continuously monitored or do not represent a value to the team at that moment.

When facing problems related to software usage, for instance, the team may need to check specific issues. The team is suspicious of some flaws in the system, but they have no idea about the dimension of the problem, nor the real impact on system operation. They decide to investigate the issue through further analysis. In one-off action, they detect the problem through software analytics. Then, they define the next steps to solve the problem and put the process used to collect and analyze information on hold. The team can suspend measurement of the issues with a low possibility of recurrence. However, some issues may need monitoring for an extended period to prevent any flaw in the system's operation. At that moment, however, the team has defined that, for some reason (e.g., effort, cost, or other project constraints), the monitoring of these issues cannot be implemented immediately.

When investigating and detecting potential problems, the team can choose metrics to monitor them continuously. But, in many cases, the team may not have a monitoring system yet, or it could be that the existing system is overloaded due to monitoring other more important issues. Or even, the monitoring system does not provide resources to monitor a particular problem. Anyway, the team will have a certain cost to prepare the monitoring system.

The cost of collecting data either manually or in a "one-off" way can also be very costly for the team. For instance, consider data extracted from the database using an SQL query or information extracted from a log analysis using a simple script. Both solutions need to be developed and implemented by the team. However, the team needs to assess the feasibility of measurement of a given issue, taking into account the list of priorities and the cost of implementation. At this stage, the guiding question is "Should we proceed with this measurement?"

As a practical example of when to SUSPEND MEASUREMENT, *let's suppose that a team is using software analytics to know about the consistency of the information stored in the database where data are provided daily (minute by minute) from a distributed sensors network. The team suspects data inconsistency caused by sensor failures, but they do not know the extent of the problem. From the analysis of data, the team has obtained evidence to prove their suspicions and make some decisions about what to do to resolve this problem. In contact with the domain experts, they discuss mechanisms to normalize the data before the information is delivered to the end-user of the application. They envisage the possibility of implementing continuous monitoring of the issue, but currently, they have other higher priorities and demands. Because of this, they decide to put the measurements on hold. As an advantage, after this experience, the team already knows how to collect and analyze sensor data any moment they need to in the future.*

As a consequence, the team should act quickly to gather evidence on issues of concern, which can have an irreparable effect if they are ignored for a long time. As an immediate action, the team can mitigate a problem by using corrective methods. In the future, they may implement preventive actions. Knowing how to do it, the team can use the same means to fix a problem when it occurs. However, the team can forever postpone a definitive solution to a problem, the installation of an alert program, or the implementation of a continuous monitoring system for the most critical issues.

◇ ◇ ◇

Shull [46] presented a discussion between two ways to handle software data. The first advocate that analysts need to be intentional and to work on what is useful, not just what is convenient to collect, and the other argue for reflecting and learning more from collected data before collecting something new.

Ram et al. [40] reported challenges faced in operationalizing metrics based on multiple case studies conducted at four Agile software companies. The main challenges found were the lack of data or appropriate tools to produce that data, the existing process inhibiting change, and difficulty in deriving actionable inputs.

Huijgens et al. [27] investigated how strong metrics for agile (Scrum) DevOps teams can be set in an iterative fashion strong agile metrics. Strong agile metrics refer to metrics with high predictive power to be able to support a highly effective monitor and control capability within a continuous delivery context.

◇ ◇ ◇

The RECALIBRATE THE LANDING ZONE pattern [56] is related to this pattern by addressing the implementation of decisions when resources are incrementally implemented. Naturally, some criteria adopted in the course of the project need to be adjusted over time. These decisions can affect or limit the ability to achieve new goals and meet other demands. Thus, measurements may be provisionally suspended and then refined in future actions. The ARCHITECTURAL TRIGGER pattern [55] suggests that when the team does not know when to evolve the architecture, they can develop architectural triggers. Similarly, the team can define triggers to warn them when a certain condition may require immediate action to treat a particular issue. If WHAT YOU NEED TO KNOW resulted in a satisfactory solution, the team can SUSPEND THE MEASUREMENT to focus on more pressing issues.

5   Conclusions

Software analytics provide means to support Agile teams gain and sharing insight from software data to understand and improve their processes. Although much research has been conducted on software analytics about how to extract, process, and visualize data, still very little has been explored about how to implement analytics in practice.

This paper presents a Pattern Language for supporting software analytics activities implementation in Agile teams in practice. The proposed patterns focus on recurring solutions about how to incorporate software analytics on an interactive and continuous basis to inform the decision-making process of software practitioners.

Considering different levels of decision-making, these patterns can address different issues by using a software analytics approach, such as the ones related to source code quality, testing methods, bug treatment, runtime software properties, reuse of components, maintenance and software evolution, development practices, teamwork and productivity, customer and requirements, user experience, and services. The key idea behind the patterns is for the team to be able to develop software analytics activities lightly in order not to hinder the production process.

The main contribution of this work is to encourage small and medium-sized Agile teams to incorporate data-based approaches into their development process to make better decisions. As a result, we have applied these patterns in the building of an artifact named Software Analytics Canvas (SA Canvas) to support Agile teams in conducting software analytics activities in software projects. Taking into account how teams communicate and collaborate in Agile contexts, the SA Canvas works as a hub in terms of information flow related to software analytics projects and a situation awareness channel, which considers how people are kept informed about what is happening [6]. Canvas artifacts are visual maps – structured and preformatted – used to support collaborative teamwork in their communication processes. The proposed canvas for software analytics is composed of seven blocks based on the pattern language presented in this work. For more details of the canvas components, see [12].

The patterns presented in this paper are the basis of our pattern language in software analytics. However, as we identify new practices, new patterns may be added to this pattern language. Recently, for instance, we empirically investigated the use of SA Canvas with experienced agile teams from two software companies and identified two new patterns that were submitted to the PLoP'21 conference. Currently, these patterns are in the publication process. Furthermore, as far as we know, there are still no sub-patterns that show specific strategies to identify key issues and means to explore the issues related to software analytics. Such sub-patterns could be investigated in future work.

Acknowledgments. We are grateful for the financial support from the Coordenação de Aperfeiçoamento de Pessoal de Nível Superior (CAPES - Brazil) - Finance Code 001. We also thank the PLoP'17 shepherd Filipe Correia and SLPLoP'18 shepherd Rebecca WirfsBrock for reviewing our patterns and giving us feedback to improve them. Furthermore, we thank all the friends we made at PLoP Conferences, especially those who gave us precious feedback at the writers' workshop, like Joseph Yoder, Lise Hvatum, Ademar Aguiar, Andreas Seitz, and Hernán Astudillo. Finally, we thank all TPLoP reviewers, whose comments and suggestions contributed to the maturity of our work.

References

1. Aalst, W.V.D.: Big software on the run: in vivo software analytics based on process mining. In: Proceedings of the 2015 International Conference on Software and System Process, pp. 1–5. ACM (2015)
2. Alexander, C.: A Pattern Language: Towns, Buildings, Construction. Oxford University Press, New York (1977)
3. Baysal, O., Holmes, R., Godfrey, M.W.: Situational awareness: personalizing issue tracking systems. In: Proceedings of the 2013 International Conference on Software Engineering, pp. 1185–1188. IEEE Press (2013)
4. Baysal, O., Kononenko, O., Holmes, R., Godfrey, M.W.: Extracting artifact life-cycle models from metadata history. In: 2013 1st International Workshop on Data Analysis Patterns in Software Engineering (DAPSE), pp. 17–19. IEEE (2013)
5. Beck, K., Beedle, M., Bennekum, A., et al.: The agile alliance. manifesto for agile software development (2001)
6. Berndt, E., Furniss, D., Blandford, A.: Learning contextual inquiry and distributed cognition: a case study on technology use in anaesthesia. Cogn. Technol. Work **17**(3), 431–449 (2015)
7. Buschmann, F., Henney, K., Schimdt, D.: Pattern-Oriented Software Architecture: On Patterns and Pattern Language, vol. 5. Wiley (2007)
8. Buse, R.P., Zimmermann, T.: Information needs for software development analytics. In: Proceedings of the 34th International Conference on Software Engineering, pp. 987–996. IEEE Press (2012)

9. Cerulo, L., Di Penta, M., Bacchelli, A., Ceccarelli, M., Canfora, G.: Irish: a hidden Markov model to detect coded information islands in free text. Sci. Comput. Program. **105**, 26–43 (2015)
10. Choma, J., Guerra, E.M., Silva, T.S.: Patterns for implementing software analytics in development teams. In: Proceedings of the 24th Conference on Pattern Languages of Programs, p. 12. ACM (2017)
11. Choma, J., Guerra, E.M., Silva, T.S.: Learning from experiments, define quality standards, suspend measurement: three patterns in a software analytics pattern language. In: Proceedings of the 12th Latin American Conference on Pattern Languages of Programs (SLPLoP), p. 10. ACM (2018)
12. Choma, J., Guerra M, E., Silva, T.S., Zaina, L.M., Correia, F.F.: Towards an artifact to support agile teams in software analytics activities. In: Proceedings of the 31st International Conference on Software Engineering & Knowledge Engineering (SEKE 2019) (2019)
13. Coplien, J.O., Harrison, N.: Organizational Patterns of Agile Software Development. Pearson Prentice Hall, Upper Saddle River (2005)
14. Davenport, T.H.: Make better decisions. Harv. Bus. Rev. **87**(11), 117–123 (2009)
15. Destefanis, G., Counsell, S., Concas, G., Tonelli, R.: Software metrics in agile software: an empirical study. In: International Conference on Agile Software Development, pp. 157–170. Springer (2014)
16. Downey, S., Sutherland, J.: Scrum metrics for hyperproductive teams: how they fly like fighter aircraft. In: 2013 46th Hawaii International Conference on System Sciences (HICSS), pp. 4870–4878. IEEE (2013)
17. Feldt, R., Staron, M., Hult, E., Liljegren, T.: Supporting software decision meetings: heatmaps for visualising test and code measurements. In: 2013 39th Euromicro Conference on Software Engineering and Advanced Applications, pp. 62–69. IEEE (2013)
18. Foidl, H., Felderer, M.: Data science challenges to improve quality assurance of internet of things applications. In: International Symposium on Leveraging Applications of Formal Methods, pp. 707–726. Springer (2016)
19. Giger, E., Gall, H.C.: Effect size analysis. In: 2013 1st International Workshop on Data Analysis Patterns in Software Engineering (DAPSE), pp. 11–13. IEEE (2013)
20. González-Torres, A., García-Peñalvo, F.J., Therón, R.: Human-computer interaction in evolutionary visual software analytics. Comput. Hum. Behav. **29**(2), 486–495 (2013)
21. Gonzalez-Torres, A., Theron, R., Garcia-Penalvo, F.J., Wermelinger, M., Yu, Y.: Maleku: an evolutionary visual software analysis tool for providing insights into software evolution. In: 2011 27th IEEE International Conference on Software Maintenance (ICSM), pp. 594–597. IEEE (2011)
22. Gousios, G., Safaric, D., Visser, J.: Streaming software analytics. In: Proceedings of the 2nd International Workshop on BIG Data Software Engineering, pp. 8–11. ACM (2016)
23. Guerra, E., Aniche, M.: Achieving quality on software design through test-driven development. In: Software Quality Assurance, pp. 201–220 (2015)
24. Haron, N.H., Syed-Mohamad, S.M.: Test and defect coverage analytics model for the assessment of software test adequacy. In: 2015 9th Malaysian Software Engineering Conference (MySEC), pp. 13–18. IEEE (2015)
25. Hartmann, D., Dymond, R.: Appropriate agile measurement: using metrics and diagnostics to deliver business value. In: Agile Conference, 2006, pp. 6–pp. IEEE (2006)

26. Hassan, A.E., Xie, T.: Software intelligence: the future of mining software engineering data. In: Proceedings of the FSE/SDP Workshop on Future of Software Engineering Research, pp. 161–166. ACM (2010)

27. Huijgens, H., Lamping, R., Stevens, D., Rothengatter, H., Gousios, G., Romano, D.: Strong agile metrics: mining log data to determine predictive power of software metrics for continuous delivery teams. In: Proceedings of the 2017 11th Joint Meeting on Foundations of Software Engineering, pp. 866–871. ACM (2017)

28. Kim, M., Zimmermann, T., DeLine, R., Begel, A.: The emerging role of data scientists on software development teams. In: 2016 IEEE/ACM 38th International Conference on Software Engineering (ICSE), pp. 96–107. IEEE (2016)

29. Liechti, O., Pasquier, J., Reis, R.: Supporting agile teams with a test analytics platform: a case study. In: Proceedings of the 12th International Workshop on Automation of Software Testing, pp. 9–15. IEEE Press (2017)

30. Lou, J.G., Lin, Q., Ding, R., Fu, Q., Zhang, D., Xie, T.: Software analytics for incident management of online services: an experience report. In: 2013 IEEE/ACM 28th International Conference on Automated Software Engineering (ASE), pp. 475–485. IEEE (2013)

31. Martínez-Fernández, S., Jedlitschka, A., Guzmán, L., Vollmer, A.M.: A quality model for actionable analytics in rapid software development. In: 2018 44th Euromicro Conference on Software Engineering and Advanced Applications (SEAA), pp. 370–377. IEEE (2018)

32. McGrath, S., Bastola, K., Siy, H.: Concept to commit. In: 2013 1st International Workshop on Data Analysis Patterns in Software Engineering (DAPSE), pp. 6–8. IEEE (2013)

33. Melegati, J., Goldman, A.: Seven patterns for software startups. In: Proceedings of the 22nd Conference on Pattern Languages of Programs, p. 20. The Hillside Group (2015)

34. Merson, P., Aguiar, A., Guerra, E., Yoder, J.: Continuous inspection: a pattern for keeping your code healthy and aligned to the architecture. In: 3rd Asian Conference on Pattern Languages of Programs, Tokyo, Japan, pp. 6–8 (2014)

35. Minelli, R., Lanza, M.: Samoa-a visual software analytics platform for mobile applications. In: ICSM, pp. 476–479 (2013)

36. Musson, R., Richards, J., Fisher, D., Bird, C., Bussone, B., Ganguly, S.: Leveraging the crowd: how 48,000 users helped improve lync performance. IEEE Softw. **30**(4), 38–45 (2013)

37. Nord, R.L., Ozkaya, I., Koziolek, H., Avgeriou, P.: Quantifying software architecture quality report on the first international workshop on software architecture metrics. ACM SIGSOFT Softw. Eng. Notes **39**(5), 32–34 (2014)

38. Pachidi, S., Spruit, M., Van De Weerd, I.: Understanding users' behavior with software operation data mining. Comput. Hum. Behav. **30**, 583–594 (2014)

39. Pinto, A.F., Fontes, N., Guerra, E., Terra, R.: Archci: an architectural verification tool into continuous integration. In: Proceedings of the 2016 Brazilian Conference on Software: Theory and Practice (CBSoft) – Tools Session, pp. 121–128 (2016)

40. Ram, P., Rodriguez, P., Oivo, M.: Software process measurement and related challenges in agile software development: a multiple case study. In: International Conference on Product-Focused Software Process Improvement, pp. 272–287. Springer (2018)

41. Ramarao, P., Muthukumaran, K., Dash, S., Murthy, N.B.: Impact of bug reporter's reputation on bug-fix times. In: 2016 International Conference on Information Systems Engineering (ICISE), pp. 57–61. IEEE (2016)

42. Rising, L.: Small experiments. Better Softw. (Jan-Feb), 13–44 (2011)
43. Rising, L.: Patterns mining. In: Handbook of Object Technology, pp. 38–31 (1999)
44. Robbes, R., Vidal, R., Bastarrica, M.C.: Are software analytics efforts worthwhile for small companies? The case of amisoft. IEEE software **30**(5) (2013)
45. Robles, G., González-Barahona, J.M., Cervigón, C., Capiluppi, A., Izquierdo-Cortázar, D.: Estimating development effort in free/open source software projects by mining software repositories: a case study of openstack. In: Proceedings of the 11th Working Conference on Mining Software Repositories, pp. 222–231. ACM (2014)
46. Shull, F.: Data, data everywhere. IEEE Softw. **31**(5) (2014)
47. Souza, R., Chavez, C., Bittencourt, R.: Patterns for cleaning up bug data. In: 2013 1st International Workshop on Data Analysis Patterns in Software Engineering (DAPSE), pp. 26–28. IEEE (2013)
48. Souza, R., Chavez, C., Bittencourt, R.A.: Rapid releases and patch backouts: a software analytics approach. IEEE Softw. **32**(2), 89–96 (2015)
49. Suonsyrjä, S., Systä, K., Mikkonen, T., Terho, H.: Collecting usage data for software development: selection framework for technological approaches. In: Proceedings of The Twenty-Eighth International Conference on Software Engineering and Knowledge Engineering (SEKE 2016) (2016)
50. Sureka, A., Kumar Singh, H., Bagewadi, M., Mitra, A., Karanth, R.: A decision support platform for guiding a bug triager for resolver recommendation using textual and non-textual features. In: 3rd International Workshop on Quantitative Approaches to Software Quality, p. 25 (2015)
51. Taipale, T., Qvist, M., Turhan, B.: Constructing defect predictors and communicating the outcomes to practitioners. In: 2013 ACM/IEEE International Symposium on Empirical Software Engineering and Measurement, pp. 357–362. IEEE (2013)
52. Turhan, B., Kuutti, K.: Simpler questions can lead to better insights. In: Menzies, T., Williams, L., Zimmermann, T. (eds.) Perspectives on Data Science for Software Engineering. Morgan Kaufmann, Boston (2016)
53. Wang, C., Akella, R., Ramachandran, S., Hinnant, D.: Knowledge extraction and reuse within "smart" service centers. In: 2011 Annual SRII Global Conference (SRII), pp. 163–176. IEEE (2011)
54. Weiss, D.M., Mockus, A.: The chunking pattern. In: 2013 1st International Workshop on Data Analysis Patterns in Software Engineering (DAPSE), pp. 35–37. IEEE (2013)
55. Wirfs-Brock, R., Yoder, J., Guerra, E.: Patterns to develop and evolve architecture during an agile software project. In: Proceedings of the 22nd Conference on Pattern Languages of Programs, p. 9. The Hillside Group (2015)
56. Yoder, J., Wirfs-Brock, R.: QA to AQ part two: shifting from quality assurance to agile quality. In: 21st Conference on Patterns of Programming Language (PLoP 2014), Monticello, Illinois, USA (2014)
57. Zhang, D., Dang, Y., Lou, J.G., Han, S., Zhang, H., Xie, T.: Software analytics as a learning case in practice: approaches and experiences. In: Proceedings of the International Workshop on Machine Learning Technologies in Software Engineering, pp. 55–58. ACM (2011)
58. Zhang, D., Han, S., Dang, Y., Lou, J.G., Zhang, H., Xie, T.: Software analytics in practice. IEEE Softw. **30**(5), 30–37 (2013)

Bridging the Gap Between Business Process Modellers and Domain Experts by Variability Patterns

Ralf Laue[1]([⊠]) [iD], Kathrin Kirchner[2] [iD], Birger Lantow[3] [iD], and Kasper Edwards[2] [iD]

[1] University of Applied Sciences of Zwickau, Zwickau, Germany
Ralf.Laue@fh-zwickau.de
[2] Technical University of Denmark, Kongens Lyngby, Denmark
{kakir,kaed}@dtu.dk
[3] University of Rostock, Rostock, Germany
birger.lantow@uni-rostock.de

Abstract. Communication between business process modellers and domain experts can be aided by business process models. However, this communication can become difficult if the domain experts have no deep knowledge of the formal modelling language and the processes include variable elements, i.e. when several ways exist to reach the goal of a process. We propose to support the communication by means of a lightweight and rather informal language. It is based on building blocks that express different patterns of variability. In addition to discussing these patterns, we also show how they can be expressed in the formal modelling languages BPMN and CMMN. This allows to communicate on an informal, but easy-to-understand level without loosing the possibility to create computer-interpretable formal business process models.

Keywords: business process modelling · variability · patterns

1 Introduction

In a project involving many stakeholders (in other words: in almost every relevant project) processes need to be discussed with several people. For this purpose, business process models have to be presented to a variety of audiences. Not all stakeholders will have a profound knowledge of business process modelling languages. This results in time loss by the need to learn a modelling language and/or frustration when discussing.

In this paper, we present a number of patterns that can be used for discussing business processes without requiring the knowledge of such languages. The patterns describe typical building blocks of process models. The aim of these building blocks is to discuss about variable parts of a process (model) using a vocabulary that is close to domain experts' understanding. This means that we

© The Author(s), under exclusive license to Springer-Verlag GmbH, DE, part of Springer Nature 2025
E. Wallingford et al. (Eds.): TPLOP V, LNCS 14630, pp. 190–225, 2025.
https://doi.org/10.1007/978-3-662-70810-1_5

do not want to speak in technical terms such as "gateways" or "sentries" – which would be the vocabulary of the modelling language (BPMN and CMMN in this case).

We also do not want to speak in terms of the traditional workflow patterns [35] which require a deep understanding of process modelling. For example, we wish to say that certain activities are executed in parallel instead of referring to the pattern PARALLEL SPLIT in combination with another pattern SYNCHRO-NIZATION as it would be the terminology of workflow patterns. The patterns should be named in a language that can be used intuitively by domain experts. To give another example: Instead of speaking about the INTERLEAVED ROUT-ING workflow pattern (which would be hard to understand without explanatory notes), we use the term "in any order".

Our process variability patterns are useful for the following groups of readers:

1. **Designers of a modelling language** can discuss for which situation their modelling language should have its own symbols/constructs. While it is not often the case that a new modelling language standard is developed, the term "design of a modelling language" can be interpreted in a broader sense: It can be useful to develop proprietary (or even domain-specific) notations for business process modelling. For the purpose of discussing about the processes, it is not important that the syntax of such a language conforms to a standard as long as all stakeholders in an organization understand the meaning of the notation.
2. **Designers of Modelling Tools** may be interested in introducing support for the patterns into their tools (see [31]).
3. **Researchers** can make use of the patterns for detecting typical situations in process models for purposes such as process mining or the comparison of process models.
4. **Business Process Modellers** who can use our discussion on implementing the patterns in the standardized modelling languages BPMN and CMMN for looking up how to model commonly occurring situations by means of those modelling languages. While it can be assumed that business process modellers are familiar with the scenarios described in the patterns, our experience indicates that the notation elements to be used in BPMN and CMMN (such as the ad-hoc subprocess in BPMN) are not well-known. Furthermore, the patterns help them to discuss and model business processes together with domain experts.

The motivation for our patterns came from the language CUTA4BPM [12] which turned out to be useful for developing process descriptions in collaboration between domain experts and modelling experts. The core element of CUTA4BPM is the so-called *SimpleActivity Card* which contains an activity description in natural language. Additionally, several building blocks (in the form of cards) are defined, that display the typical flow elements (parallel execution, case, loop, multiple choice). Those cards are arranged to build a process model which can be later translated to the standard modelling language BPMN

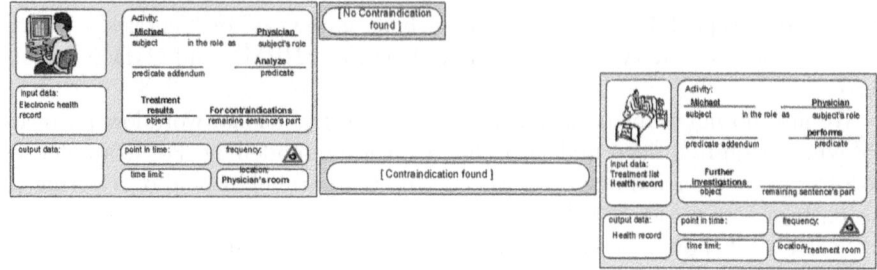

Fig. 1. Example process segment modelled with CUTA4BPM cards

[13]. This way, it is possible to discuss (informal) process models with domain experts who do not have to know formal business process modelling languages.

Figure 1 shows a segment of a hospital process modelled with CUTA4BPM. The first element is a *SimpleActivity Card*, explaining one activity in a treatment process in a hospital. Afterwards, a *Case Block* is used to show an alternative additional execution of an activity (again displayed as a *SimpleActivity Card*). Only if the physician decides after an analysis of the patient health record that a contraindication for certain treatment was found, additional investigations are performed in the treatment room.

CUTA4BPM has been used with process experts working in healthcare, farming, pharmacy, university administration and production. We found – especially in a project at the University Hospital of Jena (Germany) [11] – a need for expressing variability in the process model. However, the activity cards in CUTA4BPM do not support many aspects of process variability. While it is possible to express an alternative execution or multiple choice, no options exist for modelling complex variability rules. By the term variability, we mean that – as stated in [21] – many processes exist "that are not so predefined and repeatable, but instead depend on evolving circumstances and ad hoc decisions by knowledge workers regarding a particular situation". Based on the experience in the mentioned projects (in particular those from the healthcare sector), we identified different types of process variability for which we will discuss patterns in this paper.

- First, it can be unknown until runtime whether an activity has to be executed and whether it has to be repeated after being executed unsuccessfully, i.e. activities can be skipped or it can be necessary to repeat an activity until the desired outcome has been achieved.
- Second, there can be more than one way to reach a certain goal, and one out of many possible activities can be selected for this purpose.
- Third, the order between activities does not have to be known before the process is actually executed.
- And fourth, the execution of a business process can depend on whether certain activities (such as tests, authorizations or approvals) have been executed successfully which does not always have to be the case.

To identify the patterns, we analysed the processes in our own projects and systematically discussed the patterns described in the literature that investigate changes to business process models based on graph operations (see [5]). This discussion focused on understanding the type of variability that makes such changes necessary. Furthermore, we studied 142 samples of process models and guidelines from the medical domain, details of this study can be found in [10].

We propose using process building blocks to describe scenarios that involve variability. Using process building blocks should be sufficient for discussing the process with the stakeholders (who do not have to be fluent in formal modelling languages). Those building blocks can be transformed into a more formal language if the need arises. In Fig. 2 we see an example process depicted in BPMN as well as by using our process building blocks. The latter show the situation in a more concise form which is still easy to understand.

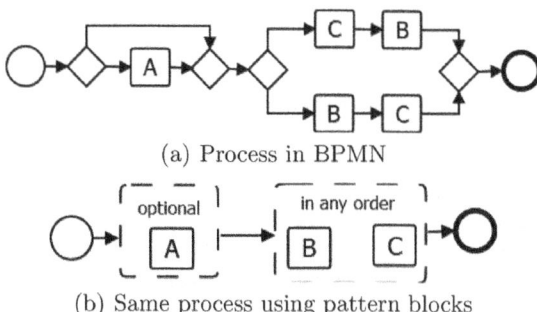

(a) Process in BPMN

(b) Same process using pattern blocks

Fig. 2. Process example in BPMN and using pattern blocks

The remainder of this paper is structured as follows: In Sect. 2, we define basic terms that will be used throughout the paper. The patterns for expressing variability are discussed in Sect. 3. Section 4 deals with different ways to modify those patterns. Section 5 discusses related work before Sect. 6 comes to a conclusion and lists challenges for future work.

2   Definitions

In the rest of this paper, we will make use of the following terms:

Activity. The term "activity" can refer either to a single (atomic) task or to a set of tasks that must be executed together.

Participant. Participants are persons, groups of persons or computer programs that carry out an activity. *Workflow engines* can be used to coordinate process execution between participants. A workflow engine can provide human participants by presenting a so-called *worklist* which displays them the activities that can be performed. *Knowledge workers* are human participants who are not required to execute all activities in the worklist. For them, the worklist just suggests possible activities. They have the possibility to select appropriate activities from the worklist based on their experiences and the properties of a specific case.

Goal. A goal is a desired state that can be reached by executing a set of activities.

Success/Failure. We say that activities are executed successfully if they contribute to the desired goal in a positive way. Note that this is more than just saying that the activity came to an end without being cancelled and without raising an exception at runtime. For example, an activity "rate credit status of the customer" that has been executed correctly is still be regarded as a failure with respect to the goal "sell real-estate property to the customer" if it came to the negative result that the customer is not creditworthy.

3   Patterns

We introduce block symbols for expressing different patterns of variability. In this section, we will discuss these patterns. For each such pattern, we will describe:

- The problem (i.e. a type of variability occurring in business processes),
- one or more examples,
- the block symbol(s) for depicting the pattern in an informal visual language,
- possible ways to model the pattern using the languages BPMN or CMMN,
- related patterns.

We decided to discuss a mapping to BPMN and CMMN because both rely on an international standard [20,21]. BPMN is regarded as the most widespread process modelling language while CMMN has been explicitly designed for dealing with variability in processes. In the discussions on implementing the patterns using BPMN and CMMN, we assume familiarity with those languages. However, readers who are not interested in these implementation details can simply skip these paragraphs without loss of information about the patterns in general. In the paragraphs discussing the implementation we will write terms that have been defined in the BPMN or CMMN standard document [20,21] in italics and using the same spelling that has been used in the standard, e.g. *CaseFileItem*.

Types of Variability. The types of variability we discuss in this paper are:

- The optional execution of an activity (Sect. 3.1)
- The need to repeat an activity when not finished successfully (Sect. 3.2)
- Dealing with many possible ways to reach a goal (Sect. 3.3)
- Several variants where a number of activities have to be executed altogether (Sect. 3.4)
- Applying multiple tests to an object (Sect. 3.5), repeating an activity if a test shows the need to do so (Sect. 3.6) and confirming the result of a testing/analysing/measuring activity by another one (Sect. 3.7).

Variants. Most of these patterns exist in a number of variants. These variants can be obtained from the "core" pattern by adding one or more of the following requirements:

- When being unsuccessful after a given period of time or based on a certain condition, all processes within the pattern block have to be stopped. Instead, an escalation or substitution process can be started.
- The activities belonging to one pattern block have to be executed in a given order.
- Parallel execution of activities can be forbidden.

Section 4 discusses how these variants can be added to the core patterns. However, before dealing with those variants, we will present the core patterns in the following subsections.

Pattern Template. The template used in this contribution for describing patterns differs from the formats used by other authors (such as the Design Patterns by the GoF [6]).

The beginning of each pattern is indicated by a black sidebar and the bold-printed name of the pattern. Below that, there is a "Use when" statement that briefly describes a scenario to be modelled. In the paragraph "Problem", this scenario is described in more detail, and the actual problem is stated as "How to model the following scenario:..."

Since the scenario to be modelled already clearly specifies what needs to be modelled, leaving no room for discussion about alternative ways to design a scenario, we did not see a reason for a paragraph "Forces" commonly found in other pattern papers.

To describe the solutions to the "How to model"-question, we use the paragraph "Implementation" in accordance with the literature on workflow patterns [27]. There exist a paragraph "Implementation (BPMN)" and/or a paragraph "Implementation (CMMN)", depending on whether meaningful solutions exist in the mentioned modelling languages. In most cases, there will be multiple ways to model a scenario in the mentioned modelling languages. We have strived to provide the most efficiently modelled diagram in the "Implementation" sections. In addition, the paragraph "block symbol" provides a visual representation that is meant to depict the given scenario in a manner that aims to be easy to comprehend for all involved stakeholders.

3.1   Optionality

This is a very common element of process variability. Natschläger et al. [19] pointed out that BPMN needs too many constructs to depict an optional execution and suggested to use a marker at a BPMN activity symbol to depict optionality. Our pattern blocks work in a similar fashion. We distinguish between two patterns based on whether the decision to execute an activity can be made automatically or not.

Pattern 1: Execute only if – Workflow engine decides on execution
  Use when: A certain activity has to be executed in certain cases
only. The decision on execution can be made automatically.

Also Known As: POSSIBILITY [19], SKIP SEGMENT [4], SKIPPING ACTIVITIES [25], SKIPPED ACTIVITY [34], REJECT [30].

Problem: How to model the following scenario: An activity has to be executed for certain cases only. The decision whether or not the execution is necessary can be made by a workflow engine based on data that are associated to a case.

Example: During evaluation for a liver transplantation, only women need to undergo a gynaecological investigation.

Block Symbol:

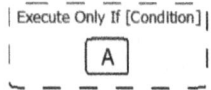

Fig. 3. EXECUTE ONLY IF – Workflow engine decides on execution

Implementation (BPMN):
The implementation of this pattern in BPMN is straightforward as shown in Fig. 4. Note that the while in the model, the conditions are expressed by means of labels in natural language, they have to be implemented in a formal language too in order to be executed by a workflow engine. If the decision rules are complex, it can be useful to model them using the Decision Model and Notation (DMN) standard [22].

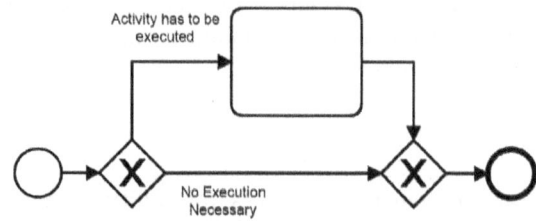

Fig. 4. EXECUTE ONLY IF pattern in a BPMN diagram

Implementation (CMMN):
A *Sentry* makes the *Task* active or enabled if a *Condition* evaluates to true. In the graphical CMMN model, this condition should be given as a comment. The *Task* has a *Required Decorator*, the ! symbol, because it has to be executed (to be more precise: must reach the Completed, Terminated, Failed, or Disabled state) before its parent *Stage* can complete, i.e. the user is not allowed make a decision to skip the activity (Fig. 5).

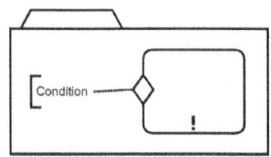

Fig. 5. CMMN model for EXECUTE ONLY IF...

Related Patterns: This pattern differs from OPTIONAL pattern described below as pattern 2. In EXECUTE ONLY IF... , a workflow engine can decide whether the activity has to be executed and hence, whether it has to be shown in the worklist of a human participant. In the case of the OPTIONAL pattern, the activity is always shown and it is the knowledge worker who decides whether or not it will be actually executed.

Pattern 2: Optional – Knowledge worker decides on execution
Use when: A certain activity has to be executed in certain cases only. The decision on execution can not be made automatically.

Also Known As: OPTIONAL ACTIVITY [1].

Problem: How to model the following scenario: An activity has to be executed for certain cases only. The decision whether or not the execution is necessary can **not** be made by the workflow engine based on known data. Instead, the workflow engine should show the option to perform an activity in the worklist of a knowledge worker who decides about the execution.

Example: When deciding about accepting a client for a health insurance, the underwriter can decide to ask a doctor for additional information (Fig. 6).

Block Symbol:

Fig. 6. OPTIONALITY – Knowledge worker decides on execution

Implementation (BPMN):
It is a common anti-pattern to use the textual labels of an activity to depict optionality. Examples for such labels could be "send invoice if necessary" or "send invoice (optional)". The disadvantages are that automatic comparison between models becomes more difficult and that the decision whether the activity should be executed, is hidden [16,24].

Instead, there should be a separate *User Task* "Decide whether the activity has to be executed", followed by an *Exclusive Gateway* that allows to skip the activity as shown in Fig. 7. Note that such a *User Task* is not necessary if the workflow engine decides whether the activity should be executed as shown in Fig. 3.

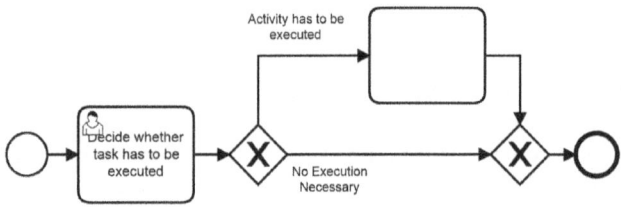

Fig. 7. BMPN model for the OPTIONAL Pattern

Implementation (CMMN): The presence of a *ManualActivationRule* (indicated by the symbol ▷)[1] shows that the *Task* waits for a human to start or disable it (Fig. 8).

Related Patterns: This pattern differs from EXECUTE ONLY IF... ; the differences are explained in the paragraph "Related Patterns" of the EXECUTE ONLY IF... pattern (see pattern 1 above).

---

[1] Unfortunately, the CMMN standard document is misleading when it comes to the meaning of this symbol. Our text follows the recommendation on how to read the standard given by leading CMMN experts at https://issues.omg.org/issues/CR-148.

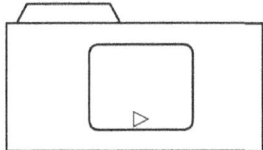

Fig. 8. CMMN model for the OPTIONAL Pattern

3.2   Pattern 3: Repeat Until Success

Use when: An activity must be repeated when its execution has failed.

Problem: How to model the following scenario: An activity does not have to be successful at the first try. If it is unsuccessful, it has to be repeated. Another "testing" activity may be necessary for deciding whether or not the first activity can be considered as "being successful".

Example: An election process has to be repeated until one candidate has collected a majority of the votes.

Block Symbol: The symbol for expressing the pattern is shown in Fig. 9.

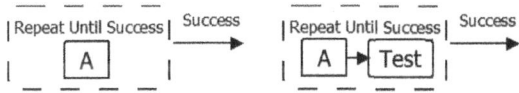

Fig. 9. REPEAT UNTIL SUCCESS; the right image explicitly models the test whether A has been executed successfully

The right variant makes explicit that a special test activity may be necessary to decide on the success or failure of activity A. As REPEAT UNTIL SUCCESS would literally mean that the activity can be repeated arbitrary often, there is in practice actually always a limit either on the number of repetitions or on the time. Therefore, in practice, there will often be another outgoing arrow leading to what has to be done when the execution of the activity is still unsuccessful when this limit is reached. This is discussed in Sect. 4.1,

Implementation (BPMN): The easiest way to model the repeated execution of an activity is to use the "loop" marker ($\circlearrowleft$) which indicates its looping behaviour.

The attribute *loopCondition* can contain a Boolean expression, and the activity is repeated as long as this expression evaluates to true. The BPMN standard does not provide a standardized way for this expression to access the state of an activity in order to express something like "loop if the activity is in the state *Failed*". Instead, the modeller would have to take care about using and evaluating such a "Failed" flag. The loop condition is not visible in the visual notation of a BPMN model.

The decision whether a failure actually means that the same activity has to be repeated should be taken with care. If e.g. an activity "Fill out form" is followed by an activity "Check form for completeness", there are two possibilities to model the correction: Either the situation can be modelled such that "Fill out form" has to be repeated. Alternatively, another activity "Complete missing part" could be used. This difference becomes important if execution times are calculated, for example by means of simulation runs. As it is likely that filling out the form takes more time than just adding missing parts, a model that simply repeats the activity would be inappropriate.

Furthermore, the modeler should decide whether after the "correction" step, one more round of validation is necessary. Usually, this will be the case. A sequence "Do something" – "Validate Something" and (if necessary) "Correct something" (without another round of validation) would be correct only if it is guaranteed that the correction will always lead to an acceptable result.

It can be useful to depict the process for the decision whether the execution of the activity will be considered as being correct by means of DMN.

Implementation (CMMN):
The implementation depends on how "success" can be determined. If the fact that "success" can be claimed is documented by the fact that the *Task* has been executed at all (formally: reaches the state COMPLETED or TERMINATED), it is sufficient to add a *RepetitionRule* to the *Task*. Such a model is shown in Fig. 10. The *RepetitionRule* contains an *Expression* that evaluates to true as long as there is a need for repeating the *Task*. An alternative way to model the situation would be to add the *RepetitionRule* to a *Stage* in which the *Task* is contained (see Fig. 11).

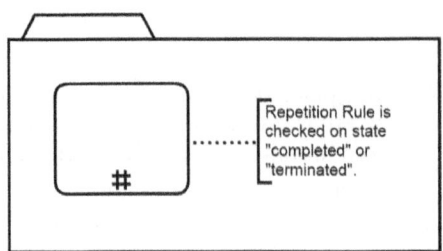

Fig. 10. CMMN model for REPEAT UNTIL SUCCESS

However, often the fact that an activity has been completed does not yet mean that it has been completed correctly. Instead, the correctness of the execution has to be checked afterwards by a separate activity "Test". In the model in

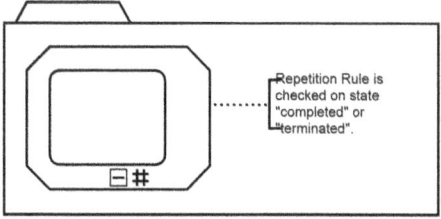

Fig. 11. CMMN model for REPEAT UNTIL SUCCESS, using a Stage

Fig. 12, the *Task Test* writes a *Property* which contains the Boolean value true if and only if the test showed that the *Task* has been executed to full satisfaction. The *IfPart* of the *Sentry* for the *Task A* specifies a condition that evaluates this *Property*, and *Task A* is repeated only if the property evaluates to true. This results in *Task A* being enabled as often as *Task Test* detects a need to do so.

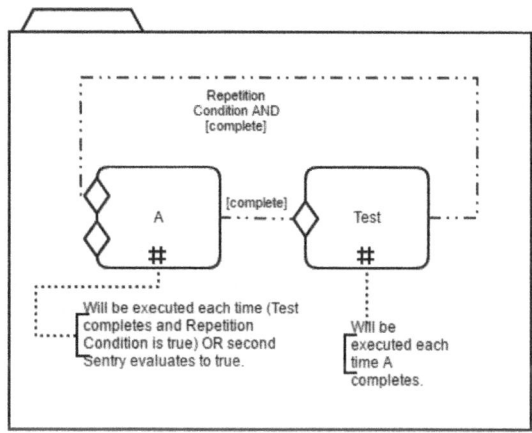

Fig. 12. CMMN model for REPEAT UNTIL SUCCESS, contains separate Test task

Related Patterns: In practice, it will be rarely the case that an activity can be repeated arbitrarily often. Therefore, the modeler should consider to include either a time restriction (repetition has to stop when it takes too long, see pattern variant TERMINATION BY TIMEOUT in Sect. 4.1) or a restriction of the number of tries, see pattern variant TERMINATION BY CONDITION in Sect. 4.1.

The pattern is different from the CYCLIC ELEMENTS pattern discussed in [15]. CYCLIC ELEMENTS describes the planned repetition of an activity after some time span. In our pattern, the repetition of an activity is the unwanted result of an unsuccessful execution.

Also, pattern is not identical to the workflow pattern STRUCTURED LOOP [28] (also called LOOP SEGMENT [38] or REPETITION [26]). While both can be expressed as a kind of loop in a process model, the difference is a semantic one: Our pattern deals with the case that an activity has to be repeated due to a failure, while the STRUCTURED LOOP pattern also allows scenarios such as "repeat the activity while there are remaining unprocessed work items".

A similar pattern FIX AND RETEST will be discussed in Sect. 3.6 as pattern 11. This pattern assumes that in addition to repeatedly executing a task, we have the possibility to actively make a correction of the factors that made it fail.

3.3   Try Alternatives Until Success

This subsection addresses scenarios where multiple alternative activities can be chosen to achieve a goal. As soon as one activity has been executed successfully, there is no need to try another alternative, and the process can continue with its next step.

In this subsection, we will discuss three patterns. They differ in what we know about the chances of the activities to be executed successfully. The first pattern can be applied if we know for sure that one of the alternatives will be successful. The second pattern deals with the case that for each activity it can happen that it will fail, and repeating its execution would not help either. This means that it can happen that all activities fail and the goal will not be reached. Finally, in the third pattern each activity can fail, but it can be tried again as often as necessary with the chance to come to a successful result next time.

Variants: In the discussion below, we will refer to the most basic case of the patterns: No restrictions on the order of the alternative activities is given. The activities can, but do not have to be executed in parallel. In our block symbols, this is denoted by the text *In any Order*. In Sect. 4.2, we will show how we deal with additional restrictions:

- if an order between the alternative activities is given, and
- if it has to be enforced that activities are not executed in parallel.

> **Pattern 4: Try Alternatives Until Success – One Alternative Will Be Successful**
> **Use when: One out of many alternatives must be successful. We know for sure that at least one of the alternatives will be successful when executed once (but we do not know which one).**

Problem: How to model the following scenario: We know that one out of many activities will lead to the goal, but we do not know which one. The alternatives should be tried without a preferred order, but no activity should be executed more than once. Note that this pattern should rather be avoided because usually we should have an idea about the costs and chances of success for each activity and hence an preference in which order the alternatives should be tried.

Example: A technical system consisting of several modules has to be repaired. We suppose that it can be ruled out that more than one module is defect. Therefore, for repairing the system the modules are exchanged one by one. The modules do not differ in probability of failure and cost to be replaced, hence they can be replaced in arbitrary order.

Block Symbol: We indicate all TRY ALTERNATIVES UNTIL SUCCESS patterns by writing "Try Alternatives Until Success" into the block. If deemed useful, the word "success" can also be replaced by a more concrete description of what is regarded as success (e.g. "Try Alternatives Until Car Repaired"). In Fig. 13, there are no arrows between the activities *A*, *B* and *C*. In our block symbols, this always means that no specific order has to be enforced between the activities. A note "Parallel Execution" can be added as a reminder that parallel execution of tasks is allowed (if this is the case).

If it can be taken for granted that one activity *will* be successful, there has to be only one outgoing arrow from the block. It leads to whatever happens after one of the activities has been executed successfully.

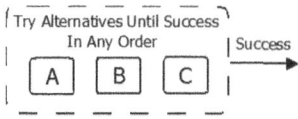

Fig. 13. TRY ALTERNATIVES UNTIL SUCCESS – ONE ALTERNATIVE WILL BE SUCCESSFUL

Implementation (BPMN): BPMN does not provide a comfortable way to express this pattern (as already discussed in [37] in the context of the INTERLEAVED PARALLEL ROUTING workflow pattern). Using an *Ad-hoc Sub-Process* – as discussed in [37] – is just a compromise because this would allow the same *Task* to be enabled more than once. Of course, in case of *User Tasks*, "being enabled" just means that an activity is shown in the worklist and is up to the knowledge worker to execute the activity or not. Anyway, it would be better if an activity that has already be executed unsuccessfully would not show up in the worklist again.

Implementation (CMMN):
An implementation of this pattern is shown in Fig. 14. All *Tasks* are available until they complete or the *Stage* terminates. An *ExitCriterion* for the *Stage* tests for success and terminates the *Stage* children, i.e. the *Tasks*.

> **Pattern 5: Try Alternatives Until Success – Each of the activities can fail, Failure is final.**
> **Use when: One out of many alternatives must be successful. Each of the alternatives can fail. Executing it once again would not help either.**

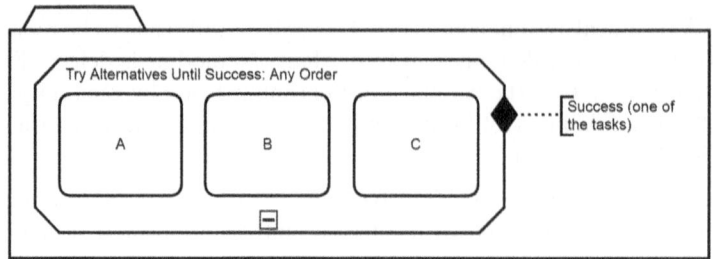

Fig. 14. CMMN model for Try Alternatives Until Success, One out of many activities will always be successful

Problem: How to model the following scenario: There are different activities that can be tried to achieve some goal, each one can fail. This situation often occurs if we need to achieve the goal quickly: we try all alternatives in parallel, taking into account the disadvantage of performing some of them needlessly.

Example: To find a bone marrow donor for a patient, a request is sent to several national bone marrow donor centres who process a search for a donor in parallel.

Block Symbol:
If all activities fail, the goal will not be reached. To denote this, there is a second arrow originating from the block, leading to what should be performed in the case that all activities fail. Figure 15 contains the note "In any order". If the order is restricted as discussed in Sect. 4.2, this note is omitted. A note "Parallel Execution" can be added as a reminder that parallel execution of tasks is allowed (if this is the case).

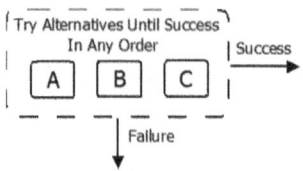

Fig. 15. Try Alternatives Until Success – Each of the activities can fail, Failure is final

Implementation (BPMN):
As already discussed in Sect. 3.3, an *Ad-hoc Sub-Process* would come close to an implementation for this pattern, however this would allow an *Activity* that has already been executed unsuccessfully to be enabled again. Hence, BPMN does not provide a proper means to model the pattern.

Implementation (CMMN):
An implementation of this pattern is shown in Fig. 16. The *Stage* has two *ExitCriteria*: The *Stage* ends (and terminates all *Tasks* inside the *Stage*) if either one of the *Tasks* has been executed successfully or all of them have been tried without success. As this logic is "hidden" into the implementation of the *ExitCriteria*, a *Text Annotation* should be used as a comment for the human reader of the model.

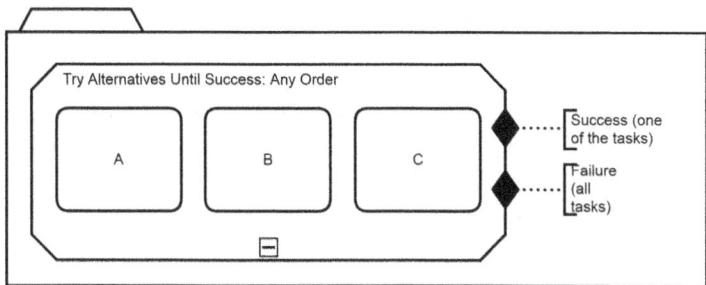

Fig. 16. CMMN model for Try Alternatives Until Success, Each Activity Can Fail, Repeating Does not Help

Pattern 6: Try Alternatives Until Success – Each of the Activities Can Fail, but be Successful Next Time
 Use when: One out of many alternatives must be successful. Each activity can fail. However, it can be repeated arbitrary often with the chance that it will succeed next time.

Problem: How to model the following scenario: There are several alternatives to reach a goal. A goal can be achieved by several means (i.e. by executing one of several activities). Each of those activities can fail, but it is possible that it will be successful when being executed once again.

Example: We attempt to reach one out of several contact persons by telephone (in no specific order). We have to repeat calling until the first one actually responds.

Block Symbol: To indicate the possibility to repeat an activity, the text "Can Be Redone" is added. A note "Parallel Execution" can be added as a reminder that parallel execution of tasks is allowed (if this is the case) (Fig. 17).

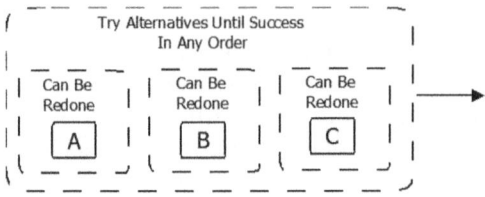

Fig. 17. TRY ALTERNATIVES UNTIL SUCCESS – EACH OF THE ACTIVITIES CAN FAIL, BUT BE SUCCESSFUL NEXT TIME

Implementation (BPMN):
This pattern can be modelled by means of an *Ad-hoc Sub-Process* (indicated by the $\sim$ symbol) as shown in Fig. 18. The attribute *completionCondition* of the *Ad-hoc Sub-Process* that defines when the process ends has to be defined such that it evaluates to true as soon as one activity has been performed successfully.

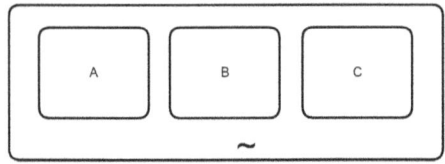

Fig. 18. BPMN implementation for TRY ALTERNATIVES UNTIL SUCCESS – EACH OF THE ACTIVITIES CAN FAIL, BUT BE SUCCESSFUL NEXT TIME

Implementation (CMMN):
An implementation of the pattern is shown in Fig. 19.

To denote that an activity that has been executed unsuccessfully can be retried, each activity has a #-marker which shows that it can be started more than once.

If we have to deal with the variant that the activities should be tried and repeated in a given order (see Sect. 4.2), the #-marker has to be assigned to the whole *Stage* as shown in Fig. 20.

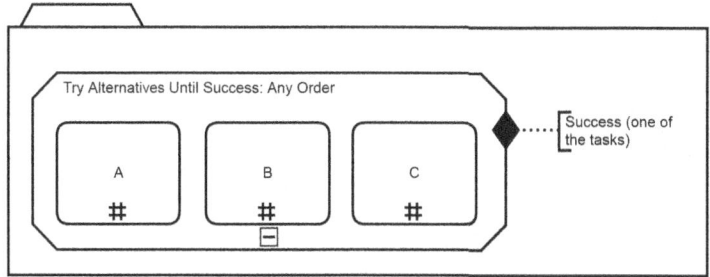

Fig. 19. CMMN model for TRY ALTERNATIVES UNTIL SUCCESS – EACH OF THE ACTIVITIES CAN FAIL, BUT BE SUCCESSFUL NEXT TIME

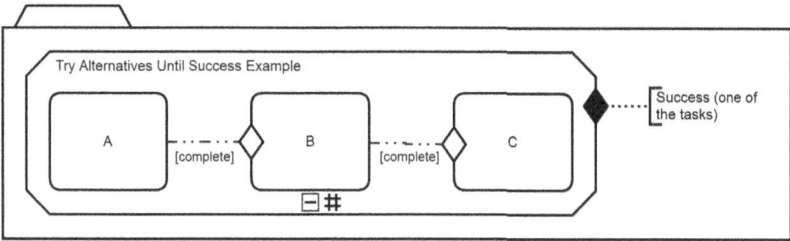

Fig. 20. CMMN model for TRY ALTERNATIVES UNTIL SUCCESS, IN A GIVEN ORDER, EACH ACTIVITY CAN FAIL, BUT BE SUCCESSFUL NEXT TIME

3.4   Do All

The patterns in this subsection deal with situations where a goal can be reached successfully if and only if a number of activities has been completed successfully (also known as PROCESS CHECKLIST [10]). The failure of a single activity means that the goal is not reached.

We will discuss three patterns: The first pattern deals with the case where it can be assumed that the activities always succeed, hence a possibility of a failure does not have to be taken into account. If an activity can fail, we again distinguish between two patterns. The second pattern in this subsection deals with the case that for each activity it can happen that it will fail, and repeating its execution would not help either. This means that it can happen that all activities fail and the goal will not be reached. Finally, the last pattern discussed in this subsection deals with the case that each activity can potentially fail, but it can be tried again as often as necessary with the chance to come to a successful result next time.

Variants: As it was the case for the pattern "Try Alternatives Until Success", we will first discuss the basic case that no restrictions on the order of the activities is given. The activities can, but do not have to be executed in parallel. In our block symbols, this is denoted by the text *In any Order*. In Sect. 4.2, we will show how we deal with the case that it has to be enforced that activities are not executed in parallel.

> **Pattern 7: Do All – Failure of an activity has not to be considered**
> **Use when: A number of activities must finish successfully in order to reach a goal. Activities are known to be always completed successfully.**

Problem: How to model the following scenario: Several activities have to be performed. In the general case, no order between them is given. If the goal should be reached quickly, the activities can be executed in parallel.

Example: In motor-sports, a pit-stop has to be executed as fast as possible. Therefore, the mechanics do services such as refuelling, changing tyres and cleaning the windscreen in parallel.

Block Symbol: Assuming that all activities will always be executed successfully, the block just needs one outgoing arrow which leads to what has to be done after the goal has been achieved. If space permits, it can be helpful to place the activity symbols not side by side because the reader who is used to read from left to right should not implicitly assume that the activities are to be performed starting from the leftmost one. Figure 21 contains the note "In any order". If the order is restricted as discussed in Sect. 4.2, this note is omitted. A note "Parallel Execution" can be added as a reminder that parallel execution of tasks is allowed (if this is the case).

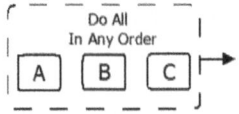

Fig. 21. Do All – Failure of an activity has not to be considered

Implementation (BPMN):
As long as no restrictions on the order of the activities are given, we can simply model them in a block between *Parallel Gateways* as shown in Fig. 22. Note that this does not necessarily enforce parallel execution (which means that the execution times of different activities overlap), but it also does not forbid it.

Implementation (CMMN):
An implementation of the pattern is shown in Fig. 23. The stage has an Auto-Complete marker (■), i.e. the stage closes when all activities have been completed.

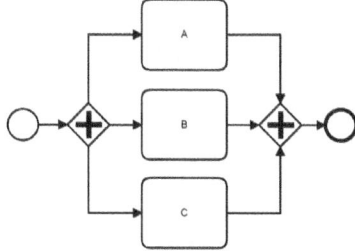

Fig. 22. BPMN Model for Do All - Activities Cannot Fail

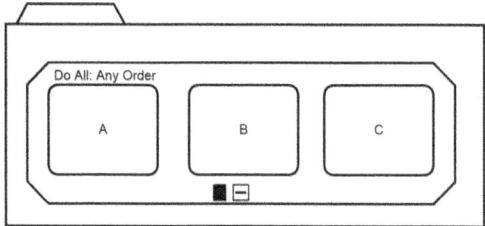

Fig. 23. CMMN model for Do All - Activities Cannot Fail

Related Patterns: In terms of workflow patterns [35], the block of parallel activities can be expressed as a combination of Parallel Split and Synchronization.

> **Pattern 8: Do All – Each of the activities can fail, with no option to succeed next time**
> **Use when: A number of activities must finish successfully in order to reach a goal. Each activity can fail, and executing it once again would not help either.**

Problem: How to model the following scenario: Several activities have to be executed in order to achieve a goal. If one of them fails, the goal cannot be reached this way anymore. The activities do not depend on each other. There is no restriction on the order between the activities, and they can be performed in parallel. This means that we accept the disadvantage of performing an activity despite the fact that it can become unnecessary because another activity fails in the meantime.

Example: If an order request arrives, both the availability of the article as the credit status of the customer are checked. These activities are done in parallel by different departments. The order will be fulfilled only if both come to a positive result.

Block Symbol: If all activities fail, the goal will not be reached. To denote this, there is a second arrow originating from the block, leading to what should be performed in the case that any of the activities fails. Figure 21 contains the note "In any order". If the order is restricted as discussed in Sect. 4.2, this note is omitted. A note "Parallel Execution" can be added as a reminder that parallel execution of tasks is allowed (if this is the case) (Fig. 24).

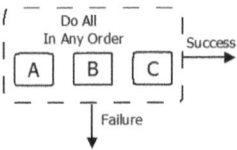

Fig. 24. Do All – Each of the activities can fail, with no option to succeed
next time

Implementation (BPMN):
The implementation shown in Fig. 22 (where failure of an activity does not have to be considered) can be enriched by *Error Events* as shown in Fig. 25. In Fig. 25, two alternative ways to model unsuccessful process execution by means of *Error Events* are shown. *Activity* A and B have an attached *Boundary Event* that reacts on an error while executing A or B. From this event, an outgoing sequence flow leads to the an *Throwing Error Event* which is an *End Event*. For activity C, the fact that the activity has not been executed successfully is revealed only after a test that follows C. Once again, in case of a negative test result, an *Error Event* is thrown. Those error events are caught by a corresponding *Error Event* at the *Sub-Process* boundary.

Implementation (CMMN):
An implementation of this pattern is shown in Fig. 26. The *Stage* closes if either all *Tasks* have been executed successfully – denoted by the *AutoComplete* decorator (■) – or one of the *Tasks* has been executed unsuccessfully (by means of the *ExitCriterion* of the stage). As already discussed in the paragraph on BPMN, it is possible to add a test activity that reveals whether a preceding *Task* has been executed successfully.

Related Patterns: A possibility to model this pattern by standard modelling languages is shown as pattern All Or Nothing in [7]. In the same paper the case that the activities are to be executed in a previously known sequence is discussed under the name Straight Road with Exits.

Pattern 9: Do All – Each activity can fail, with the option to succeed next time
 Use when: A number of activities must finish successfully in order

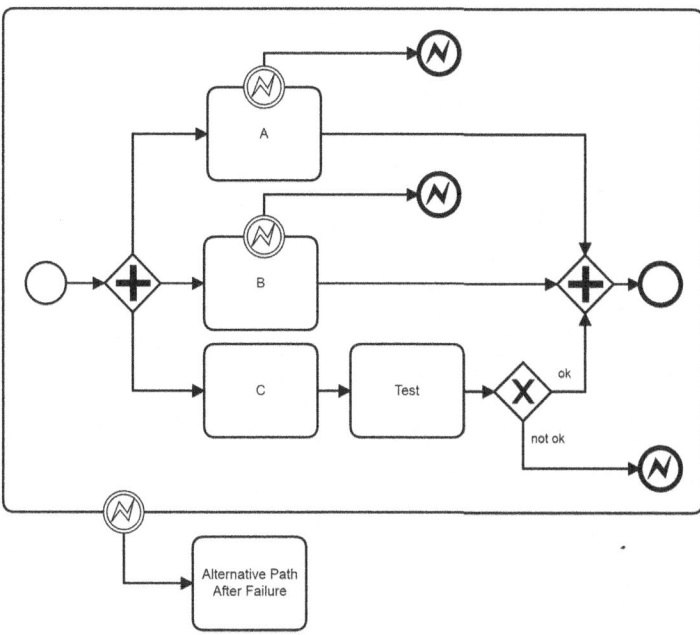

Fig. 25. BPMN Model for Do All – All Activities Must be Successful, Each Can Fail, Repeating Does Not Help

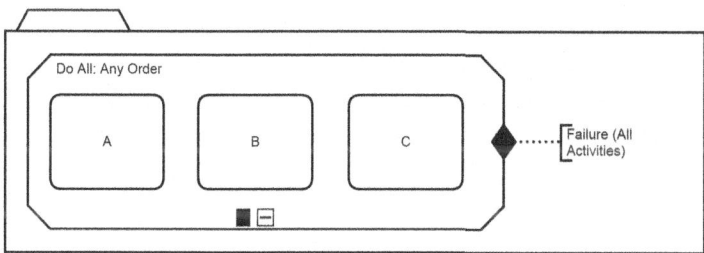

Fig. 26. CMMN model for Do All - Each Activity Can Fail, Repeating Does not Help

> **to reach a goal. Each activity can fail. However, it can be repeated arbitrary often with the chance that it will succeed next time.**

Problem: How to model the following scenario: Several activities have to be executed successfully in order to achieve a goal. Each one can be repeated if it failed. The activities do not depend on each other.

Example: A publisher wants to initiate a book project on some popular subject (such as a travel destination). For this purpose, the activities "ask author for availability", "ask photographer for availability" and "ask illustrator for availability" are executed until an appropriate person is found for each of these positions.

Block Symbol: To indicate the possibility to execute an activity more than once, the blocks include the text *Repeat Until Success*. A note "Parallel Execution" can be added as a reminder that parallel execution of tasks is allowed (if this is the case). Without additional outgoing arrow, the activities can be executed arbitrary often. For this reason, another outgoing arrow to indicate an abandoning condition can be used as discussed in Sect. 4.1 (Fig. 27).

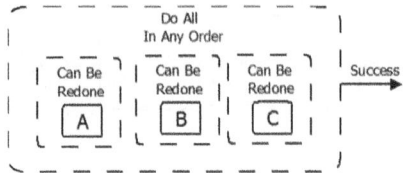

Fig. 27. Do All – Each activity can fail, with the option to succeed next time

Implementation (BPMN):
The BPMN diagram for an implementation of this pattern looks exactly as Fig. 18. However, the attribute *completionCondition* of the *Ad-hoc Sub-Process* that defines when the process ends is defined differently: it evaluates to true only if *all* activities have been completed successfully.

Implementation (CMMN): An implementation of this pattern is shown in Fig. 28. Instead of having a condition for success and another one for abandoning, a *RepetitionRule* is defined by the *Expression* ((NOT success) AND (NOT abandoning)).

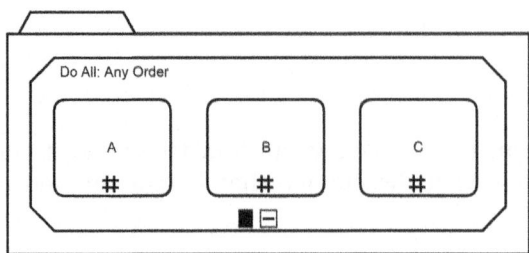

Fig. 28. CMMN model for Do All - Each Activity Can Fail, But Can Be Successful When Repeated

3.5   Pattern 10: Pass All Tests

Use when: An object must pass multiple tests.

Problem: How to model the following scenario: Some object has to undergo a series of tests. However, we do not simply have a DO ALL situation, because the tests depend on each other: As soon as the first test fails, another path in the process flow is taken, and no further tests are necessary. The process can proceed by executing the next activities only if all tests have been passed successfully.

Example: The European Payment Services Directive (PSD-2) requires multi-factor authentication. A user is granted access only if two or more pieces of authentication (independent of each other) are presented correctly.

Block Symbol: As shown in Fig. 29, the block has two outgoing arrows: one dealing with the case that all tests have been passed successfully and another one for the case that at least one test was unsuccessful.

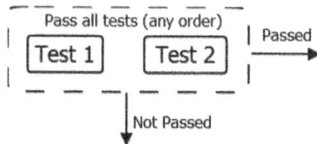

Fig. 29. PASS ALL TESTS

Implementation (BPMN/CMMN): As will be discussed in the paragraph "Related Patterns" below, this situation can be modelled in the same way as pattern 8 (DO ALL – EACH OF THE ACTIVITIES CAN FAIL, WITH NO OPTION TO SUCCEED NEXT TIME) described in Sect. 3.4.

Related Patterns: In fact, this is not a new pattern: PASS ALL TESTS is just a variant of the pattern DO ALL – EACH OF THE ACTIVITIES CAN FAIL, WITH NO OPTION TO SUCCEED NEXT TIME discussed in Sect. 3.4 as pattern 8. In this case, the activities to be executed are the tests. Anyway, as the wording "Do All" does not make explicit that we are dealing with tests that make a decision, we added PASS ALL TESTS as a pattern with a separate name. This name is closer to the verbal description of the given situation.

The iterative approval of an object is addressed in [18] using the patterns SEQUENTIAL APPROVAL and PARALLEL APPROVAL (depending on whether the test activities can be executed in parallel). The special case of an iterative approval by multiple organizational roles is described as ITERATIVE APPROVAL pattern in [33]. In [32], the iterative approval of a document by multiple organizations is discussed.

See the next subsection for a discussion of the related pattern FIX AND RETEST

3.6   Pattern 11: Fix and Retest

Use when: In case of a negative test, some "repair" activity has to be executed.

Also Known As: RETRY [30], CORRECT & RESTART PROCESS [18].

Problem: How to model the following scenario: In Sect. 3.5, nothing is said about what happens in the case of "not passed". In reality, it is often the case that some activity has to be performed that aims to fix the problems. This is followed by another round of tests.

Example: For ensuring software quality, unit tests are run. In case of failure, the code will be corrected and the tests (in this case: all of them) are repeated. This is repeated until all tests run successfully.

Block Symbol: The block symbols introduced in Sect. 3.5 are complemented by the problem fixing activity that follows the "not passed" arrow. From this activity, another arrow points back to the test block (see Fig. 30). There are two different options: Either all tests have to be repeated after the fixing activity or just those that did not yet complete successfully before. For the latter case, the text "Pass remaining tests" is used instead of "Pass all tests".

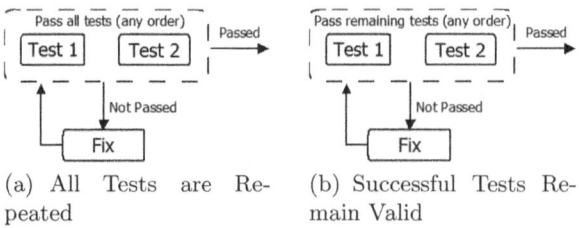

(a) All Tests are Repeated   (b) Successful Tests Remain Valid

Fig. 30. FIX AND RETEST: Multiple Tests have to be passed. If one fails, a fix and another round of tests are executed.

Implementation (BPMN/CMMN): If all tests have to be repeated, this is just a combination of PASS ALL TESTS (pattern 10, see Sect. 3.5) and REPEAT UNTIL SUCCESS (pattern 3). Otherwise, the activities to be performed in the case of failed tests must explicitly be modeled. An example using BPMN for the latter case is shown in Fig. 31.

Related Patterns: This pattern is an extension of pattern PASS ALL TESTS (pattern 10, see Sect. 3.5). If only a selected subset of the activities have to be repeated, subtle problems related to the execution semantics can occur; a detailed discussion can be found in the description of the PARTIAL REDO pattern in [7].

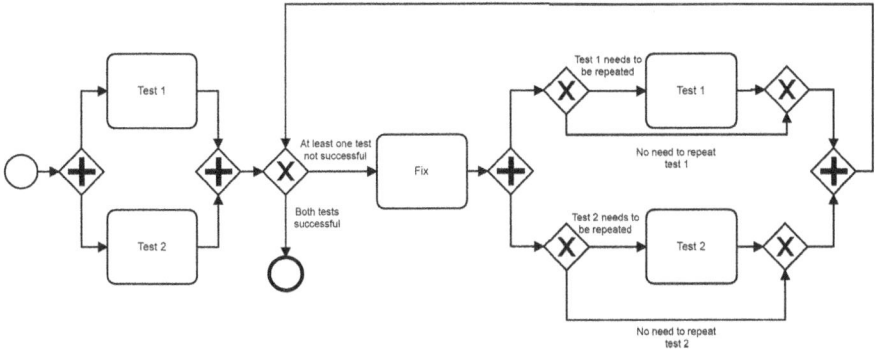

Fig. 31. An example for FIX AND RETEST

Note that a difference between this pattern and REPEAT UNTIL SUCCESS (pattern 3) is that there is a possibility to overcome the obstacles for successful execution by executing the "Fix" task.

3.7   Pattern 12: Double Check

Use when: Several Activities Must Come to Consistent Results

Also Known As: CONFIRM [10], 4-EYES PRINCIPLE [18].

Problem: How to model the following scenario: A number of activities has to be executed, and each activity is expected to deliver some result. The goal is only reached if all activities have been completed successfully and their results do not contradict each other. Although the pattern is named DOUBLE CHECK, it is not restricted to two activities.

Example: A medical guideline requires that blood group testing must take place by two different methods. Blood typing is regarded as being successful if and only if both methods deliver the same result. If this is not the case, either the testing has to be repeated, another test has to be applied or the result is that no conclusive result can be given.

Block Symbol:
Figure 32 shows the block symbol for the DOUBLE CHECK pattern – in this case for two activities A and B.

Implementation (BPMN):
Figure 33 shows the test activities as well as an activity that subsequently compares their results. The *Data Objects* make clear that the activity "Compare Results" needs data from both test activities. In the case that the tests come to

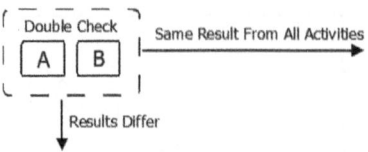

Fig. 32. FIX AND RETESTDOUBLE CHECK

different results, the process in Fig. 33 simply ends with an *End Event* named "Tests have to be repeated". In a real case, it would be necessary to model what actually happens (repeat test 1 or 2 or both or do another test 3,...).

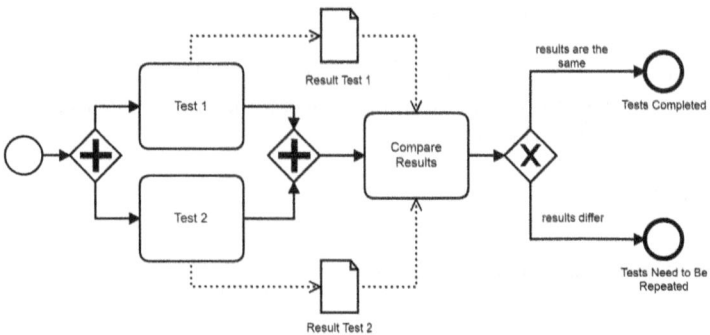

Fig. 33. BPMN Model for DOUBLE CHECK

Implementation (CMMN):
Figure 34 shows the core implementation of this pattern in CMMN. To make the data-based decision explicit, a *Case File Item* has been used which contains the results of the comparison between the results of Test 1 and Test 2. Whether a *Repetition Rule* is added to Test 1, Test 2, both tests or the *Stage* as a whole depends on the actions to be taken if the test results differ from each other. In the simple form of Fig. 34, the process simply ends without any test being repeated.

Related Patterns: This pattern looks very similar to the pattern PASS ALL TESTS discussed in Sect. 3.5 as pattern 10. The difference becomes apparent when we look not only at the flow of control but also on the flow of data between the tests. In the PASS ALL TESTS pattern, the tests work independently from each other. Each test has a criterion to decide whether or not some object passes the test. These criteria are known before testing starts. DOUBLE CHECK works differently: Here the result of the first test defines the criterion for the second one. This means that there has to be a flow of data (outgoing from the test activities) which is not the case for the PASS ALL TESTS pattern. Therefore, the

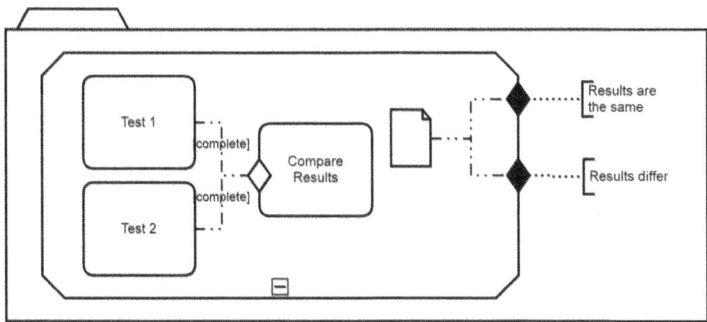

Fig. 34. CMMN model for DOUBLE CHECK

technical implementation is different even if the verbal description sounds very similar for both patterns.

DOUBLE CHECK can be combined with REPEAT UNTIL SUCCESS (pattern 3) if we regard the fact that the activities do not come to the same result as "not being successful". However, embedding DOUBLE CHECK into REPEAT UNTIL SUCCESS is the correct way to model the situation only if the reaction to the non-conclusive results is to repeat all activities. If instead another activity has to be executed, this alternative way should be modelled at the "results differ" path.

4 Pattern Variants

4.1 Pattern Variants for Terminating Activities

Termination by Timeout
Use when: An activity must be completed in a given time span.

Also Known As: TIMEOUT, UNFAILABLE TIMED HANDLER [3], DEADLINE EXPIRY [29].

Problem: How to model the following scenario: An activity must lead to a satisfactory result within a given time. After that time, the execution of the activity has to be stopped. In addition, it can be necessary to do compensation work to clean-up partly executed steps or to start an alternative activity. Often, this alternative activity is executed by another participant (escalation).

Example: The program chair of a scientific conference collects reviews from a number of reviewers. If all reviews arrive in time, a decision about the acceptance of a contribution can be made. If a reviewer fails to send back the review in time, the program chair can ask other reviewers or proceed with a limited number of reviews.

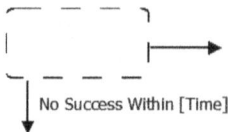

Fig. 35. TERMINATION BY TIMEOUT: The activities inside the block must succeed in a given time

Block Symbol:

Implementation (BPMN): Modelling the expiration of a deadline by means of a *Timer Event* as shown in Fig. 36 is quite common in BPMN.

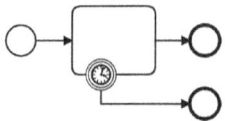

Fig. 36. Timeout in BPMN

Implementation (CMMN): CMMN provides the concept of a *TimerEventListener* to close a *Stage* or a *Case*. Its attributes *timerStart* and *timerExpression* must be set such that the event occurs if the execution of the *Task* takes too long (Fig. 37).

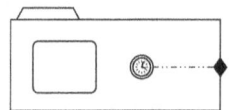

Fig. 37. Timeout in CMMN

Related Patterns: [29] contains a detailed discussion about possible reactions on exceptions (such as a deadline expiry). In particular, this paper discusses many ways how the activity can be allocated to new resources (which include the participant(s) who are involved into the processing of the activity). The handling of an activity for which a time-out occurred is discussed in [8, p. 97] as PRIORITIZATION and ESCALATION: A delayed activity becomes "more important" (prioritization) and can be reassigned to another role (escalation). For the special case of a signature workflow (where several permissions have to be collected from different participants), this escalation is discussed as JUMP SIGNATURE pattern in [9].

[3] discusses a pattern COMPENSATION WITH ESCALATION in which the expiration of the timer leads to a call of a task handler. If the task handler succeeds, the activity which took too long is restarted. This can be considered as a special case of our pattern.

Termination by Condition
Use when: The (repeated) execution of one or more activities has to be terminated because a success became unlikely or no more necessary.

Example: An investor places a buy order for a certain bond. The order becomes invalid if the price of the bond surpasses a given limit. In this case, no action is required (Fig. 38).

Block Symbols:

[Abandoning Condition]

Fig. 38. TERMINATION BY CONDITION

Implementation (BPMN): BPMN provides a rich set of *Events* that can be used to terminate the execution of activities in the same way as shown for timer events in Fig. 35.

In addition, for an activity that has a "loop" marker ($\circlearrowright$) indicating that it can be executed repeatedly, the *StandardLoopCharacteristics* can be defined. It contains an attribute *loopCondition* with a Boolean expression that controls the looping behaviour. The activity will continue to be repeated as long as the condition remains true. In addition, the `loopMaximum` attribute serves as a cap on the number of iterations. While the loop marker is shown in the visual model, the details of the *loopCondition* are not.

Implementation (CMMN): A common way to model this pattern in CMMN is by using an *Exit Criterion* that ends a *Stage* or *Case*.

4.2   Pattern Variants for Restricting the Flow of Control

Force Order
Use when: In one of the patterns TRY ALTERNATIVES UNTIL SUCCESS, REPEAT UNTIL SUCCESS, ONE OUT OF MANY ALTERNATIVES MUST BE SUCCESSFUL **or** ALL ALTERNATIVES MUST BE SUCCESSFUL, **more than one activity can be executed. We want the activities to be executed in a given order.**

Block Symbol: For expressing the need of a fixed order between activities, we use arrows that depict the control flow. An example can be seen in the right diagram in Fig. 9 where the test must be executed *after* the completion of the preceding activity.

Implementation (BPMN): In BPMN, it is quite normal to model a well-defined order between the activities. This can be done by means of *Sequence Flow* arrows. In an *Ad-hoc Sub-Process* (as used in Fig. 18) it is allowed to have a sequence flow between some of the activities within the *Ad-hoc Sub-Process* while other activities are not connected by *Sequence Flow* arrows. This allows to specify constraints for the execution order without enforcing an order between all activities at modelling-time.

Implementation (CMMN): Order dependencies among elements in CMMN can be depicted by means of *Connectors*. Formally, those connectors represent an *OnPart* of a *Sentry*. In Fig. 39, *Task* B cannot be executed until *Task* A has been completed while no restrictions are defined for the execution of *Task* C.

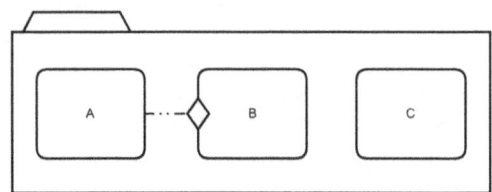

Fig. 39. CMMN model with a connector between tasks

Disallow Parallel Execution
Use when: In the pattern TRY ALTERNATIVES UNTIL SUCCESS, REPEAT UNTIL SUCCESS, ONE OUT OF MANY ALTERNATIVES MUST BE SUCCESSFUL **or** ALL ALTERNATIVES MUST BE SUCCESSFUL, **more than one activity can be executed. We want to restrict the execution of activities such that at most one activity is executed at any point of time.**

Example: In medical guidelines, one can often find a recommendation like the following: "prescribing medication X is indicated in patients who remain symptomatic even after treatment with medication Y". It may be important to emphasize that both medications should not be administered simultaneously.

Implementation (BPMN): When an *Ad-hoc Sub-Process* is used as recommended for a version of pattern 6 in Sect. 3.3, the attribute *ordering* of the *Ad-hoc Sub-Process* can be set to sequential. This means that an *Activity* can be selected for execution only if the previous one has terminated.

Implementation (CMMN): In general, CMMN allows different *Tasks* to be executed at the same time. Restricting this behaviour would be possible by placing *Sentries* on each *Task.* Those *Sentries* can evaluate a *Condition,* and it would be possible to define this *Condition* such that it is true only if no other *Task* is active.

5   Related Work

Before the concept of patterns was introduced in the field of business process modelling, semantic patterns have been used for creating unambiguous textual use case specifications. [26] discusses four patterns SEQUENCE, CONSTRAINT, CONCURRENCY and REPETITION which can be regarded as patterns occurring between activities in a process. In the area of business process modelling, the most popular work on patterns are the workflow patterns [27, 28, 35]. They are helpful for selecting a workflow system that corresponds to the needs of an organization and for evaluating the expressiveness of modelling languages [36]. Our patterns have a higher abstraction level than the workflow patterns. We are convinced that this makes it easier to communicate business situations with the stakeholders. However, our patterns are not so specific that they are restricted to a well-defined type of activities. This is a difference to patterns that address the actual meaning of an activity with patterns such as INFORMATION REQUEST in [33].

Patterns for differences/changes between business process models have been discussed for various reasons and using different terminologies (an overview can be found in [5]). As explained in [17], "High-level change operations provide richer syntactical meanings than change primitives." This means that a difference between two models is not simply explained as a difference between graphs (on a by-node and by-vertex-level), but rather by its meaning, e.g. an activity is moved from one place to another. Those change patterns have been developed for a different purpose than the patterns in our paper. However, in many cases they are highly related to our patterns. When we in our terminology say that, e.g. "activities can be executed in any order", this is related to a change pattern such as CHANGE ORDER between one model and another. Change patterns describe variability on a technical level while the aim of our patterns is to use typical business vocabulary only.

A pattern collection that shares some goals with our patterns are the exception handling patterns in [30]. They discuss ways to express exceptions and failures in a business processes. The tree-like modelling language LittleJIL [2] (developed by the same group) has built-in support for many of those patterns. The same is true for the tree-based language Concur Task Trees [23]. Several situations that we have included into our pattern catalogue are built-in notational elements in this language, allowing a terse notation. [14] discusses the use of this language as a stakeholder-centred form of process modelling.

6   Conclusion and Future Work

In this paper, we suggested a visual modelling language that can express variability in business processes. It is simple enough for being understood without much training. We do not present our block symbols as a recommendation or even a "standard". Our goal was to highlight the observed variability patterns. If different labels contribute better to understanding within an organization, we encourage adapting the labelling of the building blocks. Block-based modelling is essentially intended as a temporary aid for discussion during the modelling process, not for creating final models.

A first piece of evidence that the patterns are useful for discussing variable processes with practitioners was provided when we discussed the applicability of our patterns with medical professionals at Rigshospitalet, the leading university hospital in Denmark. Three medical doctors were asked whether they could give an example of each pattern from their work and explain how their example matched the pattern. They could translate the patterns into their daily work practice. Afterwards, we applied the patterns in an interview with a nurse, wherein she explained the highly-variable process of a planned patient admission to a hospital. It was found that the process building blocks described by our patterns could be used to create a model of this process that was understood by everyone involved into the modelling (researchers and nurse). More details about the experiments with medical practitioners can be found in [10].

Figure 40 shows the process of the evaluation of a potential living liver donor in a hospital. It can be seen that using our patterns, the process can be depicted in a condensed way even if it contains several points of variability. If necessary, building blocks can also be nested into each other. We think that such a notation is very helpful for the communication with domain experts (who are not business process modelling experts).

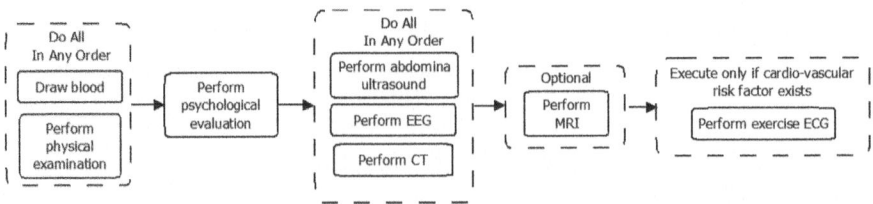

Fig. 40. Process for evaluation of a living liver donor in a hospital

However, we also acknowledge the value of standard modelling languages – in particular if our ultimate aim is to produce executable process models. Therefore, we hope that the mapping of our patterns into constructs in standard modelling languages given in this paper can be helpful when formal models have to be constructed. It would be an interesting goal for future research to construct a automatic transformation from "informal" models as shown in Fig. 40 into models in standardized languages such as BPMN or CMMN. For the building blocks that do not include variability, the basic concepts for such a transformation into BPMN have already been published in [13]. We would like to emphasize that although a model as the one in Fig. 40 is an "informal" one, it can show some information more clearly than BPMN or CMMN diagrams do. The reason is that several properties and constraints in these standardized languages are "hidden" in attributes of the models that are not shown in the diagrams (unless comments have been added, which is of course recommended).

Acknowledgments. We want to gratefully thank the anonymous reviewers, our shepherd Frank J. Frey and all participants of the workshop at EuroPLoP 2018 for their feedback.

References

1. Bauer, T.: Anforderungen an vormodellierte Flexibilität für den Kontrollfluss von Geschäftsprozessen. In: INFORMATIK 2017, pp. 799–813. Gesellschaft für Informatik (2017)
2. Cass, A.G., Lerner, B.S., Jr., S.M.S., McCall, E.K., Wise, A.E., Osterweil, L.J.: Little-JIL/Juliette: a process definition language and interpreter. In: Proceedings of the 22nd International Conference on on Software Engineering, ICSE 2000, pp. 754–757. ACM (2000)
3. Döhring, M., Zimmermann, B., Godehardt, E.: Extended workflow flexibility using rule-based adaptation patterns with eventing semantics. In: INFORMATIK 2010. LNI, vol. 175, pp. 195–200. Gesellschaft für Informatik (2010)
4. Döhring, M., Zimmermann, B., Karg, L.: Flexible workflows at design- and runtime using BPMN2 adaptation patterns. In: Abramowicz, W. (ed.) BIS 2011. LNBIP, vol. 87, pp. 25–36. Springer, Heidelberg (2011). https://doi.org/10.1007/978-3-642-21863-7_3
5. Fellmann, M., Koschmider, A., Laue, R., Schoknecht, A., Vetter, A.: Business process model patterns: state-of-the-art, research classification and taxonomy. Bus. Process. Manag. J. **25**(5), 972–994 (2019)
6. Gamma, E., Helm, R., Johnson, R., Vlissides, J.: Design patterns: abstraction and reuse of object-oriented design. In: Nierstrasz, O.M. (ed.) ECOOP 1993. LNCS, vol. 707, pp. 406–431. Springer, Heidelberg (1993). https://doi.org/10.1007/3-540-47910-4_21
7. Gruhn, V., Laue, R.: Good and bad excuses for unstructured business process models. In: 12th European Conference on Pattern Languages of Programs, EuroPLoP 2007 (2007)
8. Havey, M.: Essential Business Process Modeling. O'Reilly (2005)
9. Hsu, H., Tsai, M., Wang, F.: Simplifying the design of signature workflow with patterns. In: 36th Annual IEEE Computer Software and Applications Conference Workshops, pp. 290–295. IEEE Computer Society (2012)

10. Kirchner, K., Laue, R., Edwards, K., Lantow, B.: Patterns for modeling process variability in a healthcare context. Bus. Process. Manag. J. **30**(1), 1–27 (2024)
11. Kirchner, K., Malessa, C., Scheuerlein, H., Settmacher, U.: Experience from collaborative modeling of clinical pathways. In: Modellierung im Gesundheitswesen: Tagungsband des Workshops im Rahmen der Modellierung 2014, pp. 13–24 (2014)
12. Kirchner, K., Nešković, S.: Using CUTA4BPM to support participative development of expert-driven processes. In: 2nd International Conference on Information Society Technology (2012)
13. Kirchner, K., Nešković, S., Stojimirović, D.: From user-understandable to technical process model: a model-driven approach using CUTA4BPM. In: 3nd International Conference on Internet Society Technology and Management (2013)
14. Kolb, J., Reichert, M., Weber, B.: Using concurrent task trees for stakeholder-centered modeling and visualization of business processes. In: Oppl, S., Fleischmann, A. (eds.) S-BPM ONE 2012. CCIS, vol. 284, pp. 237–251. Springer, Heidelberg (2012). https://doi.org/10.1007/978-3-642-29294-1_19
15. Lanz, A., Weber, B., Reichert, M.: Time patterns for process-aware information systems. Requirements Eng. **19**(2), 113–141 (2014)
16. Laue, R., Koop, W., Gruhn, V.: Indicators for open issues in business process models. In: Daneva, M., Pastor, O. (eds.) REFSQ 2016. LNCS, vol. 9619, pp. 102–116. Springer, Cham (2016). https://doi.org/10.1007/978-3-319-30282-9_7
17. Li, C., Reichert, M., Wombacher, A.: On measuring process model similarity based on high-level change operations. In: Li, Q., Spaccapietra, S., Yu, E., Olivé, A. (eds.) ER 2008. LNCS, vol. 5231, pp. 248–264. Springer, Heidelberg (2008). https://doi.org/10.1007/978-3-540-87877-3_19
18. Lübke, D.: Design patterns for approval processes. In: Proceedings of the 28th European Conference on Pattern Languages of Programs, EuroPLoP 2023, Irsee, Germany, 5–9 July 2023, pp. 1:1–1:22. ACM (2023)
19. Natschläger, C., Geist, V., Kossak, F., Freudenthaler, B.: Optional activities in process flows. In: EMISA 2012. LNI, vol. 206, pp. 67–80. Gesellschaft für Informatik (2012)
20. Object Management Group (OMG): Business Process Model and Notation (BPMN) Version 2.0. Technical report (2011)
21. Object Management Group (OMG): Case Management Model and Notation, CMMN 1.1. Technical report (2016)
22. Object Management Group (OMG): Decision Model and Notation (DMN), Version 1.1. Technical report (2016)
23. Paternò, F.: Model-based Design and Evaluation of Interactive Applications. Springer (2000)
24. Pittke, F., Leopold, H., Mendling, J.: When language meets language: anti patterns resulting from mixing natural and modeling language. In: Business Process Management Workshops 2014. LNBIP, vol. 202. Springer (2015)
25. Reichert, M., Bauer, T., Fries, T., Dadam, P.: Modellierung planbarer Abweichungen in Workflow-Management-Systemen. In: Modellierung 2002. LNI, vol. 12, pp. 183–194. Gesellschaft für Informatik (2002)
26. Rolland, C., Achour, C.B.: Guiding the construction of textual use case specifications. Data Knowl. Eng. **25**(1–2), 125–160 (1998)
27. Russell, N., van der Aalst, W.M.P., ter Hofstede, A.H.M.: Workflow Patterns: The Definitive Guide. MIT Press (2016)
28. Russell, N., ter Hofstede, A.H.M., Mulyar, N.: Workflow controlflow patterns: a revised view. Technical report, BPM Center Report BPM-06-22, BPMcenter.org (2006)

29. Russell, N., van der Aalst, W., ter Hofstede, A.: Workflow exception patterns. In: Dubois, E., Pohl, K. (eds.) CAiSE 2006. LNCS, vol. 4001, pp. 288–302. Springer, Heidelberg (2006). https://doi.org/10.1007/11767138_20
30. Staudt Lerner, B., Christov, S., Osterweil, L., Bendraou, R., Kannengiesser, U., Wise, A.: Exception handling patterns for process modeling. IEEE Trans. Software Eng. **36**(2), 162–183 (2010)
31. Thom, L., Reichert, M., Iochpe, C.: On the support of workflow activity patterns in process modeling tools: Purpose and requirements. In: 3rd Workshop on Business Process Management. Brazilian Symposium on Multimedia and the WEB (2009)
32. Thom, L.H., et al.: On the capabilities of BPMN for workflow activity patterns representation. In: Dijkman, R., Hofstetter, J., Koehler, J. (eds.) BPMN 2011. LNBIP, vol. 95, pp. 172–177. Springer, Heidelberg (2011). https://doi.org/10.1007/978-3-642-25160-3_18
33. Thom, L.H., Reichert, M., Iochpe, C.: Activity patterns in process-aware information systems: basic concepts and empirical evidence. Int. J. Bus. Process Integr. Manag. **4**(2), 93–110 (2009)
34. Uronkarn, W., Senivongse, T.: Change Patterns Detection and Traceability Impact Analysis of Business Process Models, pp. 441–455. Springer (2015)
35. van der Aalst, W.M.P., ter Hofstede, A.H.M., Kiepuszewski, B., Barros, A.: Workflow patterns. Distrib. Parallel Datab. **14**(3), 5–51 (2003)
36. van der Aalst, W.M., ter Hofstede, A.H.: Workflow patterns put into context. Softw. Syst. Modeling **11**(3), 319–323 (2012)
37. Wohed, P., van der Aalst, W.M.P., Dumas, M., ter Hofstede, A.H.M., Russell, N.: On the suitability of BPMN for business process modelling. In: Dustdar, S., Fiadeiro, J.L., Sheth, A.P. (eds.) BPM 2006. LNCS, vol. 4102, pp. 161–176. Springer, Heidelberg (2006). https://doi.org/10.1007/11841760_12
38. Zimmermann, B., Döhring, M.: Patterns for flexible BPMN workflows. In: 16th European Conference on Pattern Languages of Programs, EuroPLoP 2011, p. 7. ACM (2011)

Pattern Discovery and Validation Using Scientific Research Methods

Dirk Riehle[1]([⊠]), Nikolay Harutyunyan[1], and Ann Barcomb[2]

[1] Friedrich-Alexander-University Erlangen-Nürnberg, Erlangen, Germany
dirk@riehle.org, nikolay.harutyunyan@fau.de
[2] University of Calgary, Calgary, Canada
ann@barcomb.org

Abstract. Pattern discovery, the process of discovering previously unrecognized patterns, is often performed as an ad-hoc process with little resulting certainty in the quality of the proposed patterns. Pattern validation, the process of validating the accuracy of proposed patterns, remains dominated by the simple heuristic of "the rule of three". This article shows how to use established scientific research methods for the purpose of pattern discovery and validation. We present a specific approach, called the handbook method, that uses the qualitative survey, action research, and case study research for pattern discovery and evaluation, and we discuss the underlying principle of using scientific methods in general. We evaluate the handbook method using three exploratory studies and demonstrate its usefulness.

Keywords: Pattern discovery · pattern validation · the handbook method

1 Introduction

A design pattern, in the context of the computer science and related research and practice communities, is an abstract problem solution derived from similar recurring problem solutions in a defined context (Gamma et al. 1994; Buschmann et al. 2007). This definition is an adaptation from the field of (traditional) architecture (Alexander 1977). In computer science, pattern authors usually present their patterns in an easily digestible format, the pattern form, and assemble larger sets of patterns into pattern languages, handbooks, or catalogs. As of today, thousands of patterns have been written and published, all proposing common problem solutions.

The process of extracting and abstracting patterns from expert experience, which we call pattern discovery, as well as the initial evaluation and ultimate validation of proposed patterns or pattern languages has seen little research, however. Pattern authors seek feedback on their patterns in writers' workshops, but such feedback is often only about the presentation of the pattern. Technical discussions of patterns can happen in writers' workshops and can provide important feedback to authors, but do not constitute technical validation of the content. While Gabriel (2008) argues that writers' workshops can be seen as a scientific method, nobody has ever evaluated them as such. Hence, their outcome is uncertain and the reliability as a method is unclear.

© The Author(s), under exclusive license to Springer-Verlag GmbH, DE, part of Springer Nature 2025
E. Wallingford et al. (Eds.): TPLOP V, LNCS 14630, pp. 226–253, 2025.
https://doi.org/10.1007/978-3-662-70810-1_6

Pattern authors, as this article's related work section discusses, have received little guidance on how to discover patterns and validate their findings. Pattern authors generally rely on their own experience, and pattern readers have little indication of the validity of the presented patterns but to trust their authors.

Researchers employ a large array of methods and approaches to build theories and to validate them. Following an established and validated method correctly helps scientists achieve rigor and quality in results. In the context of this article, a theory is the knowledge captured about some phenomena of interest; its value or usefulness lies in how well it allows users of the theory to predict the outcome of events and actions. At any point of time, there may be many competing theories to describe the phenomena of interest; these will all be put to the test and over time those theories that fail to predict correctly will be put aside as invalid.

In this article, we describe how to apply scientific methods to pattern discovery, evaluation, and validation. We call the combination of traditional scientific methods with the pattern presentation form the handbook method, a derivative research method. We focus on the domain of software engineering in this article and in the demonstration of our approach, because this is what we are most familiar with.

- From the perspective of the patterns community, the main contribution of this article is to provide a start-to-finish process of discovering, codifying, evaluating, and validating patterns.
- From the perspective of the scientific community, the main contribution is a derived research method that utilizes the work of the patterns community for theory presentation, a sorely neglected topic.

The focus of this article is to introduce and demonstrate the usefulness of our approach to the patterns community. In other work, we intend to show the usefulness of using patterns for theory presentation to the scientific community.

This work, our approach, and its validation, is in an exploratory stage. The proposed method has been developed by the first author and has been explored in several projects by all authors. We believe that our work brings the patterns and the scientific community closer together by more clearly (than before) showing the usefulness of the respective work for each other.

The structure of this article is as follows: After this introduction, Sect. 2 reviews related work. In Sect.3, we describe our approach to pattern discovery and validation using scientific research methods. In Sect. 4 we discuss several exploratory studies, in which we have applied our approach to demonstrate its usefulness. Section 5 follows with a discussion of this work and Sect. 6 presents an outlook and concludes the article.

2 Related Work

We discuss the pattern community's work on pattern discovery and validation, the pattern community's work on relating patterns to the scientific method, and the scientific community's work on theory building and validation as related to this article.

2.1 Pattern Discovery and Validation

Pattern discovery is the discovery of previously not as-such recognized patterns, usually from examples. Pattern discovery is also called "pattern mining". Validation of such discovered patterns is often reduced to applying a simple heuristic, the so-called "rule of three". According to this rule, a pattern author must present three known (and significantly different) instances of the pattern to substantiate the claim that a new pattern has been found. As such, pattern discovery and validation is an inherently inductive process.

Iba et al. discuss pattern mining (in the sense of pattern discovery) in a series of articles (Akado et al. 2015; Iba and Isaku 2012; Iba & Isaku 2016). In these articles, Iba et al. reflect on their experiences with discovering patterns in various domains. Specifically, they use four pattern languages that they wrote as the empirical base for presenting their approach to pattern discovery. Not entirely surprisingly, the approach is presented using the pattern form. Iba et al. perform example processes to illustrate how to discover patterns. They utilize different forms of reasoning during the process.

Iba et al.'s approach to pattern discovery, presented as a pattern language, references their own pattern discovery and development work as examples in which the patterns of pattern discovery have been applied. Their approach consists mainly of creativity techniques, and does not utilize any traditional scientific research methods. Iba et al. apply the rule-of-three heuristic to substantiate their findings.

The rule-of-three, from a scientific perspective, this can be euphemistically called "convenience sampling". The pattern authors use what they have at hand. However, the purpose of the rule-of-three is to support the claim of generalizability (from known examples) to a more general principle, the pattern. For this, a pattern author should employ a sampling strategy that supports claims of generalizability (Baltes & Ralph 2020) rather than use what is conveniently at hand.

From a scientific perspective, Iba et al.'s work remains in proposal status, as the patterns (of pattern discovery) have not been validated using an established scientific method.

In contrast to Iba et al.'s work, our approach utilizes established scientific methods rather than inventing new ones. At this stage, we present a preliminary exploratory evaluation of the validity of our approach using three non-trivial studies, leaving a full validation of the handbook method to later work.

Outside of Iba et al.'s work, in software engineering, the term "pattern mining", in the literature typically refers to the identification of existing known patterns in software system design and code. On this topic, Dong et al. (2009) present a survey of known techniques for identifying applied design patterns in source code. Such techniques are used in reverse engineering to unearth previously lost or poorly documented design decisions. Dong et al.'s survey discusses a range of techniques drawn from the literature. In addition to this survey, further design pattern mining articles in the sense of reengineering design decisions have been published, for example, Gupta (2011), Gupta et al. (2011), Marco (2012), Alhusain et al. (2013), and Dwivedi et al. (2018).

Another relatively less used but relevant method for pattern mining is through literature reviews, employed, for example, by Fehling (2011) and Correia (2013).

2.2   Patterns and the Scientific Method

Our epistemological base is critical rationalism, the mainstream theory of science under-lying most of engineering and computer science. We assume that an outside world exists, about which we develop theories and which we continue to test until we find flaws and replace old theories with newer ones.

Already Christopher Alexander, the architect who inspired much of the computer science patterns community, was looking for analogies or metaphors to explain what patterns are (Alexander 2007). As an architect, his view on patterns and "the nature of order" was formed not only by facts, but also by more elusive concepts like "beauty" and "belonging", for which he does not provide definitions that would fit a critical rationalist's paradigm. As a consequence, his views on patterns and science are incommensurable with our epistemological base and stand in parallel to ours.

Fitting into the paradigm that our work is based on is Kohls and Panke's work of equating patterns with scientific theories and that the process of pattern mining can be equated with scientific discovery (Kohls & Panke 2009). We share the same underlying assumptions but differ in their extension and in the details.

Kohls and Panke consider an individual pattern a theory. We argue that pattern handbooks and their domains can be equated with scientific theories, if derived using scientific methods. We don't equate individual patterns with theories, but rather view them as an outgrowth of theory, that is, hypotheses. This difference may appear to be subtle, but is important, because the validation of theories proceeds by testing hypotheses.

Without hypotheses to test, there is no (good) theory. Later in their article, after introducing patterns as theories, Kohls and Panke also equate patterns with hypotheses.

Kohls and Panke list "usefulness to the practitioner" as the main test of a pattern. While we obviously agree that patterns should be useful, to us usefulness is a property of a well-working theory and not a test of it. Scientists validate theories by testing hypotheses, which are predictions about the future derived from the theory. If such predictions keep becoming true, the theory becomes useful for its increasing likelihood of making correct predictions next time again.

We agree that pattern mining is similar to scientific discovery. In our book, however, it should only be equated with scientific discovery, if such mining is performed using proper scientific research methods. Simply stating the similarity and then assuming that pattern mining is the same as scientific discovery is not sufficient because it lacks the depth and rigor (so far) that has been spent on developing scientific methods. The article does not list specific research methods or common research designs used for pattern mining.

Kohls and Panke's article is noteworthy for articulating an important question: Are patterns anything new? We have argued before that pattern instances may be well known, but that the abstraction step from instances to the underlying pattern is a noteworthy (i.e. publishing-worthy) achievement. This matches the approach taken in this article: Known pattern instances are primary materials that feed into the scientific theory building process, and pattern handbooks including their constituent patterns are the (novel) output.

By discussing constructivism at some length, Kohls and Panke seem to imply that their work is rooted in constructivism. The consequences of this are unclear to us, because their arguments seem to work as well, if one were to take a traditional rationalist approach to science, as we do. Later in the article, they indicate inductive empiricism as their epistemological base. Whichever, rationalism is still the workhorse assumption of most of engineering and natural sciences and has not been displaced despite competing approaches, and it seems to work well as a base for their work as much as ours.

In an essay, Gabriel (2008) argues that writers' workshops, as practiced by the patterns community, can be viewed as a scientific methodology. Most of the essay is dedicated to explaining how writers' workshops work, but at the end of the essay, Gabriel equates the activities of the patterns community with "making science". Gabriel's use of words is similar to ours, when he talks about theory building, experimentation, and observation, among others. The essay, however, devotes only a few paragraphs to this analogy and does not provide any detailed mapping of how writers' workshop could be interpreted as a scientific method.

Rising (2020), in a recorded speech (keynote address at PLoP 2020), asks for gradual improvement through testing. Patterns come with promises, like improving our surroundings, but the patterns community has yet to spend effort on testing and validating patterns. She uses scientific terminology, and like Kohls and Panke relates patterns to hypotheses. However, she stays on a rather general level, as may be appropriate for a speech, without getting into details as to what experimentation and testing might mean. We view her insights as encouragement for our work in making a scientific approach to patterns concrete and specific, as we are doing it here with our handbook method.

2.3 Theory Building and Validation

The approach presented in this article puts together established research methods for the purposes of pattern discovery and validation. Pattern discovery is carried out using (mostly qualitative) research methods of theory building, and pattern validation is carried out using research methods of theory validation.

Theory building is generally viewed as an iterative process of theory creation and evaluation, where the creation of new theory is followed by (sometimes only partial) evaluation, feeding back into the next iteration of theory creation and evaluation.

Prominent representatives of theory building research methods are:

- The qualitative survey, e.g. Jansen (2010). This comparatively simple theory creation method focuses on qualitatively surveying stakeholders and analysing the primary materials gathered using methods of qualitative data analysis, as, for example, defined by Mayring (2000) or Kuckartz (2014). The qualitative survey tries to stay neutral of other research methods and techniques so that it can be combined well, where necessary.
- Grounded theory, e.g. Glaser & Strauss (1967), Corbin & Strauss (2014), Charmaz (2006). This heavyweight start-to-finish method of theory building provides a comprehensive set of further methods and techniques of theory building. Arguably, it is better considered a research methodology, forging research methods and techniques into a coherent whole. An important practical contribution by grounded theory is the open coding approach of qualitative data analysis, as discussed by Corbin & Strauss (2014) and as widely used in practice.

- Case study research, e.g. Yin (2003), Runeson et al. (2012). This other heavyweight of theory building methods focuses on selecting cases for data gathering and analysis. Unlike grounded theory, which goes broad, case study research can go deep on the usually small number of selected cases. Like grounded theory, case study research is suitable for both theory creation and evaluation, but most authors suggest research should focus either on exploration (i.e. creation) or evaluation of theory, not on both at the same time.

These three methods informed our research. Beyond these three, many other theory building methods exist, for example, action research, e.g. Davison et al. (2004), ethnographies, e.g. Robinson et al. (2007), and critical theory, e.g. Horkheimer (1972).

In computer science, the predominant epistemological stance is positivistic or rationalistic: Most researchers believe that we can not only build theories, but can also validate or invalidate them using appropriate research methods. Unlike the iterative process of theory building, theory validation consists of a large number of hypothesis tests that probe a theory. Hypotheses are predictions of the theory being tested, and if they turn out to be true, the likelihood of the theory being correct increases, otherwise it decreases. Therefore, each hypothesis test contributes to the truth value to the overall validation or (ultimate) invalidation of a theory.

The original research method is the controlled experiment. It is often informally equated with "the scientific method", though this is too simplistic today. The defining characteristic of controlled experiments is that using statistical methods, you can make truth statements about the correlation between input and output variables (independent and dependent constructs), and that this gives definitive answers about the truth value of the hypothesis within the limits of the experiment's definition (Wohlin et al. 2012).

Controlled experiments are a possible approach for testing individual patterns: In general, the pattern's applied context is the experimental set-up, the problem statement is the independent variable, and the solution is the dependent variable. Controlled experiments can go beyond this general set-up and focus on individual aspects of a pattern, like the impact of a particular force. The challenge, as with most experiments, is to rigorously control for the set-up to avoid confounding factors that influence the outcome.

Another research method of theory validation is the hypothesis-testing survey (Fowler 2013). Unlike the controlled experiment, which goes deep in a specific situation, the hypothesis-testing survey broadly surveys experts or stakeholders as to their thoughts on a particular topic. What may sound subjective is not: Using defined instrument creation and calibration methods, the questions on a hypothesis-testing survey allow for precise statistical analysis and corresponding answers to the underlying hypothesis. As such, the hypothesis-testing survey can be used to broadly query an expert community on the validity of a pattern.

3 The Handbook Method

This section describes an approach to using scientific research methods for pattern discovery, codification, evaluation, and validation. We use a running example to illustrate our approach.

3.1 Process Overview

Patterns are discovered ("mined"), codified ("written"), and applied, where initial applications often also serve to evaluate and refine the pattern definition. These activities are usually performed in sequence, but eventually also iterated over, until the results seem satisfactory to the pattern author.

Table 1 displays the equivalence of these activities to the matching scientific terminology. This article covers the complete process, and presents exploratory studies of using scientific methods for pattern discovery and evaluation. Terms from theory building have a white background, terms from theory validation have a gray background.

Table 1. Terminology and processes of the scientific and the patterns community compared

#	Patterns Community		Scientific Community
1.	Pattern discovery ("mining")	↔	Theory creation
2.	Pattern codification ("writing")	↔	Theory codification
3.	(Reflective) pattern application	↔	Theory evaluation
4.	Proposed pattern	↔	Hypothesis
5.	Pattern testing	↔	Hypothesis testing
6.	Pattern validation	↔	Theory validation

Example. As an example, we will use scientific methods for the development of a patterns handbook of open source governance (Harutyunyan 2019).

Open source governance is the governance of using open source code in a company's software projects and products. Using open source makes the company depend on the code being used, and this dependency needs to be managed. Such governance includes the selection, integration, monitoring and maintenance of open source code and components as well as being compliant with their license.

Until recently, there were no comprehensive scientific theories nor practical pattern handbooks on how to do this. Some patterns about legal issues of using open source in software products have been published (Hammouda et al. 2010; Link 2010), but their discovery has not been documented and they have been presented as self-evident without much clarification of how they were derived.

3.2 Pattern Discovery

Pattern discovery is the identification of new patterns, typically from an author's experience. Ideally, the author not only invents the patterns, but rather bases them on instances (examples) that they have seen.

The first activity for pattern discovery using scientific methods is to use methods of theory creation to identify new patterns and to develop an understanding of their properties. We say theory creation rather than the more general theory building, because theory building in scientific methods not only includes creation, but also evaluation, which we view as a separate activity.

To discover new patterns, the author applies an appropriate (theory-building, qualitative) research method to the domain of interest. Examples of research methods are the qualitative survey (Jansen 2010) or grounded theory (Glaser & Strauss 1967; Corbin & Strauss 1998).

Table 2 illustrates an example research design for developing a theory of open source governance in software companies.

Table 2. Example research process for developing a theory of open source governance

#	Activity	Example
1	Define research question	What are patterns of open source governance?
2	Choose research method	Use the qualitative survey (Jansen 2010)
3	Write research protocol	Lay-out steps to be taken, assumptions made, …
4	Build sampling model	Model companies using dimensions like age, size, …
5	Sample relevant population	IBM, MySQL, Bosch, …
6	Gather primary data	Interview stakeholders in companies
7	Analyse data	Perform qualitative content analysis (Mayring 2000)
8	Repeat 5.-7. until saturation (stopping criterion) is reached (Corbin & Strauss 2014)	

With the exception of Iba et al.'s creativity techniques, there are no established methods for the process of pattern discovery that step through the details as illustrated in the research design of Table 2. Only scientific methods, here the qualitative survey, come with detailed guidance and textbooks that instruct researchers what to do. This is a significant gain over the pattern community's sole reliance on an author's experience.

Taking this approach, any scientific research method suited to the domain of software engineering can be used, as long as it helps gather the data needed for theory creation. Research methods can be combined, if desired, as long as they don't conflict with each other but strengthen the outcome. The output of such methods must be primary data that can be analyzed.

The analysis of primary data is called qualitative data analysis (QDA) (Corbin & Strauss 2014) or qualitative content analysis (Mayring 2000) or qualitative text analysis (Kuckartz 2014). Common types of primary data are stakeholder interviews, workshop notes, and artifact documentation. The research method defines how to get to this data.

In our example of open source governance, we choose

"What are the patterns of open source governance?"

As the driving pattern discovery question. The underlying assumption is that such patterns exist and can be determined using appropriate theory-building research methods.

Next, we choose the qualitative survey as the simplest applicable research method.

We then determine companies that are experts in open source governance. For this, we develop a sampling model structured by relevant dimensions like size and age of a company, types of products or markets, etc. Using purposive sampling, sufficient coverage of variation can be achieved. Example companies to investigate could be IBM (large, established, traditional products) or Chef (medium-size, challenger, open source product).

Figure 1 presents an excerpt from the sampling, including its model.

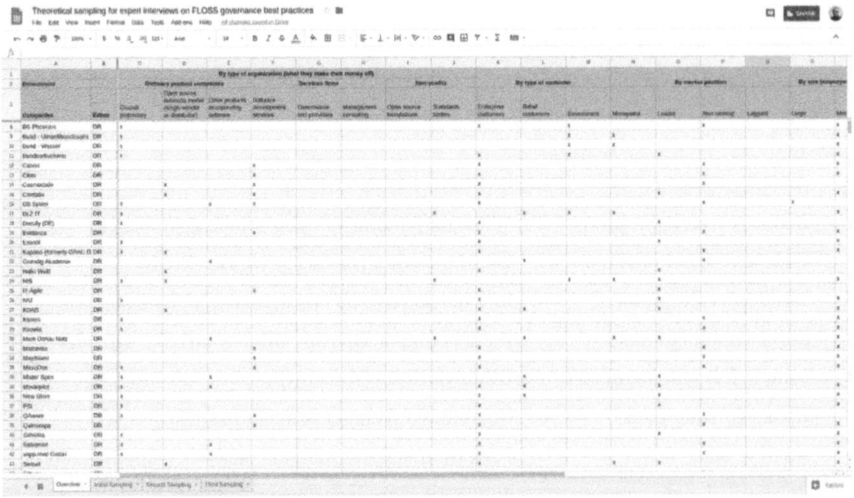

Fig. 1. Example sampling model and population

Within those companies we sample relevant stakeholders, for example, engineering managers, software architects, software developers, the legal counsel, and staff like an open source program officer. We then perform open interviews and ask for supplementary materials like written policies.

With these materials in hand, we start the QDA process and develop the theory. If it becomes apparent that important aspects have not been covered enough, we go back to gathering more materials, either with companies that we already visited or with new companies.

3.3 Pattern Codification

Pattern codification is the process of describing a pattern in written form.

Scientific methods usually have little to say about presentation of theories; they focus on rigorous and traceable derivation of results from primary materials. As such, pattern codification and scientific methods complement each other well.

Data Analysis. To go from primary materials like expert interviews to patterns, the material has to be analyzed and the patterns to be derived.

The previous section showed how to gather the primary materials within which the patterns are waiting to be discovered. The next activity in the pattern discovery process is data analysis, from which the patterns emerge. There are many approaches to qualitative data analysis, see the aforementioned ones (Corbin & Strauss 2014; Mayring 2000; Kuckartz 2014).

In general, qualitative data analysis consists of annotating the primary materials in such a way that insights emerge incrementally. Initial steps are usually called open coding, because the researcher annotates primary materials with labels ("codes") that represent what seem to be interesting information or distinct concepts. Over time, codes are grouped to become higher-level abstractions through axial and selective coding (Corbin & Strauss 2014) or thematic coding (Mayring 2000), leading to a multi-rooted tree structure of codes, the so-called code system.

The specific coding paradigm does not matter here, as long as it allows relevant abstractions, here the patterns, to emerge.

Code Systems. An important step of going from primary materials to patterns is the creation of a code system.

A code system consists of codes (representing, for example, key concepts) and their sources (codings, which are links into primary materials like statements from stakeholders) with associated memos and other materials. It is the result of qualitative data analysis performed during theory building.

As an artifact, a code system is a hierarchical structure of codes, where each code has zero, one, or more references into the primary materials. Each reference is an annotation of the primary material, and the code is the label of that annotation. Thus, a code can have many instances, called codings. Codes emerge from the primary material, specifically, when the researcher recognizes something of significance and creates a corresponding code for the first time.

The researcher is usually free in how they structure the hierarchy of codes, but it should follow from their research question and a defined coding process provided by their research method. In general, the higher up in the code system, the more general a code is. Often, a code system has multiple root codes, called core categories, that represent major insights into the theory under development.

Associated with a code is a memo that explains important aspects of the code in general as they can be learned from the codings. Here, the researcher takes notes that can't be represented in the code itself.

Qualitative data analysis is often performed using a so-called CAQDAS (computer-assisted qualitative data analysis software) tool. Figure 2 shows a screenshot of parts of the code system in our running example together with a memo and some primary material.

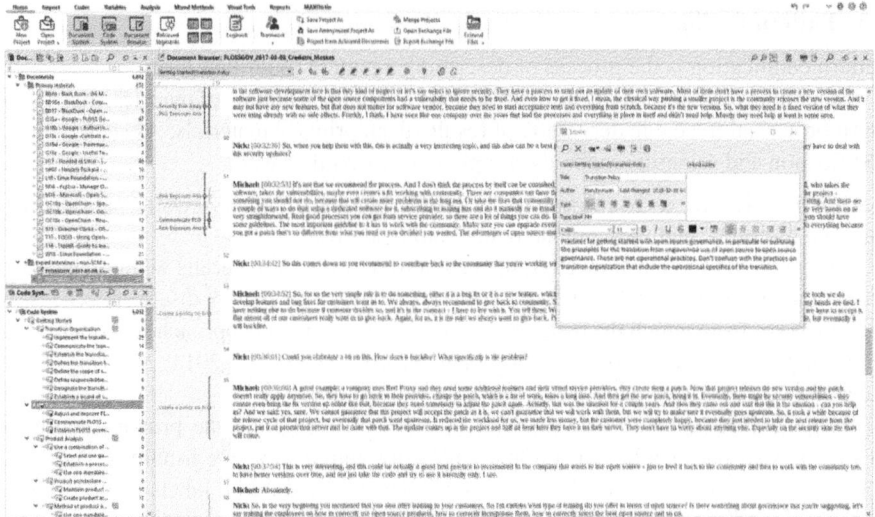

Fig. 2. Screenshot of example code system, memo, and primary material

Coding Process. The data analysis process is usually an iterative process of creating the theory and going back for more primary materials until a stopping criterion is reached.

For this, the researcher works through the primary materials, as discussed. Doing so, they recognize connections between open codes and abstract them into more general codes as part of building a multi-rooted hierarchical code hierarchy, the code system.

The initial observation and the subsequent abstraction through open and axial coding constitute the initial pattern discovery. Since the coding process is iterative, discovering patterns is an on-going process of refining the code system.

Abstract intermediate codes or codes at the root of the hierarchy, commonly called core categories, are prime candidates for patterns. Patterns could be capturing

- whole processes and domains,
- individual workflows and architectural structures, or
- single activities or design structures.

Whatever way a researcher decides to write down as a pattern, eventually, they will always have traceable links to original stakeholder statements by way of codings that justify the pattern at hand.

Pattern Handbooks. In the definition of our approach, we have found a particular structure useful, which we call pattern handbooks. Our handbooks are similar to pattern languages, and we are striving for the holistic generative flow expected of pattern languages, but to avoid confusing or alienating industry we are calling them pattern handbooks.

Table 3 presents a mapping of the key concepts underlying a code system and related materials to the different parts of a patterns handbook.

Summarizing Table 3, different codes that emerge as core categories represent different domains in the handbook. Subcodes of the core categories further structure the

Table 3. Code system to patterns handbook mapping

Code System Concept		Patterns Handbook
Core category	↔	Domain chapter
Intermediate or leaf code	↔	Process pattern, practice pattern
Parent/child relationship between codes	↔	Subsections in handbook
Codings	↔	Instances of patterns in primary materials

domains into subdomains and, eventually, process templates and best practice patterns. Codes that represent process templates or best practice patterns should not have subcodes that are different process templates or best practice patterns, but they can have variants of the same process or pattern as subcodes. Codings represent identified instances of the codes in the primary materials.

The current template handbook structure is a reflection of our specific projects and may change over time. Other types of handbooks may have a different overall structure and it is possible that ultimately we will find a way (back) to the classic format of a pattern language as a single graph-like structure of patterns and pattern relationships.

Continuing our example of a pattern handbook for open source governance, Fig. 3 shows an excerpt from our initial role and responsibility section.

Next, Fig. 4 provides an overview of key domains which structure the handbook as well as some patterns within the domain. We often use a mind-map to visualize the hierarchical structure of domains, subdomains, and patterns, as derived from the code system.

- The **CEO** has final responsibility for the company and thereby for best open source governance and compliance; typically he or she delegates this task to a program officer.
- The **program officer** is responsible for establishing and evolving best open source governance and compliance at the company; they may be on their own or lead a team.
- The **legal counsel** is responsible for providing legal advice including license interpretation, but they are not (or should not) be responsible for business risk assessment.
- An **engineering manager** is responsible for the development and delivery of a software prod-

Fig. 3. Part of a list of roles and responsibilities (short) in open source governance.

The hierarchical breakdown of domains and subdomains and patterns as the leaves does not necessarily reflect the way patterns are linked. Using the handbook by applying patterns one after another happens by following forward references from one pattern to the next.

Within a domain, we have found different types of patterns, for example, those which serve as entry gateways to the domain, those that serve as exit patterns, or pairs of alternative patterns. These types of patterns are in line with prior investigations of writing patterns (Meszaros & Doble 1997; Buschmann et al. 2007).

Figure 5 shows a short example best practice description in pattern form.

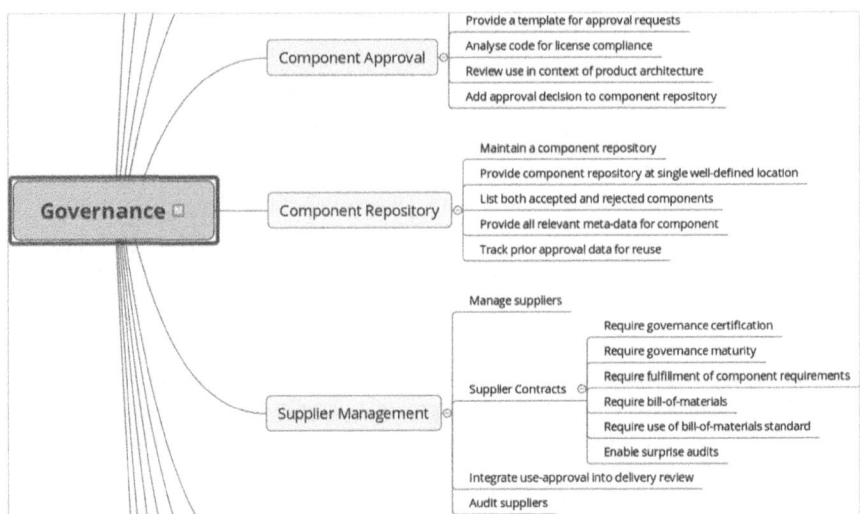

Fig. 4. Example break-down of domain into subdomains and best practices (patterns)

The maturity status describes the scientific evaluation status of the pattern and not the writer's certainty about its presentation quality. The maturity is similar to Kohls and Panke's (2009) confidence. The next subsection explains how the maturity status can evolve from proposed to evaluated to validated (or invalidated, that is, rejected).

5.7.1 Manage suppliers

Name	Manage suppliers
Actor(s)	Engineering manager
Context	Your product includes not only open source components, but also third-party components that are supplied to you by other software vendors. In contrast to open source projects, you are paying for the component (license) and you are receiving it from a corporate entity. You previously → *defined (your) component requirements* and they must be met by any component, open source or not.
Problem	How to ensure that a third-party component delivery meets your requirements?
Solution	First, before you select a supplier, you may → *require governance certification* or at least → *require (a minimum) governance maturity* of them. Once you have decided for a supplier, in any delivery contract, you should → *require fulfillment of your component requirements* and you should → *require a bill-of-materials* upon delivery for which you → *require they use a bill-of-materials standard*. Upon delivery, you have to → *ensure requirements are met* and for this, you have to → *integrate use-approval into the delivery process*. If the supplier isn't certified and having to reject a component delivery is too expensive, you may want to → *enable surprise audits* and consequently also → *perform surprise audits* as to best governance practices.
Maturity	Proposed

Fig. 5. Example best practice, here for managing suppliers in software supply chains

3.4 Pattern Evaluation

Pattern evaluation, as we define it, is the evaluation of the quality of a pattern. There are no methods for pattern evaluation in the patterns community, but one could argue that the actual reflective use of a pattern leads to its reevaluation and rewriting. In fact, some patterns, like the value object pattern (Cunningham 1995; Fowler 2002; Evans 2004; Riehle 2006), have been written over and over again, with different authors addressing different aspects.

Evaluation vs. Validation. In scientific research, there is a difference between theory evaluation and theory validation. Evaluation is usually baked into the theory building process and helps steer the researcher towards increasing the quality of the theory being built. Methods like grounded theory have made theory creation and evaluation complementary but integral parts of the theory building process.

Theory validation, however, is the classic process of making predictions from the theory and testing the resulting hypotheses. Theory building and validation can be kept distinct by the different quality criteria applied to their results. In case of theory building and qualitative work, "trustworthiness" (Guba 1981) is often used, and in case of theory validation and quantitative work, the traditional reliability and validity metrics are usually used.

Consequently, we distinguish pattern evaluation by application in real-world contexts from pattern validation in laboratory-controlled experiments or similar methods.

Using Case Studies. We have found Yin's approach to case study research useful for the evaluation of our pattern handbooks. Other approaches like action research work as well. In general, action research allows the pattern author to engage with and guide pattern users, while the case study researcher is more hands off, observing and analyzing only.

For this, we apply the handbooks as part of case study research. According to Yin (2003), case study research applies well to phenomena that are

- contemporary,
- occur in real-life, and
- cannot be tightly controlled.

These conditions are a good match for applying our handbooks with their intended audience, for example, software companies. In the following, we walk through the major steps in applying case study research, but keep it short and refer the reader to the original literature.

For theory creation, the pattern author has to sample experts from which to learn. For theory evaluation, the author samples subjects that want to learn and are open to using patterns for this. Thus, they must not be experts of the domain being investigated. Purposive sampling applies like for expert selection; even the same model can be used. As a rule of thumb, at least three independent and ideally polar ("opposite") cases along relevant dimensions should be selected. In our own use of our approach, we have only ever used multiple-case designs, embedded or holistic.

The units of analysis depend on the domain, but for software engineering process phenomena they are often the company, specific departments, or the people involved.

The research questions are tied to the effectiveness or "truth" of the handbook and its components. They start with a broad question that gets refined with more detailed questions:

1. Is the domain adequately and completely captured?
2. Is process template X adequate and common?
3. Is best practice Y correct and effective?

To answer these questions, appropriate data need to be gathered. How to do so depends on the pattern handbook's domain and data gathering methods. In general, however, data triangulation is a good idea. Thus, relevant data that can be gathered includes, among others, direct observation, participant observation, and interviews, during or after establishing and applying the processes and practices described by the handbook.

Please note that the research questions are about the actual content of the theory, that is, the practices the patterns describe, and not about the presentation quality of the patterns.

A case study protocol should be written before a specific case investigation is started.

Following the case study protocol, the pattern author provides the handbook to the case subjects, for example, companies, or to whoever needs to apply the handbook as part of the case study.

The author may have to be available to help case subjects in applying the handbook. If the author has to spend significant time helping implement the handbook, action research may be a more suitable research method than case study research. In any case, the author should stay close to the subjects, allowing them to collect necessary data as outlined in the case study protocol.

With data in hand, the author proceeds to evaluate the handbook and answer the questions mentioned above. A challenge will be to separate the following two main dimensions within the materials:

1. Quality of presentation (understandability, applicability, etc.)
2. Quality of content (completeness, correctness, etc.)

The quality of the presentation is the original domain of the patterns community. While intertwined with the correctness of the handbook, it should be dealt with separately from answering the research questions. The data on the quality of content, that is on the correctness and completeness, among other quality criteria, is the main concern, and the research uses it to review the handbook, annotate the maturity of a section, and possibly to trigger a reevaluation and future incremental theory building to improve the handbook.

3.5 Pattern Validation

As discussed above, using approaches like grounded theory and case study research for theory evaluation only gives us limited certainty about the quality of the theory (hence the choice of words of evaluation rather than validation). Such broad evaluation is nevertheless useful, because full-blown validation is usually not possible.

To illustrate the point, consider a fully developed patterns handbook with multiple domains, dozens of process templates and hundreds of best practices. Effectively, each element is its own hypothesis. To validate each hypothesis, an appropriate method like a hypothesis-testing survey or controlled experiment has to be applied. This is usually not feasible:

- For a hypothesis-testing survey, not only does a survey have to be created, but the respective constructs and their instruments need to be developed first. Given the broad variety of domains and their specificity, we don't expect that theoretical constructs and their measurement instruments can be used off-the-shelf. Together with a potentially large survey, the amount of work to be performed for validating a full pattern handbook is likely to become prohibitively large.
- For controlled experiments to serve as comprehensive validation of the pattern handbook, every single best practice, including its interconnections, needs to be cast as a hypothesis and tested. Given the number of hypotheses and their interactions, this also quickly becomes prohibitively complex and expensive.

In an open world, we can only approach (but never reach) a fully validated theory. Thus, we judiciously choose specific best practices for validation, in such a way that we continuously increase coverage of the theory and incrementally build our trust in its validity.

The set of patterns in a given domain can be viewed as a network of interlinked best practices. Within this network, best practices of a high network centrality are a good choice for hypothesis testing. Examples of such high-centrality best practices are entry and exit (to the domain) best practices. To maximize the impact of hypothesis testing, these best practices should be tested first.

Hypothesis testing, applied this way, buttresses the theory evaluation of other research methods and helps incrementally build trust in the validity of the handbook.

3.6 Incremental Process

Sections 3.1 to 3.5 present a rationalized process of pattern discovery, evaluation, and validation. This might suggest a simple linear execution of the handbook method, with resulting patterns at the end. In reality, however, pattern discovery and validation usually proceed incrementally.

We distinguish two different dimensions of incremental pattern discovery and validation:

1. The incremental discovery of the overall pattern domain structure. Usually, in a first project, one pattern author approaches the overall domain broadly to develop the initial domain structure. The same author or those who follow them later might incrementally change the domain structure based on new knowledge gathered.
2. The in-depth development of a particular domain (chapter) in the patterns handbook. The pattern discovery and evaluation of a particular domain proceeds incrementally, in that after the initial pattern discovery, there usually are learnings gained from the evaluation of the patterns that feed-back to and motivate extended pattern discovery and refinement.

Such incremental development is in line with most theory building methods mentioned so far, in particular, the qualitative survey, action research, and case study research. It depends on the method, however, when another iteration or increment can be started.

This doesn't mean that our approach can be applied carelessly and without planning. In particular, if specific aspects like important best practices are selected for in-depth validation, costs can go up significantly. If the tested hypothesis turns out to be invalid, less may have been learned than what was expected and hence resources will have been wasted.

3.7 Industry Collaboration

A particularly interesting aspect of our approach is that it lends itself well to collaboration with industry. Let's assume that a particular domain of practice has not been covered well yet by usable patterns. Then, while there certainly might be companies who know how to perform the processes and practices in question well, there will be many other companies who don't know how to do this and have no established body of work to learn from.

This second set of companies, who recognize that they lack some desired capabilities, contains the companies who might be willing to serve as evaluation case studies for the research. They might also be willing to fund the research. These companies would benefit from being given a patterns handbook of process templates and best practices that helps them build the desired capabilities. This is the opening for a principal investigator to motivate a collaboration with these companies.

From our approach's perspective, companies which already possess the desired capabilities can serve as experts for pattern discovery, and companies wanting to acquire the capabilities can serve as case studies for pattern evaluation.

At the same time, as our work shows, does the equivalence of pattern discovery and theory building allow researchers to perform and publish scientific work as well.

4 Exploratory Studies

At this stage of our work, we have formulated our approach and explored it in several studies. These studies are not full-fledged evaluation case studies, but rather exploratory studies that helped us understand and refine the approach.

4.1 Overview of Studies

Using scientific research methods for pattern discovery and validation has been applied in three exploratory studies and is currently being applied in others more. The three exploratory studies are:

1. User experience design in product lines. We applied our approach to eliciting and codifying industry best practices of user experience design for software product lines (Harutyunyan & Riehle 2019a).
2. Episodic volunteering. We applied our approach to eliciting and codifying best practices of managing episodic volunteers in open source projects (Barcomb 2019).

3. Open source governance. We applied our approach to eliciting and codifying best practices for open source governance in software producing companies (Harutyunyan & Riehle 2019b; Harutyunyan & Riehle 2019c, Harutyunyan 2019).

The example used in this article draws on exploratory study 3 just listed. Other handbooks currently in work are on microservice integration in software architecture and pre-requirements traceability in requirements engineering.

4.2 Evaluation Model

To assess the effectiveness of using our approach for pattern discovery, we defined an evaluation model to review the results of the exploratory studies. Table 4 presents the evaluation model.

Table 4. Evaluation model for effectiveness of using the handbook method for pattern discovery

Quality Criterion	Measurement/Evaluation Metric
Correctness of individual pattern	• Expert found no inconsistencies • Application showed no inconsistencies
Completeness of individual pattern	• Expert found no omissions • Application showed no omissions
Correctness of patterns in domain	• Expert confirmed patterns belong to domain • Application showed patterns belong to domain
Completeness of patterns in domain	• Expert found no missing patterns • Application showed no missing patterns
Correctness of pattern connections	• Expert found no incorrect links • Application showed no incorrect links
Completeness of pattern connections	• Expert found no missing links • Application showed no missing links

Effectively, for three main dimensions (any individual pattern, the patterns within one domain, and the connections between patterns within one domain), we evaluated correctness and completeness. We did so by reviewing the handbook both from the pattern discovery side (asking an expert) as well as the pattern evaluation side (asking users about the handbook application).

Asking an expert meant going back to the experts who we interviewed for pattern discovery. This practice of reviewing the output of pattern discovery is one of the most common quality assessments in theory-building research, called member checking (Creswell & Miller 2000).

Asking users about the handbook application meant evaluating how well they did in practice by working with our case study partners. At this stage, we are reporting only preliminary findings.

With this evaluation model, we are evaluating the output of three specific pattern discovery studies, and only by extrapolation can suggest that using our approach for pattern discovery actually improves the state of the art. As mentioned, a more rigorous evaluation will have to be done in the future.

Please note that we omitted quality criteria for pattern presentation. While presentation quality is also important, scientific methods have little to say about achieving high presentation quality and we refer the reader to established approaches of the patterns community like writer's workshops (Coplien & Woolf 1997; Gabriel 2008).

4.3   Study 1: User Experience Design in Product Lines

Our first foray into using the handbook method both for scientific research and delivering a practically useful handbook was in the domain of user experience design for software product lines (Harutyunyan & Riehle 2019a). We conducted multiple-case case study research using two different product lines within the multinational company Siemens AG: In a healthcare software division and in an industrial automation software division. We performed an exploratory study that resulted in a handbook of industry best practices covering the design, implementation, and management of user experience design in the context of software product lines. An example pattern from the study, from the category of UXD Definition, is shown in Table 5.

Table 5. An example pattern drawn from a study on UXD in product lines

Practice UXD-DEF-2: Develop SPL-wide templates for new UXD concept definitions, improve them over time and use them consistently	
Problem	How to create and formulate new UXD concepts in a detailed, consistent and efficient way across an SPL?
Context	UXD definition is considered a creative process, so definition teams often don't have templates for suggesting new UXD components. Each UXD engineer in the SPL uses the tools they prefer to create UXD concepts and mock-ups, for example PowerPoint presentations. However, often there is a need to compare various UXD concepts in the SPL, which can be difficult, if presentation formats and levels of detail are very different

(continued)

Table 5. (*continued*)

Practice UXD-DEF-2: Develop SPL-wide templates for new UXD concept definitions, improve them over time and use them consistently	
Solution	Even though templates are often considered as creativity killers, according to our case studies, if well designed, they can improve the creative process, by stimulating it and putting the necessary limitations and technical constraints in place. The best practice is the development of templates for UXD concepts that would include the technical details of the concepts, its mock-ups and description consistent across the SPL. These templates need to be evaluated and improved continuously to ensure that they are a stimulating tool for the concept development and not another documentation step that is perceived unnecessary and time consuming. The SPL-wide usage of such templates ensures that they evolve and lead to better UXD design. In an SPL such templates will ensure a common approach to the conception of new features and a common UXD definition. Templates save time by avoiding redesigning the basic concept structure every time. This can be a significant benefit. However, the use of the templates for UXD concepts should not eliminate the use of more sophisticated prototypes in the further phases of development. Beyond the UXD concept, there is a need for prototypes, static or dynamic. For these instances, our data suggest a freer approach in terms of the toolset used to formulate the UXD. In these stages the use of templates is not recommended
Traces in our data:	[Case 1, Interview 3] [Case 2, Interview 1]
Example trace in data:	The head of UXD team from Case 1 explains the practice: "So we have a template for concept definitions. Basically, all UXD changes are done with the use of these concepts. Not only do we define concepts, but there are also some technical aspects to be clarified and there is basically a template that explains what the contents are on the information that needs to be gathered." [Case 1, Interview 3]

4.4 Study 2: Episodic Volunteering

We also performed a study on the subject of episodic volunteering in free/libre and open source software communities (Barcomb et al. 2018; Barcomb et al. 2019). Building on this earlier work, we conducted a Delphi study to determine and confirm best practices. Community managers were asked to describe their concerns about episodic volunteering and the practices they employ to address these concerns. The handbook method was chosen as the best method for relaying the responses to participants to allow for the incremental development of practices over multiple rounds. The final result is a handbook consisting of 65 interrelated practices grouped into five categories: Community Governance, Community Preparation, Onboarding Contributors, Working with Contributors, and Contributor Retention. An example pattern from the study, from the category of Community Preparation, is shown in Table 6.

Table 6. An example pattern drawn from a study on episodic volunteering

Practice P.8: Create working groups with a narrow focus	
Context	The project is too complex for participants to easily comprehend it in its entirety. It is not possible to readily identify stand-alone tasks in the project
Concerns	• 2.C Episodic contributor lacks awareness of opportunities to contribute
Solution	Create specialized working groups that people can identify with. With a narrow focus and defined outcomes, episodic contributors will be able to find tasks more readily
Related practices	• P.6 List current areas of activity is a possible alternative step • P.18 Write modular software is a possible alternative step • P.18 Write modular software is a complementary practice • P.18 Write modular software is a possible preceding step • O.1 Learn about the experience, preferences, and time constraints of participants is a possible preceding step
Challenges	Contributions within the working groups will need to be reported back outside of the group
Used by	CM2, CM3, CM4, CM5, CM6, CM16
Example trace	"By focusing the working group on a topic that people can identify with, we hope that episodic contributors have an easier time identifying what is useful to them and then have a place to contribute."—CM4

4.5   Study 3: Open Source Governance

Our main study, presented here only in its initial exploratory stage (and later as part of full-fledged qualitative survey research), is about open source governance. We define open source governance as a set of processes, best practices, and tools employed by companies to govern the use of open source software components as parts of their products while minimizing their risks and maximizing their benefit from such use. Our work resulted in a theory of industry best practices on the core topics of open source governance in companies:

- Getting started,
- inbound governance,
- outbound governance,
- general governance, and
- supply chain management.

Using the handbook method, we presented our findings in an actionable and industry-friendly format of interconnected best practice patterns that formed a handbook for open source governance. We published parts of the handbook focused on getting started with open source governance (Harutyunyan & Riehle 2019b) and parts focused on inbound governance (Harutyunyan & Riehle 2019c). Further parts of the handbook focused on supply chain management were published in Nikolay Harutyunyan's dissertation (Harutyunyan 2019). An example pattern from the latter is shown in Table 7.

Table 7. An example pattern drawn from a study on open source governance

Practice OSGOV-SUCHMA-BOMMAN-4	
Use machine-readable and standard format for BOM upon software supply	
Actor	OSPO (Open Source Program Office), Supply chain management responsible role
Context	You have used the bill of materials and code scanning of the supplied code to → identify open source components and metadata from the supply chain. You have → tracked, documented and updated BOM in a consistent and complete manner
Problem	How can you improve the performance of managing your BOMs?
Solution	Software supply chains are complex and cannot be handled manually. You need to → use tools to improve the performance of BOM management. Most importantly you need to establish a machine readable and standard format for BOMs. An example of such a format is called Software Package Data Exchange (SPDX). It enables the documentation and exchange of data and metadata for open source components and BOMs made of such components

4.6 Evaluation of Studies

As explained in Sect. 4.2, the evaluation model, we used two different methods to assess the quality of our approach with respect to the generated output:

- Member checking
- Case study research

The results confirmed the specific handbooks. Member checking was carried out in all three exploratory studies and domain experts confirmed the individual patterns, the set of patterns, and the connections between the patterns with respect to correctness and completeness.

As mentioned, exploratory study 2 employed the Delphi method, in which a panel of experts over three rounds of questioning and commenting helped us define the practices they knew as patterns (Dalkey & Helmer 1963). This highly structured elicitation and reviewing process ensures a high degree of confidence in the quality of the patterns that were determined.

Please note again, that such member checking increases our confidence, but does not represent a full-fledged validation due to the inherent biases of asking domain experts flat out to provide feedback.

The exploratory study 3 was evaluated not only through expert member checking but in several full-fledged case studies, using case study research. In this case, the case study researcher observed the use of the handbook within companies which were not experts, and reviewed the patterns, the overall set of patterns, and their connections for correctness and completeness. While we found a few blank spots, the case studies overwhelmingly confirmed the handbook.

5 Discussion

In this paper, we bring together traditional scientific research methods with the methods developed and refined by the pattern community. This has led us to the proposition of the handbook method, a novel approach to discovering and validating patterns.

To demonstrate the viability and applicability of the proposed method, we present three exploratory evaluation studies that show different applications of the handbook method and position it for future use by others.

The handbook method is highly versatile: It can be used by pattern authors, researchers, and practitioners. Pattern authors can use the method to more rigorously discover and validate their patterns. Researchers can use the method to better describe the result of their work, a theory, using pattern handbooks. And practitioners create or receive handbooks grounded in empirical data that they can use in their daily practice in industry. In fact, two case study companies from Harutyunyan's dissertation (Harutyunyan 2019) decided to implement the best practice handbooks based on our studies.

We also published and presented parts of our work including selected patterns at the European Conference on Pattern Languages of Programs, one focusing on component approval in open source governance (Harutyunyan & Riehle 2020) and one focusing on component reuse (Harutyunyan & Riehle 2019b). This work can be considered as a foundation for a pattern language covering different aspects of open source governance in companies, which can be extended by our own future research or that of others in the pattern community.

Finally, the proposed handbook method can be used by other researchers from the software engineering research community, opening up to them the rich toolset of the pattern community, especially for presenting their theories. Such future research has the potential to better structure the research findings published by multiple authors on a given domain, while also enabling an easier applicability of the research results by the practitioners.

At this stage we evaluated the trustworthiness of the exploratory studies as presented in the previous chapter. The main evaluation method was member checking with experts whose input was used to create the theories and discover the patterns. In addition, for one exploratory study, we performed substantial multi-case case study research.

The evaluation of exploratory research for theory building is not served well by the classic four criteria of test validity (internal validity, external validity, reliability, and objectivity). In response to this, Lincoln and Guba (1985) defined trustworthiness of qualitative research using four new criteria which they called credibility, transferability, dependability, and confirmability, in analogy to the four criteria of test validity.

- Credibility. Credibility is often demonstrated using member checking and triangulation. To make this possible, we would have to give this method to other independent researchers and see them apply it. Then we can check back with them to learn how well the approach worked for them. The second and third author of this article applied the method as conceived by the first author, but because of their relationship (professor and their Ph.D. students), the conclusions that can be drawn from the positive feedback are limited. We argue, however, that the success of the exploratory case studies suggests that the method worked as intended.

- Transferability. At this stage, we can't confirm anything about the transferability of our work to other studies than those presented. However, any break-down in transferability can only come from the particular way of how we put established methods together, because the individual pieces have already been validated separately (as established methods). Our current research will add new studies to the portfolio.

- Dependability. When we performed the exploratory studies, our approach itself was only in the process of being formulated. We therefore view potential variation in approach definition as well as potential inconsistencies in their application across the exploratory studies as the biggest possible problem with our evaluation and the quality of the results. However, we did not observe any effects of the evolution of the approach on the evaluation of its effectiveness, as presented in the previous section. We suspect that the reason is that the researchers most of the time simply followed the particular research method at hand, e.g. qualitative survey, action research, or case study research, which are well-defined and have been validated in their own right.

- Confirmability. As explained, the approach as presented here is still in an exploratory stage. There is no audit trail for the research method but the dissertations of Harutyunyan and Barcomb, and they focus more on their specific research question than the approach. As such, we postpone claims of confirmability to the next set of handbooks, currently in work as part of a new set of dissertations. These are being written in a constrained research harness with the purpose of demonstrating confirmability of the approach.

As a final note, we would like to point out that given that there are no other rigorous methods for pattern discovery and validation that utilize established and validated scientific methods, we already improved over the state of the art simply because we provide a new approach for it.

6 Conclusions

This article presents a new approach for pattern discovery and validation. The key innovation is to use established scientific research methods for pattern discovery and validation in ways that they have not yet been used before, and complement them with pattern handbooks as a novel way for presenting theories.

We also present three exploratory studies that suggest the usefulness of the proposed approach. In addition to the three studies, the proposed method was employed to study industry best practices for corporate open sourcing including why and how companies contribute to open source communities.

When compared with previous approaches to discovering patterns, our approach is both significantly more rigorous and laborious due to its scientific underpinnings. However, such detailed work is justified, and as mentioned, may even be paid for by industry without interfering with any research goal of the studies. It is also highly effective in new and emerging domains, where relevant knowledge exists, but is hard to get to. In such circumstances, organic pattern discovery, which depends on an observer encountering multiple examples of the solution, is unlikely to occur.

In future work, we will subject the method to more rigorous testing to confirm that it reliably delivers what it promises, which are patterns handbooks that adequately capture a domain and help the practitioner in solving problems in that domain. Next, we will therefore take a step back and perform theory building and evaluation of the handbook method, for example, by applying the method itself to developing a handbook for using the handbook method.

We aim to provide the patterns community with a rigorous method for pattern discovery and have taken the first step of method definition and exploration with this article.

Acknowledgments. We would like to thank Joseph Yoder for introducing us to Takashi Iba's work as part of a pattern writing workshop. We also would like to thank Michael Dorner and Julia Krause for participating in a writer's workshop that helped us improve this article. Finally, we would like to thank the reviewers for their extensive suggestions on how to improve this article, which is better off because of these.

References

Akado, Y., Kogure, S., Sasabe, A., Hong, J.H., Saruwatari, K., Iba, T.: Five patterns for designing pattern mining workshops. In: Proceedings of the 20th European Conference on Pattern Languages of Programs, p. 9. ACM (2015)

Alexander, C.: A Pattern Language: Towns, Buildings, Construction. Oxford university Press, Oxford (1977)

Alexander, C.: Empirical findings from the nature of order. Environ. Archit. Phenomenol. Newsl. **18**(1), 11–19 (2007)

Alhusain, S., Coupland, S., John, R., Kavanagh, M.: Towards machine learning based design pattern recognition. In: 2013 13th UK Workshop on Computational Intelligence (UKCI), pp. 244–251. IEEE, September 2013

Ampatzoglou, A., Michou, O., Stamelos, I.: Building and mining a repository of design pattern instances: practical and research benefits. Entertain. Comput. **4**(2), 131–142 (2013)

Baltes, S., Ralph, P.: Sampling in software engineering research: a critical review and guidelines. arXiv preprint arXiv:2002.07764 (2020)

Barcomb, A., Kaufmann, A., Riehle, D., Stol, K.J., Fitzgerald, B.: Uncovering the periphery: a qualitative survey of episodic volunteering in free/libre and open source software communities. IEEE Trans. Softw. Eng. (2018)

Barcomb, A., Stol, K.J., Riehle, D., Fitzgerald, B.: Why do episodic volunteers stay in FLOSS communities? In: 41st International Conference on Software Engineering (2019)

Barcomb, A.: Retaining and managing episodic contributors in free/libre/open source software communities. Ph.D dissertation. University of Limerick (2019). https://ulir.ul.ie/handle/10344/8166

Buschmann, F., Henney, K., Schmidt, D.: Pattern-Oriented Software Architecture: on Patterns and Pattern Language, vol. 5. Wiley, Hoboken (2007)

Charmaz, K.: Constructing Grounded Theory: A Practical Guide Through Qualitative Analysis. Sage, Thousand Oaks (2006)

Coplien, J.O., Woolf, B.: A pattern language for writers' workshops. C Plus Plus Rep. **9**, 51–60 (1997)

Coplien, J.O., Gabriel, R.P.: A Pattern Definition. Web-published (1999). http://www.cs.unc.edu/~stotts/COMP723-s15/patterns/gabriel.html

Corbin, J., Strauss, A.: Basics of Qualitative Research: Techniques and Procedures for Developing Grounded Theory. Sage Publications, Thousand Oaks (2014)

Correia, F.F., Aguiar, A.: Patterns of flexible modeling tools. In: Proceedings of the 20th Conference on Pattern Languages of Programs, pp. 1–17, October 2013

Creswell, J.W., Miller, D.L.: Determining validity in qualitative inquiry. Theory Pract. **39**(3), 124–130 (2000)

Cunningham, W.: The CHECKS pattern language of information integrity. In: Pattern Languages of Program Design, pp. 145–155. ACM Press/Addison-Wesley Publishing Co. (1995)

Dalkey, N., Helmer, O.: An experimental application of the Delphi method to the use of experts. Manag. Sci. **9**(3), 458–467 (1963)

Davison, R., Martinsons, M.G., Kock, N.: Principles of canonical action research. Inf. Syst. J. **14**(1), 65–86 (2004)

Dong, J., Zhao, Y., Peng, T.: A review of design pattern mining techniques. Int. J. Softw. Eng. Knowl. Eng. **19**(06), 823–855 (2009)

Dwivedi, A.K., Tirkey, A., Rath, S.K.: Software design pattern mining using classification-based techniques. Front. Comput. Sci. **12**(5), 908–922 (2018)

Evans, E.: Domain-Driven Design: Tackling Complexity in the Heart of Software. Addison-Wesley Professional, Boston (2004)

Fehling, C., Leymann, F., Retter, R., Schumm, D., Schupeck, W.: An architectural pattern language of cloud-based applications. In: Proceedings of the 18th Conference on Pattern Languages of Programs, pp. 1–11, October 2011

Fowler, M.: Patterns of Enterprise Application Architecture. Addison-Wesley Longman Publishing Co., Inc. (2002)

Fowler Jr., F.J.: Survey Research Methods. Sage Publications, Thousand Oaks (2013)

Gabriel, R.P.: Patterns of Software. Oxford University Press, Oxford (1996)

Gabriel, R.P.: Writers' workshops as scientific methodology. DreamSongs, Inc. (2008). https://www.dreamsongs.com/Files/WritersWorkshops.pdf

Gabriel, R.P.: The structure of a programming language revolution. In: Proceedings of the ACM International Symposium on New Ideas, New Paradigms, and Reflections on Programming and Software, pp. 195–214 (2012)

Gamma, E., Helm, R., Johnson, R., Vlissides, J.: Design patterns: elements of reusable object-oriented languages and systems (1994)

Glaser, B.G.: Doing Grounded Theory: Issues and Discussions. Sociology Press (1998)

Glaser, B.G., Strauss, A.L.: Discovery of Grounded Theory: Strategies for Qualitative Research. Routledge (1967)

Guba, E.G.: Criteria for assessing the trustworthiness of naturalistic inquiries. Ectj **29**(2), 75 (1981)

Gupta, M., Rao, R.S., Pande, A., Tripathi, A.K.: Design pattern mining using state space representation of graph matching. In: Meghanathan, N., Kaushik, B.K., Nagamalai, D. (eds.) CCSIT 2011. CCIS, vol. 131, pp. 318–328. Springer, Heidelberg (2011). https://doi.org/10.1007/978-3-642-17857-3_32

Gupta, M.: Design pattern mining using greedy algorithm for multi-labelled graphs. Int. J. Inf. Commun. Technol. **3**(4), 314–323 (2011)

Hammouda, I., Mikkonen, T., Oksanen, V., Jaaksi, A.: Open source legality patterns: architectural design decisions motivated by legal concerns. In: Proceedings of the 14th International Academic MindTrek Conference: Envisioning Future Media Environments, pp. 207–214. ACM, October 2010

Harutyunyan, N., Riehle, D.: Industry best practices for component approval in FLOSS governance. In: Proceedings of the 25th European Conference on Pattern Languages of Programs. ACM (2020)

Harutyunyan, N., Riehle, D.: User experience design in software product lines. In: Proceedings of the 52nd Hawaii International Conference on System Sciences. ScholarSpace (2019a)

Harutyunyan, N., Riehle, D.: Industry best practices for FLOSS governance and component reuse. In: Proceedings of the 24th European Conference on Pattern Languages of Programs. ACM (2019b)

Harutyunyan, N., Riehle, D.: Getting Started with FLOSS governance and compliance: a theory of industry best practices. In: Proceedings of the 15th International Symposium on Open Collaboration, pp. 1:1—1:10. ACM (2019c)

Harutyunyan, N.: Corporate open source governance of software supply chains. Ph.D dissertation. Friedrich-Alexander-Universität Erlangen-Nürnberg (2019). http://nbn-resolving.de/urn:nbn:de:bvb:29-opus4-122727

Harutyunyan, N., Riehle, D., Sathya, G.: Industry best practices for corporate open sourcing. In: Proceedings of the 53rd Hawaii International Conference on System Sciences. ScholarSpace (2020)

Horkheimer, M.: Traditional and critical theory. Crit. Theory Sel. Essays 1, 188–243 (1972)

Iba, T., Isaku, T.: Holistic pattern-mining patterns. In: Proceedings of the 19th Conference on Pattern Languages of Programs. The Hillside Group (2012)

Iba, T., Isaku, T.: A pattern language for creating pattern languages. In: Proceedings of the 23rd Conference on Pattern Languages of Programs, p. 11. The Hillside Group (2016)

Jansen, H.: The logic of qualitative survey research and its position in the field of social research methods. In: Forum Qualitative Sozialforschung/Forum: Qualitative Social Research, vol. 11, no. 2 (2010)

Kohls, C., Panke, S.: Is that true...? Thoughts on the epistemology of patterns. In: Proceedings of the 16th Conference on Pattern Languages of Programs, pp. 1–14 (2009). https://doi.org/10.1145/1943226.1943237

Kuckartz, U.: Qualitative Text Analysis: A Guide to Methods, Practice and Using Software. Sage, Thousand Oaks (2014)

Lau, F.: Toward a framework for action research in information systems studies. Inf. Technol. People 12(2), 148–176 (1999)

Lincoln, Y.S., Guba, E.G.: Naturalistic Inquiry. Beverley Hills (1985)

Link, C.: Patterns for the commercial use of open source: legal and licensing aspects. In: Proceedings of the 15th European Conference on Pattern Languages of Programs, p. 7. ACM, July 2010

Mayring, P.: Forum: qualitative social research. In: Qualitative Content Analysis, vol. 2 (2000)

Meszaros, G., Doble, J.: A pattern language for pattern writing. In: Proceedings of International Conference on Pattern Languages of Program Design, vol. 131, p. 164, October 1997

Noble, J., Biddle, R.: Notes on postmodern programming. In: Proceedings of the Onward Track at OOPSLA, vol. 2, pp. 49–71, March 2002

OMG: Business process model and notation specification version 2.0.2 (2014). https://www.omg.org/spec/BPMN

Riehle, D.: Value object. In: Proceedings of the 2006 Conference on Pattern Languages of Programs, vol. 30. ACM, October 2006

Rising, L.: Patterns and experiments: next steps. In: Invited Talk at the 27th Conference on Pattern Languages of Programs (PLoP 2020) (2020)

Robinson, H., Segal, J., Sharp, H.: Ethnographically-informed empirical studies of software practice. Inf. Softw. Technol. 49(6), 540–551 (2007)

Runeson, P., Host, M., Rainer, A., Regnell, B.: Case Study Research in Software Engineering: Guidelines and Examples. Wiley Hoboken (2012)

Wagner, S., Mendez, D., Felderer, M., Graziotin, D., Kalinowski, M.: Challenges in survey research. arXiv preprint arXiv:1908.05899 (2019)

Wohlin, C., Runeson, P., Höst, M., Ohlsson, M.C., Regnell, B., Wesslén, A.: Experimentation in Software Engineering. Springer, Heidelberg (2012)

Yin, R.K.: Case Study Research and Applications: Design and Methods. Sage publications, Thousand Oaks (2003)

Zanoni, M.: Data mining techniques for design pattern detection. Dissertation, Universita degli Studi di Milano Bicocca (2012)

Configuring Patterns and Pattern Languages for Systemic Inquiry and Design

Helene Finidori[✉]

Centre for Systems Studies, Business School, University of Hull, Hull HU6 7RX, UK
h.finidori-2016@hull.ac.uk

Abstract. The present paper explores how a systems approach to patterns and pattern language could support systemic inquiry and systemic design, and more broadly, the advancement of pattern language. It examines the multiple facets and definitions of the concept of pattern and proposes reconciling them to include the affordances that patterns bring both to inquiry and design within a larger systems framework. In particular, it discusses extending the act of design to encompass the inquiry that motivates a design and the ongoing monitoring of the fitness of this design to its intended purpose in a systems perspective. Considering complexity and the notion of generativity, this approach challenges the appropriateness of patterns expressed in problem-solution form and suggests ways forward for extended definitions and pattern forms. This work contributes to bringing pattern thinking and systems thinking, or pattern science and systems science, closer to each other. The purpose is to further integrate pattern thinking and pattern language in the design, assessment, and orientation of our socio-technological and socio-environmental systems, both large and small, to better address the societal challenges of our time. It complements various initiatives aimed at harnessing pattern languages for sustainability and societal change and at developing pattern literacy in support of systems literacy.

Keywords: Pattern Language · Patterns · Design · Problem-solving · Complexity · Pattern Literacy · Systems Literacy · Systems Thinking · Complex Systems

1 Introduction

This paper builds upon previous work on pattern literacy as a foundation for systems literacy [1] and the future of pattern languages [2] presented to the Systems Science and Pattern Language communities between 2015 and 2017. It complements various initiatives aimed at harnessing pattern languages for sustainability and societal change, and at introducing pattern thinking and pattern language into systems thinking and systemic design. These efforts include contributions within the pattern language community, notably at PLoP (Pattern Languages of Programs), Purplsoc (Pursuit of Pattern Languages for Societal Change) and PUARL (Portland Urban Architecture Research Lab) conferences, and the work of influential figures such as Mehaffy [3, 4], West and

© The Author(s), under exclusive license to Springer-Verlag GmbH, DE, part of Springer Nature 2025
E. Wallingford et al. (Eds.): TPLOP V, LNCS 14630, pp. 254–297, 2025.
https://doi.org/10.1007/978-3-662-70810-1_7

Quillien [5], Iba [6], Schuler [7], as well as Atlee [8]. In the realm of systems thinking and systemic design, communities such as the ISSS (International Society for the Systems Sciences), and the work of Ing [9], Henshaw [10], Ulrich [11], Mobus and Kalton [12], Troncale [13, 14], Palmer [15, 16], Tuddenham [17], McNamara [19], Silverman [21], Smith [22], Jones [23] and others provide valuable insights into the interplay of patterns and systems.

The author, working at the intersection of the pattern language and systems communities, seeks to bridge these domains. The core idea is that the advancement of pattern thinking and pattern literacy is essential to understanding and orienting, if not designing, complex systems. Improving the detection and monitoring of the mechanisms underlying our socio-environmental and socio-technological systems can significantly enhance our responses to them. Moreover, the proactive development of our various ways of understanding and representing these mechanisms and of assessing the extent to which they can be controlled, influenced, or simply acknowledged [22], will lead to more effective and sustainable solutions to tackle societal and environmental challenges. The collective intelligence derived from such pattern and systems literacies could help design healthier regenerative systems, and re-orient current systemic trajectories, which, according to recent studies[1], are leading us towards potential environmental and social disasters, faster than expected.

Developing pattern thinking and pattern literacy in support of systems literacy and systemic design involves a pattern-centric approach to systems, coupled with a systemic perspective in designing patterns and pattern languages. Pattern literacy can be understood as the ability to identify, learn, assemble, represent, and mobilize patterns. Pattern literate individuals are better equipped to make sense of, discuss, and act upon the order of things and how they change. Systems literacy can be defined as the capacity to comprehend and influence systems behavior through inquiry into the relationships and interactions between and among systems and their components, and to gain insights into systems processes and effects. By viewing patterns as both static embodiments of systems organization and as dynamic expressions of systems in action and transformation, the author argues that a deep understanding of systems requires a foundational pattern competence.

This paper, aimed at the pattern language and design communities, explores how a systemic approach to patterns and pattern language within a larger systems framework could help develop more effective and adaptive pattern forms and practices in order to support systemic inquiry and design. A systemic approach, as defined by the author, is the study of systems within their wider contexts, considering both the organization and effectiveness of a system within its boundaries, and its interactions with and impacts on surrounding systems, even those it is indirectly related to. Systemic design adopts this comprehensive approach, understanding the act of design not only in terms of its immediate outputs —the system being built—, but also in terms of the system's repercussions on its environment and on other systems it may affect. For example, while systems thinking may be well suited to design operational efficiency and minimize cost, it may lead to greater resource depletion or environmental harm. Such outcomes, especially when

---

[1] For example, IPCC Special Report on Global Warming of 1.5 °C (SR15), Oct. 2018, https://www.ipcc.ch/report/sr15/.

resulting costs are externalized, i.e. supported by society, do not align with systemic design principles. Similarly, a building designed for the enjoyment of its sole residents, but which negatively impacts the local social fabric, or a software system that delivers efficient outputs but alienates its users, does not qualify as systemically designed. In a way, pattern language and systemic design share the philosophy and goal of achieving what Christopher Alexander named the 'Quality Without a Name' [24], which the author identifies with the ongoing regeneration of commons [25].

Asking questions more than providing answers, the author lays theoretical ground-work to initiate conversations for the further development of practical applications. Section 2 examines pattern language and its evolution in the context of systemic design. It starts with an analysis of state-of-the-art pattern languages and introduces the con-cept of a systemic pattern language as a next generation of pattern languages designed to address complex issues systemically. Section 3 reviews the multiple facets of the concept of pattern, with a focus on the cognitive and semiotic properties of patterns. This section underscores the crucial role of patterns in inquiry and meaning-making processes, and in constructing our realities, emphasizing their importance as media for encoding and decoding. Building on Christopher Alexander's work, Sect. 4 challenges how well the multifaceted nature of patterns and their potential for systemic design are currently leveraged in pattern language form and practice. It critically examines the prevailing definition of patterns built upon concepts such as context, problem and solu-tion, and their association, and extends it to include the notion of generative processes fundamental to systemic design. Finally, Sect. 5 suggests directions for configuring and using patterns and pattern languages for systemic design, inviting the pattern language community to engage further.

2   Pattern Language and Systemic Design

The concept of systemic pattern language as a next-generation pattern language intro-duced here is built upon the fourth-generation pattern language concept presented at the 2015 Purplsoc conference [2] as an extension of Takashi Iba's inquiry into the evolution of pattern languages.

2.1   The Evolution of Pattern Languages

Iba's framework [26] identifies three generations of pattern languages since Christopher Alexander introduced the concept in the 60s. This framework differentiates genera-tions by object of design—the types of forms designed—, act of design—the nature of the design process over time—, and purpose—the types of connections generated among stakeholders throughout the design process—. Finidori et al. [2] introduced a fourth-generation pattern language, adding orientation—the broader systemic aim of the design—as a new differentiating criterion. Figure 1 illustrates this evolution, showing each generation building upon the features and possibilities of the previous and adding relational and adaptive components to address more complex design challenges. The fourth generation, systemic in nature, integrates multidimensionality and multimodal-ity by construction, for more effective problem identification and solutions design in complex situations. In a conversation with the author, Mehaffy [27] suggested his own interpretation of this evolution he calls the 'sliced pie', which will be referred to as well as we delve further in the following description of generations of pattern languages.

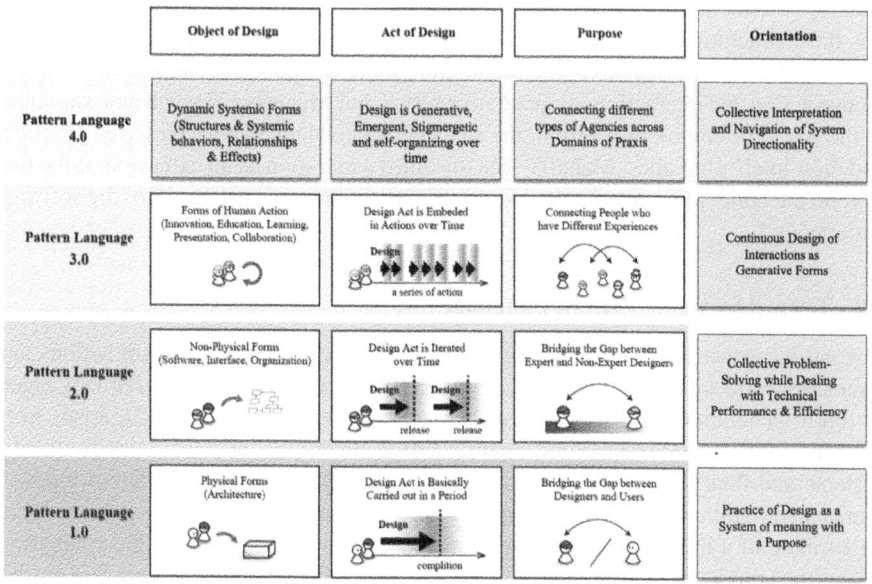

Object of Design	Act of Design	Purpose	Orientation
Pattern Language 4.0 — Dynamic Systemic Forms (Structures & Systemic behaviors, Relationships & Effects)	Design is Generative, Emergent, Stigmergetic and self-organizing over time	Connecting different types of Agencies across Domains of Praxis	Collective Interpretation and Navigation of System Directionality
Pattern Language 3.0 — Forms of Human Action (Innovation, Education, Learning, Presentation, Collaboration)	Design Act is Embedded in Actions over Time — a series of action	Connecting People who have Different Experiences	Continuous Design of Interactions as Generative Forms
Pattern Language 2.0 — Non-Physical Forms (Software, Interface, Organization)	Design Act is Iterated over Time — Design release / Design release	Bridging the Gap between Expert and Non-Expert Designers	Collective Problem-Solving while Dealing with Technical Performance & Efficiency
Pattern Language 1.0 — Physical Forms (Architecture)	Design Act is Basically Carried out in a Period — Design / complition	Bridging the Gap between Designers and Users	Practice of Design as a System of meaning with a Purpose

Fig. 1. Four Generations of Pattern Languages—Adapted with permission from Comparison among generations of pattern Languages [26]

Iba's first generation of pattern languages starts with Alexander's initial pattern language. With this first generation, the object of design is a physical tangible form related to its environment or place: a building or a town. The act of design is carried out in a single time period, with an identifiable start and end. The purpose is to bridge the gap between designers and communities of dwellers or users. First generation pattern languages are meant to generate event and space 'piecemeal', through single acts of design, with the whole in mind, enabling 'structure-preserving transformations' Alexander [28], where each additional part strengthens the whole. The orientation added here is that of a practice with a meaning and a purpose, working towards a Gestalt. Mehaffy [27] describes the design produced as largely static configurations of design forces that are resolved in the most preferred way for designers and users.

With Iba's second generation, the object of design is a non-physical, intangible form: software, a human-computer interface, an organization, a process. The purpose of the design is to bridge the gap between expert and non-expert designers. The act of design is iterated over time, with the intention of adapting the design to changes in the context. The orientation added here is collective problem solving in connection with technical performance and efficiency of the objects transformed. For Mehaffy [27], the design produced is a process-oriented collection of code that also generates preferred results without crashing or producing unintended outcomes.

With the third generation, the object of design is human action. The purpose is to connect people with different experiences around a shared goal or practice. Group participatory processes such as collaborative discovery and sense-making, pattern languages of learning or creativity, pattern languages for dealing with organizational change, earthquakes, or dementia, or pattern languages for democracy fall under this category. With this third generation, the act of design, built from the mining of human experience, is embedded in action over time. The orientation of the design is the continuous design of human action and interactions as generative forms. For Mehaffy [27] such patterns allow, in the world of community action, the sharing of knowledge about preferred practices and their likely outcomes. Mehaffy sees this third generation as an extension of the first beyond the built environment, incorporating some of the process aspects of the software patterns.

2.2   Toward Systemic Pattern Languages

Beyond the construction of meaningful or efficient wholes, or of human actions and interactions towards shared goals, the prospective idea of systemic pattern languages, or fourth-generation pattern languages, as proposed by Finidori et al. [2], arises from the need to better understand and orient socio-technological and socio-environmental systems and their underlying behaviors, which emerge from many different types of human and non-human systems in interaction. One commonly understands behavior as an attribute of a living organism, but systems also exhibit behaviors in the changes or effects they produce and the processes they generate, whether or not living organisms are involved. In software also, behavior is the manifestation of a change of state in the system or a sequence of events generated by or within the system. The underlying organization and behaviors of these multiple systems in interaction—whether forms and relationships, or processes and mechanisms—are manifestations of these systems at work, which can be identified and recognized as patterns. Discovering these patterns can help understand and model or design systems in their multiple aspects.

Examples of systems behavior include stock market crashes or booms, traffic congestion, pandemics spreading, or the expansion of social networks. Systemic patterns are the recurrent and recognizable forms that these behaviors take. Examples of systemic patterns include 'preferential attachment', which demonstrates the 'network effect' by which the largest network attracts subscribers in greater proportions until it reaches and maintains a state of monopoly. Preferential attachment is also at work in the 'Matthew effect', also known as 'the rich get richer', allowing those with an initial advantage or privilege to accumulate further benefits over time. Another notorious systemic pattern is the self-fulfilling prophecy whereby actors or agents adjust their behavior to match a prediction, such as buying more stock based on rising value forecasts, which can inflate the market until it crashes due to overevaluation. These and additional examples are documented in [25]. While these examples are quite prominent or easy to observe, most systemic patterns remain, however, hidden from view or unfold in places and at paces that make them less visible.

Typically, fourth-generation pattern languages are intended to help tackle complex challenges or situations where natural, technological, social, and psychological factors are entangled to create emergent phenomena that cannot clearly be related to determined causes, where conditions are in constant change, and where single goals cannot clearly be established. In particular, they are meant to help address issues for which adopted solutions could generate unintended consequences in areas beyond the context for which the design was initially created. Examples at the societal level include public health or addiction concerns, criminality or conflicts, financial volatility, urban development, climate change, and its consequences such as migration and droughts, or risks inherent to the development of artificial intelligence, cybercrime or big data exploitation, to name a few. Complex challenges also arise in business management, supply chains, transportation systems, or policymaking. In practical terms, a fourth-generation pattern language would consist of networks of patterns that could describe existing configurations, mechanisms of power and change, interaction between causes and their possible effects, and variations or transformations in response to evolving contexts across multiple levels and scales.

Systemically complex challenges cannot be resolved through a single solution or device, tangible or intangible, or merely by change of behavior. They require systems of solutions of multiple types operating synergistically on multiple leverage points [29] in more or less controlled or self-organized ways, to modify existing patterns of systems behavior or generate new ones.

Coming back to Iba's framework, with fourth-generation pattern languages, the object of design is a dynamic systemic form that results from many systems and processes in interaction. The purpose is to federate different forms of agency—defined as capacity to act—and constructs across domains of practice. The act of design is generative, emergent, and self-organizing over time. The orientation is the collective interpretation and navigation of systems directionality as an 'enactment' of collective federated agency. Mehaffy [27] sees fourth-generation patterns as relationships in the wider world, between elements in a system that generate specific kinds of forms, whether designed or natural, which combine process and structure, united within a systems perspective. The fourth generation includes patterns of the first three generations, working together.

Let's consider a simple example around the car and transportation. The first-generation pattern language focuses on designing the car, the object itself, in its material form, the infrastructures to support it such as roads, energy supply, or servicing and the quality of the direct driving experience. The second generation extends to the services connected to or around the car, including the software, enriching the driving experience further. The third generation caters to the lifestyle enabled by the car, such as mobility and connectivity, the driver's behavior, and the social implications of driving. Finally, the fourth generation tackles broader societal challenges related to collective mobility and transportation, their environmental impact, the ethical implications of new technologies such as driverless vehicles, and how the different aspects of the 'car experience', from the perspective of the driver, the community, the infrastructure, the social system, and the environment, can function sustainably together.

2.3 Constraints and Novelty

Systemic design and systemic pattern languages address the complex challenges that require, to be resolved, an aggregation of emergent solutions involving different types of agencies and generative processes. These aggregated emergent solutions cannot be proactively orchestrated because there is no universal or all-encompassing viewpoint nor unified vision and goals around which to devise common action, but only disparate purposes and actions at multiple local levels. In such cases where things cannot be directly designed, it may be possible to identify and nurture conditions for generative or regenerative forces to orient vectors of actions towards convergent outcomes. The intention is to use participatory heuristic methods [30], towards [re]generative processes that synergistically work together at multiple systemic levels and scales. This approach is designed to produce 'whole' outcomes that are greater than the sum of the parts [25], tending towards QWAN, Alexander's Quality Without a Name [24], a hallmark of systemic health.

Of course, this is exactly what Christopher Alexander was after with QWAN, keeping wholes whole and alive, at the different levels and scales of patterns. However, the author argues in the following sections that current patterns and pattern languages and their practice are not presently defined and configured to achieve this optimally, particularly in the context of socio-technological and socio-environmental systems. A significant constraint is the difficulty of identifying and capturing the essence of 'good design', 'fit', quality or QWAN given the variety of generative processes and systems in interaction.

Systemic approaches and expertise are often highlighted for their potential misuse towards nefarious objectives, and fourth-generation pattern languages could serve these objectives as well. Nefarious approaches are often applied top-down, or 'inside out' by a select few who know how to manipulate systems to their advantage, producing outcomes that favor or protect specific interests. Examples include various forms of propaganda through social media to interfere in elections, the creation of culture wars or addictions, the acquisition of monopoly via billion-dollar venture capital investments exploiting the network effect, or the externalization of certain risks and costs onto the broader system. It is far more difficult to unite so-called 'forces for good' that are diffuse and distributed, than it is to deceive and divide, hence the need to find ways to aggregate different expressions of 'good willing' agency towards systemic health. A systems dynamics analysis by Jack Harich [31] shows how an investment in deceit produces a greater return than an investment in truth. This quote from the 'finance hacker' Brett Scott [32] is particularly illustrative of the powerlessness which may be experienced in the face of complex dynamics: "The large part of the complexity and opacity we are faced with is that it neutralizes political action. There is… a large diffuse body of people who can't really articulate what they don't like about the [financial] system and how to change it…". To some degree, pattern languages for systemic design engage with the concepts of a system's purpose or directionality, and power—defined as the capacity to assess, influence or control the mechanisms or forces at play over time. The interplay of purpose and power, and the framework of appreciation, influence, and control (AIC) and their interrelations are further explored in Smith [22].

The proposed systemic form of pattern language transcends its role as merely a tool for design, serving also as a medium for inquiry and a heuristic device. This dual functionality enables, in the same act of design, the simultaneous generation of new insights into systemic mechanisms and interacting forces, and the anticipation or envisioning of new desired ones, thus extending Christopher Alexander's vision for Pattern Language to encompass socio-technological and socio-environmental systemic scales.

Thus, it functions more as an instrument for collective intelligence and empowerment, facilitating the emancipation of the multitude, rather than serving as a means for coercion. This resonates with Ulrich's Critical Systems Heuristics (CSH) oriented towards supporting critical and emancipatory practice, to liberate users from those who control knowledge [33], an approach akin to Alexander's. The proposed systemic pattern language can therefore be seen as a tool for 'hacking the system' in the good sense: taking the system apart to understand its hidden mechanisms (decoding) to rebuild it anew or transform it with new mechanisms (encoding). It includes sense-making components that guide both participatory inquiry and design, with ways to explore and interconnect diverse epistemological perspectives so that solutions can be coherent and converge in self-organized ways, without a need to explicitly share and proactively align goals [1, 25, 30].

Through the evolution of pattern languages up to the third generation, the nature of design has transformed. Initially perceived as a single definitive endeavor with a clear beginning and end, completing a tangible whole, the act of design has evolved into a process iterated over time, geared toward perpetually efficient constructs and processes. In further stages, it becomes an act embedded in and driven by action, guiding behavior towards collective objectives. With the fourth generation, a new evolutionary step is reached, where the act of design encompasses generative dynamics and the life that our designs may take themselves as they interact with their environment, transforming contexts, in a continuously recursive and emergent process. This process is characterized by self-reorganization over time as a result of decisions and implemented solutions that transform the existing structures and forces in play. Specifically, fourth-generation pattern languages focus on illuminating, as anticipated by Mehaffy [34], how parts in a system differentiate themselves and change their structure and relationship to one another, as the whole goes through each phase of a process of transformation.

The expanded act of design discussed here extends far beyond the completion of a design's construction and adaptation. It is broader than the conception-to-delivery of a designed object, project, or system, and even than the generative process that produces it. It involves a constant monitoring of the forces and underlying mechanisms that drive or affect a system and its transformations both in part and as a whole, as well as a continual reassessment and adjustment through monitoring of successive states of both the design and the ideal state it seeks to achieve—a target which may itself shift over time.

In this context, the notions of problem and solution, which are inherent to current design pattern form and practice may be difficult to capture or circumscribe, and may be variable in time, as described later in Sect. 4.2. The fit between a solution and the problem it is meant to solve may rapidly become obsolete; therefore, 'hardcoding' problem and solution in an interlocked way might end up inadequate. Considering patterns as current and desired configurations and mechanism, producing current or desired systems behavior, which may be evaluated and adjusted over time, may reveal to be preferable.

In this view, design patterns are not only to be seen as ideal configurations, templates for design, captures of best- or good practices, or proven solutions to recurring problems, where they implicitly signal quality or 'fit', as they currently are in pattern language practice. Instead, they should be configured in more granular and modular ways so as to track and readjust the configurations and forces discovered and captured within the design pattern. These configurations and forces may change over time, as the design itself, in interaction with other designs, may generate processes and effects which recursively affect and modify, as they unfold, the initial contexts they arise from. These evolving configurations and forces are patterns themselves.

Patterns, in this context, are expressions of systemic activity or behavior across multiple levels, which can be assessed and monitored on an ongoing basis to ensure the systemic validity and fitness to purpose of a design, as well as its sustainability and evolution over time. This continuous evaluation enables the identification and implementation of necessary adjustments or transformations. With this extended act of design, which interweaves systemic inquiry and design, patterns function as recognizable signs upstream in the context that motivates or triggers a design, and downstream in the behaviors generated by the design in interaction with others, as well as in the effects the design may produce on initial contexts and behaviors. This perspective requires a reexamination of the definition, form, and role of the pattern in an act of design extended over time and space, as well as a reflection on the role and responsibilities of the designer and on their margin of maneuver and capacity to navigate and leverage positive societal change.

3 The Multifaceted Nature of Patterns, Largely Untapped

Much of Alexander's work sought to capture the 'systemic' order and directionality of how we build things—towards QWAN—into pattern language and design. The novelty of the approach suggested here lies in the extension of the application of pattern language to complexity that manifests in other domains than the built environment, where 'place' is more difficult to locate. It also resides in the way patterns and pattern languages are configured and operationalized to do so effectively. The following sections examine possible reasons why, although the systemic intention is there and well stated in current pattern language epistemology, practice does not follow. One of the main reasons suggested here is that current pattern language form and practice do not leverage the full properties and potential of patterns [30], although these properties were implicitly acknowledged by Alexander. In particular, pattern language practice has not taken the full measure of the potential of patterns as a manifestation of systemic order and activity, and it has not fully leveraged the role of patterns in cognitive processes, in the way meaning and perception of the world are decoded and encoded, and in the way form and meaning are recursively transferred from the world, to our minds, to the traces we leave in the world through our actions and productions. Developing systemic pattern languages requires a reflection on pattern definitions, their various functions and attributes, and on the manner in which they can work together in practice.

3.1 Pattern Definitions

Pattern definitions, however diverse they may be, can be grouped into two fundamentally distinct functional categories:

(1) Observational Patterns: These patterns are recurring signs, forms, or arrangements in space and/or time that are observed or observable. This category encompasses patterns that are descriptive, revealing structure, behavior, and function/direction of

a design, and therefore the result of a design, whether natural or created. The term "observational" here includes not only what is recognized, but also what is cognized, imagined, intuited, invented, anticipated.

(2) Design Patterns: These patterns encapsulate captured experience or best practices, formalized processes or standards intended to guide design. This category includes templates or blueprints, or any normative form that describes or shows how to generate a design and to what end.

Patterns of the first category are renderings of reality, an expression of how things are inferred to be configured and unfold, which can serve for comparison and evaluation, such as in the scientific approach. They imply some form of objectivity, although they are subject to observer bias. Patterns of the second category inherently involve judgments of value or quality, and a decision about what ought to be formalized. These patterns must be worth capturing and serve a purpose.

The two categories overlap when an observational pattern becomes a model to be reproduced proactively. In the case of biomimicry for example, the documented observational pattern describes structures, behaviors, functions, or mechanisms observed, which themselves may be designed by natural forces, physical or biological, or by the actions of agents. Such a pattern may also describe, as Alexander suggests [24], why an arrangement in space or time is effective, and must be reproduced. The design pattern describes the structures, processes and sequences of steps, necessary to bring about the observed or sought out structure, behavior, function or mechanism. In some cases, the observed pattern may serve as a model to build the design and therefore may also itself become the design pattern. However, it is crucial to not conflate an observed structure or generative process with the structure or process necessary to generate and implement it. For example, the generative processes involved in the design of a genetically modified organism (GMO) differ significantly from the generative processes enabled by the newly designed genes. This is a vital distinction that will be further explored later in the paper.

'Alexandrian' patterns are typically of the mimicry type, an overlap between the two categories. Christopher Alexander referred to the pattern as, at the same time, a "thing" (from category 1), and the steps required to build the thing (from category 2) [24]. However, as discussed in the following sections of this paper, there is a tendency within the pattern language community to favor design patterns as forms over observational patterns as means for systemic inquiry through which structure, behavior, function and direction can be identified and assessed. The observational/inquiry aspect is often assumed to be contained, implicitly, in the design pattern. While this assumption may make intuitive sense from a design pattern perspective, this paper argues that such integration is neither systematic nor explicit enough. Especially when the forces and contexts considered are complex, some signs may be left out. Furthermore, when the integration between the two categories exists, it fails to leverage the full potential of the pattern as an observable, recognizable, or anticipable, and assessable sign of systemic order or activity.

3.2 The Pattern as Sign and the Construction of Our World(S)

In the realm of systemic design, patterns and pattern languages provide much greater affordances than what being confined to the process of design itself as rules or proven ways combined into steps towards achieving specific outcomes or qualities may enable. Patterns offer more than this through the critical role they play in our cognitive processes. They are involved not only in our ability to create but also in our ability to discover and to understand, to create meaning, and to confront interpretations and representations. These cognitive and semiotic properties of patterns are not currently leveraged to their full potential.

Patterns exist at the same time in the world, in our minds, and as representations, artifacts, or other traces in our environment, resulting from the interacting and co-evolving behaviors of many entities or systems. The essence of pattern literacy and patterning, or pattern thinking, in the broad sense intended here, as a competence of the observer and designer, can be understood as our ability as humans to grasp, assemble, represent and mobilize patterns in both our thought and action, in order to make sense of, converse about and shape our world(s). Are we not, in the pattern community, referring regularly to patterns being discovered rather than created? It is this essence that Alexander captured so well, and the reason why, probably, despite frequent critiques regarding the application of his work highlighted in the literature or at conferences and by Alexander himself, his concepts and theories continue to resonate and gain traction.

We humans are inherently an 'agent' species, evolved as natural designers who constantly create and construct, initially for survival in hostile environments and subsequently to thrive in an environment we have come to 'master'—or so we think—engaged in a perpetual quest to understand the world and extend our capabilities through tools. Patterns, as we understand them in their extended role, are key to these construction processes, whether cognitive, social, or material. They are the raw material, the building blocks, as well as the connectors of the meaning we construct and make sense of through our communications, actions, and productions. Alexander calls them the atoms of our man-made universe [24].

Our understanding of the world begins with the sensorial perception of forms by our embodied minds—shapes, sounds, textures, tastes, smells—which we then assemble to give them meaning. The individual components and the assembled forms we cognize and recognize are patterns. The partial image of a house glanced by each of our eyes, the sound of a bird, and we recognize our home in the dark. A strand of hair, an eye, a voice, and we recognize a friend. A few notes of music and we hear a whole symphony. Patterns as recognition or anticipation of repetitive form are at the basis of our making sense of objects as we piece perceptions together [35]. However, this extends beyond mere objects. Promising research with infants in developmental psychology suggests that we humans are born with five core innate pre-linguistic knowledge systems, which give us the ability to recognize and process percepts: forms and their relations of length and angles; quantity, numbers, and their arithmetic relations; objects and their motions; agents and their goal-directed actions; places, and their relations of distance and direction, and we make inferences from them [36]. Lakoff also identified similar innate schemas that we build both our physical motions and our metaphors upon [37]. These schemas can be seen as systemic operators that help us make sense of organization in space and time, and the associated outcomes and transformations, that ultimately help us orient ourselves. While other mammals share some of these knowledge systems, what we humans have that other animals don't is a unique capacity to recognize, assemble, and envision representations from across these independent systems into increasingly complex structures, as our mind/body develops [38]. This pre-linguistic associative capacity, possibly what Chomsky referred to as 'universal grammar', underlies not only natural languages, but all forms of our cognitive encoding and decoding systems and languages, or the codes we may use, including mathematics and music [38]. Pattern language as intuited by Alexander is one of these also.

Our minds appear to be hard-wired with a form of pattern language comprising systemic operators at its core, and therefore systemic in nature, which allows us to recognize and differentiate structures, relationships, dynamics, flows, feedback, recursions, all characteristic of working systems. How this works will be developed in the following subsection and is detailed further in the author's Plop 2020 paper titled "The Biosemiotic Underpinnings of Patterning and Languaging" [39]. This innate capability that humans have exhibited throughout history to varying degrees of awareness could valuably be nurtured and further developed into a pattern literacy [1]. Cultivating and operationalizing this pattern literacy to enhance systems literacy and effectiveness in systemic design is the primary focus of the author's doctoral research.

The process of cognitive construction operates recursively at multiple levels and on multiple dimensions. It begins with our personal inner worlds before extending into our social worlds and the broader socio-technological and environmental contexts we evolve in, which include the tangible objects we construct.

First, assembling percepts allows us to detect and infer the arrangements in space and time, forms, movements, magnitudes, directions, and outcomes, systemic in nature, which help us orient ourselves. As we continue to encounter and engage with these patterns, we organize them in our minds and build concepts around them to create increasingly complex structures. This process, essentially a continuous form of learning, lays the foundation of our inner worlds, shaping our identities, and our modes of expression. By parsing reality as we observe and interact with it—both individually and collectively—we develop the frames of reference and mental models that we use to further parse and make sense of the new phenomena we encounter and the new patterns in the world we perceive [40]. Then, expressed through language and other communicative forms, these frames contribute to shaping our external social worlds as we reflect and exchange with others and co-individuate in recursive interactions. The resulting virtual and material transactions, generate recurrent habits, patterns of understanding, and behavior characteristic of cultures at social scales.

The frames of mind and action logics we develop through these processes—our mental models—determine the form and direction of our designs and actions, and the artifacts we produce which in turn shape our social worlds, and influence the socio-technological and socio-environmental systems that emerge in the process. The systems we contribute to designing may take a life of their own, either empowering or constraining us, and in a way, designing us back, a phenomenon referred to as immergence by Bourgine [41]. An agent is both a designer and designed, a principle rooted in the reciprocal nature of feedback, where observation alters both the observer and the observed. At wider scales, the thing being designed is a partner in its own design, and leads the other designers along, which is, according to Gabriel, what Alexander was getting at with the objectivity of QWAN or Wholeness [42]. For Alexander [24], "All acts of building are governed by a pattern language of some sort, and the patterns in the world are there, entirely because they are created by the pattern languages which people use." (p.193).

Through the assembling and enactment of more or less complex, and more or less conscious patterns, meaning and direction are generated in the world at various levels of recursion, affecting natural phenomena as well. This impact has never been as significant and visible as it is today. Welcome to the Anthropocene era.

Patterns are involved in our perception of the world and our experience of reality. They contribute to shaping not only the material things we create, but also our multiple social worlds, and the world at large. In concrete terms, patterns can be found and studied at multiple levels: the level of forms we perceive in 'reality' or in the objects/phenomena/behaviors we observe; the level of observation itself and of our interpretations; and the level of our expressions, representations, and productions. As such, they play an active role in the recursive dynamics between our inner and outer worlds, between the subjective, the intersubjective, and the objective realms, as well as between the natural and the constructed, between the material and the conceptual. Quite appropriately characterized as *Patterns That Connect* by Bateson [43], patterns hold a vast untapped potential as connectors of multiple components, dimensions, modalities, that characterize complex systems. They can serve as mediators across experiences (phenomenologies), forms of knowledge (epistemologies) and modes of perception of reality (ontologies), helping individuals and communities understand and design systems across domains of knowledge and practice, and across worldviews and ways of understanding things [44].

3.3 Language, Composability and Symmetry: Patterns as Encoding and Decoding Media

The patterns discussed here, as fundamental units of construction of our realities and through which meaning is 'encoded' in our worlds, are also the units that enable us to make sense of and decode meaning from our worlds and interactions with others, through a natural, embodied process. Patterns are at the center of the processes of semiosis and construction of our worlds. They enable the transfer of form from the world, to our minds and to the traces we leave in the world through our actions, communications, and productions. The semiotic properties [1, 39, 45] of patterns as objects observed in the world, interpreted as percept or concept in the mind and represented or expressed, and enacted in our socio-technological and socio-environmental systems, support this decoding/encoding process.

For Michael Mehaffy [34], the universe is compositional, and so is the structure of the brain. Both display structural relationships and isomorphic properties, irrespective of any epistemological or ontological assumption. Moreover, both are connected via partial symmetric relations and isomorphic correspondences. A similar symmetry can be found in the structure and processes of language. Mehaffy suggests [46] that patterns "are consistently created by the interactive movements of other patterns—and made comprehensible by the symmetrical patterns of our own language and thinking." (p. 16).

Mehaffy [34] sees language as "the architecture of possibility" (p.113) enabling us to mirror and model the parts of the world we are most familiar with and to generate new possibilities in the process. He suggests [47] that "we are ourselves structures immersed in a world of structures, and our linguistic structures (and the brain structures in which they're evidently rooted) are in a continuous process of mapping symmetries and transformations, some of which we can bring about with our chosen actions. (But the choices are limited by—even created by—the mapping of the structures. They have generative power, but also limitations and dangers.) PLs are simply formal extensions of this same process into another logical system."[2]

The central question here is how pattern languages could help further enhance and leverage the potential offered by patterns as signs or manifestations of systemic activity, to better understand and design our world. By enhancing this capability, we could help bridge our constructed categories and concepts and their representations, allowing us to see/sense in multiple dimensions across various logical systems, thereby developing both understanding and creativity.

In the introduction to the Nature of Order [48], Alexander mentions a "slightly modified vision of science, which includes mechanisms as understood in the past, but also includes a powerful new kind of structure, coupled with a new form of observation, that transforms the range and extent of the experience which science can illuminate" (p.22), wondering whether the "order observed in science, and the order created in art might ultimately be treated as one phenomenon" (p.24). Clearly Alexander was onto something here. We could probably venture much further now, combining recent advances in both patterns and systems research.

We see encoding and decoding resulting from an iterative integration of inquiry and design at work in scientific inquiry where patterns are units of observation probed and turned into laws after successful experimentation— the pattern is for example the first of seven crosscutting concepts in science [1, 49]. This process occurs in psychology, where the pattern is altogether trigger, habit, archetype. It has also been well understood by computer scientists who emulate the patterning capability of humans into AI [35, 50, 51], and who use patterns both to model and to generate human-machine interactions. In the sense used here, patterns are also very close to schemata described in schema theory[3], used by linguists and cognitive scientists as units of knowledge and theories of reality.

3.4   Envisioning the Multi-faceted Pattern at Work

Our engagement with the world is a perpetual act of design, whereby we and our worlds co-evolve. What we experience in the world is not a succession of events resulting from individual acts of design or iterations, even though we may perceive them as such. Our experiences, rather, are continuous processes that we are participants in, consciously or not, emerging from our various designs in interaction. In this logic, action can be seen as an act of design, an idea encapsulated in the concept of 'ontological design' [52]. This perspective was explored by the author in a dialogue with Gabriel [42]. It resonates with the notion of Husserl's lifeworld [53], as referenced by David Seamon in his Keynote at PUARL2018.

---

[2] Group conversation on social media. PLs: Pattern languages.

[3] Ref https://en.wikipedia.org/wiki/Schema_(psychology).

Intervention for change in the context of wicked problems and complex systems requires making sense of all these patterns in interaction through constant processes of observation, interpretation, orientation, design, action, monitoring, and adaptation across various levels and scales. These cycles of inference and action, which themselves participate in the construction of our worlds are captured in a variety of frameworks such as Charles Peirce's cycle of pragmatism—observation, induction, abduction, deduction, testing, action—[45], John Boyd's OODA loop for situational awareness—observe, orient, decide, act—[54] and more recently, Dave Snowden's Cynefin approach to complex adaptive systems—probe, sense, respond—[55], as well as the human needs centered approach of design thinking—empathize, define, ideate, prototype, test—[56]. Each framework encompasses the principles of ongoing sense-making and adjustment. These constant iterative adaptive processes of sense-making and design, which may occur consciously or unselfconsciously, at various paces, levels, and scales, and in fractal types of manners, are applicable across all types of activity. By making these processes and iterations more conscious through pattern thinking—actively seeking, revealing, and mobilizing different types of patterns at these various iterative stages—we could enhance and further internalize the skills associated with pattern literacy. Such an approach would make these capabilities more innate and automatic, akin to the unselfconscious forms of design described by Alexander [57].

Pattern thinking can help make different types of inferences, and move through these cycles using heuristic, iterative, and interpretative approaches, identifying structure, behavior, function, and potentially hidden mechanisms at multiple levels, and designing to adjust, if necessary, along the way. It can help distinguish, during interventions, the different levels of observation (standpoints) and construction (objects of focus) involved, to better cross different types of boundaries and tackle specific challenges when seeking to transform or design systems.

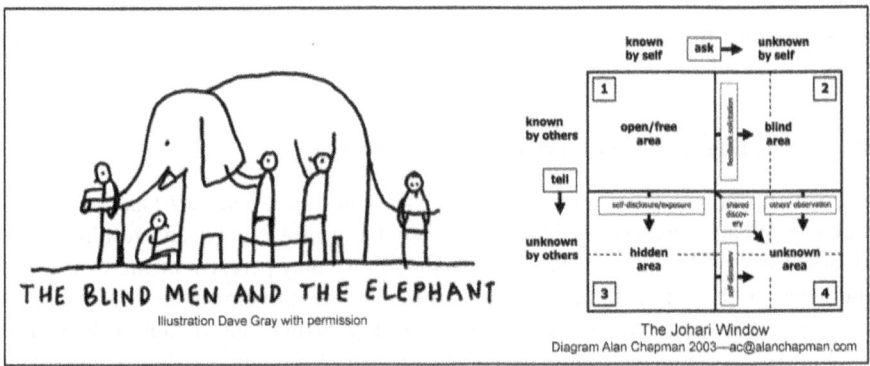

Fig. 2. The blind men and the elephant fable [58, 59], and the Johari window [60] illustrate how patterns could be used as boundary objects, mediating and connecting multiple interpretations and representations in participatory inquiry. A way to explore, confront and record different views and interpretations, points of convergence and controversies jointly discovered in our shared experiences. Getting a collective grasp of the elephant…

In this context, and because complex problems do not have clear boundaries, a systemic pattern language is not seen as a closed set of domain-related patterns, but rather as a generative ability to identify, and assemble patterns as needed, in an open and probing way, just like in natural language, with what seems an infinite set of words at our disposal—even if our vocabulary is arguably finite. In this respect, Mehaffy's [34] observation that "There is a corollary with languages, which have a limited set of words, and yet produce a vast set of complex meanings" (p.63) invites further reflection. The finiteness of vocabulary is not set by construction, but by opportunity. New words can emerge at any moment. Some languages, such as German, Bahasa Indonesia, or Finnish, have explicit rules for the creation of new terms, to various extents. Only the alphabets that serve to construct words in a given language are truly finite.

This potentially infinite composability enables new forms of literacy. In this sense, we can see such new generations of pattern languages as much more open than Christopher Alexander may have originally envisioned. This expansive nature allows for an unbounded number of patterns, and possibilities of representing them, that together could be combined to 'explain the universe', and design it at the same time. Mehaffy [34, 46] describes the universe as an "endless compositional structure" that is only partly comprehensible. One can think of mathematics here, as the language par excellence for explaining the universe, and note that within the scientific methodology, patterns serve as foundational elements to identify or recognize phenomena, from which laws and theories are derived.

Seeking to explain and design the universe should, however, be viewed here as an ideal, rather than an achievable goal—a process that can help uncover unknowns, perhaps even reveal some of the currently unknowable (see Fig. 2 above). In this context, fourth-generation pattern languages could be seen as a proto-language, a systemic language affording greater 'performing' or 'systems behavior generating' capabilities than natural spoken language, with a reduced dependence on assumed shared meaning. This could be seen as a kind of perceptual or inferential code used to describe, simulate, or even enact, in adaptive ways, the systemic operations of the world, bringing the focus on processes and networks of complex systems interrelationships and their manifestations, rather than on categories, and how things are named by convention.

This approach, as Henshaw suggests with the distinction between systems thinking and systems making [10], shifts the focus more directly onto the individual subjects and organizational designs found in nature, along with their overlaps, cross-linkages, and ambiguities, rather than on "invented categories". Such pattern languages become a medium for systemic conversation and mediation, with patterns serving as boundary objects or objects of research within and across different realms of interpretation and representation, as proposed by Cunningham & Mehaffy [61].

Patterns are altogether the recurring or anticipated signs and cues that we pick-up to 'grasp' something, the clues we look for, combine, and follow to understand our world, ourselves, and others in various contexts, and ultimately the elements we assemble to express and share this understanding. Found in the habits we develop, and in the ways in which we shape the world through our actions and the design of objects, organizations, and experiences, patterns are particularly well suited for transferring form and meaning from the world, to the mind, and into tangible forms, thanks to their versatility and semiotic properties. In the broadest sense, patterns act as units of 'meaning-making', facilitating both the understanding (decoding) and the design or transformation (encoding) of systems characteristics across levels, as illustrated in Peirce's triadic semiotic relation [62] and Rosen's modeling relation [63]. Their role is essential as connectors and mediators among diverse experiences of reality, knowledge forms and ontological views of the world [44], proactively fulfilling the function assigned to them by Bateson [43], of "patterns which connect" (p. 8).

The potential for pattern-based tools and methods that could leverage interpretative aspects in learning and action research interventions is vast, using participatory heuristics such as explored by the author at Plop 2017 [1], and by Takashi Iba at PUARL 2018 on The Future of Pattern Language [64].

The challenge of evolving pattern definitions, pattern language structure and the formulation of patterns to explicitly incorporate the multifaceted nature of patterns, and the expansion of pattern language practice into a comprehensive and continuous act of systemic inquiry and design, are key questions for both the pattern language and systems communities.

4   How Well is the Versatility of Patterns Leveraged?

As suggested earlier in the paper, from an epistemological perspective, although Alexander did capture the multiple facets of patterns and their systemic implication, the execution or practice did not follow. This is due to the fact that in their current form, patterns and pattern languages are not fully leveraged for their inherent properties and potential. They are not currently configured to be systemic, and therefore, they are not methodologically suited for systemic design.

Specifically, the quality of patterns as observational signs, indicative of current or aspired behavior of systems in action (category 1), is overlooked in favor of viewing patterns primarily as guides for design (category 2). This slippage away from systemic fitness is exacerbated by the prevalent problem-solution structure of patterns, which locks patterns in an instruction mode where they lose their recognizable 'performative' and 'evaluative' properties, namely their potential to render what 'is' and unfolds, as observed or anticipated. Pattern practice is also hindered by a view of generativity that does not seem to support the multidimensionality and multimodality of various generative processes in interaction, which are characteristic of complex systems.

Thus, developing and maturing systemic pattern languages requires rethinking pattern definitions and how problems, solutions, and generative processes are approached within an act of design that seeks to integrate the processes of inquiry and design effectively.

4.1   Alexander's Own Versatility: Getting the Various Definitions of Patterns to Work Together?

In his writings, Alexander explores both roles of patterns: as signs or forms to be discovered (observational patterns / descriptive, category 1) and as rules or guides for design to be followed (design patterns / prescriptive, category 2). This duality encompasses both the thing 'in the world'—the thing designed—and the process for designing it. Alexander's perspectives on patterns vary not only over time, as his work progresses, as highlighted by West and Quillien [65], but within individual texts, like the "Timeless Way of Building" [24], sometimes leading to inconsistencies [65].

In both his early and later works, Alexander describes patterns as observed signs/forms more than as rules or guides for design. In "Notes" [57] he describes a pattern as an extension of the diagram: an "[a]bstract pattern of physical relationships which resolves a small system in interacting and conflicting forces"[4], congruent with Herbert Simon's [66] "nearly decomposable systems" (p.473). Similarly, Michael Mehaffy suggests [34], the fifteen fundamental properties of wholeness Alexander introduces in his later work [67] could be expressed as sign/form patterns, as they describe the basic structural outcomes of the symmetry-breaking process inherent to any unfolding, and thus the structure of any part-whole relation, applicable in principle to any phenomenon.

Let us explore how, according to Alexander, 'patterns in the world', and 'patterns in our minds' inter-relate, and work together in the documented pattern and pattern language approach.

In the "Timeless Way of Building" [24] Alexander refers to a pattern as something "in the world" that we learn to see, belonging to the first category of patterns mentioned above:

> …a unitary pattern of activity and space, which repeats itself over and over again, in any given place, always appearing each time in a slightly different manifestation (p.181).

He goes on to relate patterns in the world and patterns in our minds:

> When we ask, now, just where these patterns come from, and also where the variation comes from, which allows each pattern to take on a slightly different form each time that it occurs, we have been led to the idea that these patterns "in the world" are created by us, because we have other, similar patterns in our minds from which we imagine, conceive, create, build, and live these actual patterns in the world. These patterns in our minds are, more or less, mental images of the patterns in the world: they are abstract representations of the very morphological rules which define the patterns in the world (p.181).

This is the "symmetry" Mehaffy applies to reality and language, which mirror each other. Alexander acknowledges here the constructed nature of the world, along with the existence of an external phenomenological order, and the recursive semiotic relationship between patterns in the world and their equivalent patterns in our minds. How, then, does he shift from acknowledging patterns in the world which 'appear' in any given place, and from referring to the 'very morphological rules which define both patterns in the world and their abstracted form in our minds', to collapsing this idea altogether in the next paragraph, subsuming the representation or image of order to a know-how or even to an urge to build?

---

[4] Preface to the paperback edition.

However, in one respect they are very different. The patterns in the world merely exist. But the same patterns in our minds are dynamic. They have force. They are generative. They tell us what to do; they tell us how we shall, or may, generate them; and they tell us too, that under certain circumstances, we must create them (p.182).

… highlighting that we retain and nurture in our minds the forms that are the strongest and the most meaningful to us, and therefore recognizing the strength of the pattern in its cognitive dimension and a drive to mimic in design the patterns in the world, but then immediately shifting the focus to a definition of a pattern as rule:

Each pattern is a rule which describes what you have to do to generate the entity which it defines (p.182).

…the pattern in the world morphs into a guide for design, which Alexander later announces as an 'extension of the definition of the pattern'. It seems the extension now prevails over the original intent.

This shift probably explains the current tendency within the pattern language community to narrow the definition of patterns to their design functions, overlooking the patterns observed in the world which gave rise to design patterns in the first place. These overlooked patterns are crucial as they are the signs or manifestations of systemic configurations or events, which can serve as tools to identify and assess form and process, and their inherent quality. The concept of observational pattern, from which the design pattern originates, however, and quite paradoxically, seems to not fit the pattern community's definition of a pattern. The author often receives feedback that questions the validity of these observational patterns as 'patterns' in the traditional sense, and suggestions for alternative naming to avoid confusion, with comments such as *"your" patterns are not "patterns"… "Could we name these differently than patterns, so as not create confusion?"…. "but then, everything is a pattern!"*.

It is understandable that not every random pattern in the world may serve as an ideal model for good design or action, or embody QWAN. But does this justify a complete disregard of patterns 'in the world', deeming them unworthy to be called patterns, or to be discussed as part of a systemic inquiry and design? Turkish carpet patterns and patterns of embryogenesis, before being celebrated by Christopher Alexander as epitomizing beauty and the order of nature, or QWAN, are first and foremost patterns of the first category: recurrent forms and processes that can be observed and discussed independently of any value judgment and formalization. These usually bear the name of pattern candidates in the pattern language community.

Most people understand patterns as repeated forms, of the first category, without introducing a value judgment a priori, using them as meaning-making and evaluating devices. How could we reconcile the two definitions, and leverage the full potential of patterns?

Patterns indeed are ubiquitous and multifaceted. They mean different things to different people, but these different meanings or functions are not random. They are interconnected through the semiotic relation linking the form in the world, the form in the mind, and the expression or representation of these forms. Embracing and leveraging this multifaceted and versatile nature of patterns is exactly what could bring pattern languages to a next level as far as collectively addressing complex socio-technological and environmental issues is concerned.

Alexander offers the following four consecutive statements on patterns in "The Timeless Way of Building" [24], as an introduction to the properties living patterns must have in order to be documented and shared:

Each pattern is a three-part rule, which expresses a relation between a certain context, a problem, and a solution.

As an element in the world, each pattern is a relationship between a certain context, a certain system of forces which occurs repeatedly in that context, and a certain spatial configuration which allows these forces to resolve themselves.

As an element of language, a pattern is an instruction, which shows how this spatial configuration can be used, over and over again, to resolve the given system of forces, wherever the context makes it relevant.

The pattern is, in short, at the same time a thing, which happens in the world, and the rule which tells us how to create that thing, and when we must create it. It is both a process and a thing; both a description of a thing which is alive, and a description of the process which will generate that thing (p.247).

We do find here the multiple definitions or facets of patterns. Alexander articulates in the pages following these statements how patterns in the world can be 'discovered' from observing the context, revealing systems of forces, and inferring or inventing the configuration and processes that produce them, and from there deriving the instructions for building them, to ultimately produce the patterns in their documented form. What is absent, however, is a reflection on how these different facets of patterns might complement each other in their 'pattern-ness', and how they could 'work' together, while preserving their functional specificity, in an extended act of design. In other words, there is a lack of reflection on how to better leverage all the properties and functions of patterns that Alexander has captured so well. Specifically, there is a gap in considering how patterns in the world, and our various ways of interpreting and enacting them, could be more effectively acknowledged as patterns in their own right, endowed with their observational, mediating, and generative quality.

Kohls [68] stands out among pattern language researchers for his comprehensive integration of the diverse properties of patterns, while addressing elements of potential confusion. He makes the semiotic distinction between patterns in the world, patterns in our minds, and patterns formalized as descriptions, highlighting the frequent shifts between these semiotic aspects, from the phenomenological aspect to the cognized and recognized and to the formal. By acknowledging the constructed nature of our worlds and the epistemological aspects of patterns, Kohls emphasizes the importance of differentiating the expression of patterns—essentially a mediating tool—from patterns themselves. He conceptualizes the documented form of the pattern as a double projection: the projection (expressed) of the projection (in the mind) of the pattern in the world, an explicit description of a 'form' in the world together with practical knowledge about this form. Gabriel characterizes this as a genre [69], specified further as a text genre by Kohls

[68], aimed at documenting practical knowledge. Kohls views the documentation of patterns as a scientific endeavor aimed to reveal hidden structures, echoing Cunningham and Mehaffy's idea of patterns as research objects [61], where quality is collaboratively assessed and discussed, and convergences or divergences of interpretation are systematically recorded, just as they are, for example, in Wikipedia.

Alexander described the versatility of patterns—in their material, functional, conceptual, and practical dimensions—quite effectively, as shown in Finidori [30]. However, he did not fully reconcile perspectives and demonstrate how they could work together and complement each other in practice, through an explicit "pattern methodology" [27] or framework. This versatility ought to be further explored and embraced rather than simplified or confined within strict boundaries. The work of Kohls, Mehaffy, and other pattern and systems thinkers, as well as the ongoing doctoral research of the author, aim to develop such a comprehensive pattern framework or methodology. Practitioners within the pattern language, systems science and systems thinking communities are encouraged to engage in these discussions and to explore tools and methods that could enhance the contribution of patterns and pattern languages to systemic design.

4.2   The Inquiry/ Design Integration and the Problem/Solution Association

Let us focus now on the configuration of patterns and how they capture interacting generative forces and problematiques. If we look at the current prevalent structure of documented patterns, we predominantly find a problem/solution structure, derived from the definitions of the pattern that Alexander et al. provided in "A Pattern Language" (APL) [70]:

> Each pattern describes a problem which occurs over and over again in our environment, and then describes the core solution to that problem, in such a way that you can use the solution a million times over, without ever doing it the same way twice (p. x).

> … and in "The Timeless Way of building" [24]:

> Each pattern is a three-part rule, which expresses a relation between a certain context, a problem, and a solution (p.247).

Patterns and pattern languages are regarded as problem-solving tools par excellence. How well do they help accomplish this task?

A key challenge in design and problem-solving is the difference in the nature of the skills they require, which makes their integration difficult.

Addressing general problem-solving strategies, Ing [9] highlights Peña and Parshall's [71] emphasis on the importance of the "search for sufficient information to clarify, to understand, and to state the problem." They further point out the "confusing duality of problem-solving methods," especially in "finding out what the problem is and trying to solve it at the same time", suggesting that these are "two distinct processes, requiring different attitudes, even different capabilities" (p.15).

These distinct attitudes and capabilities reflect a historical split of human motivation into two specific drives we humans have built different types of skills around, only indirectly alluded to in the earlier discussion on pattern categories. This split includes:

1. A critical drive, which focuses on understanding the world around us and 'how things work'. It is an epistemic quest characteristic of scientific inquiry, seeking 'truth', by identifying the order of things and the laws that govern them. Traditionally, this quest was viewed through the various epistemic lenses of siloed scientific disciplines. However, it is increasingly approached transversally through transdisciplinary studies, systems science, and systems thinking, which aim to consider things as more complete wholes, and to bridge disciplines and domains of practice.
2. A creative drive, centered on the production of technologies, tangible objects, services, or experiences, involving collaboration or competition to achieve specific goals. It is both an aesthetic and technical endeavor that goes hand in hand with a drive for problem-solving, construction and action, aimed at creating new 'orders', and producing new outcomes. While historically approached through comprehensive master plans, more fluid and 'need-centered' design methods have emerged, such as design thinking and pattern language, which support step-by-step adaptable designs.

The critical quest for understanding focuses on questions, on the inquiry process, on the problem. The creative construction endeavor concentrates on the responses, on the design process, on the solution. The distinction of pattern as sign (observational pattern) versus pattern as guide (design pattern) highlighted earlier in this paper aligns with this dichotomy. Henshaw [10] suggests that the two drives and competencies evolved in connected ways. In Henshaw's view, our systematic ways of thinking arose from the process of learning and teaching systematic ways of making things. Describing this as a general pattern for how humans operate, Henshaw [10] calls it "Systems thinking for systems making," suggesting an intrinsic connection between the cognitive quest for understanding, and the tangible act of making. Henshaw actually described semiosis at work there.

When comparing systems thinking and design as problem-solving methods, Jones [23] and Ing [9] point out a tendency towards specialization in either the problem aspect or the solution side of the equation. They note that neither approach appears to have fully integrated both aspects and their corresponding skills, with the focus remaining predominantly on one or the other. They critique systems thinking for its lack of accessibility, which hinders its practicality, and highlight inconsistencies in the problem-seeking dimensions of design. Ing dedicates a whole chapter to problem-seeking vs. problem-solving [9], which other authors call 'problem setting' [72, 73], in an attempt to shift the focus back on the inquiry.

Does pattern language bridge this gap? Fundamentally designed to achieve this integration, pattern language emphasizes problem-seeking by describing contexts and forces that generate problems, and addresses the resolution aspect through a proposed configuration or solution. At the pattern level, the 'problem-solution' association may seem an effective way to achieve this integration from the ground up. Within the "architecture of possibility" that pattern language enables, as Mehaffy [27] describes, patterns can be selectively combined and applied in granular, piecemeal ways at various levels and scales, which allows for an adaptive approach to problem-solving and design. Pattern language is thus relevant to systemic design because its relational, nested, network-like structure, and the focus on forces and configurations in specific contexts are congruent with and can mirror the structure and workings of systems, and facilitate implementation in agile ways. Kohls notes that "design patterns [which] document tested solutions, **reason**[5] about the problems solved and the contexts in which they can be applied", using the metaphor of the "path" to illustrate the pattern [68], which can also be seen as "a means to an end". This analogy emphasizes the journey towards a solution, influenced by context—such as the starting point, type of environment and terrain—a progression in space and time which incorporates a heuristic exploratory method embodying inquiry.

Critical questions arising in this context are whether the integration of competences and the focus on both inquiry and design are achieved and effective in practice, and to what extent the problem-solution association 'hard-coded' in the pattern form itself is relevant in addressing complex challenges.

The ambition of the inquiry-design integration is widely acknowledged. In his 2006 review of Alexander's "The Timeless Way of Building" [24], critical systems thinker Ulrich [11] praises the powerful concept of combined observational and design quality embodied by patterns and pattern language, which he views as an art of "seeing and sharing patterns that are alive," engaging observers across all disciplinary and professional boundaries. He sees the Timeless Way as an invitation to re-create our observational languages in order to address systemic issues. Ulrich highlights the potential of pattern languages for the continued development of action- and user-centered research approaches. Along similar lines, Henshaw discusses how the general pattern of how humans learn and make things "Systems thinking for systems making," can be interpreted as a "general language for all kinds of work," which "joins together systems of thought and action in a back and forth between conceptual thinking and practical thinking, studied and refined as a universal form of action research applicable to any science or practice [10].

Manns & Yoder [74], referencing Jackson [75] and Dave Ungar's response to Alexander's OOPSLA '96 presentation [76] regret, however, the lack of a systems perspective in conventional approaches to patterns. They argue that the emphasis on the structured form of documented patterns as objects, rather than processes, over-focuses attention on solutions and overlooks the systemic nature of problems. Pattern language, thus, seems to not have escaped the dichotomy of specialization discussed earlier.

We noted, in the previous section, that observational patterns had been neglected in favor of design patterns, not recognized as 'patterns' within the current discourse and practice of pattern language, and were not exploited as such. The pattern as a rule for design which was, in Alexander's own terms, an extension of his initial pattern definition, became predominant, setting the initial broader definition aside. It is likely, as a result, that the observational quality embodied in observational patterns as seen by Ulrich was overlooked in practice as well, possibly hindering the capacity to 'see', anticipate, and assess systemicity, and therefore the capacity to generate life or QWAN, in both systemic problems and solutions.

Alexander himself [57] correlates the form to be designed to the context, and the fit of the solution to the problem, in a quite loose way:

---

[5] Author's highlighting.

In the case of a real design problem, even our conviction that there is such a thing as fit to be achieved is curiously flimsy and insubstantial. We are searching for some kind of harmony between two intangibles: a form which we have not yet designed, and a context which we cannot properly describe (p.26).

As Wirfs-Brock suggests, patterns and pattern languages describe nuances of problems and possible approaches to solving them; they are tools for inquiry when things cannot be clearly and absolutely defined [77]. They are heuristic tools.

Wirfs-Brocks defines heuristics as offering "plausible approaches to solving problems, not infallible ones,, embodying characteristics adapted from Billy Vaughn Koen's philosophy of engineering heuristics [78]:

1. A heuristic does not guarantee a solution.
2. A heuristic may contradict other heuristics.
3. A heuristic reduces the search time for solving a problem.
4. The acceptance (or applicability) of a heuristic depends on the immediate context instead of an absolute standard.

The challenge with a problem/solution pairing, especially in the realm of complex systems, lies in the fact that the notions of problem and solution and their fit are not very stable. A situation deemed a problem from one perspective may not be considered as such from another, varying across individuals and groups, and often requiring negotiation and trade-offs. Jones, drawing on Latour [23] points out that problems, and in particular complex ones, rarely have clearly and unanimously (and therefore objectively) definable and agreed-upon boundaries. They are social agreements on issues of concern. Ormerod [73] references Schön describing "problem setting" as a way to select the "thing" that will be treated as the situation, and to "set boundaries of our attention to it," so as to define a coherence and a direction to what needs to be changed. Kohls elaborates further, suggesting that a problem—or question awaiting an answer that defines the task at hand—can exist on multiple levels. It may involve identifying the system of forces requiring resolution or defining the steps necessary to build a resolving configuration. Similarly, a solution could consist of a desired systems behavior or in the steps for achieving it. Kohls highlights, moreover, the potential for multiple solutions to address the same problem, and the many different ways to develop a particular solution. This multiplicity requires clarification on the level of engagement, and the decisions made or being considered.

Additionally, not all solutions can be repeatedly applied as contexts shift as a result of applying solutions. Any solution can become 'toxic' if over-applied. This raises the question of how a pattern might account for unintended consequences, for aggregated effects resulting from disparate causes, or for cumulative effects of a repeated solution over time. A medication that becomes lethal if overdosed, an antibiotic that loses its efficacy over time as bacteria develop resistance, or a parasite that overwhelms its host are all examples of such dynamics. Similarly, prioritizing efficiency to the extreme, thus eliminating waste entirely, can remove necessary buffers and undermine resilience in case of breakdown, as seen in lean supply chains that falter during major transport disruptions.

In terms of human behavior, incentives intended to eliminate undesirable habits or nuisances may paradoxically encourage them. A well-known example is the bounty for cobra kills in India, which led people to breed cobras for compensation, making the problem worse. Similarly, fines for late pick-up at kindergartens, as identified in Israeli research, can be interpreted as paying for a service, resulting in an increase in late pick-ups. In the agricultural sector, the construction of the Aswan Dam in Egypt aimed to control irrigation and provide electricity, but it also trapped the Nile's fertilizing sediment in Lake Nasser, preventing these sediments from enriching the riverbanks, diverting a large amount of the dam's electricity to produce artificial fertilizers. Moreover, the cumulative effect of extensive monoculture, use of chemical fertilizers and pesticides, and runoff along furrow lines leads to both topsoil erosion and the pollution of groundwater tables. These examples illustrate the limitation of simplistic monolithic views of problem-solution approaches.

To navigate complexity, Jones [23] introduces the concept of problem systems, as co-occurring problem manifestations. This concept builds on the idea of "problematique", originally proposed by Özbekhan in a Club of Rome report that aimed to confront the emergent global challenges that came to the world's awareness in the 70s [79]. This seminal report questioned the conventional notions of problem and solution, and the relevance of decomposing a complex problem into discrete independently solvable problems. It brought forward the concept of meta-problem, or meta-system of problems inherent to complex situations or problematiques, also called wicked problems [80]. The characteristics of problematiques or wicked problems are highlighted in Fig. 3.

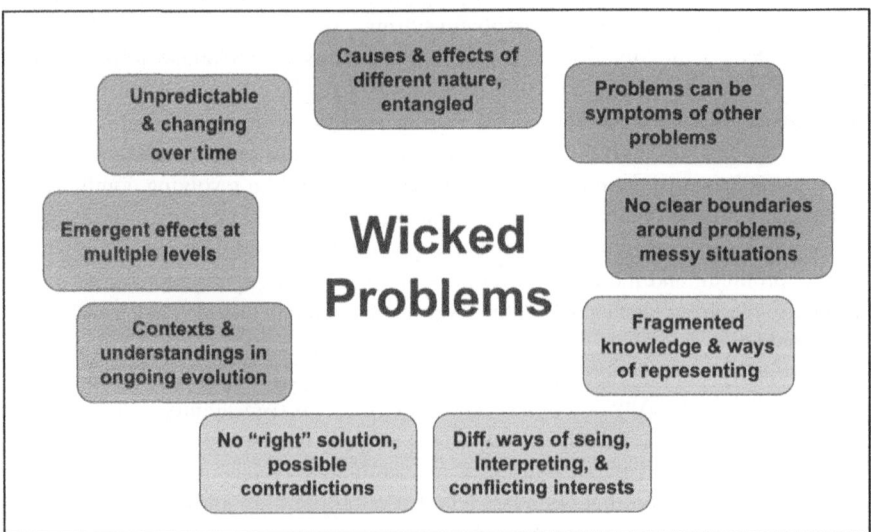

Fig. 3. Problems, solutions and knowledge in the context of complex problematiques or wicked problems [80].

Systems thinking offers strategic approaches for addressing complex problems, exemplified by Donella Meadows' work identifying leverage points for systemic intervention [29], and the development of the concept of systems archetypes by Peter Senge [81]. These archetypes capture recurring patterns of behavior in both organizational and natural systems, providing a framework for understanding causal relationships and guiding interventions.

We can observe that the common systems archetypes, as summarized in Table 1. Directly attend to the issues related to wicked problems highlighted in earlier examples and depicted in Fig. 3. While the textual form in Table 1. Bears resemblances in style to pattern language, systems archetypes are most commonly represented through systems dynamics diagrams that depict simulation cycles of nested feedback or causal loops mapping the interplay of multiple causalities. An example is the diagram illustrating the 'tragedy of the commons' archetype (Fig. 4). It is important to note, however, that the validity of this well-known archetype has been challenged by Nobel Laureate Elinor Ostrom's research on effectively managed commons [82].

Table 1. Summarized Systems archetypes. Many are targeted to problem/solution issues. Saybrook University Blog [83]

The eight most common system archetypes are:

1.   **Fixes that fail**—A solution is rapidly implemented to address the symptoms of an urgent problem. This quick fix sets into motion unintended consequences that are not evident at first but end up adding to the symptoms.

2.   **Shifting the burden**—A problem symptom is addressed by a short-term and a fundamental solution. The short-term solution produces side effects affecting the fundamental solution. As this occurs, the system's attention shifts to the short-term solution or to the side effects.

3.   **Limits to success**—A given effort initially generates positive performance. However, over time the effort reaches a constraint that slows down the overall performance no matter how much energy is applied.

4.   **Drifting goals**—As a gap between goal and actual performance is realized, the conscious decision is to lower the goal. The effect of this decision is a gradual decline in the system performance.

5.   **Growth and underinvestment**—Growth approaches a limit potentially avoidable with investments in capacity. However, a decision is made to not invest resulting in performance

The more successful effort gets a disproportionately larger allocation of the resources to the detriment of the others.

7.   **Escalation**—Parties take mutually threatening actions, which escalate their retaliation attempting to "one-up" each other.

8.   **Tragedy of the commons**—Multiple parties enjoying the benefits of a common resource do not pay attention to the effects they are having on the common resource. Eventually, this resource is exhausted resulting in the shutdown of the activities of all parties in the system.

The presence of causal loops makes probing and adjusting relationships within systems dynamics diagrams more challenging than with pattern languages, which are discrete and 'grammatical', and therefore composable in nature.

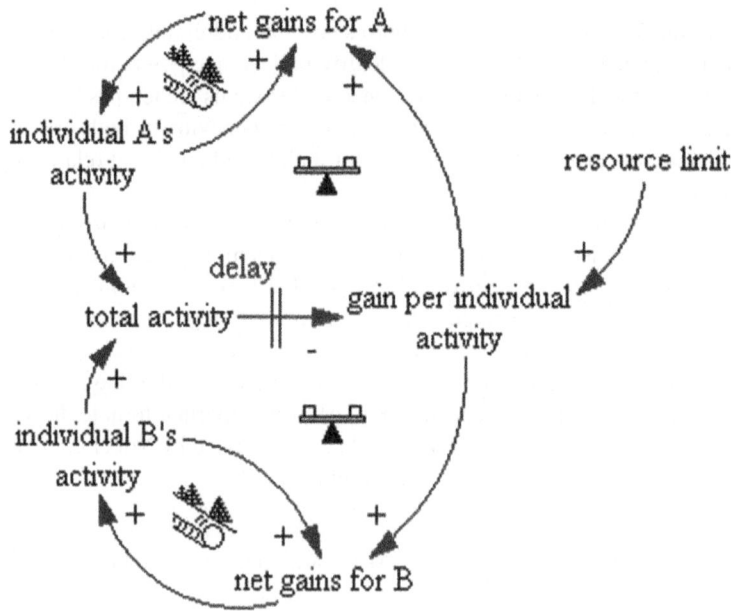

Fig. 4. Diagram of the Tragedy of the Commons systems archetype—CC BY-SA [84]

This raises the question of whether—and how—a pattern language, currently structured as a system of composable problem-solution units, could be integrated to offer a comprehensive systemic solution—or solution system—that 'fits' a problematique in all its dimensions and evolves over time.

There is a latent ambiguity in pattern language work, marked by the contrast between the claimed fluidity and adaptability of patterns in their composability into pattern language, and the potentially rigid, prescriptive nature of the problem/solution relationship embedded in the pattern form, which might not be effective in practice to support ongoing probing and adjustments, crucial for addressing complex evolving problems over time.

Complex systems are in constant process of transformation as agents continuously adapt to each other's behaviors and changes in context. Instead of enabling the monitoring of how context/problem and solution co-evolve, the problem/solution structure of patterns risks 'freezing' this relationship into configurations that may not remain relevant in changing, uncertain contexts. The association could indeed take a prescriptive / normative twist, preventing an actual inquiry in the definition of a problem and adjustment of its solution. Wirfs-Brock [77] points out that this association may impede the assessment of the validity of a solution over time. With problem-solution patterns, a slippery slope may lead to an "unfreeze-change-refreeze" cycle, quite different from a piecemeal approach aimed at producing a well-fitting form [74] that ensures the plasticity of the whole over time.

Plasticity, defined as the quality of being easily shaped or molded, is fundamental but also paradoxical. It implies malleability but does not inherently guarantee resilience.

While the brain can adapt and reconfigure itself to some degree, plasticity in physics denotes irreversible changes in shape, pointing to a kind of rigidity. Patterns are the "matter" for plasticity, embodying its dual nature. They can be remarkably malleable, allowing fluid adaptations. Yet, they also risk 'crystallizing' and remaining fixed in their form, similar to some materials or entrenched habits that confine us to rigid worldviews, biases, or hard-to-get-rid-of behaviors. The challenge here lies in harnessing patterns to promote continuous adaptation, rewiring and repurposing when needed, while preventing them from locking us into obsolete forms.

The question of the 'aliveness' and life cycle of patterns is a recurrent topic within the pattern language community [85–89]. Alexander himself [76] reflected on whether the traditional context-problem/solution format promoted in "A Pattern Language", didn't inadvertently reduce design to sequences of good ideas assembled into static forms rather than into generative entities, alive and evolving over time, able to address complex societal challenges effectively.

4.3   The Pattern as Thing and Process, Interweaving Inquiry and Design

Before examining the generative aspects of patterns, let us get back for a moment to the last paragraph of Alexander's [24] pattern definition set, shared earlier in the paper:

> The pattern is, in short, at the same time a thing, which happens in the world, and the rule which tells us how to create that thing, and when we must create it. It is both a process and a thing; both a description of a thing which is alive, and a description of the process which will generate that thing (p.247).

A pattern is at the same time a thing and a process, generative of that thing. What does this entail?

Considering this from a systemic perspective, it seems there may be several levels of 'things', several 'processes', several levels of generativity involved, as illustrated in Fig. 5.

First, the 'thing' that happens in the world, to be created, can be many things. Is it a structure? A configuration? A pattern in the world? A quality? An experience? A systems behavior? A process, itself generative of something else? The fact it 'happens' supposes, as we saw earlier, some form of phenomenon or event unfolding over time, potentially generating aggregate or ripple effects when combining with other phenomena and events, therefore involving movement and change in context as well. Then, there is the "rule that tells how to create the thing", which is a process itself, embedded in the larger process generated by the pattern language. Which of these processes generate the quality? Is quality or QWAN the 'thing' being built? Or is it embodied and enacted in all processes involved?

> This quality in buildings and in towns cannot be made, but only generated, indirectly, by the ordinary actions of the people, just as a flower cannot be made, but only generated from the seed (p.157).

If we consider this from Alexander's perspective of generating systems [90], which produce systems that are whole, a pattern language as a sequence of patterns would be

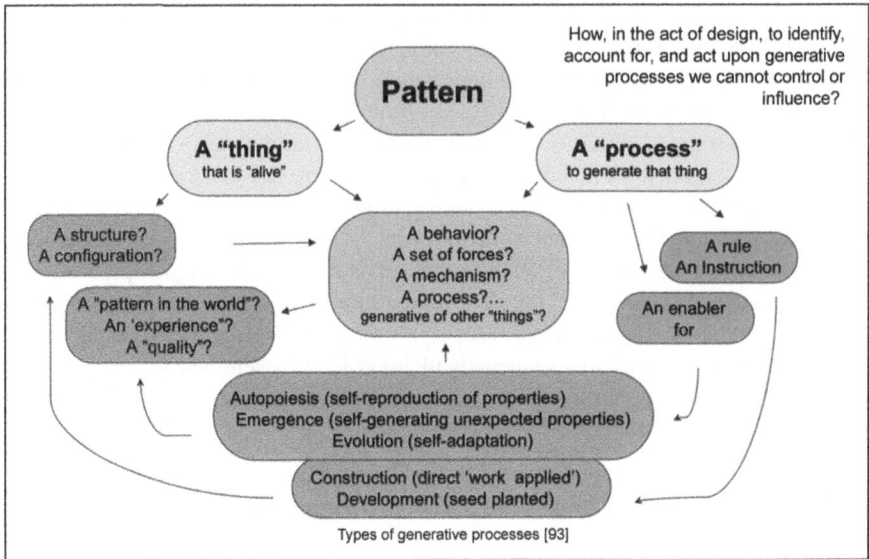

Fig. 5. Pattern as thing and process, and the different types of generative processes.

a generating system that generates the thing (a building), that itself generates a system that is whole (the system of social activity and interactions occurring in and around this building), this systems in turn being generative of other processes and qualities (increased awareness, environmental and social continuous regeneration, aliveness, wellbeing), themselves generative of changes in paradigm and thus of other more whole systems.

These different levels of generative processes occur also in socio-environmental and socio-technological systems, including software systems which are themselves socio-technological systems. They can be found not only at the operational or execution level but also within user-machine interactions and the resulting transformations within organizations using a software directly, or those indirectly involved and affected by the outputs of the system. Computer systems have the power to impact the bigger picture over time as well by generating new types of data, events or habits, which may have transformative effects on society as a whole, as seen with big data, AI or social networks in recent years.

All ordinary actions are generative acts of design which shape the systems they are embedded in. The structure and behaviors of systems and all their outputs and outcomes, whether generated directly or indirectly can be captured as observational patterns. Integrating observational patterns more explicitly into pattern language practice would enhance our ability to unpack and evaluate the different changes in systems structures, processes and relationships at different levels and scales, and the various processes they generate.

To pursue this idea further, it is necessary to make distinctions between a 'thing' designed and the generative processes and forces observed as a result of a design—both describable using observational patterns (category 1)—and further differentiate these from the design process itself, or steps to proactively realize a design, encapsulated in patterns as rules for design (category 2). We must be aware, however, that a generative process which indirectly designs a tangible object or another generative process may also be observed and described as a sequence of steps—nature's designs—akin to a design pattern. This may create some confusion in how terms such as structure, configurations, forces, behavior and process, are used and understood in relation to design process, sequence or steps. These distinctions and confusions are underlined in Kohls' [68] and Leitner's [91, 92] work.

A variety of generative processes may be involved at various levels. Mehaffy [34] refers to "coded processes that generate form", but he does not elaborate on the recursive nature of these processes. Patterns and pattern languages as we know them, in their 'process generative of the thing' dimension, clearly cover the process of building a thing or planting seeds for the development of a thing, and nurturing the thing (first to third generation pattern languages), which involve a rather direct act of design.

How effectively do current patterns and pattern languages capture and articulate other generative processes that unfold without direct intervention, those that are indirectly triggered, and that play out or 'run' on their own, such as fractal, emergent or self-replicating processes, that may combine to produce various types of unexpected aggregated effects? Software as a 'black box' may generate some of these also! This question is particularly important to examine from the perspective of wicked problems and the ways to approach complex systems of forces that may aggregate in the background at different levels. How would we identify and distinguish these generative processes of different nature and their synergetic effects when we discuss and describe patterns?

Roy and Trudel distinguish five types of generative processes [93]: construction, development, autopoiesis, emergence, and evolution, also identified by Mehaffy [34]. Construction involves deliberate work aimed at producing a given direct output. Development transforms a system through the realization of its potentials, applying work towards generating capacity/capability. With autopoiesis, the system (re)generates itself in interaction with its environment, maintaining its properties and continuously regenerating its own organization. Emergence brings forth unexpected properties or synergies resulting from the interaction between parts which do not prefigure these properties when taken individually. With evolution, the system transforms itself through adaptations and transformations at different levels and scales of diversified processes which interact with one another.

All these processes interact at various levels and scales to generate the reality we encounter, producing signs which may be more or less observable, and interpreted and represented in different ways. Pattern languages such as the first to third generation described in the first section capture construction and development processes quite effectively. But how well do they capture autopoietic, emergent, or evolutionary processes, and the combinations of multiple generative processes of different kinds in interaction? The processes which do not involve or result from the proactive application of 'work' or the planting of 'seeds', but simply 'unfold' 'in the world', most of the time in unpredictable ways, as not-so-visible underlying mechanisms and causal interactions which would require astute 'eyes', how are they recognized? They constitute the contexts and configurations of forces that shape a given problem or situation that could be expressed, interpreted, and understood using observational patterns. A number of systems science/systems thinking researchers and practitioners are using patterns in this fashion [12, 14, 94].

The application of such a systemic approach to software systems, particularly in addressing complexity and adaptive design within contexts of fragmented knowledge and agency, is detailed in Wirfs-Brock's exploration of design heuristics drawing on examples from Domain Driven Design (DDD) [95].

In the context of Event Sourced Architecture within DDD, events are treated as records or traces of occurrences, which are interpreted to understand how a given system is impacted. Changes in the system are captured as sequences of events, which set possibilities for the system to move into next states, generating new events. Sets of heuristics are applied, such as understanding how events flow around a system, tracking different kinds of events generated by the same process, or looking for patterns of events to drive systems behavior.

To navigate differences in meaning and interpretation, and in mental and operating models, DDD uses a concept particularly relevant here, that of bounded context, defined by Wirfs-Brocks as an entity driven by a unified model that operates with domain concepts which have congruent interpretation and meaning. Multiple bounded contexts coexist within a system, potentially using domain concepts with identical names but with significantly different meanings, information, and models associated with them. Sets of heuristics are applied to identify the various bounded contexts involved and the relationships between them. These bounded contexts are examples of cohesive knowledge domains that were mentioned as our different worlds previously, which resist unification for problem-solving purposes. This approach allows navigation among fragmented knowledge and agency domains.

The heuristics and patterns involved in event sourced architecture are not problem-solution centered. They render structures, flows, and changes that can help nudge a system toward desired behaviors, while addressing differences in operation, meaning, and interpretation. A similar heuristic could be applied more broadly to track the various dynamic patterns that transform and orient socio-technological and socio-environmental systems. These dynamic patterns involve many processes of the autopoietic, emergent, and evolutionary type, while also dealing with semiotic discrepancies: differences in knowledge, interpretation and representations across various modalities and forms.

Systemic pattern languages as envisioned here would enable the design or orientation of complex systems through the identification of patterns across multiple dimensions of complexity, dealing with a variety of generative forms, at different levels and scales. This interweaving and integration of inquiry and design, which involves new ways of seeing and envisioning in a single act of systemic design, brings together the drive for understanding and modeling how things work and how they transform and change as they unfold (scientific approach), with the drive to create and build solutions (design approach), thereby addressing the fragmentation of knowledge and meaning highlighted earlier. This involves integrating the inquiry —the scientific approach—into the practice—the art—and feeding back the practice or art, back into the science. Ultimately, encouraging such heuristics and pattern observation methods would help develop a pattern discovery- and design capability, and thus a pattern literacy that would enable the effective orientation of systemic trajectories.

Achieving this ambition fundamentally requires [re]extending the definition and form of the pattern back to Alexander's initial intent. It also demands the cultivation of methodologies for pattern language that embrace the semiotic properties of patterns. By establishing pattern language more assertively both as an observational and design language, we will be able to better assess and discuss the systemicity of problems, and the potential and sustainability of solutions.

5   Configuring Patterns and Pattern Languages for Systemic Design in Practice: Ways Forward

The previous sections highlighted the critical role pattern language could play in addressing complex systemic issues, and the questions raised about current pattern language form and practice to effectively support systemic design. In particular, the focus was set both on the semiotic and cognitive properties of patterns and pattern languages which could be leveraged to enhance our understanding of systems relationships and dynamics, their imbrications, and their implications, and on our capacity to envision transformations and design new forms in participatory ways.

The forms and methods to operationalize pattern language for systemic assessment and societal transformation on a larger scale are still at an exploration and experimental stage. Some directions for such operationalization were shared by the author in pattern language and systems thinking contexts [1, 25, 30]. Other initiatives are underway to broaden the usability, use, and reach of pattern languages, such as the Pattern Manifesto introduced by Yoder and Manns at Plop2017 and further workshopped at Plop 2018 [74]. The development of shared repositories and community practice are part of these also [96]. The questions that were formulated during the Future of Pattern Language session at the PUARL2018 conference are captured in Table 2. A similar inquiry is currently taking place in the systems community, particularly regarding how Systems Science and General Systems Theory could inform Systems Thinking and Systems Engineering practices more directly. Patterns and pattern languages have a role to play in this endeavor, as isomorphy and cross-cutting science concepts are brought center stage in an attempt to revisit General Systems Theory for the 21st century.

The present section focuses on possible ways forward in terms of architecture of patterns and pattern languages that would support sharing, retrieval, semantic interconnection, and composition of patterns from different sources into pattern languages, to inform the Future of Pattern Language discussions.

5.1   Making Patterns Accessible: The 'Good Form' for the Pattern

Two types of questions arise about the formalization and use of patterns in systemic and trans-disciplinary contexts. One, which was covered quite broadly above, is whether pattern language methodology and pattern forms are systemic and 'semiotic' enough to enable effective navigation of complex systems in a context of fragmented knowledge, agency, and language. The other, which is addressed here, is whether design patterns are not too complex or complicated to apprehend, store, retrieve, use, and keep alive.

Table 2. The Future of Pattern Languages World Café questions, as kick-off for the PUARL 2018 conference.

• What is important about a pattern language approach? Why does it matter in the real world?   • What can be done to make the pattern language approach more useful and popular?   • How can we integrate the wide diversity of pattern language approaches into collaborative efforts—particularly given the wide diversity of pattern languages (applications in architecture, software, civic well-being, group dynamics, organizations and companies, etc.)?

Alexandrian patterns are complex elaborate structures with many related parts or sections describing different elements and angles, which Leitner calls pattern aspects [92]. The most comprehensive structure includes context, problem, forces and counter-forces, solution, examples, resulting context, rationale, related patterns, known uses, pros, cons, figure. Other aspects can be found in software patterns, such as intent, motivation, applicability, structure, participants, collaborations, consequences, implementation...

Leitner [91, 92] suggests that pattern writing may sometimes blur the lines among pattern aspects, particularly between context, forces, problem, solution, resulting context, or consequences. Wirfs-Brock points out [77], in the context of creating libraries of patterns for cross-community reuse, that the abundance of details to go through when reading a new pattern may overwhelm users, making it difficult to determine its applicability. Especially, discrepancies that are too broad among pattern formats and sets of pattern languages at many levels complicate the selection and combination from different sets. Too many levels of abstraction and detail also make it difficult to compare and choose among patterns. As a result, pattern authors stick to their own pattern languages or collections of patterns, and reinvent the wheel, so to speak, when they don't find what they are looking for on their own shelves.

Addressing the complexity of pattern formalization and the broadening or even scaling of pattern production and use, while limiting potential shortcomings, such as too much abstraction, reduction, or 'freezing', and confusion in the terms or processes, is the main challenge.

The following questions provide opportunities for discussion about how to evolve the pattern languages of the future:

• How can clarity in articulating and distinguishing the various 'aspects' of patterns be achieved?
• How can the different processes involved be identified, along with the building steps that need to be actively undertaken?
• How can descriptive elements be differentiated from prescriptive ones?
• How could this be done in such ways that the key elements of a situation, context, and solution stand out so as to efficiently evaluate what applies?

Incorporating systemic components into the structure of design patterns and pattern languages could offer valuable insights into how to 'peel the onion' or unpack the 'ball of knots' of a problematique or wicked problem. This includes further exploration of agency: for example, identifying 'who' or 'what' generates processes and forces in play, in which manner and at which level. Addressing differences in expressions or representations and interpretations, and in particular identifying 'how' and 'why' these processes are generated, is part of the endeavor.

This involves a pattern ontology, not quite to place things in categories or boxes, but rather seen as perspective taking to facilitate meaning-making and the differentiation of things, as a way to capture not only the multidimensional nature of what is or what is to be designed, but also the multi-level nature of observation itself.

Kohls describes the pattern as 'reasoning' about context, problem, and solution pathway. Cunningham and Mehaffy [61] suggest that patterns be considered as research tools. To expand the reach and use of patterns, this would have to be undertaken at the community and cross community level. The architecture of such patterns would support community design and the collaborative or collective discussion and evaluation of patterns, with an ability to record different interpretations and perspectives, and points of agreement as well as controversies. Wikipedia, and its editorial structures and processes, currently supports this type of organization of knowledge, and its 'meta-stabilization'.

5.2   A Modular Form for Interconnected Patterns?

The discrete, versatile, and composable nature of patterns in their broadest definition enable the description of different layers of components or aspects interacting in systems, and the comparison of the different ways in which we understand and represent them. With a modular structure within the pattern form itself, the versatile properties of patterns would further be leveraged to support the methodologies mentioned above.

It seems that Alexander, even if he didn't use modular structures explicitly, paved the way for a modular approach. His descriptions of pattern language and individual patterns containing other patterns illustrate the recursive process through which both our worlds and our mental representations of them are constructed. This recursion and the resulting structures enable deconstructions and (re)constructions of patterns at various scales, and therefore individual and collective pattern-based sense-making processes [24]:

Each one of these patterns is a morphological law, which establishes a set of relationships in space.

...And each law or pattern is itself a pattern of relationships among still other laws, which are themselves just patterns of relationships again.

For though each pattern is itself apparently composed of smaller things which look like parts, of course, when we look closely at them, we see that these apparent "parts" are patterns too (p.90).

The smaller things that *are patterns too*, Alexander also referred to as the atoms or molecules from which a building or a town is made. These are manifestations or signs of systems at work, the 'signs' evoked by Rebecca Wirfs-Brock [95], that can be tracked and "stringed together" to form 'trails' in the discovery of larger structures and processes. Wirfs-Brock suggests that patterns have the potential to be trails if one can navigate from one 'sign' or pattern to the next. Pattern language in its form as well as in its practice has the potential to enable this process.

Stringing signs and trailing are a form of ongoing adaptive unself-conscious modeling, which could be undertaken self-consciously using micropatterns to construct or deconstruct structures and processes as well as meaning, in order to describe and explain observed phenomena and/or design something new. Comparable to a 'hacking' session or a Lego Serious Play activity, this method allows for combinations of discrete objects, where each relation within a model can be examined, probed, and ultimately transformed in participatory ways. Examples of such adaptive techniques, which enable comparison and confrontation of different modelling processes and languages, and ultimately address differences in natural languages, cultures, and knowledge domains, can be found in Finidori [30] and Finidori & Tuddenham [1].

Experiments with patterns as atoms or molecules constitutive of trails were conducted by the author at Purplsoc 2015 and Plop 2016 using a set of systemic interpretation cards [1]. Participants were invited to model situations and patterns they observed or experienced using these cards, and then share their insights and discuss these patterns with the group. The diversity of situations described in these sessions was broad, with cards applied in various ways to model known patterns, workplace dynamics, organizational challenges, power relations, new business models, business processes, scaling of good practices, continuous improvement initiatives, new technologies, good journalism practices, and urban development processes, among others. Some participants described the experience as 'telling systemic stories' through patterns. The primary insight from these activities is the participatory nature of the process, where the patterns expressed and the trails they compose are in focus as boundary objects, allowing comparison and confrontation, beyond concepts and the language that describes them: a way of building trails co-operatively as we go. This participatory process does not necessarily involve alignment, agreement, or consensus. It may be adversarial or confrontational when interpretations and purposes diverge, in which case using patterns as signs and trails can help minimize misunderstandings due to divergence in representation, interpretation, and value judgment.

Reconstruction of trails could be further operationalized and systematized through tools and methods designed to interconnect various instances of pattern representations from various fields within semiotic maps. This would enable the navigation of patterns and the reconstitution of trails across multitudes of symbolic reference systems or languages.

Viewing patterns as heuristic elements that help recognize, distinguish, and describe the structures, behaviors and processes or mechanisms involved in what we seek to unravel in complex systems, including those that are less visible, allows comparisons between actual, observed system behaviors and states, with ideal or desired ones. Ulrich acknowledged the heuristic potential of pattern language [11]. He considered his conceptual framework for boundary critique, in the realm of what he referred to as critical systems heuristics, as a new pattern language aimed at facilitating reflective practice among researchers and professionals of diverse fields.

In this logic, observational patterns—understood as identifiable configurations of elements in space or time and the dynamics of their transformations—could serve as critical components formative of design pattern aspects, bringing into focus the trails in the contexts, problems, and driving forces of a system under study. This applies also to desired configurations or sought quality, highlighting the generative processes and potential pathways towards building systems that are 'whole'. Figure 6 is an illustration of how the possible emerges from the actual as possibilities are explored, showing the transformation from the actual to the new through modular structures.

A problem could be expressed as a set of patterns that require transformation. A solution could be expressed similarly as a set of patterns of desired systems behavior, they themselves generating emergent qualities. Other patterns aspects could be expressed as patterns also and serve as building blocks for other patterns, enabling the mix and mash of pattern aspects in the pattern representation, suggested by Leitner [91].

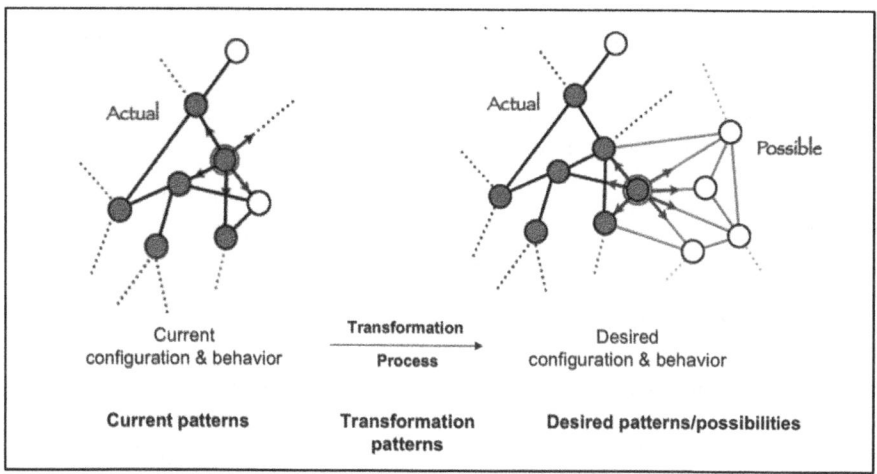

Fig. 6. Adapted with permission from Dynamics on expanding spaces: modeling the emergence of novelties—Mathematical illustration of the adjacent possible. [97]

Then, there is the design pattern acting as a rule for design guiding the transformation from a set of patterns A (the current systems behavior, and the configuration and forces that drive it) to a set of patterns B (the desired or possible future systems configuration, processes, and behavior, and the generative processes they may enable at various levels). These can then be combined into larger design patterns and further into sequences or networks—the pattern language—forming a system of design elements that function together to produce a design, or to enable the conditions for new generative processes.

Kohls and Scheiter [98] proposed an approach transposed from schema theory, where a pattern schema is composed of a problem schema and a solution schema, each divided into sub-schemata, with the solution schema encapsulating a cognitive activation: a succession of inferences and actions that echoes the cycles referred to in Sect. 3.4. The schema as described here is quite close to the pattern, understood as a recognized arrangement in space and/or time, which triggers further inference and action, and as a result, further patterns.

However, patterns are often regarded merely as 'proven paths' from point A to point B. This perspective may constrain them within rigid boundaries, overlooking their potential for adaptation and reconfiguration, or in other words, their plasticity. By incorporating observational/sense-making patterns at both the problem and solution levels, it becomes possible to consider the problem, solution, and transition pathway in a more systemic, integrated, and adaptable manner. Such an approach allows the fit between these components to be more easily probed and adjusted, addressing the problem-solution challenge described above. Increasing pattern adaptability and usability is vital for advancing pattern language methodologies, and remains a key topic for further discussions on the future development of pattern languages.

Additionally, configuring design patterns more systematically using observational patterns opens up further possibilities for collaboration and for the extension of the use of patterns across domains of application, in relation for example with General Systems Theory, which strives to find isomorphies and invariants or general systems principles that cut across domains.

5.3 Making Patterns Searchable and Reusable

Alexander's life work, which culminated in the articulation of fifteen principles of wholeness [48], and Bertalanffy's pursuit of General Systems Principles to achieve the unity of sciences [90], reflect a widespread quest for invariants or universal principles across domains and disciplines. In his "Quest for General Systems Principles", Rousseau [99] notes, however, that "although the existence of principles is inferred from the existence of isomorphic systems patterns… knowing more isomorphisms only increases confidence in the existence of principles without making them easier to find" (p.9). Focusing energy on agreeing on the most abstract and synthetic forms of invariants detached from any context seems indeed a daunting task, given the fragmentation of contexts and related vocabularies and worldviews. Semantically interconnecting representations and interpretations of systemic patterns, as will be explored below, may be a way to get there.

When considering the reuse of patterns from different origins, Wirfs-Brock [77] notes that existing patterns, usually confined within application-focused or even author-proprietary libraries, are hard to locate, remember, and parse when trying to find a fit with new situations, and thus they are difficult to reuse. She suggests that "Perhaps, instead of categorizing our patterns we should characterize, that is, tag them with multiple characteristics, and let these characterizations emerge as we build our collections and share them with others" (p.6). These characterizations or tags could be the sub-patterns contained in the larger pattern as described earlier: the 'recognizable' chunks shared across patterns and pattern languages that could be used to articulate pattern aspects, as suggested by Leitner, and interconnect patterns semantically. The author's systems interpretation elements [25]—the small patterns referred to in the above section—in addition to their use as sense-making and modeling components, were initially designed as pattern indexing or tagging system. Semantic interconnection could be further operationalized through approaches such as Kenneth Lloyd's category theory [100] and Troncale's linkage propositions.

Innovative methods and tools that systematize semantic interconnections between patterns through pattern-based indexing are necessary to enable navigation within a growing body of patterns and pattern languages stored across a variety of pattern repositories. An easier retrieval of patterns from different databases via dedicated pattern search engines would open up opportunities for sharing and reusing patterns across domains of activity and communities of practice, as called for by Wirfs-Brock [77] and Manns and Yoder [74] who see it as a breakthrough for collaborative and transdisciplinary work.

Such linked data would generate clusters of semantically or morphologically related patterns and systems characteristics, enabling the connection of multiple expressions and representations of similar realities, and therefore multiple contexts, without losing critical information. One can think of a thesaurus, which relates synonyms along multiple vectors of similarity, without trying to select a single word that captures an idea to the detriment of others. The Visual Thesaurus [101], for example, provides a graph of synonym relationships, allowing the formation of clusters of meaning, and navigation within or across them.

These semantic networks and the clusters of isomorphy or homomorphy that emerge from them could become objects for study and discussion across disciplines and domains of practice that would refine our understanding of invariants and isomorphies, in line with the objectives of General Systems Theory. Adopting an interlinked pattern approach to invariants and homomorphy or isomorphy supports the idea of a quasi-infinite and open-ended pattern language rather than a finite one, circumventing the challenge of the quest for a finite set of general systems principles. Ultimately, this approach to linked data could lay the ground to enable new processes of abstraction and synthesis, opening pathways to identifying operationalizable invariants, not through unattainable consensus such as set forth by Rousseau, but based on emergent similarities between interconnected patterns observed in different contexts. This would open up whole new avenues for both the practice of pattern languages and systems science.

Configuring patterns and pattern languages for systemic design in concrete practical terms is a whole topic of research. Some substantial steps need to be accomplished to put this endeavor on tracks. Summarizing the strategies proposed throughout this paper, these steps include:

1. Working towards a pattern definition that acknowledges the semiotic nature of patterns as 'thing' in the world, 'thing' in the mind and expression thereof, and proactively using patterns as connectors of multiple dimensions.
2. Establishing a pattern ontology, a set of heuristic tools, and methodologies for pattern exploration that help distinguish and discuss systems in focus, levels of generative processes, different systemic aspects, and perspectives under consideration, enabling individual and participatory sense-making and orientation.
3. Designing a modular pattern form that supports the embedding of smaller patterns, and a system allowing the detailed documentation of distinctions and discussions around patterns, to be used as a research tool.
4. Developing methods and tools for semantically interconnecting and navigating through diverse pattern forms based on multiple criteria, enhancing the discoverability and applicability of patterns across contexts, and the formation of clusters of isomorphy.

Addressing this challenge is a collaborative effort and it is the author's hope that members of the systems science, the pattern language, and the software development communities will engage in this endeavor.

6 Conclusion

The questions raised in this paper on the role and form of patterns and pattern languages meet some of those formulated by others at Plop 2017 and 2018. They focus in particular on the role of patterns as heuristics for complex decision-making and moving complex designs forward, and as structure, process and community within larger systemic frameworks. Reflecting from a systemic perspective, it becomes clear that the work of the designer extends beyond the completion of the designed object [74, 77], acknowledging that the designed entity itself has agency. This resonates with Alexander's original aspirations to create an impact in the world, expressed forcefully at Oopsla '96 [76].

The author's long-term endeavor is to explore how patterns and pattern languages systematize cognitive processes for systemic inquiry in order to support ongoing adaptive design within contexts where dynamics are entangled, the subjective and objective are co-related, and parameters shift constantly. Addressing this challenge involves incorporating patterns and pattern languages in an extended act of design entailing larger and more complex systemic processes, and using patterns for sense-making as well as for generating forms and dynamics. A key objective of this research is to outline the conditions and requirements for tools and methods aimed at enhancing the heuristic role of patterns and pattern languages and at keeping them in use and alive while making them more accessible.

Structuring patterns and pattern languages of the next generation in ways that support systemic understanding and design; tapping more explicitly into the observational and semiotic nature of patterns and pattern languages that connect the phenomenological, cognitive, and representational aspects of patterns; and enabling the leverage and enhancement of pattern knowledge in view of pattern literacy as a means to empower and build capacity and ways for cooperation among researchers and users, all these are directions for future collaborations with and across the pattern language and systems communities. The software community also has a key role to play, as the tools to operationalize this vision and enable this enterprise are yet to be developed.

Acknowledgments. The author extends her thanks to her shepherd, Matt Griscom; to Rebecca Wirfs-Brock, who moderated this paper's writers' workshop session with thought-provoking questions; to her writers workshop group members: Lisa Hvatum, Tomoki Kaneko, Yuki Kawabe, Maged Khalil, Julio Moreno, and Ayaka Yoshikawa, who all provided valuable and appreciated feedback; to Richard Gabriel, Pini Reznik, and all the students of the Iba Lab who attended her Writing Systemic Patterns Mining workshop, and to Joe Yoder, who helped facilitate it; and finally, to Takashi Iba for his continuous inspiration and support on her journey in pattern language and complex systems research, and in particular for the conception of the fourth generation pattern language.

References

1. Finidori, H., Tuddenham, P.: Pattern literacy in support of systems literacy: an approach from a pattern language perspective. In: Proceedings of the 24th Conference on Pattern Languages of Programs (PLoP). Hillside (2017)
2. Finidori, H., Borghini, S., Henfrey, T.: Towards a fourth generation pattern language: patterns as epistemic threads for systemic orientation. In: Baumgartner, P., Gruber-Muecke, T., Sickinger, R. (eds.) Pursuit of Pattern Languages for Societal Change (PURPLSOC). Designing Lively Scenarios in Various Fields, pp. 62–86. epubli, Berlin (2016)
3. Mehaffy, M.W.: Urban form and greenhouse gas emissions: findings, strategies, and design decision support technologies (2015)
4. Mehaffy, M.W.: Horizons of pattern languages: software, cities, planet. In: Proceedings of the 24th Conference on Pattern Languages of Programs (PLoP). Hillside, Vancouver (2017)
5. Quillien, J., West, D.: Culture under the microscope. In: Notes from the presentation at Code Freeze (2013)
6. Iba, T.: Sociological perspective of the creative society. In: Zylka, M., Fuehres, H., Fronzetti Colladon, A., Gloor, P. (eds.) Designing Networks for Innovation and Improvisation. Springer Proceedings in Complexity, pp. 29–42. Springer, Cham (2016). https://doi.org/10.1007/978-3-319-42697-6_4
7. Schuler, D.: Liberating Voices: A Pattern Language for Communication Revolution. MIT Press, Cambridge (2008)
8. Atlee, T., Rausch, M.: The Wise Democracy pattern language. The Co-Intelligence Institute, Eugene (2017)
9. Ing, D.: Open Innovation Learning: Theory Building on Open Sourcing While Private Sourcing. Coevolving Innovations Inc., Toronto (2017)
10. Henshaw, J.L.: Systems thinking for systems making: joining systems of thought and action. Systemic Practice and Action Research (2018)
11. Ulrich, W.: The art of observation: understanding pattern languages. J. Res. Pract. 2(1) (2006)
12. Mobus, G.E., Kalton, M.C.: Principles of Systems Sciences. Springer, New York (2015)
13. Troncale, L.: Systems processes and pathologies: creating an integrated framework for systems science. INCOSE Int. Symp. 23(1), 1330–1353 (2013)
14. Troncale, L.R.: Linkage propositions between fifty principal systems concepts. In: Klir, G.J. (ed.) Applied General Systems Research, pp. 29–52. Plenum Press, New York (1978)
15. Palmer, K.: Foundations of systems architecture design: steps toward and ecology of emergent design (2018)
16. Palmer, K.D.: Schemas theory overview—part 7: exploring patterned forms (2019)
17. Tuddenham, P.: Observations on systems literacy at the International Society for Systems Sciences (ISSS) 2016 conference. Syst. Res. Behav. Sci.Behav. Sci. 34(5), 625–630 (2017)
18. Edson, M.C., Metcalf, G.S., Tuddenham, P., Chroust, G. (eds.) Systems Literacy: Proceedings of the 18th IFSR Conversation 2016. Johannes Kepler University, Sankt Magdalena, Linz (2017)
19. McNamara, C.: Patterns in Nature, Systems, and Design. INCOSE Natural Systems Working Group (2018)
20. McNamara, C., Troncale, L.: How to find and map linkage propositions for a general theory of systems from the natural sciences literature. In: In: Proceedings of the 56th Annual Conference, International Society for the Systems Sciences (ISSS) (2012)
21. Silverman, H., Hill, G.M.: The dynamics of purposeful change: a model. Ecol. Soc. 23(3) (2018)

22. Smith, W.E.: Making the invisible visible: the dynamic interplay between purpose, power and leadership in organizing complexity. In: Finidori, H. (ed.) Systemic Change, vol. VI, p. 1. Spanda Foundation, The Hague (2015)

23. Jones, P.H.: Systemic design principles for complex social systems. In: Metcalf, G. (eds.) Social Systems and Design. Translational Systems Sciences, vol. 1, pp. 91–128. Springer, Tokyo (2014). https://doi.org/10.1007/978-4-431-54478-4_4

24. Alexander, C.: The Timeless Way of Building. Oxford University Press, New York (1979)

25. Finidori, H.: A Pattern LAnguage for Systemic Transformation (PLAST) (re)generative of commons. In: Baumgartner, P., Sickinger, R. (eds.) The Workshop 2014: Designing Lively Scenarios with the Pattern Approach of Christopher Alexander—Pursuit of Pattern Languages for Societal Change (PURPLSOC) Conference, pp. 58–86. epubli, Berlin (2015)

26. Iba, T.: Pattern languages as media for the creative society. In: Proceedings for COINs13 (2013)

27. Mehaffy, M.: Private email conversation on pattern types and Iba's Pattern Generations, 6 August 2018

28. Alexander, C.: The Nature of Order—Book 2: The Process of Creating Life. The Center for Environmental Structure, Berkeley, California (2002)

29. Meadows, D.H.: Leverage Points: Places to Intervene in a System. The Sustainability Institute, Hartland (1997)

30. Finidori, H.: Patterns that connect: exploring the potential of patterns and pattern languages in systemic interventions towards realizing sustainable futures. In: Proceedings of the 60th Annual Meeting of the International Society for the Systems Sciences: Realizing Sustainable Futures. ISSS Journal, University of Colorado (2016)

31. Harich, J.: Analysis of the change resistance subproblem. In: Harich, J. (ed.) Common Property Rights: A Process Driven Approach to Solving the Complete Sustainability Problem, pp. 202–273. Lulu Press, Clarkston (2011)

32. Scott, B.: Open sourcing finance keynote. In: Ctrl Alt Currency Conference (2014)

33. Ulrich, W.: A brief introduction to critical systems heuristics (CSH) (2005)

34. Mehaffy, M.W.: Cities Alive: Jane Jacobs, Christopher Alexander, and the Roots of the New Urban Renaissance. Sustasis Press, Portland (2017)

35. Hawkins, J., Blakeslee, S.: On Intelligence: How a New Understanding of the Brain will Lead to the Creation of Truly Intelligent Machines. Times Books, New York (2004)

36. Spelke, E.S., Kinzler, K.D.: Core knowledge. Dev. Sci. **10**(1), 89–96 (2007)

37. Lakoff, G.: Mapping the brain's metaphor circuitry: metaphorical thought in everyday reason. Front. Hum. Neurosci.Neurosci. **8**, 1–14 (2014)

38. Dehaene, S.: Consciousness and the Brain. Penguin Books, New York (2014)

39. Finidori, H.: From pattern language to pattern literacy: the biosemiotic underpinnings of patterning and languaging. In: Proceedings of the 27th Conference on Pattern Languages of Programs (PLoP). Hillside (2020)

40. Husserl, E.: Ideas Pertaining to a Pure Phenomenology and to a Phenomenological Philosophy: First Book General Introduction to a Pure Phenomenology. Martinus Nijhoj Publishers, The Hague (1982)

41. Chavalarias, D., Bourgine, P., Perrier, E., Amblard, F., Arlabosse, F., et al.: French roadmap for complex systems 2008–2009: second issue of the French complex systems roadmap. The French National Network for Complex Systems (2009)

42. Gabriel, R.: Private email conversation on the act of design, 15–24 May 2018

43. Bateson, G.: Mind and Nature: a Necessary Unity. E.P. Dutton, New York (1979)

44. Finidori, H.: Patterns as connectors of multiple realities. In: Proceedings of the 62th Annual Meeting of the International Society for the Systems Sciences (ISSS), Corvallis, Oregon (2018)

45. Peirce, C.S.: Pragmatism as a principle and method of right thinking. In: Turrisi, P.A. (ed.) The 1903 Lectures on Pragmatism. SUNY Press 1997, Albany (1903)
46. Mehaffy, M.W.: Quality of life by design: the science of a structuralist revolution. Athens Dialogues E-J. (2010)
47. Mehaffy, M.: Group conversation on pattern forms and formats initiated by Finidori on Facebook. Pattern Science Group, 21 April–11 May 2018 (2018)
48. Alexander, C.: The Nature of Order—Book 1: The Phenomenon of Life. The Center for Environmental Structure, Berkeley, Caliornia (2002)
49. A Framework for K-12 Science Education: Practices, Crosscutting Concepts, and Core Ideas. National Research Council, The National Academy Press, Washington DC (2011)
50. Kurzweil, R.: How to Create a Mind: the Secret of Human Thought Revealed. Durckworth Overlook, London (2013)
51. Goertzel, B.: The Hidden Pattern: a Patternist Philosophy of Mind. BrownWalker Press, Boca Raton (2006)
52. Willis, A.-M.: Ontological designing. Des. Philos. Papers **4**(2), 69–92 (2015)
53. Husserl, E.: The Crisis of European Sciences and Transcendental Phenomenology: An Introduction to Phenomenological Philosophy. Northwestern University Press, Evanston (1954, 1970)
54. Boyd, J.: The essence of winning and loosing (1996)
55. Kurtz, C.F., Snowden, D.J.: The new dynamics of strategy: sense-making in a complex and complicated world. IBM Syst. J. **42**(3), 462–483 (2003)
56. Hasso-Plattner Institute of Design at Stanford (d.school): An Introduction to Design Thinking—Process Guide
57. Alexander, C.: Notes on the Synthesis of Form. Oxford University Press, London (1964)
58. Gray, D.: Liminal Thinking: Create the Change You Want by Changing the Way You Think. Two Waves, Brooklyn (2016)
59. Practical Sanskrit: The fable of the elephant. http://blog.practicalsanskrit.com/search/label/elephant
60. Luft, J., Ingham, H.: The Johari window: a graphic model of interpersonal awareness. In: Proceedings of the Western Training Laboratory in Group Development. UCLA, Los Angeles (1955)
61. Cunningham, W., Mehaffy, M.: Wiki as pattern language. In: Proceedings of the 20th Conference on Pattern Languages of Programs (PLoP). Hillside (2013)
62. Peirce, C.S.: The Collected Papers of Charles Sanders Peirce, vols. I–VI. Harvard University Press, Cambridge, MA (1994). Online Version
63. Rosen, R.: The modelling relation and natural law. In: Mickens, R.E. (ed.) Mathematics and Science, pp. 183–199. World Scientific (1990)
64. Iba, T.: The future of pattern language: soft social infrastructure to allow freedom of creation in the creative society. In: Portland Urban Architecture Research Lab (PUARL) Conference (2018)
65. West, D., Quillien, J.: The mystery case of undiscovered patterns. In: Pursuit of Pattern Languages for Societal Change (PURPLSOC) Conference (2017)
66. Simon, H.A.: The architecture of complexity. Am. Philos. Soc. **106**(6), 467–482 (1962)
67. Alexander, C.: The Nature of Order—Books 1 to 4. Center for Environmental Structure, Berkeley (2001–2005)
68. Kohls, C.: The theories of design patterns and their practical implications exemplified for e-learning patterns. Mathematisch-Geographischen Fakultät, PhD. Katholischen Universität Eichstätt-Ingolstadt, Eichstätt (2014)
69. Gabriel, R.P.: Writers Workshops and the Work of Making Things: Patterns, Poetry. Addison-Wesley, Boston (2002)

70. Alexander, C.I.S., Silverstein, M.: A Pattern Language: Towns, Buildings, Constructions. Oxford University Press, New York (1977)
71. Peña, W.M., Parshall, S.A.: Problem Seeking: An Architectural Programming Primer. John Wiley and Sons (2001)
72. Schön, D.A.: The Relative Practitioner: How Professionals Think in Action. Basic Books, New York (1983)
73. Ormerod, R.: On the nature of OR: entering the fray. J. Oper. Res. Soc.Oper. Res. Soc. **47**, 1–17 (1996)
74. Manns, M.L., Yoder, J.W.: Patterns as structure, process, and community. In: Proceedings of the 24th Conference on Pattern Languages of Programs (PLoP). Hillside, Vancouver (2017)
75. Jackson, M.: Problem Analysis and Structure. NATO Summer School, Marktoberdorf (2000)
76. Alexander, C.: Patterns in architecture. In: Oopsla 1996, San Jose (1996)
77. Wirfs-Brock, R.: Embracing the fallibility of design heuristics: can patterns help? In: Proceedings of the 24th Conference on Pattern Languages of Programs (PLoP). Hillside, Vancouver (2017)
78. Koen, B.V.: Discussion of the Method: Conducting the Engineer's Approach to Problem Solving. Oxford University Press, New-York (2003)
79. Ozbekhan, H.: The predicament of mankind: quest for structured responses to growing world-wide complexities and uncertainties. The Club of Rome (1970)
80. Rittel, H.W.M.: Dilemmas in a general theory of planning. Policy. Sci. **4**(2), 155–169 (1973)
81. Senge, P.M.: The Fifth Discipline. Doubleday/Currency, New-York (1990)
82. Ostrom, E.: Governing the Commons: The Evolution of Institutions for Collective Action. Cambridge University Press, New York (1990)
83. Taborga, J.: Systems Archetypes and Their Application Unbound Blog. Saybrook University (2011)
84. Causal loop diagram—system archetype: tragedy of the commons. Created in Vensim Software Produced by Ventana Systems, Inc. (Harvard, Massachusetts) Creative Commons, Attribution, Share Alike 3.0 Unported License
85. Leitner, H.: Christopher Alexande: An Introduction (2016)
86. Reiners, R., Falkenthal, M., Zimmermann, A.: Requirements for a collaborative formulation process of evolutionary patterns. In: Proceedings of the 20th Conference on Pattern Languages of Programs (PLoP). Hillside, Monticello (2013)
87. Salingaros, N.: Living structure comes from (living) patterns—parts 1 and 2 (2015). e-architect.co.uk
88. Salingaros, N.: Living Patterns as Tools of Adaptive Design. Metropolis Magazine (2016)
89. Salingaros, N.: Living Structures Should Come from Living Patterns. Metropolis (2015)
90. Alexander, C. (ed.): Systems Generating Systems, vol. 38. John Wiley & Sons, Chichester (2011)
91. Leitner, H.: Social network conversations on pattern formats, aspects and the problem solution, 27 March–14 April 2017
92. Leitner, H.: A bird's-eye view on pattern research. In: Baumgartner, P., Sickinger, R. (eds.) Pursuit of Pattern Languages for Societal Change (PURPLSOC) Conference—The Workshop 2014: Designing Lively Scenarios with the Pattern Approach of Christopher Alexander. Neopubli (2015)
93. Roy, B., Trudel, J.: Leading the 21st century: the conception-aware, object-oriented organization. Integral Leadership Review (2011)
94. Bloom, J.W.: Systems thinking, pattern thinking, and abductive thinking as the key elements of complex learning. In: Annual Meeting of the American Educational Research Association, Denver, CO (2010)

95. Wirfs-Brock, R.: Traces, tracks, trails, and paths: an exploration of how we approach software design. In: Proceedings of the 25th Conference on Pattern Languages of Programming (PLoP). Hillside, Portland (2018)
96. Köppe, C., Inventado, P.S., Scupelli, P., Heesch, U.V.: Towards extending online pattern repositories: supporting the design pattern lifecycle. In: Proceedings of the 23rd Conference on Pattern Languages of Programs (PLoP). Hillside (2016)
97. Loreto, V., Servedio, V.D.P., Strogatz, S.H., Tria, F.: Dynamics on expanding spaces: modeling the emergence of novelties. arXiv:1701.00994v1 (2017)
98. Kohls, C., Scheiter, K.: The relation between design patterns and schema theory. In: Proceedings of the 15th Conference on Pattern Languages of Programs (PLoP) (2008)
99. Rousseau, D.: Systems research and the quest for scientific systems principles. Systems **5**(2) (2017)
100. Kenneth A. Lloyd, J.: Foundational concepts underlying a formal mathematical basis for systems science. In: Proceedings of the 62nd Annual Meeting of the International Society for the Systems Sciences (ISSS) (2018)
101. The Visual Thesaurus. https://www.visualthesaurus.com. Accessed Jul 2021

Author Index

E. Wallingford et al. (Eds.): TPLOP V, LNCS 14630, p. 299, 2025.
https://doi.org/10.1007/978-3-662-70810-1

The manufacturer's authorised representative in the EU is Springer
Nature Customer Service Centre GmbH, Europaplatz 3, 69115 Heidelberg,
Germany. If you have any concerns regarding our products, please
contact ProductSafety@springernature.com

Printed and bound by CPI Group (UK) Ltd, Croydon, CR0 4YY

24/04/2026

02096365-0005